The Second Augustan Legion and the Roman Military Machine

Birthday of the Eagle

The Second Augustan Legion and the Roman Military Machine

Edited by Richard J Brewer

AMGUEDDFEYDD AC ORIELAU CENEDLAETHOL CYMRU
NATIONAL MUSEUMS & GALLERIES OF WALES
2002

First published in 2002 by the
National Museums & Galleries of Wales,
Cathays Park,
Cardiff CF10 3NP

ISBN 0 7200 0514 0

British Library Cataloguing in Publication Data
A CIP catalogue record for this book is available from the British Library

This book typeset and laid out by Exe Valley Dataset Ltd, Exeter, Devon
Printed and bound in Great Britain by Henry Ling Limited, at the Dorset Press, Dorchester, DT1 1HD

Frontispiece
Aerial view of Caerleon from the south-west. Sited at the lowest convenient bridging-point across the tidal River Usk, the fortress was open to sea and river transport, and held a key position in the military road-system (photograph: Cadw: Welsh Historic Monuments, Crown Copyright)

Contents

	Contributors	viii
	List of illustrations	ix
	Preface	xiii
INTRODUCTION	*Legio II Augusta* and Caerleon *by Richard J Brewer*	1
CHAPTER 1	The origins and early history of the Second Augustan Legion *by Lawrence Keppie*	11
CHAPTER 2	Early Roman campaigns in the south-west of Britain *by W H Manning*	27
CHAPTER 3	Early Roman campaigns in Wales *by Michael G Jarrett* (revised by Peter Webster)	45
CHAPTER 4	The Second Augustan Legion in north Britain *by David J Breeze*	67
CHAPTER 5	The Second Augustan Legion in the west of Britain *by Michael G Fulford*	83
CHAPTER 6	Officers of the Second Augustan Legion in Britain *by Anthony R Birley*	103
CHAPTER 7	The framework of an imperial legion *by Michael P Speidel*	125
CHAPTER 8	Soldier and civilian: life beyond the ramparts *by Valerie A Maxfield*	145
CHAPTER 9	The legions in the later Roman Empire *by John Casey*	165
CHAPTER 10	The future of Roman military archaeology *by Richard Reece*	179
	Ancient Sources	193
	Bibliography	195
	Index	207

Contributors

Professor A R Birley	Vindolanda Museum, Bardon Mill, Hexham NE47 7JN
Professor D J Breeze	Historic Scotland, Longmore House, Salisbury Place, Edinburgh EH9 1SH
Mr R J Brewer	Department of Archaeology & Numismatics, National Museums & Galleries of Wales, Cathays Park, Cardiff CF10 3NP
Mr P J Casey	112 Alberta Street, London SE17 3RT
Professor M G Fulford	Department of Archaeology, Faculty of Letters and Social Sciences, The University of Reading, Whiteknights, PO Box 218, Reading RG6 6AA
†Professor M G Jarrett	Formerly of Cardiff University
Professor L J F Keppie	Hunterian Museum, The University of Glasgow, Glasgow G12 8QQ
Professor W H Manning	108 Plymouth Road, Penarth, Vale of Glamorgan CF64 5DN
Professor V A Maxfield	Department of Archaeology, School of Geography and Archaeology, University of Exeter, Laver Building, North Park Road, Exeter EX4 4QE
Dr R Reece	The Apple Loft, The Waterloo, Cirencester, Gloucestershire GL7 2PU
Professor M P Speidel	Department of History, College of Arts and Humanities, University of Hawaii at Manoa, Sakamaki Hall A203, 530 Dole Street, Honolulu, Hawaii
Dr P V Webster	Centre for Lifelong Learning, Cardiff University, Senghennydd Road, Cardiff CF24 4AG

Illustrations

Frontispiece
Aerial view of Caerleon from the south-west

Introduction
1 *Roman environs of Caerleon* 3
2 *Isca: plan of the fortress* 5

The origins and early history of the Second Augustan Legion
1.1 *The Arc de Triomphe, Orange, seen from the south* 12
1.2 *Inscribed graveslab recording Q. Luccius Faustus, who served as a standard-bearer in* legio XIIII Gemina Martia Victrix *at Mainz* c *AD 70–92* 13
1.3 *Part of a commemorative slab found at Castell Collen, Powys, in 1956. Mid-second century AD* 14
1.4 *a Building stone from near Vindolanda* (RIB *I, 1707); b building stone from Benwell* (RIB *I, 1344). Both bear inscriptions of* legio II Augusta *and figures of a pegasus and capricorn* 15
1.5 *Distance slab from Duntocher on the Antonine Wall* (RIB *I, 2203)* 15
1.6 *Inscribed graveslab recording C. Julius Niger, who served in* legio II Augusta *at Mainz, before AD 43* 18
1.7 *Inscribed graveslab recording C. Largennius, who served in* legio II Augusta *at Strasbourg, before AD 43* 19
1.8 *Bronze plaque depicting a winged figure of Victory, found at Caerleon. Probably second century AD* 21
1.9 Denarius *of Augustus issued 19–16 BC. The reverse shows the circular temple of* Mars Ultor 21
1.10 *Statue of Augustus, found in 1863 in Livia's villa at Prima Porta, just outside Rome* 22

Early Roman campaigns in the south-west of Britain
2.1 *The Late Iron Age tribes of southern Britain* 29
2.2 *Distribution of Roman military sites in south-west Britain* 31

Early Roman campaigns in Wales
3.1 *The tribes of Wales* 48
3.2 *The railways of Wales in their heyday,* c *1910* 51
3.3 *Rhyn Park (Shrops): fortress (*c *18 ha) from the south* 54
3.4 *Rhyn Park (Shrops): fort (*c *6 ha) from the north* 55
3.5 *Temporary camps, presumably of the campaigning period* 56
3.6 *Pre-Flavian forts and depots* 57
3.7 *Castlefield, Kentchurch (Herefs): fort, possibly part of a chain from Monmouth to Clyro* 58
3.8 *Abbey Dore (Herefs): fort in the Golden Valley* 58
3.9 *Walton (Rads): fort at Hindwell Farm* 59
3.10 *Llwyn-y-brain (Mont): ditches of the fort from the south* 60
3.11 *Llanfor (Mer): ditches of the pentagonal stores compound* 60

The Second Augustan Legion in north Britain
4.1 *Map of Hadrian's Wall* 69
4.2 *Milecastle 42 (Cawfields), built by* legio II Augusta 69

4.3	RIB *I, 1638 records the building of milecastle 38* (*Hotbank*) *by soldiers of* legio II Augusta	70
4.4	*Map of the Antonine Wall*	70
4.5	*The Bridgeness distance slab found at Bo'ness near the eastern end of the Antonine Wall in 1868* (RIB *I, 2139*)	71
4.6	*Distance slab of* legio II Augusta *from the Antonine Wall* (RIB I, 2204). *Found at Carleith before 1699*	71
4.7	*Map of north Britain showing forts which may have been held at the end of the reign of Septimius Severus in 211*	73
4.8	*Plan of Carpow legionary base*	73
4.9	*A fragment of a monumental building inscription found in front of the east gate of the legionary base at Carpow in 1964*	74
4.10	*A capricorn and a pegasus on a stone found at Castlesteads on Hadrian's Wall* (RIB *I, 2397* = CSIR *I.6, 398*)	74
4.11	*A pegasus on one of the Roman stones used in the souterrain at Crichton*	75
4.12	*Quarry inscriptions at Crowdundle, Cumbria* (RIB *I, 1001*)	75
4.13	*Altar, found at Auchendavy in 1771, dedicated to Jupiter Best and Greatest and Victorious Victory for the welfare of the Emperor and the welfare of himself and his family by M. Cocceius Firmus, centurion of* legio II Augusta (RIB *I, 2176*)	77
4.14	*The strong-room in the headquarters building in the Second Legion's compound at Corbridge*	78
4.15	*Altar dedicated to the Discipline of the Emperors by* legio II Augusta. *Found in the headquarters building at Corbridge*	79
4.16	*Fragmentary statue of Jupiter, and part of a sculptural panel showing Hercules. Both found in the Second Legion's headquarters building at Corbridge*	80

The Second Augustan Legion in the west of Britain

5.1	*a* *Wales: the garrison in the early second century;* *b* *Wales: the garrison in the fourth century*	84
5.2	*Distribution of stamped tiles of* legio II Augusta	85
5.3	*Tombstones of a veteran, Julius Valens, of* legio II Augusta *and his wife, Julia Secundina, from Great Bulmore* (RIB *I, 363 and 373*)	86
5.4	*Stone recording the construction of 33½ paces of seabank (?) from Goldcliff, near Newport* (RIB *I, 395*)	86
5.5	*A reclaimed saltmarsh: the Wentlooge Level, south Wales*	87
5.6	*Altar from Caerwent dedicated to Mars Ocelus by Aelius Augustinus* (RIB *I, 310*)	88
5.7	*Stone and mineral resources in the west of Britain*	89
5.8	*Lead pigs from the Mendips produced by* legio II Augusta*: a from Blagdon, Avon* (RIB *II.1, 2404.2*)*; b from St Valéry sur Somme, France of the reign of Nero* (RIB *II.1, 2404.24*)	89
5.9	*a* *Altar from Bath commemorating the restoration of a holy place by Severius Emeritus,* centurio regionarius (RIB *I, 1520*)*;* *b* *dedication from Combe Down, near Bath which records the restoration of a ruined* principia *by the freedman Naevius* (RIB *I, 179*)	90
5.10	*Distribution of inscriptions on stone of* legio II Augusta *from the west and south of Britain*	91
5.11	*Altars from Bath dedicated to Sulis Minerva: a by Gaius Curiatius Saturninus, centurion of* legio II Augusta (RIB *I, 146*)*; b for the welfare of Gaius Javolenus Saturnalis,* imaginifer *of* legio II Augusta *by Lucius Manius Dionisias* (RIB *I, 147*)	92
5.12	*Bath* (*Aquae Sulis*)*: plan of the walled area with the temple precinct and baths*	93
5.13	*Contoured distribution of BB1 pottery in the west of Britain*	94

5.14 *Distribution of inscriptions on stone of* legio II Augusta *and* legio XX Valeria Victrix *in the north of Britain* 95
5.15 *A building stone and quarry inscriptions recording the joint activities of* legio II Augusta *and* legio XX Valeria Victrix*: a from Maryport, Cumbria* (RIB *I, 852); b–c from Crowdundle, Cumbria* (RIB *I, 998 and 999)* 96
5.16 *a Altar from York dedicated to the African, Gallic and Italian Mother Goddesses by Marcus Minucius Audens,* gubernator *of* legio VI Victrix (RIB *I, 653);*
b tombstone from Chester of an optio *who died by shipwreck* (RIB *I, 544)* 97
5.17 *a Tile antefixes of* legio II Augusta *from Caerleon;*
b slab from the 'Castle' Baths, Caerleon inscribed with a cupid astride a dolphin 98
5.18 *Outline plans of: a the late first-century legionary fortress, Caerleon; b the late Roman coastal fort at Cardiff; c the late third-century coastal fort at Richborough, Kent* 99
5.19 *Lydney: mosaic pavement from the* cella *of the temple* 99
5.20 *Lydney: plan of the temple and associated buildings* 100

Officers of the Second Augustan Legion in Britain
6.1 *The letter sent by Adiutor, eagle-bearer of* II Augusta, *to Vindolanda* 103
6.2 *Silver* denarius *of the Emperor Vespasian (69–79)* 104
6.3 *Statue base of P. Anicius Maximus, camp prefect of* II Augusta. *Yalvaç, Turkey* (CIL *III 6809)* 105
6.4 *Part of a wooden writing tablet referring to soldiers' duties. Caerleon, 1985* 107
6.5 *Stones recording building work by the century of Julius Tertullianus of* II Augusta *on Hadrian's Wall* (RIB *I, 1970 and 2016)* 109
6.6 *Sacrificial scene from the Bridgeness distance slab found at Bo'ness, near the eastern end of the Antonine Wall in 1868* (RIB *I, 2139)* 110
6.7 *Altar to Jupiter Dolichenus dedicated by Rufilianus, legate of* II Augusta. *Caerleon, 1653* (RIB *I, 320)* 110
6.8 *Altar dedicated by Haterianus. Caerleon, 1602* (RIB *I, 335)* 111
6.9 *Tombstone of the centurion Vivius Marcianus found in Ludgate Hill, London, 1669* (RIB *I, 17)* 112
6.10 *Altar to Salus Regina dedicated by P. Sallienius Thalamus, prefect of* II Augusta, *and his two sons. Caerleon, 1845* (RIB *I, 324)* 115
6.11 *Statue base inscribed by the Silurian local authority at Caerwent in honour of Tiberius Claudius Paulinus, legate of* II Augusta (RIB *I, 311)* 115
6.12 *Inscription set up in the headquarters building at Caerleon by the chief centurion in 'honour of the Eagle' on 23 September 244. Found 1800* (RIB *I, 327)* 116
6.13 *Tablet recording the restoration of the Temple of Diana by T. Flavius Postumius Varus,* c *AD 250. Caerleon, 1603* (RIB *I, 316)* 117
6.14 *Inscription recording the rebuilding of barracks for the seventh cohort at Caerleon* c *AD 255–8* (RIB *I, 334)* 117

The framework of an imperial legion
7.1 *Plan of the legionary fortress at Isca–Caerleon* 126
7.2 *The ten cohorts and their* centuriae 127
7.3 *A building inscription from Caerleon* (RIB *I, 341)* 128
7.4 *Three building inscriptions from Hadrian's Wall: a Castlesteads (RIB 2001); b Drawdikes Castle, near Stanwix* (RIB *I, 2023); c Carlisle* (RIB *I, 2032)* 129
7.5 *Gravestone of Flavoleius Cordus from Mainz* 130

7.6	*Two reliefs from the first-century legionary headquarters-building at Mainz: a heavily-armed legionaries fighting in close ranks; b lightly-armed legionary with several* lanciae, *fighting in open ranks*	131
7.7	*Oval leather shield-cover from Caerleon*	131
7.8	*The cohorts in manipular lines*	132
7.9	*Two legionary* centuria-*standards and a flag on Trajan's Column*	134
7.10	*Gravestone from Chester, showing an* optio *and his staff* (RIB *I, 492*)	134
7.11	*Altar from near Stanwix, set up by a detachment from two* centuriae *of* legio II Augusta (RIB *I, 2024*)	135
7.12	*Legionary from the turn of the fourth century. Aquileia*	137
7.13	*Vegetius'* antiqua ordinatio	138

Soldier and civilian: life beyond the ramparts

8.1	*The tombstone of Tadia Vallaunius and her son, Tadius Exuperatus, soldier of* legio II Augusta. *Caerleon* (RIB *I, 369*)	145
8.2	*The tombstone of Marcus Caelius, killed in the Varan disaster. Xanten*	148
8.3	*The tombstone of Victor, a Moor, freedman of Numerianus, a cavalryman in the* ala I Asturum, *who had the stone erected. South Shields*	149
8.4	*The tombstone of Longinus, cavalryman in the* ala Sulpicia. *Cologne*	149
8.5	*Tombstone of Maris, a cavalryman in the* ala Parthorum et Araborum. *Mainz*	150
8.6	*The birthday invitation sent by Claudia Severa to Sulpicia Lepidina, wife of a commanding officer at Vindolanda*	151
8.7	*Map of Egypt*	155
8.8	*The fort, animal lines and store building at the heart of the quarry complex at Mons Claudianus*	157
8.9	*Ostracon from Mons Claudianus, a military-controlled quarry complex in the Eastern Desert of Egypt. It alludes to the writer's failure to get leave*	160

The legions in the later Roman Empire

9.1	*A bronze roundel depicting soldiers of vexillations of* legio II Augusta *and* legio XX Valeria Victrix . *The badge, of third century date, was found in France*	167
9.2	*The triumphal relief of Shapur I at Bishapur, Iran. The Sassanid king is shown holding the Emperor Valerian captive*	168
9.3	*Tombstone of Aurelius Mucianus, a trainee* lanciarius *of* legio II Parthica, *from Apamea*	169
9.4	*The new Constantinian field army in action during the war against Maxentius. The scene, from a panel of the Arch of Constantine in Rome, depicts the siege of a town in northern Italy*	172
9.5	*A silver coin, issued in 317, shows Constantine, attended by Victory, reviewing his cavalry*	173
9.6	*A late fourth- or fifth-century wooden panel, from a church door, depicting the biblical scene of the relief of the city of Gibeon by Joshua. From El Eshmunein, Egypt*	174

PREFACE

One of the most important festivals in a Roman legion was the birthday of the Eagle (*natalis aquilae*), which celebrated the anniversary of the legion's foundation. In the case of the Second Augustan Legion (the Caerleon garrison) this was 23 September, the birthday of the Emperor Augustus whose name the legion bore. The National Museums & Galleries of Wales celebrated this day with a lecture held annually at Caerleon on that date.

The following remarks prefaced the publication of the First Annual Caerleon Lecture, which was held on 23 September 1987.

IN HONOREM AQUILAE
The expression *'in honour of the Eagle'* occurs on two inscriptions from Caerleon, which can be dated precisely to 23 September AD 234 and 244. Two of a long series, they were set up in the headquarters building by the Chief Centurion of the Legion on the occasion of the Legion's birthday, which was attended by elaborate celebrations. The birthday of a Legion was taken to be that of its founder, in this case the Emperor Augustus.[1]

The emblem of the Second Augustan Legion, like that of other legions created by Augustus, was the Capricorn which (half goat, half fish) figures among the signs of the Zodiac. This was Augustus' chosen astrological sign, being one associated particularly with the fortunate enterprise. It is interesting to note, however, that the sun is not in the sign of Capricorn on 23 September, but moving into Libra – the balance – which, of course, carries a much less satisfactory connotation; however, Capricorn was rising at the time of Augustus' birth[2] and therefore was a more suitable and propitious choice.

In 1987 the Roman Legionary Museum was totally renovated, and it seemed appropriate to institute a series of annual lectures joined with a modest celebration, on 23 September, to commemorate the Second Augustan Legion. The first of these lectures was given by Professor W H Manning of Cardiff University. It is intended that each will trace an aspect of the life and history of the Second Augustan Legion or a subject closely connected therewith. Each lecture will contain fruits of the speaker's latest research, set out in a manner to a general audience, and will thereafter be available in printed form.

George C Boon 1988

* * * * * *

The series, which comprised ten lectures delivered between 1987 and 1996, proved to be very popular with large audiences attending annually. They were attracted by first class speakers, the opportunity to see a fine Museum and the Ermine Street Guard who provided a guard of honour and paraded the *vexillum,* the legionary flag. The individual publications, which followed at regular intervals, proved to be equally popular and sold out rapidly. Many requests were received from people who had part sets of the Caerleon Lectures and were anxious to complete their series. When the decision was taken to reprint the series as a single monograph, the authors were given the opportunity to update and revise their

[1] There is evidence that the legion existed before 27 BC, see Keppie this volume, 11–14.
[2] Now known not to be the case. However, Augustus was conceived under Capricorn, see Keppie this volume, 14.

contributions. These papers make a significant contribution to our understanding of the history of the Second Augustan Legion and Roman military archaeology more generally.

I wish to record my personal thanks to all the authors who willingly imparted their latest research and thoughts in delivering their papers, both verbally and for printing. They also responded enthusiastically to the invitation to revise and update their papers for this volume. I must also express my thanks to the Williams's Schools Charity who allowed us to use the Caerleon Endowed Junior School for the actual lectures and the Ermine Street Guard who by their presence added to the sense of occasion and celebration. Morag Redman and Wendy Ladd, both formerly of the National Museums & Galleries of Wales, undertook much of the initial typing of the papers, whilst Evan Chapman assisted with proof checking the texts. Tony Daly of the Department of Archaeology & Numismatics, NMGW, prepared all the illustrations for publication. The administration of the Haverfield Bequest kindly gave permission to reproduce the illustrations from *Roman Inscriptions in Britain.* The sources of the other illustrations are acknowledged in the captions and I am deeply grateful for the co-operation of all those individuals and organizations involved. Finally, I am grateful to the Department of Publications & Design, NMGW, for seeing this volume through the press.

To avoid any confusion BC and AD are used in papers which make reference to both, but no abbreviation is cited in those papers only referring to AD. Abbreviations for periodicals and monographs follow the Council for British Archaeology's 'list of standard abbreviations' in *Signposts for Archaeological Publication* (3rd edn), 1991.

Richard J Brewer 2001
National Museums & Galleries of Wales

INTRODUCTION

LEGIO II AUGUSTA AND CAERLEON

RICHARD J BREWER

Claudio principe Narcissi gratia legatus legionis in Germaniam missus est; inde in Britanniam translatus tricies cum hoste conflixit.

'In the reign of Claudius he (Vespasian) was sent in command of a legion to Germany, through the influence of Narcissus; from there he was transferred to Britain, where he fought thirty battles with the enemy'.

Suetonius, *Vespasian* 4

That the legion, commanded by Vespasian, was the Second Augustan is confirmed by Tacitus, *Histories* (3.4). Of the four legions which we assume took part in the invasion of AD 43, only *legio II Augusta* is documented in the literary sources, while the participation of *legio XX* is confirmed by epigraphic evidence.[1] That the early activities of *II Augusta* in Britain are mentioned in ancient texts is undoubtedly because its commander, Vespasian – consul in 51 – later became emperor. Our knowledge of the history and activities of *II Augusta* is drawn from these brief mentions in literary sources, epigraphic evidence and the excavation of its various bases, especially the fortress at Caerleon with which it is inextricably linked. Thus, the study of *II Augusta* is a matter for the historian and also the archaeologist and this dual interest is reflected in the lectures published here.

In 1924 Emil Ritterling wrote his magisterial article 'Legio' in Pauly Wissowa's *Realencyclopädie der classischen Altertumswissenschaft*, which included, for its time, a comprehensive entry on *II Augusta*.[2] This was followed in 1928 by a less reliable and detailed study of the legions by H M D Parker.[3] The most recent account of *legio II Augusta* in Britain was written by Michael Jarrett and published in 1964.[4] He tackled the subject chronologically, with special attention paid, naturally, to the relationship between the legion's activities and the archaeological evidence for the occupation of Caerleon. During the intervening period, almost 25 years, that spanned Jarrett's publication and the advent of the Caerleon lecture series a lot of new archaeological evidence had emerged, especially with regard to the bases occupied by *II Augusta* during the conquest period, before Caerleon was established in 74 or 75. The series of lectures makes a significant contribution to our understanding of the role and development of the Second Augustan Legion. The chapters following trace the origins of *legio II Augusta;* its activities during the conquest of the province; the role of the legion beyond the fortress at Caerleon in the northern and western parts of *Britannia* and our knowledge of the officers of the legion. More general topics include the examination of the strength and structure of the legion in the Early Empire and the later Roman 'legions', which were very different bodies from those of the earlier imperial period. The evidence for the life of soldiers beyond the ramparts and the civilians who depended on the army for their livelihood is also explored.

When *legio II Augusta* landed in Britain in 43, the unit was already almost a century old. Keppie studies the origins, the title and *emblema* of the Second Augustan Legion; its postings and campaign experience on the Continent and its part in the preparations for the Claudian invasion. Before its transfer to Britain, *II Augusta,* saw service in Gaul, Spain and finally in Germany. For most of the period between 14 and the legion's departure for Britain, its fortress lay at Strasbourg in Upper Germany; though a brief sojourn at Mainz is possible. Little is known of the earth and timber fortress constructed at Strasbourg by *II Augusta,* but several tombstones of the legion have been recovered from the cemetery 2 kilometres west of the base. In 43, the commander of the legion at Strasbourg was T. Flavius Vespasianus. On his arrival in Britain with the invading army he was given the responsibility for operations in southern England.

Two contributions concentrate on the thirty or so years prior to the arrival of *legio II Augusta* at Caerleon. Manning reviews the evidence of the activities of *II Augusta* in south-west England and south Wales during this period, drawing attention to some of the many sites whose discovery or reinterpretation in recent years has led to a clearer understanding of the progress of the conquest of Britain. He also discusses the nature of the Fosse Way, that remarkable Roman road which runs across England from south-west to north-east, as a communication and supply route rather than an early frontier dividing the new province from the tribes beyond. Jarrett/Webster move us westwards into Wales and the pre-Flavian and early Flavian campaigns there, a period that saw some bitter fighting. The first part of their paper assesses the relatively detailed historical accounts that we have of this period and examines the political, or tribal, geography of pre-Roman Wales. This is followed by a review of the archaeological evidence for the campaigns which ultimately led to the complete occupation of Wales. Some twenty-seven pre-Flavian forts/depots and twenty-five temporary camps (see Appendix pp 62–3) have now been identified and this allows the authors to suggest the likely routes of penetration used during the course of the various campaigns into south and north Wales. The system of pre-Flavian forts, so far as is known, looks incomplete and is in marked contrast to the final dispositions of Frontinus and Agricola in Wales. Jarrett considers that this must be one consequence of the Boudiccan rebellion and that the network must have been intended to extend westwards as the remainder of Wales was brought under Roman control. However, he also suggests that it may reflect the fact that Roman ideas of how to control conquered territory were still being developed at this period, and the system does seem to have served as an effective barrier between the tribes of Wales and the territory held by the Romans.

During this period of conquest, many sites have been suggested as bases for *II Augusta* during its advance across southern Britain before its transfer to Caerleon.[5] Emil Hübner, writing in 1881, located *II Augusta* at Gloucester (43–75);[6] Emil Ritterling in 1924 suggested Cirencester (43–9) and Gloucester (49–75);[7] while R G Collingwood, who placed considerable emphasis on the Fosse Way as a frontier-line, sited *II Augusta* at Seaton at its southern end (*c* 45–9), before it moved to Gloucester (49–75).[8] Ian Richmond by 1963, with increasing archaeological evidence emerging, located *II Augusta* at Exeter, but it is unclear whether he thought that the legion remained there until transferring to Caerleon in 75 or left for Gloucester (Kingsholm) in 67.[9]

A more complex situation is adumbrated by subsequent writers, such as Frere who, in all four editions of his *Britannia,* was attracted by the concept of half- or sub-size legionary fortresses.[10] In 1967, he suggested that Exeter was built for half of *legio II Augusta* (45–67) – even before the overall plan of the fortress could be reconstructed – with the other half of the legion based at Dorchester (43–67).[11] By 1978, he suggested that the first legionary headquarters – a half-fortress – was established at Dorchester or Lake Farm/Wimbourne (43–?), but that during the early years of the campaign vexillations of the legion may have been garrisoned in forts like Hod Hill; he still regarded Exeter as a possible half-legionary fortress (*c* 45–67), though with less certainty.[12] In the third edition (1987), it was proposed that the legion was probably divided into vexillations initially with fortresses at Lake Farm, North Tawton and perhaps Dorchester (43–55), while Exeter, with more known about its plan, was promoted back to full size (55–67).[13] In all four editions Frere proposed that *II Augusta* moved from Exeter to Gloucester in 67 before it took up quarters at Caerleon in 74/5. Graham Webster provides a more traditional view of changing legionary dispositions and vexillation fortresses do not appear in his scheme.[14] He proposed Chichester (45–8) in 1988 – but later favoured Silchester – as the first base of *II Augusta* in Britain, soon followed by a move to Lake Farm (48–55) and then further west to Exeter (55–66). Like Frere, Webster suggested a short occupation of Gloucester by *legio II Augusta* (66–75), before it moved to Caerleon.

Manning in this volume proposes that *legio II Augusta,* or at least part of it, was based at Chichester as it began to move through the south of England. Probably a vexillation fortress, rather than a full-size base, it would have served as a winter quarters for half a legion or for mixed groups of legionaries and auxiliaries. Chichester was easily supplied for it was in close proximity to Bosham Harbour and a possible depot at Fishbourne. When the Durotriges had been defeated and the initial phase of the conquest had been completed, the legion moved forward to a new vexillation fortress probably at Lake Farm, which also had its own harbour at Poole and a depot at Hamworthy. As the conquest progressed, Exeter became the next base of *legio II Augusta*. The establishment of Exeter can probably be seen as part of a general reorganization of the military arrangements of the province undertaken in the mid-50s by Didius Gallus, when new fortresses were also constructed at Wroxeter for *legio XIIII* and Usk for *legio XX*. The withdrawal of *legio XIIII* from the province in 66 entailed the redeployment of two of the remaining legions and Manning considers that *legio XX* most likely moved to Wroxeter, while *II Augusta* was probably responsible for the construction and garrisoning of the new fortress at Gloucester, built in the mid-60s. Others, however, have argued that *II Augusta* remained at Exeter until the mid-70s, when it moved to Caerleon. This supposition is based on the discovery by Boon and Bidwell of terracotta antefixes from exactly the same mould at Exeter and Caerleon.[15] Isca formed a pivotal position in Frontinus' campaign against the Silures. The new fortress was sited at the lowest convenient bridging-point across the tidal River Usk, and was open to sea and river transport (Figure 1).

The arrival of *legio II Augusta* at Caerleon in 74/5 is one fact that has, to date, not been disputed by scholars, other than Theodor Mommsen (1885), who erroneously suggested that Caerleon was founded in 48.[16] The importance of Caerleon cannot be overstressed in the opportunities it offers for the study of a legionary fortress. The first 'scientific' excavations took place in 1908–9 and were followed in 1926–7 by the exploration of the Amphitheatre by Dr Mortimer and Mrs T V Wheeler. Excavations have been going on in Caerleon and its environs since then and the progress of these archaeological investigations has been traced elsewhere by the writer.[17] The first comprehensive guide to Roman Caerleon, providing a record of discovery and excavation down to the end of 1938, was written by V E Nash-Williams, who had undertaken most of the excavation work.[18] The most detailed general account of the structural

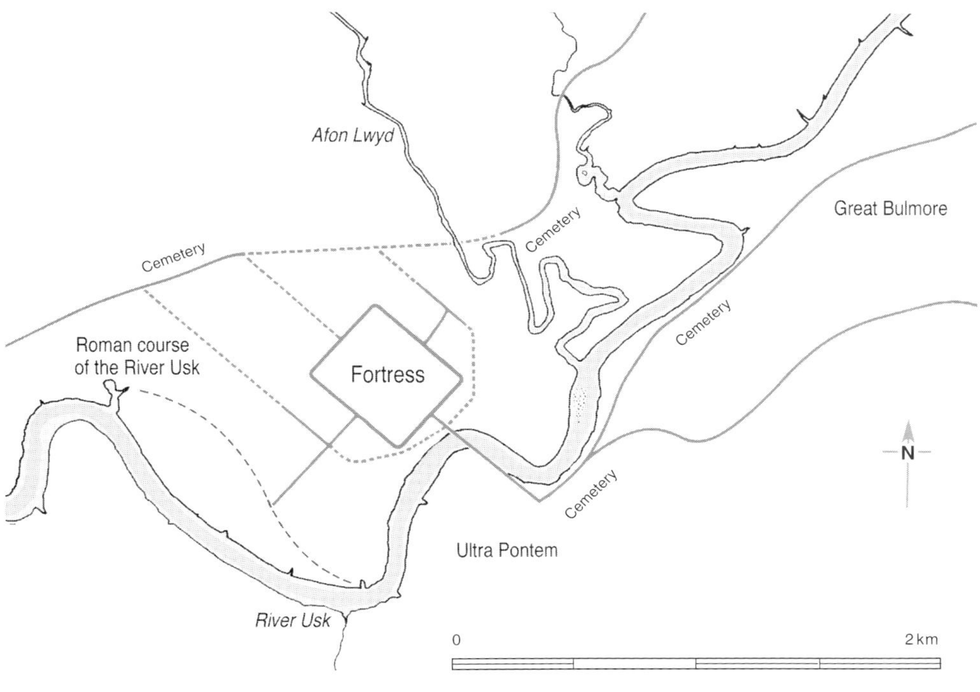

1 *Roman environs of Caerleon*

evolution and character of the fortress – *Isca* – was written by George Boon and published in 1972.[19] This edition incorporated the results of excavations undertaken during the 1960s, which revealed such notable buildings as the legionary hospital, the Fortress Baths and a substantial part of the headquarters building, as well as a re-evaluation of previous evidence. The results of this work reflect the advance of archaeological techniques over time, as well as the ability of individual excavators. The most significant subsequent development was the introduction of 'area' excavation at Caerleon from the late 1970s onwards, which has predictably led to a greater yield of information from sites. From these more recent excavations it is now realized that on many previously investigated sites the earliest buildings, mainly of timber construction, probably eluded detection. This has led to a reappraisal of the character of the Flavian occupation and the structural evolution of the fortress, which has been summarised in Boon's 1987 edition of *Isca* and elsewhere.[20] Also, this demonstrates that those sites investigated by narrow trenching would merit further excavation using modern techniques. Although the plan of Isca (Figure 2) might, at a quick glance, appear to be comparatively complete, it is worth noting that several areas still retain their secrets: the granaries remain to be located, while little is known of the tribunes' row and the accommodation for the first cohort. That we have much still to learn was starkly demonstrated by the quite recent discovery of a massive tetrapylon at the very centre of the fortress.[21]

What can we learn about the strength, structure and battle order of the legions in the Early Empire from the layout of their fortresses? These are topics which have been much argued by scholars over the years. Speidel in his paper examines these questions and attempts to throw some light on them by exploring the archaeological evidence derived from fortresses, such as Caerleon and Inchtuthil, as well as interrogating the terminology used in inscriptions and other literary sources. For example, he reviews the evidence for the survival of the three main battle-lines (*pilani, principes* and *hastati*), adopted in the early Republic, the continuing existence of maniples in the Empire and the presence of the 120 legionary horsemen. The ranking of the centurions – the *Rangordnung* – is discussed in detail and Speidel concludes that each of the sixty centurions differed in rank and that any transfer was, in effect, a promotion. He also considers the survival of the traditional names for the centuries – titles derived originally from their position in the line of battle – as evidence for their continued significance in indicating battlefield positions during the Empire. It also seems clear from epigraphic and literary sources that a legion in the first and second centuries was not one body of men all uniformly equipped and trained as frequently portrayed: instead some of its ranks were armed differently and trained for specific tasks on the battlefield. Arrian, for example – writing at the time of Hadrian – arms the first four ranks of the Cappadocian legions conventionally with *pila* and the next four ranks with *lanciae* or lighter javelins, which could be thrown over the heads of the front ranks. The ever growing differentiation in the weapons and tactics used in a legion eventually gave rise to the formation of separate specialist units, such as the *lanciarii* and the *equites promoti,* in the later Roman army.

Caerleon would have seen many comings and goings. These troop movements need not be strongly marked in the archaeological record of buildings and structures within the fortress.[22] Both Breeze and Fulford look at the role of *legio II Augusta* beyond the fortress and in times of peace. The activities of *legio II Augusta* in northern Britain are examined, not chronologically, but thematically considering evidence for subjects such as fighting, building, living and dying. It is possible that *II Augusta,* preoccupied with the situation in south Wales, did not provide any troops for the northern campaigns of Cerialis or Agricola. Indeed, the evidence for the involvement of *II Augusta* as a fighting force on the northern frontier during the second and early third centuries, though likely at times, is only circumstantial. However, when considering building activity *II Augusta* was heavily involved in the construction of both Hadrian's Wall and the Antonine Wall, as shown by the considerable number of building inscriptions. Cohort and centurial stones record the presence of seven cohorts of the legion participating in the construction of Hadrian's Wall and some forty individual centurions. The more elaborate distance slabs from the Antonine Wall demonstrate that *legio II Augusta* was present in Scotland at very nearly full strength, probably with about half the legion involved in building the

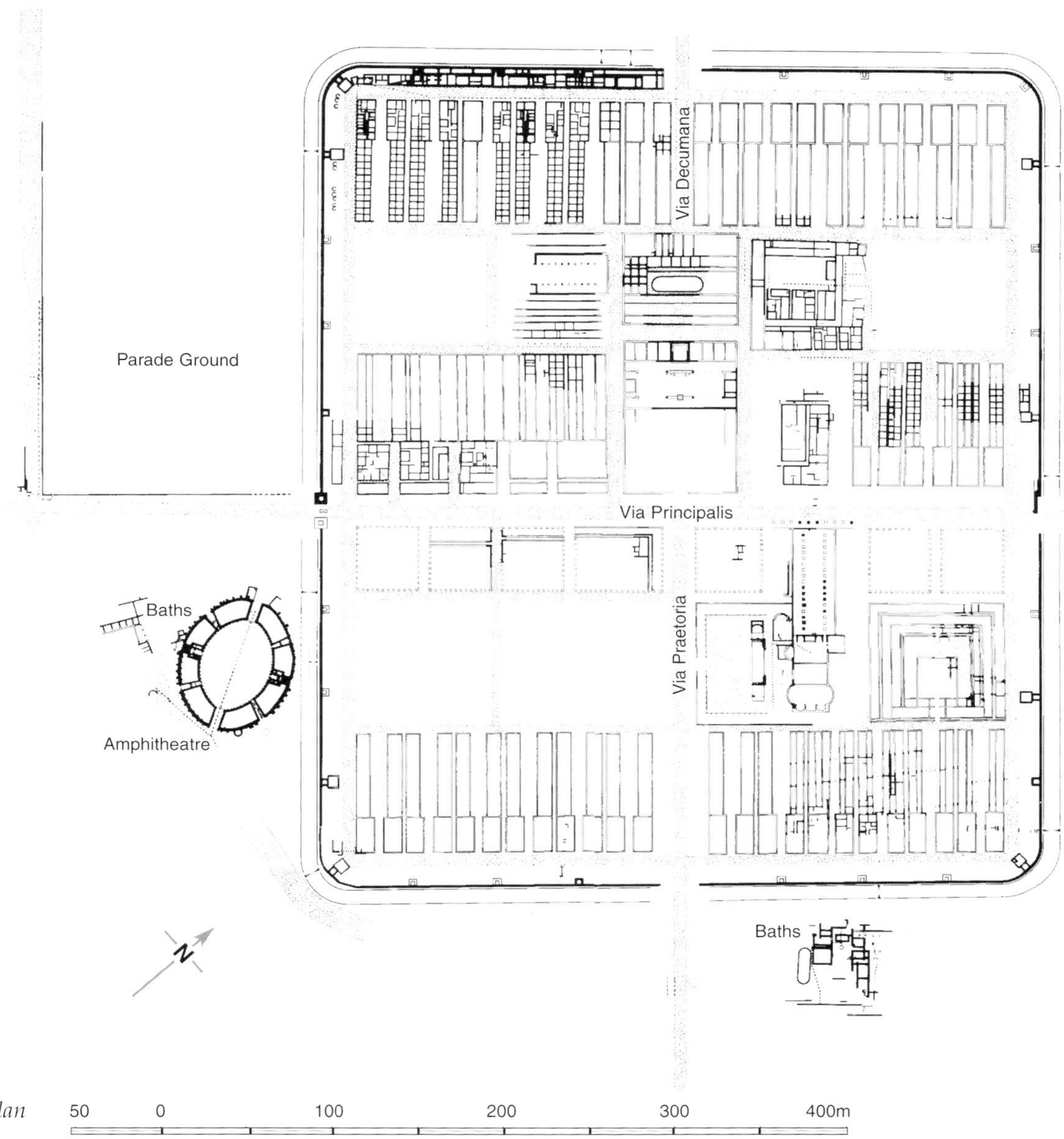

2 *Isca: plan of the fortress*

rampart and ditch of the Wall, the rest being occupied by the construction of forts. To achieve these significant engineering feats, each participating legion would have required a wide range of skilled men and an almost complete list of these specialists is recorded by Tarruntenus Paternus, a praetorian prefect under Commodus, in Justinian's *Digest*.[23]

As well as operating elsewhere in Britain, *legio II Augusta* was also called upon to send detachments abroad. As early as the latter part of Agricola's governorship a vexillation was serving in Germany with detachments from the other British legions. However, most of the evidence, assembled from literary and epigraphic sources, indicating the sorts of places where detachments of *II Augusta* were deployed overseas, belongs to the latter second and third centuries. With so many commitments beyond south Wales, there were long periods when the fortress at Caerleon would have been maintained by a caretaker garrison only. Indeed, this raises the question as to why the legion retained its home base at Caerleon when its major area of operation for much of the history of the fortress was in northern Britain.[24] Reasons of inertia on the part of the provincial government and the prohibitive cost of building a new, permanent fortress in the north have been proposed. Fulford, however, reminds us that we should not underestimate the continued threat of the mountainous hinterland beyond the lowlands of south Wales and that this perhaps influenced military thinking in retaining Caerleon for over two centuries. From its base at Caerleon, *II Augusta* would have performed a number of roles, such as overseeing imperial interests in the exploitation of a wide range of minerals and other resources in south Wales and the west of Britain and maintaining supplies to the army in Wales and northern Britain. In this latter role, Fulford argues that *legio II Augusta,* perhaps with the assistance of others, may have operated a fleet around the western shores of Britain.

Birley contemplates the officers who led the legionaries of *II Augusta* in all its duties, from the conquest of 43 up till the 250s, when the evidence runs out. During this period he records the names of a dozen legionary legates, seven *tribuni laticlavii,* eleven *tribuni angusticlavii,* five *praefecti castrorum* and about two hundred centurions (see Appendix pp 118–21 for a list of all these officers). Many of these officers, especially among the centurions, are known by name only, while for others we have details of their origins, military service and, for some, their later civilian careers. For a few, the literary sources reveal some of their exploits, such as for Vespasian, as mentioned above, and Poenius Postumus, camp prefect of *II Augusta* at the time of Boudicca's rebellion, who took his own life for failing to respond to Paulinus' call for support.[25] The frequent absence from the home base means that officers from *II Augusta* are to be found far and wide. Others joined *II Augusta* for only part of their military service and their careers are recorded on inscriptions that again can be found throughout the Empire.

Maxfield also concentrates on individuals, but rather than considering them as serving soldiers and officers, she examines the non-military side of their lives. After moving to Britain, and for most of the rest of the first century, *legio II Augusta* received its recruits from northern Italy, southern and central Gaul, Spain and the Rhineland. Maxfield, using evidence largely derived from soldier's letters surviving on papyri from Egypt, explores how those serving far away from home might have remained in contact with their families. In Egypt, as well as the possibility of using a formal postal service, relatives, friends and colleagues were frequently called upon to carry letters and sometimes goods as well if they were travelling in the right direction. Such correspondence comprised matters of private life, family affairs and business concerns. Nearer home, the numerous wooden tablets from Vindolanda are gradually revealing more about letter writing and communication within military circles in Roman Britain. One of these tablets was sent by Vittius Adiutor, eagle-bearer of *II Augusta,* but unfortunately only the initial greeting of the letter to Cassius Saecularius at Vindolanda is preserved.[26] Other connections between known personnel of the legion and those appearing on some of the Vindolanda tablets have been made, but these are of a more speculative nature. Leave of absence, at least in the case of ordinary soldiers, to visit distant families in another province appears to be rare. Soldiers no doubt spent much of their off-duty time and leave in a variety of activities in local settlements and towns, whilst others probably travelled to the popular spa complexes, such as that at Bath in the case of soldiers from *legio II Augusta.*[27]

Legionary legates were accompanied by their wives and families, who would have been accommodated comfortably in a spacious residence within the fortress. The situation was very different for the ordinary soldiery, who were legally forbidden to marry. However, as the army settled down in relatively permanent bases and a man might spend his entire service at a single station, many would have formed relationships with local women living in the civilian settlements close to the fortress. When Septimius Severus relaxed the law and allowed soldiers to contract a legal marriage, he was probably only acknowledging the existing situation and making legal relationships which had already been established. Maxfield dwells on the contacts that soldiers made with civilians living outside the camp and further afield.

At Caerleon the civilian settlement is now known to have lain on at least three sides of the fortress.[28] This also seems to be the case at the other two permanent legionary fortresses in Britain, Chester and York; at all three bases very little, if any, occupation occurs on the side of the *porta decumana*. For many years, however, it had been maintained on the evidence available that the extra-mural settlement at Caerleon was restricted to the south-west of the fortress, opposite the amphitheatre. A number of masonry buildings were investigated here in 1954 and 1955, including six or seven rectangular workshops constructed in about 140, a courtyard house of the mid-third century and a 'corridor-type' house.[29] That this assumption was incorrect, was shown by excavations undertaken between 1984 and 1990 which revealed extensive civilian occupation on the north-east side bordering the marshes through which the Afon Lwyd made its way to the confluence with the Usk.[30] The excavations uncovered evidence of twenty-two buildings, some associated with small-scale agriculture on reclaimed marshland while others produced evidence for craft activity, especially iron-smelting. A bathhouse between the east corner and the south-east gate of the fortress also probably formed part of the *canabae*. Traces of further buildings have also been found on the southern approaches to the Usk bridge.[31] Although the Caerleon *canabae* is now known to be more extensive than previously thought, it never developed into a full township, like that at York which eventually received the status of a *colonia*.

Further afield at Great Bulmore, 2 kilometres to the east of the fortress, on the left bank of the Usk (Figure 1), excavations have revealed an extensive roadside settlement.[32] Here a number of strip buildings have been identified, some of which have produced evidence of metalworking and glass making. The relationship of this settlement with the fortress is uncertain, but the inhabitants appear to have played a role in providing services and goods to the legion. Caerwent (Venta Silurum), the tribal capital of the Silures, was also in easy travelling distance of Caerleon and legionary soldiers would have been able to spend some of their leisure time there.

The impact of a legion on the local native population must have been considerable, for it would have needed huge quantities of resources to construct its fortress as well as to sustain itself. Identifying the effort and time devoted to the construction of a fortress has been the subject of recent work,[33] but the consequence of obtaining the necessary raw materials – trees and stone etc – on the surrounding landscape and the lives of the local civilian population has received little attention. Most materials would, no doubt, have been acquired locally, but some – such as Purbeck marble from Dorset and Bath stone from the south side of the Severn – were brought from some distance by sea and river and would have caused little local disruption. As well as the above, Reece also looks briefly at the massive undertaking of feeding the army as well as the operation of the legionary bathhouse and the fuel it would have consumed. These are areas which cry out for investigation, and Reece includes them among a number of suggestions which military archaeologists might like to consider in the future. The discharge of veterans, numbering 200 or so each year, from *II Augusta* would also have had some impact on local populations, for each soldier received land and/or a large donative on retirement. How many remained in south Wales is unknown. Though, as local recruitment replaced those coming from other provinces, such as Italy, Gaul and Spain, the proportion of veterans settling in Britain would no doubt have increased. Tombstones from Caerleon and Bulmore reveal that veterans settled in the *canabae* around the fortress and that some of their descendants served in *II Augusta*. Another local destination for veterans would have been Caerwent and the statue base (Figure 6.11) erected by the tribal council of the Silures in honour of Tiberius Claudius Paulinus, a former legate of *II Augusta*, suggests a close connection between town and fortress. Other direct evidence is, however, limited as noted by Fulford.

Archaeological evidence from Caerleon shows that as early as the late second century, the legion, with detachments constantly serving elsewhere, was depleted on a permanent basis. By the end of the third century a fortress the size of Caerleon had become redundant, for the role and nature of a legion had undergone significant transformation. Casey, whose theme is the later Empire, examines this fragmentation of the legions, which grew from the increasing use of vexillations, the development of specialist units, the establishment of smaller legions by Diocletian for frontier duties and from Constantine's creation of a permanent field army. The size of these later legions is a major problem in late Roman army studies, but the size and plans of newly-established fortresses, such as el-Lejjūn (Jordan), at this time would indicate a force not much larger than 1,000 men.[34] These changes in organization were the result of a long process of forced adaptation in order to defend the Empire.

The fate of *legio II Augusta,* after the closure of Caerleon, is uncertain, but Fulford proposes that the legion, somewhat reduced, was assigned in the late third century to Cardiff where, given the history of its maritime involvement, it could function more effectively. Cardiff was more accessible to the Severn Estuary than Caerleon, and from this newly-built fort the legion could have responded to the threat of seaborne raids. It is suggested that this element of the legion remained there probably until the later fourth century when, as the *Notitia Dignitatum* records, it moved to Richborough; another component, the *Secundani Iuniores,* is also listed in the *Notitia,* as part of the field army of the *Comes Britanniarum.* At Caerleon, despite the undoubted demolition of some buildings from the late second century onwards, there is evidence for continuity of occupation to the late fourth century or even later. Although the indications increasingly point to some form of military presence, the evidence is such that a partial or total civilian presence cannot be precluded.[35] This remains but one of the many questions to be resolved in our pursuit for a better understanding of both Caerleon and *legio II Augusta.* However, Reece, in his paper, suggests various approaches and models in order to take these topics and others forward.

Notes

1 *Legio XX: AE* 1924, 78. However, all four legions are recorded early in Britain.
2 Ritterling 1924/5, 1457–66 for the section on *II Augusta*.
3 Parker 1928.
4 Jarrett 1964a.
5 For an overview of the changing ideas on the pre-Hadrianic legionary dispositions in Britain, see Hassall 2000.
6 Hübner 1881, 531.
7 Ritterling 1924/5, 1460.
8 Collingwood and Myres 1936, 91–2 and 94–5.
9 Richmond 1963, 25.
10 Frere 1967, 1978, 1987a and 1999.
11 Frere 1967, 74–5.
12 Frere 1978, 90–1.
13 Frere 1987a, 59.
14 G Webster 1988, 11–23.
15 Bidwell and Boon 1976. It is uncertain whether this evidence is relevant to the argument as to whether the legion did or did not move to Caerleon via Gloucester. The mould could have travelled with the legion to Gloucester or have been left at Exeter, with a caretaker garrison, and then moved when that fortress was finally closed in the 70s or later (Manning, *in litt*).
16 Mommsen 1886, 178.
17 For a review of past excavations at Caerleon and how ideas have changed, see Brewer 2001.
18 Nash-Williams 1940; new editions of the guide appeared in 1946 and 1952.
19 Boon 1972.
20 Boon 1987.
21 See Zienkiewicz 1993, 140. This four-way arch, forming a monumental entrance to the *principia*, was first discovered by chance in 1988 with further excavations undertaken in 1992.
22 Careful excavation on the Legionary Museum site (1983–5) in the *Scamnum Tribunorum* may well reveal a sequence largely supportive of events in northern Britain involving *legio II Augusta*, see Zienkiewicz 1993, 85.
23 *Digest* 50.6.7.
24 See Breeze this volume, 81; Zienkiewicz 1990, 33.
25 Tacitus, *Annales* 14.37.
26 *Tab Vindol II*, 214.
27 Two altars from Bath refer to men from *legio II Augusta*, see Fulford this volume, 91–2 and Figure 5.11.
28 For a general discussion of the Caerleon *canabae*, see Evans 2000, 459–505. The absence of civil settlement on the north side may be an illusion. Its existence should not be discounted, for observation during the digging of a sewer trench in the 1970s revealed possible evidence of occupation (P V Webster, *in litt*).
29 A summary of the excavations 1954–5 is included in Boon 1972.
30 For a full report on the excavations 1984–90, see Evans 2000. The area to the north-west of the fortress had previously been thought to be archaeologically sterile.
31 See *Archaeol Wales* 24 (1984), 57 (Isca Grange).
32 The rescue excavations undertaken at Great Bulmore in 1983–4 were directed by David Zienkiewicz, see Macdonald forthcoming and *Archaeol Wales* 39, (1999), 103. A large-scale evaluation, conducted in 2000 by the Glamorgan-Gwent Archaeological Trust, has confirmed the probable extent of the settlement.
33 Shirley 2000; 2001.
34 For the size of legions in the fourth century, see Tomlin 2000, 169; for evidence of the size of late units based on rations, pay and donatives, see ibid, 170–3.
35 See Boon 1987, 43–4; Davies 1991, 54–5. The barrack blocks on the 'Roman Gates' site, lying north of the east gate of the fortress, were apparently still in use up to the mid-fourth century, see Evans and Metcalf 1992, 72–5.

Chapter 1

The Origins and Early History of the Second Augustan Legion

Lawrence Keppie

When *legio II Augusta* landed in Britain as part of the invasion force in AD 43, the unit was already almost a century old.[1] It had thus acquired battle honours from earlier postings, which must have remained in the memory of some of its members. Yet the early history of the legion, before AD 43, has not seemed a matter of great interest among archaeologists and historians in Britain itself. This first hundred years of its history are often passed over in little more than a single sentence.[2]

Origins of regiments and continuity of tradition are important subjects, much discussed by military historians of all periods. The oldest regiment of regular infantry in the British army is The Royal Scots, which has been continuously in service since 1633. It served first with the King of France before being finally recalled to Britain by Charles II in 1678. It did in fact claim an even greater antiquity. In Piedmont about 1643, in the course of arguments about seniority between *Le régiment de Picardie* and *Le régiment de Douglas*, otherwise the *Royal Scots*, which had been granted the privilege in the French army of standing on the extreme right of the line, the French derided the Scots' claim to seniority, with the remark that, had they really been any older than the *régiment de Picardie*, they must have served as Pontius Pilate's Bodyguard! This, I assume, was intended as an insult. However, in response, a Scottish officer expressed the view that, 'had we really been the guards of Monsieur Pontius Pilate and done duty at the Sepulchre, the Holy Body had never left it'.[3] The implication is that the Royal Scots did not sleep at their posts, whereas the French regiment often did.

About the origins of *legio II Augusta* we have no precise information. It can, however, be stated with reasonable certainty that it came first into existence in the mid- to late first century BC. I have argued elsewhere, at length, that many of the imperial legions, whose names are familiar to us, are descended from those which served Caesar in Gaul, in the years between 58 and 49 BC.[4] These legions were numbered in a continuous sequence between *V* and *XIIII*. Obviously the Second Legion does not belong to this sequence. When Caesar invaded Italy in 49 BC, he quickly formed many additional legions which were numbered from *XV* to about *XXXIII*. He did not use the numerals between *I* and *IIII* because these were traditionally reserved for the Roman consuls.

The Roman army of the earlier Republic had traditionally consisted of just four legions which were raised and disbanded each year; two were commanded by each consul. By Caesar's own time, the consuls rarely went on campaign during their year of office, but the numerals remained reserved for them to use in case any had to be raised at short notice. In 48 BC, Caesar himself was consul and it must be at this time that he did form legions numbered *I, II, III* and *IIII*, whose existence can be thereafter documented.[5] Of this sequence, legions *II* and *IIII* were stationed in Macedonia in the spring of 44 BC when the news of Caesar's assassination arrived. They were soon shipped to Italy under the command of Mark Antony. Legion *IIII* quickly transferred its allegiance to Octavian (the young Augustus), but most of legion *II* remained loyal to Antony and suffered a heavy defeat at a battle in northern Italy at Forum Gallorum, between Modena and Bologna, in 43 BC; after this nothing definite is heard of it.[6] In the same year, the consuls Hirtius and Pansa formed their own legions, numbered *I–IIII*; in this sequence it may be possible to place a legion, attested only once, with the title *legio II Sabina*. How long it continued in existence is unclear.[7]

Thus we have evidence of two legions, one formed in 48 BC, the other in 43 BC, bearing the numeral *II*. It is not at present possible to say which, if either, of these legions is the ancestor of *legio II Augusta*. After the battle of Philippi, Octavian in 41/40 BC reorganized his own forces, and where necessary filled gaps in the numerical sequence. If there was at this juncture no legion with the numeral *II*, we can quite certainly conclude that it was created now.[8]

Whatever decision is reached on the matter of foundation, it is very likely that there was a legion *II* in existence by 35 BC. At that time, on the defeat of his rival Lepidus in Sicily, Octavian settled veteran soldiers from his own army in southern France: one of the settlements was at Orange, ancient Arausio.[9] The colony's title, long known from epigraphy and from the Elder Pliny, was *Firma Julia Secundanorum*,[10] that is a colony 'of men of the Second, strong in loyalty to the Julian family', a family of which Octavian, by virtue of adoption by Julius Caesar, was now a member. An inscription found at Orange in 1953, which recalls the colony's foundation, reports the number and title of the legion as *II Gallica*.[11] This epithet surely indicates a legion which, by the time of the settlement of these veterans, had served for some years in Gaul itself. Orange was thus a suitable place for settlement of its time-served soldiers.[12]

That this *legio II Gallica* can be equated with the later *legio II Augusta* is suggested by the examination of one of Orange's most famous standing monuments – the so-called *Arc de Triomphe*, which stands outside the north gate of the town (Figure 1.1).[13] The arch is elaborately decorated with scenes of land and naval warfare. In land battles, Roman legionaries defeat Gallic infantry and cavalry, take prisoners and pile up trophies of captured equipment. The arch bears an inscription which is read as honouring Tiberius as *restitutor coloniae*, 'restorer of the colony', with the date AD 27.[14] However, a recent study of the architectural form of the arch and its sculptures has

1.1 *The Arc de Triomphe, Orange, seen from the south (photograph: L Keppie)*

concluded that it did not reach its present form until the late second or early third century AD.[15] The scenes could therefore depict a digest of the colony's, and the legion's, history over two centuries or more. In one scene, a legionary's shield bears a capricorn emblem, which further suggests a link between *legio II Gallica* and *legio II Augusta* (see below).[16]

On one of the Gallic shields the name *Sacrovir* appears. This seems to be an allusion to a revolt in Gaul in AD 21, led by Julius Florus and Julius Sacrovir, which affected large parts of the country.[17] The revolt was put down on the intervention of the Urban Cohort stationed at Lyon, and by the arrival of the Rhine legions. *Legio II Augusta* (at Strasbourg) is very likely to have been involved. Here then is a second link between the legion and events portrayed on the arch.

THE EMBLEMS OF LEGIO II AUGUSTA

Another avenue towards understanding the early history of our legion is to examine the emblems which it bore under the Empire. Each Roman legion had one or more emblems – often these were wild animals or birds of prey, reflecting the religious concerns of a primarily agricultural society.[18] Others were zodiacal signs. We cannot always say how they were acquired by individual legions and precisely what the significance was. One thing is clear: they were not mascots! We know of some Roman emblems from their appearance on building stones (eg the wild boar, a Celtic symbol, on stones of *legio XX*). In the third century AD emperors or usurpers issued 'legionary coinages', the reverses bearing the numerals and emblems of a legion, as evidence of its loyalty, or the hope of it.[19]

A legion's emblems appear on its soldiers' military equipment, on pendants, finger-rings and standards. For example, dolphins shown on helmets of legionaries in a relief from Mainz, Germany, should identify them as members of *I Adiutrix*, a legion with nautical origins stationed at Mainz in the Flavian period.[20] The monument to Q. Luccius Faustus at Mainz (Figure 1.2), standard-bearer of *legio XIIII Gemina Martia Victrix*, includes a presumably highly accurate representation of his *signum*: among the decorations and ornaments depicted is a capricorn, that legion's emblem, surmounting a globe.[21]

1.2 *Inscribed graveslab recording Q. Luccius Faustus from Pollenzo in northern Italy, who served as a standard-bearer in* legio XIIII Gemina Martia Victrix *at Mainz some time in the period AD 70–92. Among motifs on the standard is the frontal view of a capricorn, astride a globe (photograph: reproduced by permission of the Landesmuseum, Mainz)*

The emblems of *legio II Augusta* are the capricorn and the pegasus. The capricorn provides a clear link to Augustus. It appears regularly on cameos, on relief sculpture (Figure 1.3) and especially on coinage

1.3 *Part of a commemorative slab found at Castell Collen, Powys, in 1956. The Latin inscription records building work by a* vexillatio *(detachment) of a legion which can be identified as* II Augusta *from the fish-tail of the capricorn seen below. The inscribed panel was flanked by pelta-designs, the horns of which terminated in griffin-heads. Mid-second century AD (photograph: National Museum of Wales)*

issued during his reign.[22] Sometimes the capricorn is shown astride a globe, and often in naval contexts. As is well known, Augustus was born on 23 September, so that his zodiacal sign was Libra rather than Capricorn.[23] It cannot even be suggested that he was born while Capricorn was in the ascendant.[24] Certainly he had been conceived under Capricorn, and the importance of this link has been confirmed by study of the recently found Augustan sundial in the Campus Martius at Rome.[25]

It is important to note that, among Roman legions, the capricorn is borne by other legions which had a link, from the date or circumstances of their foundation, with Augustus: *IIII Macedonica, IIII Scythica,*[26] *XIIII Gemina,* and *XXI Rapax.* On the other hand, the emblem is employed also by *legio XXII Primigenia.* Formed either by Caligula or Claudius, more probably the former in AD 39–40 (see below), *legio XXII* has left numerous examples of its capricorn emblem at its long-term base at Mainz and at adjacent military sites. Another legion to use the capricorn is *I Adiutrix,* formed by the short-lived Emperor Galba in AD 68. Galba himself was a 'Capricorn', which must explain the emblem's use.[27] We are required therefore to seek different explanations for the popularity of the capricorn at different times. A capricorn appears on a standard depicted on a funerary monument found near Brescia in northern Italy; unfortunately we do not know to which legion the deceased belonged.[28]

The pegasus emblem is frequently employed with the capricorn on relief sculpture of *legio II Augusta* in Britain (Figures 1.4 and 1.5). The exact significance is uncertain. Pegasus was the winged horse of Greek mythology, the offspring of the sea god, Poseidon, and Medusa, the Gorgon.[29] The hero Bellerophon tamed Pegasus, and with his aid defeated the Chimaera monster. Afterwards Bellerophon flew up to heaven on Pegasus, but lost his balance and fell to his death. Pegasus did reach the home of the gods and was placed as guardian of Zeus' thunder and lightning. The story of Bellerophon, Pegasus and the Chimaera is a model for the legend of St George and the Dragon.

A pegasus is shown alone, that is without Bellerophon, as an emblem of the Second Legion. Precisely which elements in the story appealed to the legion, or its founder, cannot be established; the general association between the sprightly horse and the gods may have seemed adequate. Later, coins show a Roman emperor as Bellerophon astride Pegasus, slaying his foes.[30] According to the poet Claudian, Pegasus could convey a living emperor to the heavens, to consult with his peers.[31] Nowadays a pegasus is used as an emblem by military units in several countries, most obviously as a shoulder badge by British airborne forces.

Other legions too used a pegasus emblem: *III Augusta,*[32] whose history may easily parallel that of *II Augusta,* and *II Adiutrix,* formed in AD 70 by Vespasian, which served in Britain from AD 71 to 86. Long ago H M D Parker suggested that the pegasus-emblem had been given to *legio II Augusta* by Vespasian as a reward for the swift adherence of his

1.4 *a Building stone, seen before 1732 near Vindolanda, south of Hadrian's Wall* (RIB *I, 1707). A standard* (vexillum) *bearing an inscription (which has been read as* LEG II VEX, *'flag of the Second Legion') is flanked by a pegasus and a capricorn*

b Building stone, seen before 1732 at Benwell, Hadrian's Wall (RIB 1, *1344). Below the facing figures of a pegasus and a capricorn is an inscription which reads* LEG II AVG/COH X *('The 10th cohort of the Second Augustan Legion'). Both now lost (reproduced from Horsley,* Britannia Romana, *1732)*

1.5 *Distance slab from Duntocher on the Antonine Wall, recording completion of 4140 feet by* legio II Augusta, *in honour of the Emperor Antoninus Pius. AD 142–3* (RIB *I, 2203). Above the inscribed panel is a capricorn; below is a pegasus (photograph: reproduced by permission of the Hunterian Museum, University of Glasgow)*

former command in the civil wars.[33] Pegasus, he averred, was the horse of the East, from which Vespasian had emerged to challenge for power; this is ingenious, but not particularly convincing.

We cannot, I think, conclusively show either of the Second Legion's emblems in use on stone before the early second century AD.[34] However, two gemstones with capricorn motifs, and other symbols, have been recovered in what seem to be mid-first century contexts at Richborough, Kent, and at Waddon Hill, Dorset. Both, it has been suggested, could have belonged to personnel of *legio II Augusta*, who served in the invasion of AD 43 and in the ensuing campaigns.[35]

On stone, both emblems can appear together, [36] or separately.[37] On a third-century roundel, the boar of *legio XX Valeria Victrix* confronts the capricorn of *legio II Augusta.*[38] Interestingly *II Augusta* employed its emblems much more when it was away from its 'home base' at Caerleon, especially when undertaking building work at forts on the northern frontier. At Caerleon, we can cite only two or three examples of the capricorn emblem, and none of the pegasus.[39]

Modern regiments too have emblems. For example, several regiments in the British army have among their badges a sphinx, commemorating participation in the Egyptian campaign of 1801–2. The eagle-badge of The Royal Scots Greys is taken from the eagle-standard of the French 45th Regiment, captured by Sergeant Charles Ewart at the Battle of Waterloo in 1815.[40] The *Leibstandarte* regiment in 1930s Germany had a key as its emblem, but the reason for this is one which I doubt scholars could have divined, without the knowledge that the literal meaning of the surname of its first commander, Joseph (Sepp) Dietrich, is 'skeleton key' or 'picklock'.

THE TITLE OF LEGIO II AUGUSTA

It may seem to some that any search for evidence for the existence of the legion before Augustus became emperor in 27 BC is both unnecessary and misleading. I have read repeatedly that the title *Augusta*, attached to our legion, indicates its formation in or some time after 27 BC, when Octavian took his new name, Augustus.

The title *Augusta* attached to the legion certainly proves an award after that date, indeed between 27 BC and AD 14, but not that the legion necessarily had this *terminus post quem* of 27 BC for its creation. There is every reason to think that the legion existed before 27 BC. Very probably by that date it had been associated with Octavian for a decade or more; the link continued into the Empire. If it was really founded even before Octavian came on the scene, that is before March 44 BC, we can surely assume that he reconstituted it; any earlier loyalties were soon forgotten.

Under the Empire, three legions bore the title *Augusta: II Augusta, III Augusta* and *VIII Augusta. Legio VIII Augusta* can most easily be identified with the Eighth Legion which served under Caesar in his Gallic campaigns, 58–49 BC, for it bears a bull-emblem, indicative of foundation by Julius Caesar, not the capricorn of Augustus. Before becoming *VIII Augusta* it was probably entitled *VIII Gallica*, the latter title attested once only, on a tombstone at Beirut.[41] The title *Augusta* here indicates some success or victory in wars conducted during Augustus' reign, which the legion thereafter cherished.

Legions gained titles from the emperors who founded them, or after military successes in a particular province. So, for example, in Britain, *XIIII Gemina* became *Gemina Martia Victrix* (Martial and Victorious) after the Boudiccan revolt of AD 60–1; Severus gave *legio VI* the title *Britannica* in AD 211 after successes in his campaigns against the Caledonians.[42] In rather different circumstances, Claudius gave the titles *Claudia Pia Fidelis* (Claudian, Loyal and Faithful) to the two legions in Croatia in AD 42, after they had quickly returned to loyalty during an abortive coup which the legate of the province of Dalmatia had fomented.

For *legio II Augusta*, it is in fact difficult to document the use of the title *Augusta* before the legion's posting to Britain in AD 43. Two inscriptions of veterans, one from the Rhineland,[43] the other from the east coast of Italy,[44] are among the first to employ it; but the texts are not precisely datable.

The earliest securely dated occurrence of the title *Augusta* belongs in Claudian times: a text from Antioch-in-Pisidia in southern Turkey commemorates P. Anicius Maximus (Figure 6.3) who served as *praefectus castrorum* of *legio II Augusta* and was decorated *ob bellum Britannicum* ('on account of the British war') presumably in AD 43.[45] According to a roughly contemporary dedication at Arezzo, Italy, the senator L. Martius Macer was tribune in *legio II* (which lacks a title) under Tiberius or Gaius; later he was legate of legions *IIII Scythica* and *V Macedonica,* which are given their familiar titles.[46]

The lack of use of the title *Augusta* up to Claudian times, while surprising, does not of course mean that it had not yet been awarded. Exactly which episode resulted in the award remains a mystery (see below). It could be tempting to suppose that the title was awarded as a result of sterling service in the Roman invasion of Britain in AD 43! Yet in that case, the title *Claudia,* or indeed *Britannica,* would be expected. A study of the use of titles in fact suggests that (a) they were common in the civil wars fought at the end of the Late Republic, to distinguish legions with identical numerals serving in armies of different protagonists; (b) they fell out of use under Augustus and his immediate successors; then (c) reappeared under Claudius or Nero, or at latest in the new bout of civil war in AD 68–9 when legion was once again fighting legion.[47] The lack of use of an existing title finds ready parallels; the omission by *legio II* is typical of the age.[48]

THE LEGION BEFORE ITS TRANSFER TO BRITAIN

The legion's postings and campaign experience before being sent to Britain need now to be considered. In the decade after Caesar's death, if the identification with *II Gallica* (whose members were settled at Orange) is accepted, it is very likely that the legion served in Gaul, helping to consolidate the areas overrun earlier.

Thereafter, it was transferred to Spain where it helped to subjugate the northern tribes, a task usually considered complete by 19 BC.[49] Several inscriptions are reported from Spain, which may attest to its presence there in Augustan times, but they are unhelpful towards determining its precise whereabouts during these years.[50] Veterans of the legion were settled in colonies in Spain at Acci (modern Guadix, near Granada) and in Mauretania at Cartenna (modern Ténès, between Oran and Algiers).[51] I suspect that the title *Augusta* was awarded for service in Spain, but there is nothing to tell us what the circumstances were.

We can be reasonably sure that the legion was in Spain until 19 BC. Thereafter we lose track of it for two decades. Some suppose that it went straightaway to Germany.[52] Others conclude, more plausibly, that it remained in Spain until AD 9, and moved to the Rhine only in the aftermath of the disaster in which three legions under the command of Quinctilius Varus were lost in the forests between the Rhine and Elbe.[53] One inscription may record a soldier who was transferred with the legion from Spain to Germany: the veteran L. Autronius Silo, attested at Strasbourg, was born at Norba (Cáceres), in the Extremadura region of central Spain.[54]

We cannot convincingly locate the legion immediately on its arrival in Germany. If it went there before the Varus disaster, it may have lain not on the Rhine itself, but at one of the winter-camps beyond the Rhine, along the Main or the Lippe, for example at Marktbreit or Haltern. One thing is clear: it did not form part of the garrison of Lower Germany in AD 9 – the three legions of this garrison were all ambushed and destroyed in the greatest military calamity of Augustus' long reign, from the shock of which he never quite recovered.

By AD 14 the legion was based somewhere in the province of Upper Germany. Tacitus reports its quick return to loyalty in the aftermath of the military revolt on the Rhine which accompanied the announcement of Augustus' death; but he does not tell us precisely where it was stationed.[55]

For most or all of the period between AD 14 and its departure for Britain, it certainly lay at Strasbourg. However, an epitaph from Mainz may indicate a brief sojourn there. This stone reports C. Julius Niger, from Carcassonne in southern France, who died at the age of 45, after seventeen years' service in the legion (Figure 1.6).[56] The personal details are followed on the stone by a lengthy address to the passer-by; it was set up by a fellow soldier in the Second.[57] In the Early Empire Mainz was the hub of Roman military activities in the Rhineland, while expansion beyond the river was still being actively considered.[58] Later it was the gateway to the Wetterau and the *limes* forts. A fortress large enough for two legions lay on sloping ground nearly opposite the junction between the Rhine and the Main, in an area still known as Kästrich (from the Latin *castra/castrensis*). The epitaph of Julius Niger derives from Bretzenheim, one kilometre to the west of the fortress, where other early tombstones have been found.[59] We could place the Julius Niger epitaph in the last years of Augustus, around AD 14, with the legion's departure for Strasbourg following rapidly thereafter; but in reality the stone itself, and the inscription on it, cannot be dated precisely.

About the legion's sojourn at Strasbourg on the Upper Rhine, we are not very well informed: excavation within the city has never been easy, given the later occupation.[60] The Second seems likely to have been the earliest legionary garrison placed at Strasbourg, and responsible for the construction of an earth and timber fortress of 12 hectares on an island site, west of the main channel of the Rhine, on ground gently sloping to the east. Nothing meaningful is

1.6 *Inscribed graveslab recording C. Julius Niger from Carcassonne in south-west France, who served in* legio II Augusta *at Mainz, before AD 43 (photograph: reproduced by permission of the Landesmuseum, Mainz)*

known of the layout of buildings within it. In the Flavian period the site was rebuilt in stone, with an area of some 20 hectares, for *legio VIII Augusta*.

However, the Musée Archéologique at Strasbourg, in the Chateau des Rohan, preserves several tombstones of the Second Legion, reflecting its presence there prior to departure for Britain in AD 43. Five (or six) stones are known, all but one recovered from a cemetery area at Koenigshoffen, 2 kilometres west of the fortress, beyond the River Ill, to either side of the Roman road leading towards Metz.[61] None can be exactly dated, but most seem to belong in the later rather than the earlier years of the legion's sojourn at Strasbourg. The epitaph commemorating C. Largennius who came originally from Lucca in northern Italy, who served in the *centuria* of Scaeva, and died at the age of 38 after seventeen years' service, is the most notable (Figure 1.7); it is especially valuable in any study of the military equipment of legionaries at this time.[62] The slabs commemorating T. Julius, from Alba in northern Italy, who died aged 35 after sixteen years' service,[63] and T. Albius, from Bologna, who died aged 40 after seventeen years' service,[64] are plain but dignified. The inscribed panel recording Ti. Babuleius Garrulus and his family, from Milan, was part of a substantial plinth, erected to the family by a freedman not altogether familiar with Latin grammar and spelling, but with money to spend.[65] Babuleius, who died aged 45 after twenty-two years' service, served in the same *centuria* as Largennius; I assume that they knew one another and died about the same time. One of the slabs found at Koenigshoffen, recording the veteran L. Autronius Silo, was destroyed in the German bombardment of Strasbourg in 1870, when part of the museum collection was lost.[66] All the inscriptions lack the title *Augusta*. So far as I am aware, there are no stones with legionary emblems in the Museum's collections.[67] In AD 43, the commander of the legion at Strasbourg was T. Flavius Vespasianus, the future emperor.[68]

The possibility of another posting in the early Julio-Claudian period may be noted here, at Aulnay near Saintes, south of Poitiers, in the Roman province of Aquitania, south-west France. Aulnay is the site, as has recently been realized, of a large fort, or perhaps (better) a small vexillation fortress, of some 6.35 hectares. Discovered by aerial photography, it was explored in 1976–82.[69] The aerial photographs reveal at least two periods of occupation. An epitaph to a soldier from Ventimiglia in north-west Italy, who died at 27 after seven years' service in the legion, was found there long ago.[70] Two inscriptions to soldiers of *XIIII Gemina* also come from the area.[71] The exca-

1.7 *Inscribed graveslab recording C. Largennius from Lucca in northern Italy, who served in* legio II Augusta *at Strasbourg, before AD 43 (photograph: reproduced by permission of the Musée Archéologique, Strasbourg)*

vators of the military installation note, from a study of the small finds and coinage, that occupation could span the last years of Augustus and the opening years of Tiberius' reign, but after lengthy discussion concluded that it was in fact built in the immediate aftermath of the Gallic Revolt of AD 21.[72] The inscriptions fit easily in the early Julio-Claudian period, but are not precisely datable. It seems clear at any rate that detachments from at least two legions spent time at Aulnay, whatever the exact circumstances. Aulnay is among a small but growing number of military sites maintained by the Romans in Gaul into the first century AD.[73] As an alternative scenario we could envisage the presence of *legio II Augusta* at Aulnay as an intermediate posting between its sojourn in Spain and its arrival in Germany.[74]

PREPARATIONS FOR THE CLAUDIAN INVASION

It was long ago realized that we would do well to see the Claudian campaigns in the context of military manoeuvres and adventures initiated by his predecessor Caligula. In AD 40 Caligula undertook a massive military operation in Germany, in part at least to the far side of the Rhine, during a visit to the northern frontiers.[75] P. Anicius Maximus, decorated as *praefectus castrorum* of *legio II Augusta* in AD 43 (see above), had already been decorated *ob expeditionem* ('on account of the expedition'), by an unnamed emperor. Though the award could belong at a very much earlier phase of his career, it remains tempting to see this as a carefully vague reference to Caligula's adventures in Germany in AD 39–40, which were subsequently played down by his successor. After the conclusion of his German adventures, Caligula moved with his army, or part of it, to the Channel coast. At the very least this constituted a threat against the British tribes, especially (I presume) Cunobelinus and the Catuvellauni; in the view of some scholars Caligula was intending a full-scale invasion which was aborted at the last moment.[76]

The existing legions were brought up to a wartime strength, and it is very likely that two new legions were formed in Italy, named *XV Primigenia* and *XXII Primigenia* ('first born', that is of a new breed of legions) and numbered in due succession to two of the Rhine legions, *XIIII Gemina* and *XXI Rapax*; presumably the plan was that they should serve beside them in the existing 'double' legionary fortresses at Mainz and Xanten. Long ago J P V D Balsdon argued that the planned 'post-war' disposition of the legions envisaged *XX, XXI* and *XXII* in Lower Germany, and

XIIII, XV and *XVI* in Upper Germany. The 'odd men out', that is legions *I, II* and *V*, were to be despatched elsewhere, whether to Britain or to new bases across the Rhine we cannot say.[77] We shall probably never know for certain; other interpretations of the evidence are possible. At any rate, when Claudius turned to consider a suitably expansionist policy, to mark the beginning of his reign and to establish his own position as a military emperor, he would have been aware of the bloated Rhine garrison, and the army's plans for a cross-Channel adventure. The invasion force for Britain in AD 43 consisted in the end of *II Augusta* from Strasbourg, *XIIII Gemina* from Mainz (both in Upper Germany), *XX* (evidently not yet *Valeria Victrix*) from Xanten (Lower Germany), and *VIIII Hispana* from the province of Pannonia. These legions were to form the resident garrison of the new province.

The ordinary soldiers may have gone on 'strike' at the Channel ports in the summer of AD 43, but some officers were doubtless eager to be part of the invasion force. Such diversity of motivation has shown itself repeatedly, down to modern times. Later in the century officers were keen on a posting to Britain, one of the few frontiers of the Empire where glory could still be acquired.[78]

REGIMENTAL TRADITION IN THE ROMAN ARMY

We are familiar today with the importance of traditions and regimental history in the modern British army. Legions and auxiliary regiments in the Roman army were as long-lasting as any British formation. While we should not assume automatically for Roman times a veneration of past events and the passing down of regimental lore (which in modern times has become important only from the nineteenth century), it seems appropriate to scan the literary and epigraphic sources for evidence of such practices in Roman times.

Most modern regiments have a museum housing flags, captured equipment, an array of silverware, together with medals and decorations won by past members. Such regimental museums can be found in Cardiff Castle and at Brecon. Memorials to officers and soldiers can be found at regimental chapels in our cathedrals. In the National Army Museum, Chelsea, the visitor can see the top hat worn by Sir Thomas Picton when he was killed at Waterloo, and the saw used to amputate Lord Uxbridge's right leg in the later stages of the same battle.[79] Such items were adjudged worth keeping. At a level more elevated than such memorabilia and curiosities is the powerful image of the wooden hand of Capitaine Danjou, preserved by the French Foreign Legion as an emotive symbol of heroic resistance and steadfastness. Capitaine Danjou (who had lost his left hand in an earlier engagement) was the defender of an outpost at Camerone, Mexico, in 1863.[80] After the defenders succumbed to Mexican attack, the wooden hand, separated from the captain's body, was recovered in somewhat mysterious circumstances. Kept like a holy relic in the crypt of the Legion's present-day museum at Aubagne in southern France, the hand is paraded annually before the legionnaires, on the anniversary of Camerone, 30 April. In 1962, when the legion left its long-term base at Sidi-bel-Abbès in Algeria for the last time, the marching column of troops was preceded through the gates by a soldier carrying a box with the hand of Danjou inside it.[81]

We do not know, I think, very much about the Roman army's attitude to, or veneration of, heroes of past victories,[82] as opposed to mythical warriors such as Theseus, Achilles and Hercules.[83] Equipment captured from the enemy in battle was set on trophies and dedicated to the gods, but not (so far as I am aware) kept by the legions (Figure 1.8).[84] Whether there was a 'Legionary Museum' at Caerleon in Roman as well as in modern times remains a moot question! Under the Republic, some of this material was brought home by the generals, and prominently displayed in their homes, and at their doors, as an everlasting memorial to their exploits. They were still to be found there much later.[85] A regiment's standards were kept in the *aedes principiorum*, inside the headquarters building of a fortress or fort, together with statues of the emperor, and altars; the room was guarded day and night.[86]

Soldiers departing on patrol would pass, outside each legionary fortress, the tomb monuments and graveslabs of their comrades and predecessors in arms. Many were decorated in relief with eagles, standards and military decorations as well as the deceased in full uniform, painted in rich colours, and

1.8 *Bronze plaque, length 26.2 cm, found in 1986 at Caerleon. It shows the winged figure of Victory, who carries a 'trophy' of captured military equipment: body armour, a helmet and two shields set on a pole. A common theme in sculpture and on coins, it symbolises the Roman army's successes. Probably second century AD (photograph: National Museum of Wales)*

other scenes symbolising his military service. The military decorations were worn on special occasions, such as festivals and state funerals, less certainly in battle.[87] The decorations could be buried along with the ashes of a dead soldier or veteran.[88] A certain Marcus Helvius Rufus, awarded a *corona civica* for saving the life of a comrade in Africa in AD 20, adopted the extra surname *Civica* in permanent recognition of the event.[89]

Standards occasionally incorporated symbols which alluded to past successes, and were often decorated with wreaths and crowns.[90] The eagle itself might have its wings wreathed, as a symbol of victory.[91] This presumably followed upon the sending off, by a victorious general, of 'wreathed despatches' to the emperor in Rome.[92]

The loss of standards was a particular insult and embarrassment. Those legionary eagles recaptured from the Dalmatians in 35 BC found a home in the Portico of Octavius at Rome.[93] Eagles captured by the Parthians were, when recovered in 20 BC, placed in the temple of Mars Ultor on the Capitol (Figures 1.9 and 1.10); they were transferred some years later to another such temple in the brand-new Forum of Augustus.[94] The three eagles of Varus' legions, recovered one by one from the Germans, were presumably deposited in the same place; but I do not think we have any precise information.[95] Titles won in recognition of military success were retained permanently. We know that Augustus was revered as our Legion's founder into the third century AD, and presumably for as long as it continued to exist.[96] When generals harangued their troops before battle, the favourite themes reported by historians are discipline, courage, families at home, advantages of

1.9 Denarius *issued 19–16 BC at an unknown Spanish mint. The obverse shows the laureate head of Augustus; the reverse shows the circular temple of* Mars Ultor *(Mars the Avenger), within which are placed an Eagle and two military standards (photograph: reproduced by permission of the Hunter Coin Cabinet, University of Glasgow)*

1.10 *Statue of Augustus, found in 1863 in the ruins of his wife Livia's villa at Prima Porta, just outside Rome. Augustus is shown in the act of addressing his victorious soldiers. In the centre of the breastplate a Roman officer, either Augustus himself, or his stepson Tiberius, receives an Eagle from a bearded Parthian. The scene celebrates the recovery in 20 BC of military standards lost with Crassus more than 30 years before. Now in the Vatican Museum (photograph: reproduced by permission of the Mansell Collection)*

their weaponry, to be contrasted with the poor training and motivation of their opponents. Only rarely, in versions which have come down to us, is much made of the legion's or legions' own past and distinguished record; presumably because the historians were unaware of any details to be incorporated in the largely fictitious speeches. A search of the ancient sources for specific references to military tradition and memory of past glories, has produced little result. In a letter to the mutinous legionaries of Pannonia in AD 14, Tiberius reminded the soldiers of heroic deeds under his own command, in earlier years; but they were interested only in more immediate demands: better pay and an early discharge.[97] The bicentenary of the participation of *legio VI Ferrata* in Mark Antony's Parthian campaigns of 36 BC was marked by a coin issue under Marcus Aurelius in the early AD 160s.[98] The distinguished role played by *III Gallica* in Antony's campaigns, and in subsequent wars down to living memory, was recalled in AD 69 by Antonius Primus, in order to motivate the legion's soldiers in a battle against Vitellian troops.[99] When Hadrian addressed members of *legio III Augusta* at their fortress of Lambaesis in AD 128, he congratulated them on the fine quarters they occupied, despite being understrength and having had to move their permanent base twice in the past two generations.[100] Certainly Hadrian had been well briefed on the legion's history; but did the soldiers appreciate the details?

One document which might have been expected to reveal some mention of celebration of a unit's distinguished past is the *feriale Duranum*, a festivals' list compiled in the mid-third century AD, which provides dates and events for an army unit to commemorate.[101] It was found during the 1931–2 excavation season at Dura Europos on the Euphrates (in northern Iraq), the base of an auxiliary cohort, the *cohors XX Palmyrenorum*. It includes the festival of the *rosaliae signorum*, the decking out of the standards with garlands of roses, on two separate days in May.[102] This was a festival to mark the return of spring and summer. Dates of imperial victories won centuries earlier were commemorated, and the birthdays of popular emperors and members of their families, back to Augustus' reign. But there are no allusions to any success of the regiment itself during its lifetime of half a century or a little more.[103]

For *legio II Augusta*, and doubtless the others too, our evidence is very incomplete. An important annual event was the *natalis aquilae*.[104] How was it celebrated? A much restored papyrus from an auxiliary fort in southern Egypt records the celebration, in AD 232, of the birthday of the Emperor Severus Alexander: a religious ceremony in the *aedes principiorum* was followed by a distribution of gifts by the cohort commander, an inspection of troops, a march past, and a party for a select few.[105]

The lack of many categories of appropriate evidence makes it difficult to identify traditions and what they meant for the Roman army. Nevertheless, it may be worthwhile to look afresh at records of the legion.

Welsh regiments, as well as Scottish regiments and indeed Roman legions, have their traditions and a proud history. The 24th Regiment of Foot, soon to be The South Wales Borderers, featured dramatically in the film *Zulu Dawn* (1979), depicting the defeat of the 1/24th at Ishandlwana in 1879, and more heroically in the better-known film *Zulu* (1963), when a company of the 2/24th defended the mission station at Rorke's Drift against part of Cetewayo's army.[106] The successful engagement diverts attention from the defeat, though the soldiers involved in the latter displayed considerable courage, culminating in the forlorn attempt by Lts Coghill and Melvill to save the Queen's Colour of the 1/24th,[107] later commemorated in a music hall song.[108] The colour was successfully recovered, and displayed to Queen Victoria at Osborne House; she placed above it a wreath of flowers, 'immortelles'; a facsimile of the wreath was henceforth attached to the Queen's Colours of both battalions of the 24th, the only regiment in the British army to have this honour. The wreath matches those shown on the eagle-standards of legions.[109]

The past exploits of regiments have always been an important factor in the maintenance and strengthening of an army's morale.[110] Strong traditions and unit-cohesiveness have been crucial in modern times. Though we would do well not to implant modern concepts or preconceptions into any study of the Roman army, I should like to think that the *legio II Augusta* had its share of traditions well known to at least some of its members, which served as a background to its continuing success over several centuries as the Romans pacified and held their outlying province of Britain.

ACKNOWLEDGEMENTS

For their help in the preparation of this paper, I am grateful to Stephen Wood, then Keeper of the Scottish United Services Museum, Edinburgh Castle; Dr David Breeze, Chief Inspector, Historic Scotland; Lt-Col J L Wilson Smith, then curator of the Royal Scots Museum, Edinburgh Castle; Dr Bernadette Schnitzler, conservateur of the Musée Archéologique, Strasbourg; Dr Franca Maselli Scotti, director of the Museo Archeologico, Aquileia; Mike Dobson (University of Exeter); Professor Y Le Bohec (then Université de Lyon); P R Jeffreys-Powell (then University of Glasgow), Dr Martin Henig (Oxford), Dr Glenys Davies (University of Edinburgh), Dr K V Decker (then Rheinisches Landesmuseum, Mainz) and Catriona Urquhart (Caerleon). Richard Brewer invited me to give the lecture, after a visit to Orange in 1990 had whetted my interest in the legion's early history. The award in spring 1992 of the Gunning Jubilee Gift by the Society of Antiquaries of Scotland enabled me to visit museums in Strasbourg, Mainz, Köln and Bonn, in search of material relating to the early history of the legion. I must thank especially Dr Jürgen Oldenstein (Mainz) and Professor Hartmut Galsterer (Bonn) for their hospitality, advice and help at the time of these visits. Stephen Wood, Dr David Breeze and Margaret Robb read an earlier draft of this paper.

Notes

1 Ritterling 1924/5, 1457–66.

2 Jarrett 1964a.

3 Leask and McCance 1915, 9.

4 Keppie 1984, 80 ff, 199.

5 Ibid, 78, 105, 199.

6 Appian, *Bella Civilia* 3.66–69; Cicero, *Epistulae ad Familiares* 10.30.

7 *ILS* 2227 (C. Aclutius Gallus, *tribunus militum legionis primae, tribunus militum legionis secundae Sabinae*) at Venafro, an Augustan colony in south-central Italy (=Keppie 1983, no. 96). In fact there was an extra legion in this series, *V Urbana*, held back to defend the *urbs Roma*, hence its title.

8 Pompey had a *legio II* in Spain, originally raised during his consulship of 55 BC; it is last heard of in 45 BC; see *ILS* 2224=*ILLRP* 502; Brunt 1971, 475 with his n 5. Inscriptions naming a *legio II*, probably our legion, in Augustan times include epitaphs of *C. Domitius C. f. leg. II* at Cremona (*Bollettino Storico Cremonese* 20 (1955–7), 175=Keppie 1983, no. 67); *Sex. Magius C. f. Fab. Patavinus centhurio legionis secundae* at Aquileia (*Inscr Aquil* no. 64); but the museum label, on the authority of G Brusin, dates the stone to the end of the second century BC. Another early soldier is *C. Andenius C. f. centurio legio(nis) secundae* at Treviso (*CIL* V, 2114). Notice also M. Oppius, *tribunus legionis II* at the colony of Lucera (*CIL* IX, 798).

9 Appian, *Bella Civilia* 5.129; Cassius Dio 49.14–34.

10 *CIL* XII, 3203; Pliny, *Historia Naturalis* 3.36; Kromayer 1896.

11 Piganiol 1951; *AE* 1952, 44.

12 On the land allocation in the *territorium* of Orange, see Piganiol 1962. It is in my view unlikely that the Second Legion at Orange was Antonian, settled by Octavian in 30 BC in the aftermath of Actium.

13 Amy *et al* 1962.

14 *CIL* XII, 1230; see also Le Gros 1979.

15 Anderson 1987.

16 Amy *et al* 1962, 123 f with Fig 52.

17 Tacitus, *Annales* 3.42–47, 14.38; Wightman 1985, 64 ff.

18 von Domaszewski 1885; Daremberg and Saglio 1909, 4.2, 1307 ff; Ritterling 1924/5, 1371–5; Weinstock 1971, 118 ff; Keppie 1984, 136 ff.

19 Oman 1918, 80–96; 1924; Okamura 1991.

20 Selzer 1988, 64, Abb 44. For the link with *I Adiutrix*, see Kähler 1931. For dolphin antefixes at Exeter and Caerleon, see Bidwell and Boon 1976.

21 *CIL* XII, 6898; Selzer 1988, 34, Abb 17.

22 Dwyer 1973; Kraft 1967; Zanker 1988, 82 ff; *Kaiser Augustus und die verlorene Republik* (exhibition catalogue, 1988), 351 ff.

23 Suetonius, *Augustus* 5; but the same writer, ibid, 94.12, wrongly states that he was born 'under capricorn'.

24 I am grateful to Catriona Urquhart for advice on astrological complexities.

25 Bowersock 1990, 385 ff.

26 On *IIII Scythica*, see Coarelli 1967; corrected by Keppie 1984, Plate 14a, 229.

27 Suetonius, *Galba* 4.1.

28 Franzoni 1987, 74 ff, Tav 25.1.

29 Harvey 1981; Reinach 1920. Le Bohec 1989, 556. Pegasus was the emblem of the city state of Corinth in Classical Greek times.

30 Yalouris 1987, 67.

31 Claudian, *De Quart. Cons. Honorii Aug.* 558; another significance could be astronomical, in that the constellation Pegasus rises on 7 March.

32 Le Bohec 1989, 555 f; Veyne 1964, 37–40, citing *CIL* VIII, 2579e=*ILS* 3539, *CIL* VIII, 17977.

33 Parker 1928, 106.

34 On centurial stones from Hadrian's Wall, which are assumed to be contemporary with its construction in about AD 122–30 (*RIB* I, 1341, 1342, 1344, 1707, etc). But if the arch at Orange is genuinely Tiberian, the earliest occurrence would date to AD 27.

35 Henig 1971, 192. The capricorn appears only once on gems found in the excavation of the Caerleon Fortress Baths; see Zienkiewicz 1986b, 132, no. 26.

36 *CSIR*, I.1 *Hadrian's Wall East*, 91, nos 280–2; *CSIR* I.4 *Scotland*, nos 152, 154; *CSIR* I.6, *Hadrian's Wall West*, no. 398. See also *RIB* I, 340, 1341, 1342, 1344, 1707. *CSIR* I.4, *Scotland*, no. 171 shows a capricorn and two confronting pegasi.

37 *CSIR* I.4, *Scotland*, no. 41; *CSIR* I.6 *Hadrian's Wall West*, no. 399. Coins issued by Victorinus show pegasus alone.

38 Casey this volume, 167, Fig 9.1.

39 *CSIR* I.5, *Wales* nos 32, 34, 59. Boon 1984 can cite no examples among the corpus of antefixes from Caerleon.

40 Wood 1990, 45 f. The eagle is preserved in the Scottish United Services Museum, Edinburgh Castle.

41 *CIL* XIII, 14165^6.

42 A R Birley 1971.

43 *CIL* XIII, 12075.

44 *CIL* XI, 6223.

45 *ILS* 2696; Birley this volume, 105, Fig 6.3; Wiseman 1981, Pl 1; Dobson 1978, 188, no. 52.

46 *ILS* 969; *PIR*^{2}, M no. 343. The title *Augusta* is attested for *III* under Tiberius (*ILS* 6285, 9375); for *VIII* under Augustus or Tiberius (*ILS* 2466).

47 See Keppie 1984, 136 ff.
48 Notice the *legio Augusta* which Cassius Dio 54.11.5 reports as losing its title after a reverse in Spain. Syme 1933, 15 ff, proposes identification with legion *I*. But can we be sure that it was not our legion which suffered this embarrassment?
49 Syme 1933; 1970; Le Roux 1982, 61 ff; Roldan Hervas 1974, 192 ff. Jones 1976; Schmitthenner 1962.
50 Veterans at Barcelona, a Caesarian (civil) colony (*CIL* II, 6152) and at Astigi (Baetica, *CIL* II, 5053); serving soldiers at Burguillos (Baetica, *CIL* II, 985) and Osilippo (Lusitania, *CIL* II, 166). The epigraphic evidence is cited by Roldan Hervas 1974, nos 501, 502, 505, 506 and Le Roux 1982, 184, nos 48–51.
51 Acci (coins); Cartenna, see Pliny, *Historia Naturalis* 5.20. Perhaps also Tucci (Martos in Baetica); see Pliny, *Historia Naturalis* 3.12 *(colonia Gemella)*.
52 Roldan Hervas 1961, 114–60; Le Roux 1982, 84.
53 On Varus, see now Schlüter 1993.
54 *CIL* XIII, 5975.
55 Tacitus, *Annales* 1.37.
56 *CIL* XIII, 7234: *C. Julius C. f. Vol. Carc. Niger miles leg. II annor. XXXXV aer. XVII h.s.e.;* Cüppers 1990, 97, Abb 53; *Anthologia Latina* II.2, no. 1005.
57 The name of the dedicator is mostly lost, but may include the surname Gnatus or Cognatus, unless the latter has its literal meaning, 'kinsman'. P R Jeffreys-Powell very kindly commented on metrical irregularities and mixtures of tenses in the Latin text.
58 Decker and Selzer 1976; Baatz 1962; Schönberger 1969.
59 *CIL* XIII, 6855, 7232, 7234a, 7235, 7236, 7237 (a soldier from Toulouse in *leg I...*).
60 Forrer 1927, esp 272–82; Wells 1972, 147 f; Hatt 1980, 83 ff; Schnitzler and Schneider 1985, 52 ff; Petry 1985; Waton 1985.
61 *CIL* XIII, 5976, 5977, 5978, 11628, 11629. Forrer 1927, Taf xxxiv at 275 illustrates the whole group. His Pl cix at 276 shows the findspots. See also Hatt 1964, nos 1, 3.
62 *CIL* XIII, 5978: *C. Largennius C. Fab. Luc. mil. leg. II 7 Scaevae an. XXXVII stip. XVIII h.s.e.* See the discussion by Hatt 1983. Hatt suggests that Largennius died in the Gallic revolt of AD 21; but we have no good reason for linking the epitaph to any known historical event.
63 *CIL* XIII, 5977: *T. Julius T. f. Cam. Alb. miles leg. II 7 Bieni ann. XXXV stip. XVI h.s.e.*
64 *CIL* XIII, 11628: *T. Albius Lemonia Bonia ano. XL stip. XVII h.s.e.*
65 *CIL* XIII, 5976: *Tiberius Babuleius Garrulus Tibri Ofent. Medioleanio mil. leg. II 7 Scaevae Petr. ano. XXXXV stip. XXII h.s.e.*, etc.
66 *CIL* XIII, 5975: *L. Autronius L. f. Sergia Norba Silo veteranus ex leg. II heredes ex testamento.* Forrer 1927, 276, Fig 196 has a line-drawing. The same cemetery yielded a richly decorated *gladius* in its scabbard, perhaps from an officer's tomb (Hatt 1980, 118 ff, Fig 27); the excavation context suggested a Tiberian date.
67 A partially preserved slab (*CIL* XIII, 11629) is usually claimed as an early military epitaph; see Forrer 1927, 281, Fig 200. While certainly of a soldier, it may date rather later and could report a member of *VIII Augusta*. A brick (*CIL* XIII, 12137), now on display in the Musée Archéologique, inscribed by hand, reads LEG II; see Forrer 1927, 21, Pl 1.1; Hatt 1980, 121.
68 Suetonius, *Vespasian* 4.
69 Tassaux and Tassaux 1983; 1984.
70 *CIL* XIII, 1122 (*...Fa]l. Albi. mile. leg. II 7 Laenatis anno. XXVII sti. VII h.s.e.*). The stone is incomplete and damaged at the point where the numeral of the legion is recorded. See Maurin 1978, 48 ff and Fig 5. Le Roux 1982, 85 n 12 discusses the text; see his Pl IIIA.
71 *CIL* XIII, 1121 *(L. Autius L. f. Ani. For. Juli mil. leg. XIIII Gem. anno. XXXV stip. XV h.s.e.)*, 1123 *(L. Furius L. f. Ani. Crem. miles leg. XIIII G[..)*. See Maurin 1978, Figs 3–4. For another military epitaph at Saintes, of early date, reporting a C. Julius of an unknown legion, see *CIL* XIII, 1046. Note, from the same general area, an early gravestone of *XIIII Gemina* at Néris-les-Bains near Montluçon (*CIL* XIII, 1383) and a tile of *legio II Augusta* at Dax (on the route to Spain); see Tassaux and Tassaux 1984, 151 f, n 85.
72 *Loc cit* (n 69).
73 King 1990, 54 ff, 163.
74 Ritterling 1906, 173.
75 Cassius Dio 59.21; Suetonius, *Caligula* 43–45; *Galba* 6.
76 Barratt 1989, 125 ff.
77 Balsdon 1934, 13–17.
78 Statius, *Silvae* 5.2.142; Martial, *Epigrammata* 10.44.
79 The leg was buried on the battlefield, and the location marked by a small monument; see Paget 1961, 149 ff.
80 Porch 1991, 141 f, 419 f; Sargent 1981.
81 Porch 1991, Pl at 337. Other soldiers carried the ashes and coffins of dead colleagues and former commanders.
82 The centurion Crastinus, killed at Pharsalus in 48 BC, was honoured with an individual tomb monument by Caesar, on the battlefield (Appian, *Bella Civilia* 2.82).
83 Henig 1970; Maxfield 1981. Decorations were awarded for heroism and special service, as the

epigraphic evidence reveals, but the names of recipients are all too rarely reported in the surviving historical accounts.

84 Picard 1957. For commemoration of Actium, see now Murray and Petsas 1989, 92 f, 125 ff.

85 Livy 10.7.9; 23.23.6; 38.43.11; Polybius 6.39.8; Suetonius, *Nero* 38.

86 Johnson 1983, 111 ff.

87 Maxfield 1981, 141 ff; Appian, *Bella Civilia* 2.148 with Suetonius, *Caesar* 84.4; Tacitus, *Historiae* 2.89; Polybius 6.39.8.

88 Pontiroli 1971.

89 *ILS* 2637.

90 For a sculptural relief showing standards decorated with ships' prows and wreaths of victory, now in the Church of S Marcello, Rome, see G Webster 1985, Pl X.

91 Selzer 1988, 128, no. 30 (*CIL* XIII, 6901), and on Trajan's Column.

92 Pliny, *Historia Naturalis* 15.133.

93 Appian, *Illyrica* 28; Wilkes 1969, 55 n 2.

94 Cassius Dio 54.8; cf *Res Gestae* 29.

95 Tacitus, *Annales* 1.60.4, 2.25.2; Cassius Dio 60.8.7.

96 *RIB* I 327, 328.

97 Tacitus, *Annales* 1.25.

98 *Coins of the Roman Empire in the British Museum* IV (1940), *Marcus Aurelius and Lucius Verus*, nos 500–1; pl 62.17.

99 Tacitus, *Historiae* 3.24. Cassius Dio 55.23 notes the long histories of the Augustan legions still in existence in his day.

100 *ILS* 2487.

101 Fink *et al* 1940; Nock 1952; Gilliam 1954; more generally, Fink 1971, no. 117; Helgeland 1978.

102 Hoey 1937.

103 Kennedy 1983.

104 Watson 1969, 130.

105 Wicklen 1894, 83; von Domaszewski 1899. For a translation, see Johnson 1983, 112.

106 Paton *et al* 1892, 223 ff. Strictly speaking, at the time of the Zulu Wars, the 24th was the (2nd) Warwickshire Regiment; but under the territorial reorganization of 1873, it was authorised to recruit from several Welsh counties, with a depot at Brecon. In 1881, after amalgamation, it was renamed The South Wales Borderers. Brereton 1989, 157 ff.

107 According to a contemporary (Zulu) account, when Cetewayo complained that the Colour, 'a long stick, to which was attached a piece of cloth,' had not been brought to him, a chief replied that it was torn, 'and far too gaudy for you ever to have worn' (Brereton 1989, 157 ff).

108 The Noble 24th *or* Vanquished *not* Disgraced' (J W Rowley, nd).

109 Above, p 21; Maxfield 1981, 70 ff; Devijver and van Wonterghem 1990, esp Figs 25–6.

110 MacMullen 1984; among modern literature, note Royle 1990.

CHAPTER 2

EARLY ROMAN CAMPAIGNS IN THE SOUTH-WEST OF BRITAIN

W H MANNING

Ob Diem Natalem Legionis Augustae Secundae Aquilam Saluto

The archaeologist who is concerned with the early years of the Roman conquest is fortunate in that the most complete historical accounts of Roman Britain to have survived are for the half century following the invasion of 43.[1] For the invasion itself we are largely reliant on the *Roman History* of Cassius Dio written in the early years of the third century, with Suetonius' *Lives of the Caesars* adding important details, including some on the conquest of the south-west of England. But without question the greatest of all our ancient sources is Tacitus,[2] whose major work was a history of Rome which, if completed, would have covered the greater part of the first century AD. In such a survey he must have discussed the conquest of Britain, but he had another and more personal interest in the province, for his wife was the only daughter of Agricola, a man whose whole career had been bound up with Britain where he had served twice already before he returned as governor in 78. So highly did Tacitus regard his distinguished father-in-law that he wrote a short, laudatory biography of him, which effectively serves as a summary history of the first half-century of the province. Unfortunately it is terse, highly selective, and frequently imprecise. Not that it does not provide much valuable information, although in practise it has often proved extremely difficult, indeed at times impossible, to correlate this with archaeological discoveries. In the surviving fragments of his greatest works, the *Annales* and *Historiae*, his treatment of Britain was less personal, but it is often no more detailed. We are also further handicapped by the loss of large sections of his narrative, including his account of the invasion. Nor was Tacitus attempting to write the kind of history, precise in geography and minute in detail, which an archaeologist desires. His aims were grander, and perhaps we should not complain that he did not do what he never intended. Above all, it must never be forgotten that without Tacitus our knowledge of the conquest of Britain would be even less complete than it actually is.

PRE-CONQUEST BRITAIN

At the time of the Claudian invasion Britain was inhabited by a series of more-or-less independent tribes.[3] The previous century had seen the growth in power of one of these, the Catuvellauni whose capital was at Verulamium (St Albans), although by the early years of the first century AD their king had transferred his seat to Colchester (Camulodunum), the capital of the Trinovantes, probably following the conquest of that tribe. By 43 their rulers appear to have effectively controlled much of south-eastern England and exerted influence over a much wider area. Beyond them lay tribes who had good reason to fear their domination, and who may have welcomed the arrival of the Romans as the lesser of two evils. The situation was complicated by the fact that the Britons had a system of alliances whereby weaker tribes became the clients of their stronger neighbours. Such alliances, possibly aided by family relationships, probably explain how Caratacus, originally co-ruler of the Catuvellaunian empire, became the leader of the Welsh tribes in their fight against Rome.

There is no doubt that Rome had been in diplomatic contact with some of the British tribes in the century following the invasions of Julius Caesar. In the *Res Gestae*, his political testament, the Emperor Augustus listed the British kings who had fled to him for refuge: 'The following kings sought refuge with me as suppliants ... Dumnobellaunos and Tincommius, Kings of the Britons'.[4] A generation later Adminius, the exiled son of Cunobelinus, was to flee to Caligula,[5] and, a few years after, Verica (*Berikos* in the Greek text) to Claudius.[6] By then dispossessed British kings appear to have been treading a well-worn path. That this traffic was not limited to fallen rulers is shown by Strabo's comment that: 'At present some of the kings (of Britain) have gained the friendship of Caesar Augustus by sending him embassies and paying him deference. They have not only dedicated offerings in the Capitol, but have also brought the whole island under Roman control'.[7] Even allowing for a degree of exaggeration it is clear that Rome had considerable influence in certain parts of Britain long before the invasion of 43. The absence of references to similar embassies under Tiberius and Caligula is more likely to reflect the deficiencies of our sources than a cessation of formal contacts between British kings and Rome. When the invasion came Rome was probably able to rely on the support of at least some of these tribes; a number which will have increased with the rapid success of her armies. A clear example of this is given by Cassius Dio who records that after the initial defeat of the British forces following the invasion 'he (Claudius) won over a section of the Bodounni (ie the Dobunni), who were subject to the Catuvellauni'.[8] The reward for such tribes was to be allowed to retain a nominal independence as allies of Rome; an independence which usually lasted no longer than the lifetime of the ruler who made the treaty.

THE INVASION

The invading army consisted of four legions each of somewhat over 5,000 men, with a large supporting force of auxiliaries, mainly light infantry and cavalry, mostly divided into units of 500 or less, each unit being attached to one of the legions. As there were probably as many auxiliaries as legionaries, the total army will have been around 40,000 men. Its commander was a distinguished general, Aulus Plautius.[9] The beachhead was at Richborough in Kent and the forces of Caratacus and his brother Togodumnus, who between them controlled the Catuvellaunian empire, were soon defeated. After the capture of Colchester, an event directed, at least nominally, by the Emperor Claudius, the army was divided into four groups each centred on a legion. The evidence suggests that *legio XX Valeria* remained at Colchester, which became the *de facto* capital of the new province. *Legio VIIII Hispana* moved north through the East Midlands, while *legio XIIII Gemina* struck west across the Midlands until it reached the northern marches of Wales where, probably by the mid-50s, it had built a base at Wroxeter, near Shrewsbury.[10] *Legio II Augusta* under its commander Vespasian, a quarter of a century later to become emperor, conquered the south of the province; in the process, we are told by Suetonius, fighting thirty battles, reducing two powerful tribes, and taking more than twenty towns (*oppida*, which must mean hillforts) and the Isle of Wight; this last detail indicating not only his area of operations, which is otherwise unrecorded, but also the fact that his army worked in concert with a fleet.[11]

Useful though this information is it leaves many questions unanswered. Vespasian's command almost certainly ended in 47,[12] and it is perhaps unlikely, although not impossible, that he campaigned as far west as the territory of the Dumnonii of Devon and Cornwall. The evidence for the early conquest of the Durotriges is clear. The fort at Hod Hill was built soon after 43,[13] whereas the fortress at Exeter was not founded until the mid- to late 50s, and this, together with the absence of proven Claudian sites in Devon, tends to confirm that Roman control of the area had not been consolidated before the departure of Vespasian.

The northern limit of his command is uncertain, but if we are correct in assuming that *legio XIIII Gemina* was responsible for the conquest of the Midlands, the division between the two legionary territories is likely to have been in the northern Cotswolds. The alternatives would be either that *legio XIIII Gemina* held a much larger part of the country than its sister legion, or that there was an area of unoccupied territory between the two, neither of which seems likely. If these arguments are correct, then Vespasian will have been responsible for the conquest of a much larger part of southern England than is often assumed. Certainly Tacitus' statement that Ostorius Scapula, Plautius' successor, found it necessary to bring legionaries against the Silures, apparently in 49 or just possibly in 50, confirms that by then the Roman army was within striking distance of south Wales (p 38 below).

The construction of the fort at Cirencester in the late 40s suggests that *legio II* operated on more than one front. In the past the emphasis has usually been placed on the evidence of military activity in Dorset and the areas to the north have received less attention. But it is unlikely that Vespasian's army first advanced through the coastal counties before turning north into Somerset and Gloucestershire; more probably they operated on at least two fronts, although these need not have been on the same scale nor have met the same degree of opposition. Although Vespasian was the commander of a legion he would have had a roughly equal number of auxiliaries under his command, and so would have been able to use various combinations of units to deal with different problems.

If we are correct in our assumption that his theatre of operations covered a block of country to the west of London extending from the Channel coast to the north Cotswolds he will have been dealing with five main tribes, the Atrebates, the Regni,[14] the Dobunni, the Belgae and the Durotriges (Figure 2.1). Of these, the Atrebates had been ruled in the late Iron Age by the house of Commius, and Verica, the last ruler of that dynasty, had fled to Claudius immediately before the Roman invasion; indeed Cassius Dio cites Roman support for Verica (who he calls Berikos) as the reason for the invasion.[15] The little that we know of the pre-Roman history of the tribe suggests that it was firmly pro-Roman, and it seems unlikely that it will have done anything other than welcome the arrival of the Roman army, the more so as it appears to have been subject to aggression from the Catuvellauni in the years before the conquest.[16] The Regni were to form the core of Cogidubnus' client kingdom, and their loyalty to Rome seems to have been absolute.[17] The Dobunni (or Bodounni as Dio calls them) make an early appearance in the history of Roman Britain since part of the tribe, who according to Cassius Dio

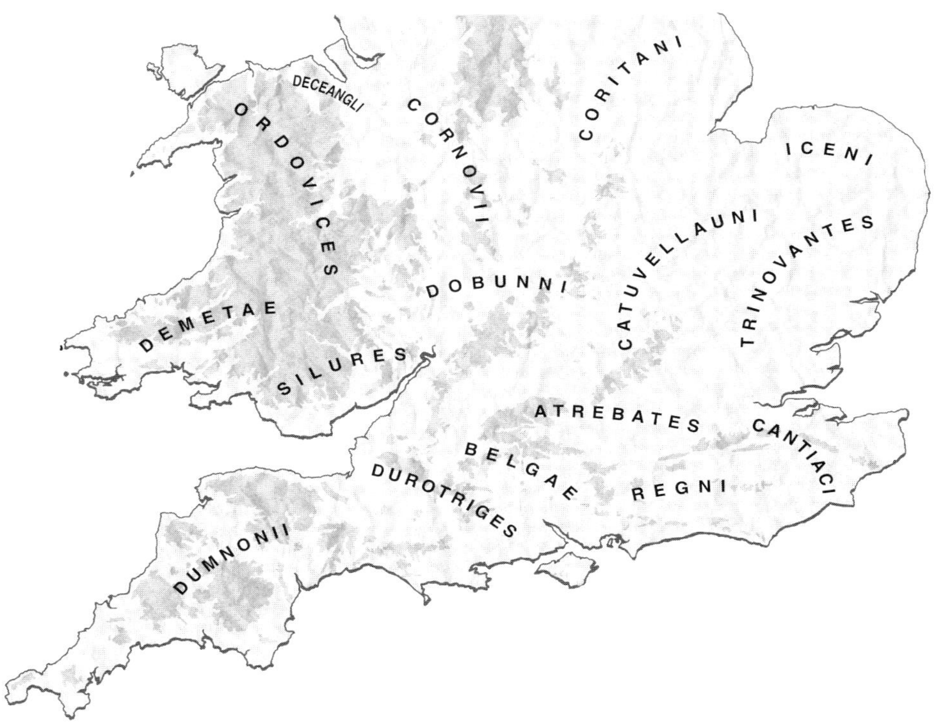

2.1 *The Late Iron Age tribes of southern Britain*

were subject to the Catuvellauni, came to terms with the Romans after the first defeat of Caratacus and Togodumnus.[18] Presumably their leader was among the eleven British kings, who according to the inscription from Claudius' triumphal arch in Rome, surrendered to him.[19] Here again opposition to Vespasian's army appears unlikely. History is silent on the Belgae and the Durotriges. In the Roman period the *civitas* of the Belgae extended from somewhere to the east of Winchester, which was their capital, to beyond Bath, if Ptolemy's *Aquae Calidae* is Bath, and it is difficult to see an alternative identification.[20] Their attitude to the Romans is not known, but with the possible, but very uncertain exception of Winchester,[21] no fort is known in the east of their territory and relatively few in the west, which suggests that the Romans did not regard them as a major problem. By contrast, the archaeological evidence makes it quite clear that the Durotriges did resist and that their territory was garrisoned. Given these facts it seems likely that most of Vespasian's military effort will have been in the southern part of his command, and that it was there that most, although not necessarily all, of the twenty *oppida*, which Suetonius tells us he captured, lay.[22] The Durotriges must have been one of the two strong tribes which Suetonius records him as conquering, but the identity of the other is less certain although the Belgae is perhaps the most likely. On the other hand if the army did reach Dumnonia under Vespasian's command that could have been the tribe in question. The question is open and will probably remain so.

Even those areas which were pro-Roman will not have been exempt from the presence of the Roman army if that was thought to be necessary, which is why we find early military activity at Chichester and Fishbourne. Later this area became part of Cogidubnus' client kingdom, but whether he assumed that status immediately after the conquest or had to wait a few years for it is uncertain; perhaps the latter is the more likely.

The suggestion that the Regni and Atrebates were not inherently hostile to the Romans is supported by the fact that there is a notable lack of Roman forts known in the area to the north and east of Dorset. The most important military establishment in this area may have been at Chichester where there is evidence to suggest that a major military site underlies the later Roman city. Unfortunately it also lies below the modern city and this has prevented both its size and the details of the early timber buildings being ascertained with certainty. Extensive, but generally small scale excavations have located fragments of Claudian timber buildings over an area of *c* 5.3 hectares, and some of the military equipment known from the site was almost certainly used by legionaries.[23] However, without large scale excavations the exact nature of the establishment is likely to remain obscure. Given its early date it is unlikely to have been a full-scale legionary fortress, for, with the exception of Colchester, these do not appear to have been constructed until the mid-50s; its apparent size suggests that it was one of the so-called vexillation fortresses which preceded them. These are large bases which could have served either as winter quarters for half a legion, or for mixed groups of legionaries and auxiliaries; effectively reflecting the situation in the field where the two types of soldier will have worked together.[24] Unfortunately, the problem of identifying the garrisons of these forts is bedevilled by uncertainties as to whether the auxiliaries and legionaries always had different equipment. If we accept, for example, that the auxiliaries could and did wear *lorica segmentata*, then the discovery of that type of armour can no longer be used as proof of the presence of legionaries at a site as it has in the past. Where there are several vexillation fortresses within an area which is likely to have been under a unitary command, which one served as the headquarters may have depended simply on the presence or absence of the legionary commander and his staff. If Chichester was the site of such a base it could well have been the headquarters of part, although not necessarily all, of *legio II* as it began to move through the south of England. The military granaries found below the later palace at Fishbourne on Bosham Harbour presumably represent the harbour and depot for the fort at Chichester, and probably of Vespasian's fleet.[25] The recent excavation of a masonry building (Building 3) resembling the *principia* of an auxiliary fort which was built in *c* 50–60 immediately to the east of the Flavian palace at Fishbourne raises some interesting questions. The fact that the site may have been the centre of Cogidubnus' kingdom complicates the matter, for, as a client king, he may have been allowed to maintain

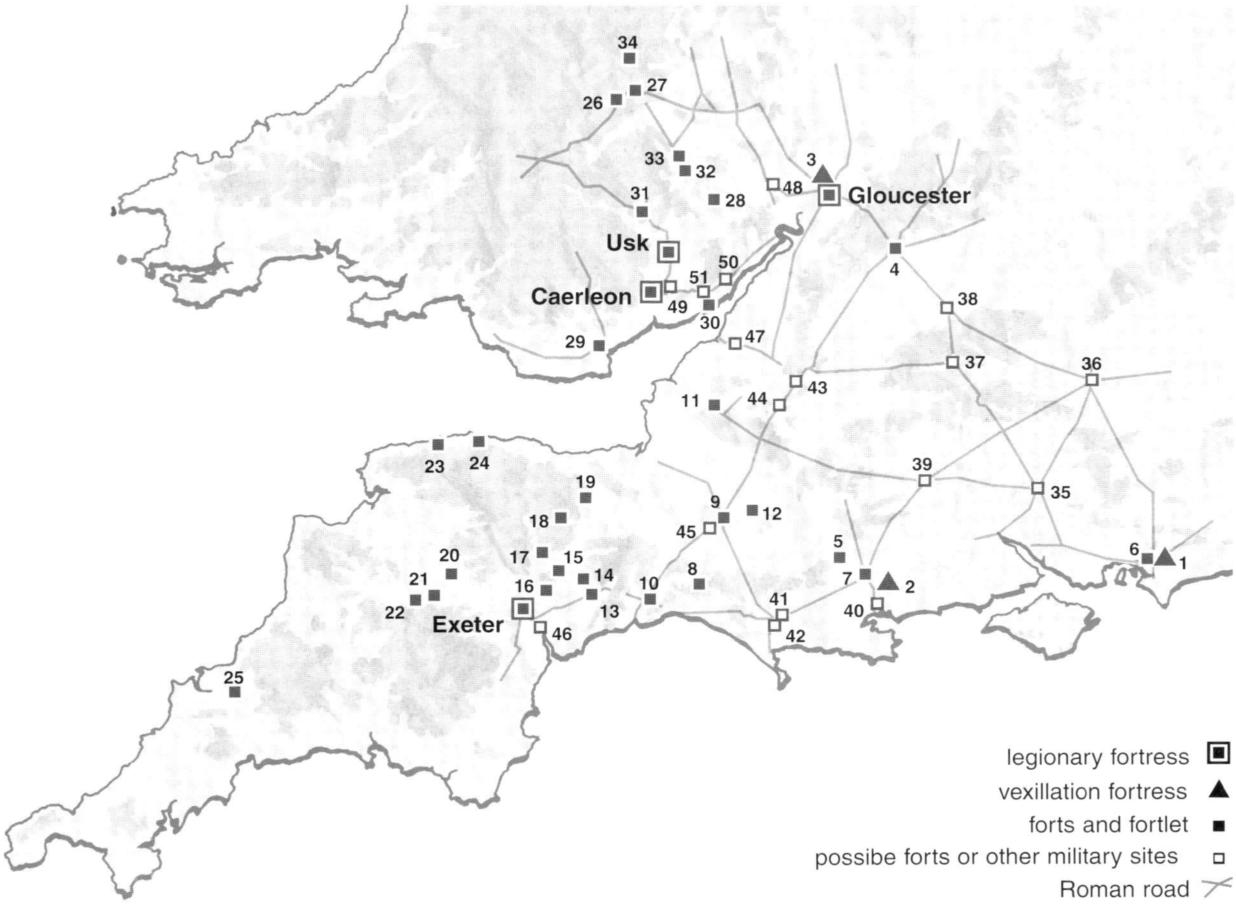

2.2 *Distribution of Roman military sites in south-west Britain. Vexillation fortresses: (1) Chichester (2) Lake Farm (3) Kingsholm. Forts and fortlets: (4) Cirencester (5) Hod Hill (6) Fishbourne (7) Shapwick (8) Waddon Hill (9) Ilchester (10) Axminster (11) Charterhouse (12) South Cadbury (13) Gittisham (14) Hembury (15) Cullompton (16) Killerton (17) Tiverton (18) Clayhanger (19) Wiveliscombe (20) Bury Barton (21) North Tawton (22) Okehampton (23) Martinoe (24) Old Burrow (25) Nanstallon (26) Clyro (27) Clifford (28) Monmouth (29) Cardiff (30) Sudbrook Camp (31) Abergavenny (32) Kentchurch (33) Abbey Dore (34) Walton. Possible forts or other military sites: (35) Winchester (36) Silchester (37) Mildenhall (38) Wanborough (39) Old Sarum (40) Hamworthy (41) Dorchester (42) Maiden Castle (43) Bath (44) Camerton (45) Ham Hill (46) Topsham (47) Sea Mills (48) Weston under Penyard (49) Coed-y-caerau (50) Chepstow (51) Caerwent*

an army of his own, albeit a small one. On the other hand a military function cannot be regarded as proven for, as the excavators note, there is an absence of military equipment and other military buildings from the site. It may also be relevant to note that a stone *principia* would be very unusual, indeed probably unique, in Britain at such an early date. It is now clear that there was a site of unusual character at Fishbourne long before the great palace was built, but it may be best to regard Building 3 as being part of the early civil development of the site. The fact that it remained in use beside the palace until late in the second century suggests that it continued to have a function in the palace phase, which is very unlikely if it had been a military *principia*.[26]

What we lack are the auxiliary forts which would indicate a full-scale occupation of Sussex and Hampshire. In the past one has been suggested at

Winchester, but the evidence is wanting; although the key position of the Roman city (Venta Belgarum) in the road system of southern England would have made it a suitable place for a short-lived fort during the conquest phase.[27] It is possible that others have yet to be found in the area, but given the long history of fieldwork in that part of England, this begins to look less and less likely, and for once the absence of evidence may reflect a genuine absence of forts. If so, it indicates that the Romans did not find it necessary to garrison the area in strength, presumably because it was pro-Roman from the beginning. The possibility of a fort at or near Silchester has been postulated, but positive evidence is again lacking. However, the fact that most of the major roads running to the south-west of Britain originated at Silchester indicates its importance to the military planners at this time and some military presence in the Atrebatic capital, whether it was pro-Roman or not, would not be surprising. However, the very extensive excavations which took place before the First World War failed to produce any significant amount of military equipment and much of what is known is later in date.[28]

The area to the north of Dorset is equally devoid of proven Roman military sites. A fort has been claimed at Mildenhall, Wiltshire where a number of pieces of military equipment and early Roman pottery have been found, but if there is a fort there it has yet to be located.[29] Slightly further north, Wanborough, on the edge of Swindon, has been suggested as the site of another fort, but the evidence is inconclusive.[30] A scatter of military bronzes and other equipment from various parts of north Wiltshire confirms that the Roman army was active in the area, but these pieces do not have to come from forts.[31] In the south of the county a fort has been suggested close to Old Sarum on the evidence of early pottery, but again it remains no more than a suggestion,[32] although its situation at the junction of two major Roman roads might be thought to strengthen the possibility.

THE DUROTRIGES

Vespasian's campaigns, which almost certainly extended over several seasons, have left their clearest traces in Dorset where he appears to have met considerable opposition. A fort is known at Shapwick, near the key road junction at Badbury Rings,[33] but this was soon replaced by the much larger establishment at Lake Farm. The two are too close together to have been occupied at the same time, and the fact that aerial photographs show a Roman road running across the Shapwick fort strongly suggests that it predates the Lake Farm site.[34] Further west a Roman fort has been sought for many years at Dorchester (Durnovaria), but it remains elusive, and as more and more of the town is examined the space available for such a fort has become less and less. The discovery of the large fort at Lake Farm has almost certainly removed the possibility of there being another of similar size at Dorchester, but a small fort remains a possibility, although by no means a certainty.

Some years ago Malcolm Todd suggested that the early Roman material from the hillfort at Maiden Castle, on the edge of Dorchester, indicated that the site had been used as a fort by the Roman army.[35] The 'war cemetery' excavated by Mortimer Wheeler provides clear evidence of the Roman army's activity there, and if the site was occupied by them it would explain the apparent absence of a fort at Dorchester. The problem is further compounded by the fact that Ptolemy cited *Dunium*, not *Durnovaria*, as the *polis* of the Durotriges.[36] *Dunium* is clearly a corruption of *Dunum*, meaning a fort, and this has usually been identified with Maiden Castle.[37] Wheeler's excavations showed that after its capture by the Romans in the mid-40s, the site remained in use for about a quarter of a century.[38] The more recent work of Niall Sharples has confirmed this, and produced at least one building which could be of Roman military type, although the dating evidence is sadly imprecise.[39] The main problem is the fact that Maiden Castle is far too large for the whole of it to have served as a Roman fort, and any fort built within it presumably would have had defences of its own which should have survived as do those of the fort built within the equally large hillfort at Hod Hill. The alternative, that the Romans garrisoned part of the site while allowing a substantial native population to remain, is not impossible but it contradicts the conventional view of how the Roman army operated. Furthermore, the general lack of Roman military equipment from the site, despite extensive excavations, does not support the idea of a garrison. Wheeler was notoriously selective in his publication of small finds even when he was not writing under the pressures of a World

War, but he is unlikely not to have recognized and published Roman military equipment.

The key site in this area is at Lake Farm.[40] This has been the subject of limited excavation and an extensive magnetometer survey which revealed that the fort covered some 12.8 hectares which would make it a large, but not abnormally large, vexillation fortress of the type already referred to. Norman Field, the excavator of the site, claimed that there was a second and larger fort on the same site, but the evidence for the defences is fragmentary and can be interpreted, with perhaps greater validity, as the external ditches associated with the proven fort.[41] Given its position Lake Farm is unlikely to have been the base for the conquest of the Durotriges, and Chichester is the more likely candidate for this, with Lake Farm being built to replace the earlier site when that phase of the conquest was complete. Like Chichester, Lake Farm probably had its own harbour and depot, in this case at Hamworthy on Poole Harbour where early Roman material is known.[42]

The well known fort in the Iron Age hillfort at Hod Hill was almost certainly contemporary with Lake Farm, and the fact that it was not rebuilt after its apparent destruction by fire in about 50 suggests that the area was regarded as reasonably pacified by then.[43] By contrast, the fort at Waddon Hill, which lies some way to the west, does not appear to have been built until *c* 50 and continued in occupation until the early 60s.[44]

THE FOSSE WAY

Until quite recently, it was widely held that the archaeological evidence indicated that there had been a change in Roman policy in the late 40s. The key to this argument was the Fosse Way, that remarkable Roman road which runs across England from south-west to north-east. This, it was suggested, marked a *limes* or frontier dividing the intended Roman province from the tribes beyond. Constructed around 47 when Plautius returned to Rome having completed the task assigned to him by Claudius, namely the conquest of the lowlands of south-eastern England, it left the more mountainous areas to the west outside the new province. That the conquest continued beyond this line was seen by the proponents of this theory as a Roman reaction to the provocation offered by the tribes of Wales. In recent years, however, a number of doubts have been raised against this interpretation.[45] One of the main objections is that there is no hint in the ancient authors that Rome intended anything other than the occupation of the entire island, albeit over a period of years. Another is the fact that Ostorius Scapula, the governor who succeeded Aulus Plautius, seems to have had no hesitation in bringing large areas to the west of the Fosse Way under Roman control almost immediately after he arrived in Britain. This does not suggest that he regarded the road as marking a permanent frontier, which had been created as imperial policy. Had this been the situation, he is unlikely to have extended his province without Claudius' permission, and there is no hint in Tacitus that this was the case. Ostorius will have been well aware that only two years before Claudius had forced Corbulo to withdraw the garrison which he had placed in the territory of the Frisii, to the east of the Rhine, without imperial permission.[46] In fact the impression given in the *Annales* is of rapid action initiated by Ostorius as soon as he had arrived in Britain and found that the situation had deteriorated in the interregnum between his predecessor's departure and his own arrival.[47] Experience dearly bought in other areas, had revealed the problems created by failing to complete such conquests, and an army which had campaigned through the mountains of three continents was not likely to baulk at the hills of Wales.

There is no doubt that the Fosse Way was constructed at an early stage in the conquest, but given the logistics of the situation, with three army groups extended diagonally across England, the construction of such a road for communication purposes would be no more than common sense. That some forts will have been constructed either on or near it was inevitable, and as we will see, the Roman army appears to have constructed linear systems of forts in both Devon and south-east Wales. On its southern length, with which we are concerned, there are forts at Cirencester, Ilchester and Axminster with another, smaller one, some way in front of it at Charterhouse on Mendip.[48] A fort has been suggested at Bath, mainly on the evidence of military tombstones found there. Two of these were erected as memorials of men who were serving in *legio XX* at the time of their death. However, one of these omits all of the legion's titles and so cannot be dated to either before or after 61 when the title *Victrix* was awarded for its part in the suppression of the Boudiccan revolt.[49] Another bears the full title *Valeria Victrix* and so must post-date 61 when it is most unlikely that any part of that legion would have been in garrison there.[50] The same argument applies to the tombstone of a man from *legio II Adiutrix*, which did not arrive in Britain until 71.[51] All of these are best explained as the memorials of soldiers who were in Bath for medical reasons at the time of their death. The only auxiliary tombstone from the city, that of Lucius Vitellius Tancinus, a trooper of the *ala Vettonum*, has been dated to the late Claudian or early Neronian period.[52] At first sight this would seem to offer better evidence for the presence of an auxiliary garrison there in the pre-Flavian period. However, the other military tombstones from the city make it clear that Bath cannot be regarded as a typical site, and it would be unwise to place great weight on a single auxiliary tombstone without supporting evidence. The hoard of military metalwork from Camerton greatly strengthens the argument for a military site there,[53] but if so it remains elusive despite various excavations in the area.[54]

As a result of Malcolm Todd's recent excavations, the fortlet at Charterhouse on Mendip is now known to be a two-phase site, with the earlier phase dating to the Claudian period. It lies in the middle of a lead mining area which is shown by the evidence of a now lost lead 'tablet' (almost certainly a lead pig) from Wookey Hole to have been exploited by the Roman authorities by 49. Given that the area cannot have been under Roman control for more than a year or so when the pig was cast, it seems almost certain that the work was begun under military control, and the construction of a fortlet in the area to supervise and protect the newly acquired mines does not seem unlikely. This argument is greatly strengthened by two lead pigs bearing the name of *legio II*, one from Blagdon, Somerset and the other from St Valéry sur Somme, the latter also inscribed with Nero's name.[55] These clearly show that this legion was responsible for lead mining at that time, and as it was in south-western England throughout Nero's reign there can be no reasonable doubt that the mines in question were in the Mendips. The fact that the site is 16 kilometres in front of the Fosse Way confirms that it should not be regarded as one of the forts directly associated with that road.

The date of the samian ware from the apparent Roman military occupation of the hillfort of South Cadbury, a few miles to the east of the Fosse Way, suggests that it was probably connected with the after-effects of the Boudiccan revolt of 61 rather than the conquest period.[56] The fact that the area enclosed within the defences of South Cadbury is only *c* 7.3 hectares meant that a Roman garrison did not feel it necessary to fortify a smaller area within it, as had been done at Hod Hill, but could rely on the existing defences. Nor need they have held it for very long. The existing evidence suggests that there may have been two forts at Ilchester. Fragments of a rampart and ditch found in the town have been interpreted as being part of the defences of a large fort, while a second and smaller fort of *c* 1.3 hectares is known from aerial photographs just outside the town. Unfortunately insufficient is known about either of them for any discussion of their relative dates.[57] The large Iron Age hillfort at Ham Hill, Somerset has produced Roman material, but the site itself was destroyed by quarrying in the nineteenth century.[58] In favour of it having been occupied by the Roman army is the fact that we now know that they did make use of hillforts in this way, but there are other possible explanations which would account for the material, including votive deposition, perhaps following native uprisings in the west country at the time of the Boudiccan revolt of 61. Trouble of this kind perhaps provides the best explanation for the refusal of Poenius Postumus, *praefectus castrorum* of *legio II Augusta*, to obey the governor's orders and bring the legion, at that time almost certainly at Exeter, to join him before the decisive battle with Boudicca.[59]

Cirencester (Corinium Dobunnorum) is a key site in the road system of the west country and the garrison of the fort there must have been responsible for controlling a large part of the Cotswolds. Tombstones indicate that it had a cavalry garrison at some point in its history if not throughout.[60] It probably lay within the command of *legio II*, but whether it was built by Vespasian or his successor is uncertain. In any event, when the legionary base was built at Kingsholm, a suburb of Gloucester, in *c* 49 the fort at Cirencester would probably have come under the control of the legion there, although whether that was the case with other forts further south is less certain. The existence of a fort at Cirencester need not imply that the Dobunni were hostile to Rome; the Roman need to keep control of their communications and supply routes would probably be sufficient explanation for its construction.

THE DUMNONII

In 47 Plautius was succeeded as governor by Ostorius Scapula, and Tacitus' record of events in Britain in the *Annales*, lost for the first years of the conquest, begins. His account is dramatic but imprecise, and is largely concerned with the campaigns in Wales, only occasionally referring to events elsewhere. Of the occupation of south-western England he tells us nothing.

Until quite recently the silence of Tacitus and the apparent absence of early military activity in Devon and Cornwall led to an assumption that the Roman army had by-passed the peninsula, probably because the Dumnonii were either pro-Roman or at least not openly hostile. However, the discovery of a legionary fortress at Exeter and a considerable number of forts in the area has now made that view untenable, and it is clear that the Roman army was present in some force. When this occupation began is less certain. It has been argued above that it is unlikely to have been while Vespasian was commander of *legio II* although he could have campaigned in the area. More probably it was the work either of Ostorius Scapula, governor from 47–52, or, less probably, of his successor, Didius Gallus who left Britain in 57. The key must lie in the legionary fortress at Exeter (Isca), the foundation of which will have followed the conquest of at least a large part of Devon. Unfortunately the evidence, as so often with archaeology, is ambiguous. Paul Bidwell, in his report on the excavation of the fortress baths, suggested a foundation date of between 55 and 60.[61] Subsequently Malcolm Todd, using the same material, preferred a date around 50.[62] All depends on the date of the samian ware from the site and, unfortunately, the sample is too small for statistical certainty. However, the existing evidence suggests that a construction date closer to 55 than 50 is equally probable and this is the date preferred by Christopher Henderson in his discussion of the fortress.[63] The mid-50s is also the date postulated for the foundation of the fortresses at Wroxeter and Usk, and in the case of the latter at least, the sample of coins and samian ware is sufficiently large for the results to be accepted as statistically valid.[64] In the present state of our knowledge the foundation of the fortress at Exeter is best seen as part of a general reconstruction of the military arrangements of the province, probably undertaken under Didius Gallus following the initial period of conquest under Aulus Plautius and Ostorius Scapula.

The fortress at Exeter was almost certainly built by *legio II Augusta*, for there is no evidence that Scapula's arrival resulted in any change in the legionary dispositions in the province. Additional evidence is provided by Ptolemy who stated that *legio II Augusta* was based at Isca Dumnoniorum (Exeter), rather than Isca (Caerleon) where it certainly was in the second century when he wrote.[65] For long this was thought to be a confusion on his part, but it is now clear that he was simply using an old source which reflected the position as it had been in the middle years of the previous century.[66] Archaeological support for this argument is provided by the fact that tile antefixes from both Exeter and Caerleon had been made in the same mould, strongly suggesting that the moulds had been moved from Exeter to Caerleon in the legion's baggage.[67] Taken together, this evidence is as strong as we are likely to get, in the absence of an inscription, for the presence of *legio II Augusta* at Exeter. The fortress was relatively small, some 16.4 hectares, compared with the 20 hectares or more of most of the later fortresses.[68] However, the early fortresses at Gloucester and Lincoln were of similar size, and this suggests that Exeter should not be regarded as abnormal. The siting of Exeter 16 kilometres from the mouth of a major river suggests that one of the factors, which the Roman authorities considered when they chose the site, was the desirability of being able to supply it by sea. Topsham, which lies on the Exe 6.5 kilometres below Exeter, has produced material of this date,[69] and it has been suggested that it was the site of a harbour for the fortress. Topsham was the main port for Exeter in historical times and, although the evidence is not conclusive, the existence of a pre-Flavian harbour there does not seem unlikely; the more so as there is other evidence for the Roman use of a fleet on the south coast (see above p 30).

The fortress at Exeter must have been the keystone of a system of smaller auxiliary forts extending into Dorset and Somerset as well as Devon and Cornwall. Until quite recently few of these had been identified, but the number has increased quite dramatically in recent years. To the east we have the fort at Waddon Hill, near Beaminster, Dorset, excavated by Graham Webster[70] and another fort has been identified at Axminster where the Fosse Way crosses the road from Dorchester to Exeter.[71] The dating evidence for the latter suggests that it was founded *c* 55–60. Somewhat further to the west we now know that a series of forts ran in an arc across the neck of the Dumnonian peninsula. The southernmost, at Gittisham, is a new discovery on the Dorchester to Exeter road.[72] Then comes Hembury where Malcolm Todd has shown that an Iron Age hillfort was remodelled and utilised by the Roman army to command a strategically important route to Exeter from the east.[73] Unfortunately the dating remains imprecise although it must lie within the range 50–70, and probably within the decade 50–60. A little further to the north-west two successive forts have been found at Cullompton in the Culm Valley, a site which commands an important route to Exeter from the north-east.[74] Unfortunately there is too little evidence for precise dating, but at least one of them was occupied in the pre-Flavian period. Another possible fort has been cautiously suggested on the evidence of crop marks at Killerton between Cullompton and Exeter in the same valley.[75] In the next valley to the north, that of the River Exe, a fort of 1.4 hectares with two phases of construction has been excavated by Valerie Maxfield at Bolham Farm on the edge of the Tiverton.[76] The excavations revealed that the first fort was constructed in the mid-60s and continued in use until the early 70s when it was rebuilt, remaining in use for a further decade. This is perhaps the only fort in the region where the dating evidence is sufficient for any useful attempt to relate its occupation to the history of the period. Its relatively late date of construction, some ten years after the foundation of the fortress at Exeter, is surprising at first sight, but it may be related to the removal of the legionary garrison from Exeter as part of the rearrangement of legionary forces in the west of the province necessitated by the departure of *legio XIIII* from Britain in 66 (see p 42 below). In any consideration of the troop movements which must have resulted from the departure of this legion it is necessary to remember that a large number of auxiliaries will have gone with it. On a number of occasions in the *Historiae* Tacitus refers to eight Batavian cohorts which were auxiliaries of *legio XIIII* and which had followed it to the Continent.[77] Given this, some change in the auxiliary arrangements in the province was probably inevitable. However, it is equally possible that the construction of the fort at Bolham Farm was the result of a decision to strengthen the auxiliary presence in the south-west to offset the removal of *legio II* from Exeter. Similarly its rebuilding in the early 70s could be related to changes in the dispositions of auxiliary troops necessitated by the Flavian campaigns in the north of England and Wales. Two other forts lie to the north-east of Tiverton, one at Cudmore Farm, Clayhanger[78] and another at Wiveliscombe, almost due west of Taunton.[79]

To the west of Exeter rises the high massif of Dartmoor. As yet no forts are known on its southern side, but to the north Malcolm Todd has identified a fort at Bury Barton, near Lapford to the north-west of Crediton.[80] South-west of that there is a fort at North Tawton, located from the air by J K St Joseph in 1975, where later aerial survey indicates that there are other military sites including a large enclosure which Sheppard Frere has suggested may be a vexillation fortress.[81] If so it should predate the fortress at Exeter; a fact which creates problems given their relative positions. Only excavation will resolve the problem. Finally there is a small fort at Okehampton which may be of the same date.[82] A fort between Tiverton and Bury Barton probably remains to be found.

Both of these groups of forts are supplemented by a number of marching camps, and signal stations or fortlets which may be fragments of a larger system linking the forts with the fortress at Exeter.[83]

Most of these forts have not been excavated and they are probably not all of the same date; indeed Valerie Maxfield's work at Tiverton shows this to have been the case. Taken together they form a reasonably coherent system for controlling routes in and out of the Dumnonian peninsula, but without further work it would be unwise to assume that they were a unitary system, albeit one built over a period of years. None the less, as we know them today they form linear arrangements which have many similarities to the pattern of pre-Flavian forts in south-east Wales (p 39–41 below), and it is possible that we are beginning to detect a standard pre-Flavian method of containing unconquered territory. If so, it is one with which Agricola will have become familiar when serving in Britain in 61, and it may well have influenced his decision to use a similar system in the 80s to block the Scottish glens where they open onto the eastern lowlands.

The military arrangements in north Devon remain obscure, although the existence of forts there is made virtually certain by two small fortlets, probably observation posts, overlooking the Bristol Channel at Martinhoe and Old Burrow. Excavations by Aileen Fox and William Ravenhill showed that they were occupied somewhere between 55 and 75.[84] Their position reveals an interest in the Bristol Channel by the Roman army which probably worked in conjunction with a fleet there and, as will be seen below (p 40), there is some evidence from south Wales for the existence of such a fleet. Between them and the nearest known forts in central Devon there must be other unlocated sites, for such fortlets could only have functioned in association with larger forces.

Even less is known of the forts in Cornwall. Indeed were it not for the fort which was excavated by Fox and Ravenhill at Nanstallon it would be possible to question if the Roman army ever crossed the Tamar. Nanstallon, which lies by the River Camel, is only a little over 0.8 hectares in area, but the excavations showed it to be a fort in miniature, with barracks, a headquarters building and a commanding officer's house. In the unexcavated area there must be more barracks and a granary.[85] The numismatic evidence from the site suggests a foundation in the mid- to late 60s.[86] Obviously the evidence from a single site cannot support major conclusions, but it does raise the question of when Cornwall was occupied. The foundation of the fortress at Exeter in the 50s need not imply that the Roman army held the whole peninsula by then. Indeed it would be quite logical to see the first campaigns reaching as far as Dartmoor, to be followed by a period of consolidation, during which Exeter was constructed, before the remainder of the peninsula was brought under Roman control.[87]

WALES

If historical accounts of the occupation of the south-western peninsula are lacking, that is not true of Wales. Unfortunately, Tacitus' account of the Welsh campaigns shows all the imprecision of time and place which characterises so much of his writing on Britain. None-the-less, the information which he does give is of the greatest importance and provides the framework which must control our interpretation of the archaeological evidence. The surviving account in the *Annales* begins with the arrival of Ostorius Scapula as governor late in 47 to find that an unnamed enemy had attacked unnamed Roman allies.[88] Scapula, who was nothing if not a man of action, threw back the enemy, and occupied the area between the Rivers Trent and Severn, effectively the West Midlands: the territory of the Coritani and Cornovii, either or both of whom may have been Roman allies. Had the Fosse Way ever formed a frontier, it did so no more. His next move was to attack a tribe called in our texts the Cangi or Decangi, almost certainly a corruption of the Deceangli of Flintshire.[89] Whether Scapula's actions indicate that he was responding to an attack by the Deceangli, and possibly their more powerful neighbours the Ordovices, on the Cornovii of the northern marches remains uncertain, although it must be considered probable.

Then followed a series of campaigns against the two major tribes of Wales, the Silures in the south, and the Ordovices of mid and north Wales. Where the boundary between the two tribes lay is not known, although it seems fairly certain that it was somewhere in south-central Wales. Michael Jarrett and John Mann[90] have produced convincing arguments to show that the territory of the Ordovices included much of mid-Wales, but the fact that Agricola attacked Anglesey as part of his campaign against them in 78 suggests that they controlled at least part of north Wales.[91] Both tribes fought under the command of Caratacus, the former king of the Catuvellauni. How he obtained this dominance we do not know; doubtless the explanation lay in the complexities of Celtic political and family relationships. Under his command the war moved from the Silures to the Ordovices and it was in their territory that Scapula was finally given the opportunity for a full-scale battle of the type which the early imperial army rarely lost. Nor did they on this occasion. Caratacus survived the field only to be handed over to the Romans by Cartimandua, Queen of the Brigantes, to whom he had unwisely fled.[92] Since Tacitus tells us that this occurred in the ninth year after the invasion of Britain, in other words the year 51, it is clear that he has telescoped some five years of campaigning into one short narrative.

This battle may have broken the Ordovices, but the Silures were another matter. At the beginning of his account of these wars, Tacitus remarked that 'the Silures were turned neither by brutality nor by clemency from pursuing war and required the encampment of legions to keep them down', adding that to do this a colony was created at Colchester.[93] In other words, by founding a colony for veterans at Colchester the legion previously stationed there, almost certainly *legio XX Valeria*, was released for action against the Silures. Whether his words should be interpreted as meaning that a legionary fortress was constructed on or adjacent to their territory is another matter. Tacitus frequently uses such phrases in a loose manner for rhetorical effect, and here he may mean no more than that an army was brought against the Silures. But even if this was the case, such an army must have had a base. In discussing this question elsewhere, the writer has argued that the simplest explanation of this passage is that a base was constructed for *legio XX* at Kingsholm where we know there is a major early military site.[94] Such a fortress would have been in an excellent position to exercise a measure of control over the Silures, for it would have blocked the crossing of the Severn at Gloucester, the lowest point at which they could have forded the river to raid the Dobunni, who, as we have seen, were probably Roman allies.

Whether Kingsholm was the only major site established is another matter. Tacitus' words (*castrisque legionum*) need not imply that, indeed rather the reverse, and it is possible, perhaps even probable, that Kingsholm was a vexillation fortress rather than a full legionary base. As Henry Hurst has shown we have little idea of its actual size,[95] and one of the reasons for its replacement within a few years by the fortress at Gloucester itself might be that it was too small for a full legion. An alternative, or additional site, may be located in the Wye Valley, perhaps near Weston under Penyard, a site which has produced early material.[96] There is no doubt that the Wye Valley was the key route into south Wales for any army crossing the River Severn at Gloucester, but Weston may be too far forward for a legionary base at such an early stage in the conquest of Wales; such fortresses were usually set some way back from the front line. Much depends on where the edge of Siluria lay; if on the Severn rather than the Wye, and there are good arguments for that being the case,[97] then a base at Kingsholm is as far forward as might be thought suitable in the late 40s, although as the war progressed other bases would have been created in front of it.

The defeat of Caratacus did not reduce the scale of the war against the Silures, who appear thus far to have succeeded in avoiding a major defeat, and Tacitus records a series of Roman setbacks.[98] The picture which emerges from his dramatic but imprecise account, is of groups building forts and foraging a short distance from major concentrations of troops, including legionaries, based in existing forts. The scene of these actions is as vague as ever. Modern commentators have suggested the Wye Valley, perhaps near Hay where there are large early forts at Clyro and Clifford; but if the suggestion that Siluria extended as far as the Severn is accepted, they could have taken place in Herefordshire.

It is difficult to tell from Tacitus to what extent Ostorius was initiating actions, and to what extent he was merely reacting to events. The fact that he was to die in the midst of these campaigns, in Tacitus' words, worn out by anxiety, may indicate that he was already a sick man who was having difficulty in coping with a guerrilla war which a fitter man would have been able to handle. The governor, who was, of course, the army commander, had almost total control over the direction of the campaigns, and a governor who was incapable of exercising effective control would have been a grave handicap to the efficient functioning of the army. Scapula's successor, Didius Gallus, appears to have had no real difficulty in restoring the situation, despite the fact that the Silures had succeeded in defeating a legion in the interim between Scapula's death and his own arrival.[99]

It was Gallus' subsequent lack of military action which Tacitus damned so eloquently in the *Annales*:

'For Didius being old and sluggish and surfeited with honours, was content to act on the defensive and leave everything to others'.[100] In the *Agricola* he is scarcely kinder, although somewhat more informative: 'Didius Gallus maintained what his predecessors had gained and advanced a few forts into remoter districts in order to extend his name and sphere of influence'.[101] He remained as governor until 57, and if there were no major campaigns at this time this is likely to have been on orders from Rome, which may in part have been the result of the death of Claudius in 54 and the minority of his successor Nero. Elsewhere the writer has argued that it was probably Gallus' task to consolidate the conquests made by his predecessors, and that in the west he did this by the creation of a system of forts supported by new fortresses at Exeter for *legio II*, at Usk for *legio XX* and at Wroxeter (Viroconium), in the northern marches, for *legio XIIII*.[102] Such an argument can only be made on historical grounds, for the archaeological evidence does not, and probably never will, give that degree of precision unless we are fortunate enough to obtain inscriptions or dendrochronological dates. But if this argument is correct it was the foundation laid by Gallus which enabled his successors, Quintus Veranius and Suetonius Paulinus to take the offensive so effectively in the years after 57.

Until quite recently the historian of Roman Wales was in the unusual position of having literary accounts of campaigns for which there was virtually no archaeological evidence. The discoveries which ended that state of affairs began when Jarrett showed that the large fort at Clyro in the Wye Valley dated from the reign of Claudius or Nero.[103] At much the same time George Boon observed Claudio–Neronian pottery among material found in the nineteenth century at Usk, clear evidence that there should be an early fort there.[104] The result of his discovery was a series of large scale excavations at Usk which revealed not the auxiliary fort which had been expected, but a full-scale legionary fortress, the predecessor of Caerleon. The scale of the work produced a mass of dating evidence which leaves no doubt that the fortress was constructed in the mid-50s probably early in the reign of Nero, and it may probably be assigned to the period when, as Tacitus grudgingly records, Didius Gallus was engaged in fort building.[105] The evidence for the legion which constructed it is less clear, but such as there is would suggest it was *legio XX Valeria*, the legion which we know was brought against the Silures in 49.[106]

The discovery of what must be the main fortress for the early frontier system in south Wales was clearly a major advance in our understanding of the Roman conquest of Wales, but for some time we lacked the system of forts of which Usk was the keystone. Even now only a handful of them have been identified, but the number is increasing and will continue to do so. None of those now known appears to predate Usk and we are probably safe in assuming that most of them formed part of the same system.[107]

The evidence which we now have suggests that the main route which the Roman army used to enter south Wales ran west from Gloucester, passing to the north of the Forest of Dean. As we have already noted, the evidence of early material from Weston under Penyard (Ariconium), near Ross-on-Wye, suggests that it may have been the site of an early fort.[108] Once in the Wye Valley the route will have divided with one branch running north towards Clyro and the other south along the river valley to Monmouth, where there is known to be a fort of this date.[109] From there the road turned first west and then south along the valleys of the rivers Trothy and Olway to reach Usk. From Usk the road continued south along the Usk Valley to reach the coastal levels near the site of the later fortress at Caerleon, where another early fort might reasonably be expected, although excavations within and around the fortress have produced no evidence for such a fort there. A small rectangular enclosure at Cat's Ash (Coed-y-caerau) on the hills to the south of the Usk valley overlooking Caerleon has been suggested as a Roman fort, but the question of its date is confused by the fact that it is one of several apparently interconnected enclosures most of which are clearly not Roman forts.[110]

At the moment only one fort is known for certain in the lowlands which run along the north side of the Severn Estuary and this is the large fort at Cardiff discovered by Peter Webster under the later Roman stone fort in the centre of the city.[111] Cardiff is a key site, for it controlled the mouth of the Taff Valley and effectively blocked movement along the coastal plain, as well as providing a suitable harbour for a fleet operating in the Bristol Channel. There may well have been a fort somewhere between Caerleon and Cardiff, but if so no hint of it has been discovered, and the Roman army of the mid-first century seems to have been less concerned with creating a series of regularly spaced forts than have some modern commentators. We do not know if Cardiff was the westernmost of these early forts or if there were others in the Vale of Glamorgan.

A route which ran from Gloucester to Cardiff via the Forest of Dean and the Usk Valley is unnecessarily circuitous, and there is some evidence that the Roman army made use of the Bristol Channel. Not only would it have been possible to reach Cardiff directly by ship, but the recognition of quite large quantities of Claudio-Neronian material among the finds from the pre-War excavations at Sudbrook Camp, the Iron Age fort on the Severn Estuary near Caerwent,[112] indicates that it was garrisoned by the Roman army at this time. Presumably they used it as one end of a ferry route across the Severn Estuary as well, perhaps, as an intermediate point on journeys along it. As we have seen the fortlets on the north Devon coast only make sense if they worked in conjunction with a fleet, and the forts at Sudbrook and Cardiff strengthen the arguments in favour of such a fleet operating at this time in the Bristol Channel, and probably the lower reaches of the River Severn as far as Kingsholm if not further. If a fleet did operate in the estuary it must have had harbours on the English shore, and there is sufficient material from Sea Mills on the River Avon at Bristol, to make it almost certain that there was a military site there in the pre-Flavian period.[113] Given its position, Sea Mills is perhaps the best candidate for the base for such a fleet. The fortress at Usk is too far inland to be directly accessible from the sea. Even in the early nineteenth century it was not possible for vessels to go beyond Newbridge, 6.5 kilometres downstream from Usk, where the river ceases to be tidal. However, given the great advantages of moving supplies by sea, and the evidence suggesting that a Roman fleet operated in the Estuary, it seems unlikely that the Roman army would have made no attempt to supply the fortress by water. If so docks may have existed on the river somewhere between Caerleon and Newbridge. Compared with the effort of hauling supplies around the Forest of Dean or along the north side of the Severn Estuary, the short overland route from Newbridge to the fortress would have been a minor problem.

Later in the Roman period the main route into this area was along the north side of the estuary and logic would suggest that this was utilised at this time. The possibility of a fort at Chepstow has been canvassed in the past and, as Jarrett noted, there is some evidence to support this idea.[114] Similarly the discovery below the Pound Lane site in Caerwent of a pottery kiln producing wares which would be best seen as having a military connection, and this is strengthened by the presence of brooches comparable with those from the fortress at Usk among the material found in the early twentieth-century excavations.[115] But these discoveries have to be set against the complete lack of structural evidence, and in neither case can they be regarded as more than possibilities. However, the occupation of the Sudbrook fort confirms that the Romans were in control of the coastal lowlands of Monmouthshire by this time and it may be relevant that the road from Sudbrook would have joined the main east-west road at Caerwent.

Rather more is known of the arrangement to the north and west of Usk. The fortress there gave control not only of the Usk Valley and routes into it from the east and south, but also of routes running north along the valley to the Black Mountains and Brecon Beacons. Recent excavations at Abergavenny suggest that the original fort there, which was built at much the same time as the fortress at Usk, was rebuilt in *c* 67, probably as a result of the movement of auxiliary units which followed the removal of the legion from Usk at about that time.[116] Further north there appears to be a fort at Kentchurch on the River Monnow,[117] and another fort is known at Abbey Dore in the Golden Valley,[118] although this is too close to Kentchurch for both of them to have been held at the same time. All three forts were placed in positions which will have enabled the Romans to control routes through the mountains of south Wales, for Abergavenny commands the point at which the Usk cuts between the Black Mountains and the Brecon Beacons, and Kentchurch and Abbey Dore block the Golden Valley which runs through the eastern end of the Black Mountains. Abergavenny is easily reached from Usk by following the Usk Valley, but the forts of the Golden Valley are more likely to have been approached directly either from Weston under Penyard or Monmouth.

Further north the large fort at Clyro in the valley of the River Wye must be presumed to be part of the same system. Originally identified as a vexillation fortress of 10.3 hectares, it has recently been shown to be significantly smaller, covering no more than *c* 7.3 hectares. An unpublished excavation by Jarrett led him to suggest that it was a two-phase site, but the surviving evidence is inconclusive on this point. The pottery which he found is comparable with that from Usk which would confirm a pre-Flavian date without allowing greater precision.[119] However, even if the fort is smaller than previously thought it is still much too large to be a conventional auxiliary fort. The situation is complicated by the existence of two other large forts at Clifford less than 5 kilometres north of Clyro.[120] Unfortunately the sites are unexcavated and so cannot be dated, but given their size they are almost certainly pre-Flavian. Both sites would have given control of the Wye Valley at the point where it emerged from the hills to the north to run along the edge of the Black Mountains. If Usk controlled the Usk Valley, then Clyro and Clifford were its equivalent in the Wye Valley, and it is not surprising, perhaps, that forts of this size were placed there given the importance of that valley in the communications of mid-Wales. We know too little about vexillation fortresses of this type to be able to make even an informed guess at their likely garrison, but a legionary vexillation probably formed part of it. If so it would have come almost certainly from the fortress at Usk. The obvious Roman interest in the Golden Valley suggests that this may have been the route used to reach the Clyro area, rather than the more circuitous one along the Wye Valley through Hereford. Further north there is another fort at Walton which will have blocked an important route into mid-Wales.[121]

The military sites known to the north of Walton were almost certainly part of another system of forts controlled from the fortress of *legio XIIII* at Wroxeter and they are discussed in the paper by Jarrett and Webster below.[122]

Obviously our knowledge of this system is far from complete, and any conclusions drawn from it must be tentative. With that qualification, it may be observed that it is essentially a linear system, with forts strategically placed in the river valleys where they would effectively contain the main centres of native population in south and mid-Wales. Behind the known forts there must have been others, and our knowledge of the system is clearly not complete, but the last twenty or so years have seen remarkable advances in our understanding of this important phase of the Roman conquest.

The Roman army was surprisingly willing to change its military dispositions over quite short periods of time, and hints that this was done in south Wales are now beginning to appear. At Abergavenny the fort was rebuilt on the same site, while at Clyro and Clifford, and Kentchurch and Abbeydore forts appear to have been moved relatively short distances. Whether these reflect changes in the type of garrison we cannot say; indeed we lack the evidence to comment on any of the likely garrisons in these early forts save for the legion at Usk. We must also remember that the removal of the legion from Usk following the transfer of *legio XIIII* to the Continent in 66 must have resulted in changes in the auxiliary arrangements in the area. It has been suggested above (p 36) that the construction of the fort at Bolham Farm near Tiverton may reflect a decision to strengthen the auxiliary garrison in the area after the removal of *legio II* from Exeter, and some of the changes on the Welsh frontier may have a similar explanation, as well as reflecting the need to find units to replace some of those which went to the Continent with *legio XIIII*.

The Roman army must have campaigned even further west during this period, for these forts will not have been built on the absolute edges of their conquests, and such campaigns may have left traces in the marching camps which survive in some numbers in the uplands of south Wales. But these are notoriously difficult to date with precision and too few are known for them to reveal the details of any single campaign, or for those relating to this phase of the conquest to be differentiated from those built during the wars of the Flavian period.[123]

The system which we know at the moment is strategically sensible, and may be reasonably complete. It would curb the Welsh tribes and limit their ability to raid Roman or allied territory while allowing the Romans to harass them, and it would provide an excellent springboard for further advances when the time was right. As we have seen, it is not dissimilar to the arrangement of forts found at this time in Devon, and both presage that used on the eastern edge of the Scottish highlands in the Flavian period.

Space does not permit a detailed discussion of the later history of the conquest of Wales. In 57 the army again took the offensive, striking first into Siluria and then deep into north Wales, only to have to abort the campaign when the Boudiccan revolt of 60–1 threatened their hold on the province. The major reconsideration of Roman policies, which followed this near disaster, appears to have concluded that it was necessary to consolidate the areas which they already held before attempting further advances. Had that not been the case there can be little doubt that the whole of Wales would have been under Roman control by the early 60s. By the mid-60s, when further advances might have been expected, the army in Britain was reduced by the removal of the *legio XIIII Gemina Martia Victrix*, based at Wroxeter, together with its auxiliaries; all part of a major rearrangement of troops which was necessitated by Nero's decision to assemble an army for his projected eastern campaigns. Under those circumstances further advances in Britain were probably thought neither necessary nor safe.

One effect of the removal of *legio XIIII* was to leave the northern marches of Wales and the southern Pennines without a legionary garrison, an arrangement which if made permanent would have invited disaster. It was probably to avoid this that the decision was made to move *legio XX Valeria Victrix* from Usk to Wroxeter, and *legio II Augusta* from Exeter to a new fortress at Gloucester from where it could more easily provide support for the auxiliaries garrisoning south Wales and the south-west of England than was possible from either Usk or Exeter. The original fortresses, which were not demolished, were probably garrisoned by detachments of the main legion. Much of this is speculative, of course, but there is no doubt that in the late 60s there were more legionary fortresses than legions in Britain, and not all of them could have been fully garrisoned.[124]

What was then proposed by the Roman government we do not know. The outbreak of the civil war in 69 threw everything into confusion, and when it was over, and Vespasian had emerged as victor, the situation in Britain had also changed and advances both in Wales and the north of England were the order of the day. The tribes of Wales, weakened by over twenty years of warfare, offered no prolonged resistance and by the mid-70s the Romans were in a position to create the system of forts in Wales which is familiar to all students of the Roman army.[125] As part of this reorganization the old and probably partly derelict fortress at Usk was swept away and replaced with a new legionary base a few miles downstream at Caerleon; the fortress which was to serve for so long as the home of *legio II Augusta*.

ACKNOWLEDGEMENTS

I was honoured by the invitation to deliver the first of the Caerleon Lectures and it is a pleasure to acknowledge the assistance received from my colleagues in the National Museums & Galleries of Wales and, in particular, from the late George Boon and Richard Brewer. In revising the text for this volume I have been helped by several friends, including William Britnell, Ian Dennis, Professor Michael Fulford, Howard Mason, Andrew Sargent and Janet Webster. I must also acknowledge my great debt to the late Professor Michael Jarrett, and, in particular, to Dr Peter Webster who has read this paper to its great benefit.

Notes

1 The lecture on which this paper was based was delivered in 1987 since when there have been new discoveries and new thoughts and I have taken the opportunity to revise it and include the results of recent work. Michael Jarrett devoted the Annual Caerleon Lecture for 1993 to the conquest period in Wales and the reader should consult the paper which is based on his lecture and which has been revised by Peter Webster (ch 3 below) for details of the conquest of mid and north Wales.

Translations of Greek and Roman writers quoted in this paper are taken mainly either from the relevant Loeb edition or from J C Mann and R G Penman, *Literary Sources for Roman Britain*, Lactor 11 (1990), London, with the exception of Tacitus' *Annales* where G G Ramsay's translation is preferred (*The Annals of Tacitus. Books I–VI* (1904), London and *Books XI–XVI* (1909), London).

2 For further discussion on Tacitus as a source for Roman Wales, see Jarrett and Webster this volume, 46–8.

3 For a more detailed discussion of the final years of the Iron Age, see Cunliffe 1991. For the period between Caesar's invasions and the Roman conquest and for the conquest itself, see Frere 1999.

4 *Res Gestae* 32.

5 Suetonius, *Caligula* 44.2.

6 Cassius Dio 60.19.1.

7 Strabo, *Geographia* 4.5.3.

8 Cassius Dio 60.20.2.

9 For the details of his career, see A R Birley 1981, 37–40. This book provides details of the careers of all of the governors referred to in this paper.

10 The troop movements of this period are summarized in Frere 1999, ch 4.

11 Suetonius, *Vespasian* 4.1. Suetonius does not state which legion was under Vespasian's command, this information is given by Tacitus in *Historiae* 3.44.

12 Eichholz 1972, 149 ff.

13 Richmond 1968, 119.

14 I follow Rivet and Smith 1979, 445 in accepting that this is the correct form of the name and that it was derived from a pre-Roman tribal name (Regini) as suggested by Jackson, rather than Regnenses which has often been preferred in the past.

15 Cassius Dio 60.19.1.

16 Cunliffe 1991, 154.

17 Tacitus, *Agricola* 14.

18 Cassius Dio 60.20.2.

19 *ILS* 216; Maxfield and Dobson 1995, 34, no. 22

20 Ptolemy, *Geographia* 2.3.13.

21 James 1997, 30.

22 Suetonius, *Vespasian* 4.1.

23 G Webster 1980.

24 See Frere 1999, 57 ff and map p 58 for examples.

25 Cunliffe 1971a, 38 ff.

26 The discovery of the building is reported in Cunliffe *et al* 1996, 19 ff, Figs 2.5 and 2.6. For an interim report of the more recent work, see Manley and Rudkin 1999.

27 For the evidence which led to earlier suggestions of a Roman fort, see Wilson 1972, 349, Fig 20. A more recent summary is given in James 1997, 30.

28 Boon 1974a, 68, Fig 8.

29 Annable 1966; Griffiths 1982, 53.

30 Manning 1976, 21; Anderson and Wacher 1980, 121; Griffiths 1982, 58.

31 Griffiths 1982.

32 Manning 1976, 21.

33 Field 1976.

34 Information from W Putnam.

35 Todd 1984b.

36 Ptolemy, *Geographia* 2.3.13.

37 Rivet and Smith 1979, 145 and 344 prefer to identify Dunium as Hod Hill.

38 Wheeler 1943, 65.

39 Sharples 1991, 101, 171.

40 The most convenient summary of the site at Lake Farm is Field 1992, 32 ff.

41 Ibid, 44, Fig 4.7.

42 G Webster 1958, 57.

43 Richmond 1968.

44 G Webster 1979.

45 See Manning 1981, 27 for a short discussion of this question, and Maxfield 1986.

46 Tacitus, *Annales* 11.19.

47 Tacitus, *Annales* 12.31.

48 Cirencester: Wacher and McWhirr 1982, 57; Ilchester: Leach 1982, 5, Fig 3; Charterhouse on Mendip: Todd 1995. For other forts which have been suggested in the area, see Manning 1976, 24 ff.

49 *RIB* I, 158.

50 *RIB* I, 156.

51 *RIB* I, 157.

52 *RIB* I, 159.

53 Jackson 1990.

54 Wedlake 1958. For a discussion of the problem of a fort at Camerton, see Jackson 1990, 13–14, 23–5.

55 Todd 1995; for the lead inscription, see *RIB* II.1, 2404.1 (Wookey Hole 'tablet'); 2404.2 (Blagdon pig); 2404.24 (Valéry sur Somme pig).

56 Manning 1976, 37–8.

57 Leach 1982, 5, Fig 3; Esmonde Cleary 1998, 420.

58 Manning 1976, 25.

59 Tacitus, *Annales* 14.37.5; Manning 1981, 49.
60 Wacher and McWhirr 1982, 64; McWhirr 1988, 78 ff.
61 Bidwell 1979, 13 ff.
62 Todd 1987, 196 ff.
63 Henderson 1988, 91.
64 Manning 1981, 31 ff.
65 Ptolemy, *Geographia* 2.3.3.
66 Manning 1997.
67 Bidwell and Boon 1976.
68 Henderson 1988, 95.
69 G Webster 1958, 56.
70 G Webster 1979, 51–90.
71 Silvester and Bidwell 1984; Cole and Lonford 1993; Frere 1991, 281.
72 *Devon Archaeological Society Newsletter* 70 (May 1998), 1; 71 (September 1998), 4.
73 Todd 1984a; 1987, 191.
74 Simpson and Griffith 1993; Griffith 1997, 362.
75 Griffith 1984, 25.
76 Maxfield 1991, 25–98.
77 Tacitus, *Historiae* 1.69, 2.27, 2.66.
78 Frere 1991, 281, Pl XXXI.
79 G Webster 1958–9.
80 Todd 1985.
81 Griffith 1984, 20; Frere 1999, 61.
82 Bidwell *et al* 1979; Griffith 1984, 13.
83 Details of these are given in Griffith 1984, 27, Fig 7 and Griffith 1997. For the marching camps, see Welfare and Swan 1995, 53–5, 169.
84 Fox and Ravenhill 1966.
85 Fox and Ravenhill 1972.
86 Todd 1987, 201; Manning 1976, 33.
87 Other possible fort sites in Cornwall are given in Todd 1987, 204, n 4 and Griffith 1997, 362.
88 Tacitus, *Annales* 12.31. The identity of the unnamed allies is discussed by Jarrett and Webster this volume, 47.
89 The problems presented by this and other tribes in Wales are discussed more fully by Jarrett and Webster this volume, 49.
90 Jarrett and Mann 1968.
91 Tacitus, *Agricola* 18.
92 Tacitus, *Annales* 12.33 and 36.
93 Tacitus, *Annales* 12.32.
94 Manning 1981, 34.
95 Hurst 1985, 113.
96 Manning 1981, 37 ff.
97 Ibid, 20.
98 Tacitus, *Annales* 12.38–40.
99 Tacitus, *Annales* 12. 40.
100 Ibid.
101 Tacitus, *Agricola* 14.
102 Manning 1981, 34.
103 Nash-Williams/Jarrett 1969, 77.
104 Boon 1962.
105 Manning 1981.
106 Ibid, 38.
107 Brief details of these forts are given in Manning 1981, 40 ff.
108 Manning 1981, 38.
109 Burnham 1993, 276.
110 Manning 1981, 41.
111 P V Webster 1990.
112 Nash-Williams 1939.
113 G Webster 1958–9, 56, 89.
114 Jarrett and Webster this volume, 51.
115 I am indebted to Janet and Peter Webster for this information.
116 Blockley *et al* 1993; *Archaeol Wales* 39 (1999), 98–100. I am indebted to Ian Dennis for information on the new discoveries at Abergavenny.
117 Frere 1987c, 323; *Archaeol Wales* 29 (1989), 56.
118 *Archaeol Wales* 29 (1989), 56.
119 Nash-Williams/Jarrett 1969, 77–80; Manning 1981, 41; Jarrett and Webster this volume, 52. I am indebted to William Britnell for information on the recent excavations, and to Peter Webster for details of Jarrett's excavation and the pottery from it.
120 St Joseph 1973, 238; Frere 1992, 283.
121 St Joseph 1973, 239; Frere 1977, 360.
122 Jarrett and Webster this volume, 57–61.
123 These camps are listed in Jarrett and Webster this volume, 62.
124 This is more fully discussed in Manning 1981, 45 ff.
125 For these forts, see Nash-Williams/Jarrett 1969.

Chapter 3

Early Roman Campaigns in Wales

Michael G Jarrett

revised by Peter Webster

Michael Jarrett died on 14 November 1994. With his passing, Roman Wales lost one of its leading historians. It is still hard to realize that one will never again hear his distinctive tones or enjoy his conversation, scattered, as it could be, with the occasional *bon mot* which encapsulated so exactly, if sometimes rather wickedly, a person or an event. When asked to revise this Caerleon Lecture, my first inclination was to leave the piece as it was, to serve as a monument to one of our better prose writers. However, having read the published lecture again, I realized just how much had been altered between the original lecture and the published version. Clearly, the writer's ideas had been changed as a result of discussion with many people and by further reflection in the months between lecture and final text. The chance to revise his text further in the light of another five years of research and discussion on Roman Wales is an opportunity which surely Michael Jarrett would have seized. The following version is, therefore, offered in that belief. It will not, regrettably, be the considered thoughts of one who, as he rather modestly implied in his opening lines, was making major contributions to the archaeology of Roman Wales over thirty years ago.[1] It will, however, give readers the opportunity to see how some of the lines of thought propounded in 1994 have developed in more recent years. It also provides an opportunity to keep trust with the spirit of the original opening of this lecture:

> 'I have no expectation that what is put forward here will last for another thirty years. I shall be disappointed if it does, for it will indicate that the period has produced no significant new information and even that ideas have not changed. In archaeology they do, which is one reason why the subject is so exciting.'

PVW

INTRODUCTION

The last record we have of Romans fighting the native population of Wales is assignable to 77 (or less probably 78); it involved the suppression of a revolt and the occupation of Anglesey. Later revolts there may have been, but they find no mention in the surviving documentary record. 77, therefore, is a convenient date at which to end. The starting point must, of course, be the invasion of Britain by the Emperor Claudius in 43.

Such a temporal definition is straightforward, and unlikely to be challenged. Other limits are more controversial. Wales did not exist, even as a geographical expression, in the first century. Indeed 'Wales' means nothing until 'England' comes into being half a millennium later; you cannot have Wales without England. We must, of necessity, establish arbitrary limits somewhere. Those limits may be primarily geographical or primarily political.

It is clear that the Romans had no concept of 'Wales'. All our documentary references are to political units – tribes, for short – which occupied the approximate area of what we call Wales. It was with the tribes, rather than a piece of land defined by natural features, that the Romans were concerned. Since tribal boundaries are, and are likely to remain, matters for debate we must still impose a geographical limit to the east. That is best taken as the line of the lower and middle reaches of the Severn and the Dee. It involves adding to modern Wales the whole of Herefordshire and much of Shropshire, Worcestershire and Gloucestershire to encompass the upland block of Wales and its immediate approaches.

We must recognize that our land-bound experience restricts our thinking about early campaigns. Railways and, more especially, motor transport have, within the last few generations, virtually killed river, canal and coast-wise traffic for people and goods alike. As a result, substantial areas of water, like the Bristol Channel or the Irish Sea, now divide people whom they once linked. The point is doubly important because it can easily cause us to neglect the possibility of 'combined operations' by land and sea and because we may more easily underestimate the extent to which north and south Wales each had closer links with neighbouring parts of England than they had one with the other.

The evidence available to us has a heavy Roman bias. All the usable documents reflect Roman attitudes, and the relevant archaeological material is almost entirely Roman. We may argue about the significance of a Roman fort or temporary camp, of a couple of Roman coins or half-a-dozen sherds of samian pottery; but by debating their significance we are tacitly accepting a belief that they can be fitted into an historical framework. By contrast, a pre-Roman hillfort, sacked and abandoned, is more difficult to fit into context when its inhabitants have left us little in the way of historical documentation or even material evidence.

Only one Roman author, Tacitus, provides worthwhile information about the take-over of Wales.[2] Three of his works are relevant. The *Agricola*, published in 98, is the biography of Tacitus' father-in-law, who was governor of Britain for seven years from 77, and responsible for the acquisition of Anglesey; he had also served in Britain in *c* 58–60 and 70–3. It includes a resumé of British affairs from the invasion of 43 to the beginning of Agricola's governorship. Of the *Historiae*, written *c* 105–9, little survives and nothing certainly relevant to Wales; it was a general history of Rome from 68–96, and will presumably have given a balanced assessment of the work of Frontinus (governor of *Britannia* 73/4–7) and Agricola. The last and greatest of Tacitus' writings, the *Annales*, has survived rather better. Written *c* 114–20, it covers the Roman world from 14 to 68, and gives the fullest account Tacitus wrote of Britain in the years 48–61; but it is far from comprehensive and some important items are mentioned only in the *Agricola*. There are two reasons for this, and both are relevant to any interpretation of the Tacitean narrative.

In the Roman world, history was a branch of literature. Whatever else it did, it had to hold the interest of its readers, who for financial and educational reasons – handwritten copies must have been relatively expensive to produce – were predominantly of the upper classes and living far from Britain. This probably explains Tacitus' notorious lack of geographical precision; place-names and tribes would have meant little or nothing to men who had rarely travelled north of the Alps; hence also the composition of appropriate speeches supposedly delivered before battle was joined. Their artificiality is apparent, and should warn us that the whole of the *Annales* is an elaborate literary construction. In the case of Britain, much has been sacrificed to the literary arrangement. While it is theoretically a year by year account, the reader's confusion has been reduced by placing related events together under a single year, even though they may have occupied several seasons, as Tacitus himself admits.[3] In the *Annales*, the account of Britain formed a three-act drama: *The Great Invasion* (now lost but presumably one of the sources for the surviving account by Cassius Dio),[4] *Caratacus' Last Stand* and *The Great Rebellion (of Boudicca)*. Other events were appended to these or related to them, but the years linking the 'headline' news-stories received scanty and unbalanced treatment. This poses particular problems for the period 52 to 60, and presents a contrast, if not a conflict, with the archaeological evidence, which points to considerable activity in these neglected years.

There is a further explanation. Once invasion, predestined since Caesar's campaigns of the mid-first century BC, was launched, there was, for Tacitus, only one conceivable policy: to conquer from Thanet to Cape Wrath as quickly as possible. Governors could thus be applauded or blamed according to the glory of the battles they fought and the amount of territory they added to the Empire. Nothing is said of imperial policy or British policy, of the resources available or the demands made on those resources by warfare outside Britain. Only the civil war in 68–9, the Year of the Four Emperors, is allowed in slight extenuation of inertia on the part of the governor.

Claudius invaded Britain in support of a client ruler who had been expelled by Togodumnus and Caratacus, rulers of the Catuvellauni (around the lower Thames). Presumably he intended from the first to defeat the Catuvellauni and establish a province in south-east Britain. Whether, in 43, he intended more than this is a matter of interpretation and judgement. Certainly many later advances seem to be triggered off (as the invasion itself had been) by British action rather than Roman policy. The advances into Wales in the last years of Claudius began with a British attack. Chaos greeted the new governor P. Ostorius (Scapula): 'in the expectation that a new General with a strange army, and at the beginning of winter, would not dare to meet them, the enemy had made a furious inroad into the territory of our allies'.[5] Almost certainly the attack came from Wales, and until this point Claudius may not have contemplated the conquest of the area. Certainly the comparably hilly and unprofitable terrain of northern England was the subject of a prolonged experiment with a buffer-state ruled by Cartimandua, an experiment which ended only with her expulsion by anti-Roman forces. In this context we may reasonably ask who the 'allies' were who had been invaded. While the Brigantes under Cartimandua are a possibility, a tribe on the eastern fringes of Wales seems more likely. If the phrase used by Tacitus means anything, it must surely imply that the first policy towards the Welsh Marches was one similar to that in the north, buffer states between the Roman frontier and the more warlike Welsh tribes.

The expulsion of Cartimandua coincided with the civil war and the accession of Vespasian in 69. A change of emperor was an opportunity for reappraisal, and perhaps for a change of policy. The new reign brought 'great generals, distinguished armies – and reduced hope for the enemy'.[6] For the first time it seems clear that the emperor planned for total rather than limited conquest of Britain; client rulers were now of historical interest rather than practical value. Of those known to us, only Cogidubnus survived for another decade or so.[7]

The question of imperial policy is scarcely raised in the *Annales;* it is from Suetonius' *Lives of the Caesars* that we have the report that Nero contemplated withdrawal from Britain.[8] Yet we can be certain that the emperor's policy was of far greater significance in determining what happened in Britain than was the energy or military ability of the governor. No dictator allows a general much freedom of action, and no imperial governor could show initiative with impunity. A governor had to be able to respond to an emergency, but in all normal policy matters he needed to receive imperial approval before taking action. The account of Agricola's northern campaigns implies that he reported back to Rome rather more often than perhaps stated. Doubtless these contacts involved the setting out of possible courses of action for the ensuing season of campaigns with indications of the governor's recommendations and assessments of the resources needed.[9] The emperor will have weighed these against assessments made by governors of other provinces. In the late 50s, Corbulo's campaigns in what is now Turkey had little detectable effect on Britain; but Nero's plans to lead an eastern campaign in 67 led to the withdrawal of one of the four legions in Britain and suggest that further conquest was either not then envisaged or was not high on the list of imperial priorities.

Geographical factors would certainly provide the emperor with a motive for restricting conquest, provided that his British clients were reasonably friendly and co-operative. The use of client rulers, so much a feature of the mid-first century, enabled Rome to limit the rate of expansion to what was practical. It was possible only because Britain was not a political unity but consisted of a number of tribes which, left to themselves, were in a state of more-or-less perpetual warfare. For many of their leaders the choice was between Roman rule and subservience to a neighbour, rather than between Roman rule and freedom. The rise of the Catuvellauni sparked off the invasion by removing freedom from the options available to many. If we substitute the ethnic group for the tribe we may detect some all too familiar similarities with late twentieth-century Europe.

Rome was aware of, and willing to exploit, British political disunity. That this was the case in Wales is indicated by the distribution of forts after 78. There is a conspicuous lack of them in the south-west and the north-east, the territory of the Demetae and the Deceangli respectively: by contrast forts are closely and regularly spaced in mid-Wales, the south-east and the north-west. Much of this territory belonged to the Silures and Ordovices, whose opposition to Rome is amply attested. The Romans are only recorded as fighting one campaign against the Deceangli (probably as early as 48 or 49) and no account survives of opposition from the Demetae: they may have been pro-Roman from the first, although the presence of at least one fort in their territory, at Carmarthen, suggests that we should exercise some caution in drawing such a conclusion.

THE TRIBES OF WALES[10]

To understand what Tacitus tells us of Roman campaigns we should perhaps look more closely at the evidence for tribal territory in Wales (Figure 3.1). The situation was re-evaluated some thirty years ago and the arguments still stand.[11] It is, however, perhaps time to revise and restate them.

In the mid-second century Claudius Ptolemaeus compiled, from a variety of first-century sources, a list of places with their latitudes and longitudes.[12] Some of these places can be identified from other sources. For the Demetae, Ptolemy records two places: *Maridunum* (or perhaps, more correctly, Moridunum) and *Luentinum*.[13] *Maridunum* is certainly Carmarthen, being recorded also in the *Antonine Itinerary*, a third-century road-book.[14] *Luentinum* cannot be certainly identified: Rivet and Smith follow a suggestion of Boon and place it at Pumsaint.[15] The line of forts from

3.1 *The tribes of Wales. Precise boundaries cannot be defined, and may have varied at different times*

Llanio to Pumsaint and Llandovery may be on or close to the eastern boundary of the Demetae; the new discovery of a possible fort at Llandeilo continues the line, and another fort between it and Loughor is to be expected, probably close to Ammanford.[16] The only fort certainly in Demetic territory was at Carmarthen and that, like most of the others named, was abandoned by *c* 120.[17]

The Deceangli are recorded as such on lead pigs found at Chester and Runcorn, the earliest dated to 74.[18] The name survived as Tegeingl, one of the cantrefs of Flintshire, with boundaries on the Dee and the Clwyd.[19] Clearly the Deceangli occupied at least the modern county of Clwyd. It is generally assumed that this is the tribe recorded by Tacitus as the *Decangi* who in 48 or 49 were over-run by the Roman army under Scapula.[20] Immediately after this, Tacitus says, the army had 'almost reached the shore of the sea facing Ireland' when a rebellion of the Brigantes compelled them to abandon the campaign. There is no subsequent record of fighting against the tribe and no Roman fort is known between the Dee and the Clwyd.[21] Early conquest or submission is the likely explanation.

The *Annales Cambriae,* probably compiled in the late tenth century, mention a place called *arx Decantorum*, the fortress of the *Decanti,* under the year 822. This is clearly Deganwy, on the Conway estuary; but the Decanti are otherwise unknown. They cannot be connected, philologically, with the Deceangli. Whether the Decanti existed in the first century and whether they (rather than the Deceangli) are the Decangi of Tacitus are unanswerable questions.[22]

Ptolemy records only *Bullaeum* in the territory of the Silures;[23] it is the same as the *Burrium* in the *Antonine Itinerary,* which was clearly Usk.[24] The same source gives us *Venta Silurum* at Caerwent where an inscription also records the tribal name.[25] The Silures fought against the Romans on several occasions and were not finally conquered until the governorship of Frontinus in the mid-70s;[26] they are described as strong and warlike, and occupied difficult country. To the east, their boundary was probably the Wye,[27] and the same river may have separated them from the Ordovices to the north and the Dobunni to the north-east. This latter tribe scarcely concerns us: its heartland was the Cotswolds, but a third-century inscription from Kenchester, Herefordshire was set up by R P C D, usually interpreted as *res publica civitatis Dobunnorum.*[28]

Similarly the Cornovii are of little relevance to our theme. Most, if not all, of their lands lay east of the Severn and the Dee. Ptolemy places both Wroxeter (as confirmed by an inscription[29]) and Chester within their territory. Rivet and Smith put Whitchurch, half-way between Chester and Wroxeter, in the lands of the Ordovices.[30] This seems highly unlikely, but is a logical result of equating the *Mediolanium,* said by Ptolemy to be in the territory of the Ordovices, with the *Mediolanum* of the *Antonine Itinerary* which is equated with Whitchurch on the basis of the distances given.[31] If we are not to accept an extension of Ordovician territory into northern Shropshire then we must look for alternative explanations. Rivet and Smith suggest that the site is attributed to the Ordovices because their tribal name was close by on the original map. By this argument, the site must be close to Ordovician territory, but not necessarily part of it. However, by far the simplest explanation is that the two places are not synonymous and that the *Mediolanium* of Ptolemy is not the *Mediolanum* (Whitchurch) of the *Antonine Itinerary.*

Support for this view comes from another source. The *Ravenna Cosmography* is a later and confused compilation from road-books.[32] It has two relevant sequences. First is *Utriconion Cornoviorum* [*Viroconium Cornoviorum,* Wroxeter], *Lavobrinta* [*Levobrinta*[33]], *Mediomano* [*Mediolanum*?], *Segontio* [*Segontium,* Caernarfon], *Canubio* [*Canovium,* Caerhun]. This is followed by *Mediolano* [*Mediolanum,* Whitchurch], *Saudonio,*[34] *Deva Victris* [*Deva Victrix,* Chester], *Veratino* [*Vernemetum,* ?Willoughby on the Wolds], *Lutudaron* [*Lutudarum,* in Derbyshire], *Derbentie* [*Derventio,* probably Littlechester, Derbyshire], Salionis [*Salinae,* Middlewich], *Condate* [Northwich]. In the second sequence *Mediolanum* is presumably Whitchurch in Shropshire. However, the most plausible route from Wroxeter to Caerhun via Caernarfon runs west rather than north. Surely we have here evidence for a second *Mediolanum* – by no means improbable, given the general frequency of the name. Such would make geographical sense if it were equated with Ptolemy's *Mediolanium* in the territory of the Ordovices; that has on occasion been placed at Caersws for which the name, meaning 'centre of the plain', has been considered appropriate. We must then assume error in

Ptolemy's co-ordinates, and such error is common enough.

The Ordovices represent the biggest single problem in understanding first-century Wales. Tacitus tells us that, arriving late in the summer (of 77), Agricola was faced by a rebellion of the tribe who had almost annihilated a Roman cavalry regiment *(ala)* operating in their territory;[35] Agricola then went on to invade and capture Anglesey though no preparations had been made and ships were not available. This account has led to a persistent belief that the centre of Ordovician power lay in Snowdonia. It is not an essential conclusion given the inhospitable terrain of Snowdonia and the small number of pre-Roman occupation sites in the area. The place-name Dinorwic, near Llanberis, suggests that the Ordovices may indeed have held part of Snowdonia (leaving the Decanti rather cramped), but does not prove more.

In any case we cannot take Tacitus in isolation. Within Ordovician territory Ptolemy records two places, *Branogenium* and *Mediolanium*.[36] The latter has already been discussed. The former is usually equated with the *Bravonio* of the *Antonine Itinerary* and thus with Leintwardine.[37] Rivet and Smith say that 'Ptolemy's attribution to the Ordovices may be an error', but give no evidence to support this. Error in Ptolemy is common enough, but we cannot assume it when it suits us and we should be particularly cautious in presuming that Ptolemy was in error in the case of both of the sites attributed to the Ordovices. In this instance, the name *Branogenium* is given by both Ptolemy and in the *Ravenna Cosmography* while *Bravonio* appears in the *Antonine Itinerary.* As Richmond and Crawford noted, the equation does not look very exact.[38] However, the site listed in the *Cosmography* must be on the road between *Magna* (Kenchester) and *Viroconium* (Wroxeter). Therefore, even if we do not identify *Branogenium* as Leintwardine, it must surely lie in the south central marches and there seems no reason for not accepting that Ordovician territory extended this far.

Of possible relevance here is the Tacitean account of the activities of Caratacus just prior to his final stand: '... the Silures ... put their trust in Caratacus ... he shifted the war to the country of the Ordovices'.[39] This sounds like a move north into the territory of a neighbouring tribe – surely into central rather than north Wales.

If the Ordovices extended from Leintwardine (or some site in the same general area), to Dinorwic via a site, possibly Caersws, between Wroxeter and Caernarfon, it seems probable that their power base was in mid-Wales, a more likely area than Snowdonia and one able to support a larger population.

CAMPAIGNS IN WALES

Whatever the political objectives of the Romans they could not ignore the practical problems of Welsh geography. At first sight a map of the railway system of Wales in its heyday (Figure 3.2) does not seem to have great relevance to the problems of the first century.[40] However, the needs of Roman military commanders and of nineteenth-century railway engineers had much in common. Both were looking for the easiest means of penetrating an upland mass and both will have placed 'stations' at key route centres. In fact, the railways give a fair indication of what will have been possible routes of penetration for a sizeable Roman army, though of course not all routes show evidence of use. Moreover, several Roman sites lie close to major railway junctions – Clyro/Three Cocks; Llwyn-y-brain/Moat Lane; Llanfor; Penrhos/Corwen.

The railway engineers also utilised the coastal routes and one might expect the Romans to have done likewise. It is usually assumed – though no archaeological evidence has been found to support the assumption – that the corridor along the Dee estuary was used in the campaign of 48 in which the Decangi were defeated. The incidence of both forts and temporary camps suggests that a more southerly route from the Wroxeter area to Rhyn Park and Penrhos may have been chosen.

The other main railway route, from Gloucester along the Severn Estuary and Bristol Channel to Cardiff and beyond may also reflect a line of early penetration, though there is little archaeological evidence. A base had been established at Gloucester as early as 49, and the first fort at Cardiff was occupied by the mid-50s.[41] The latter may have covered as much as 15–16 hectares and was presumably intended to be the base for further advance; but further west, although Neath and Loughor have produced small amounts of early material, excavation does not support pre-Flavian occupation.[42] How the

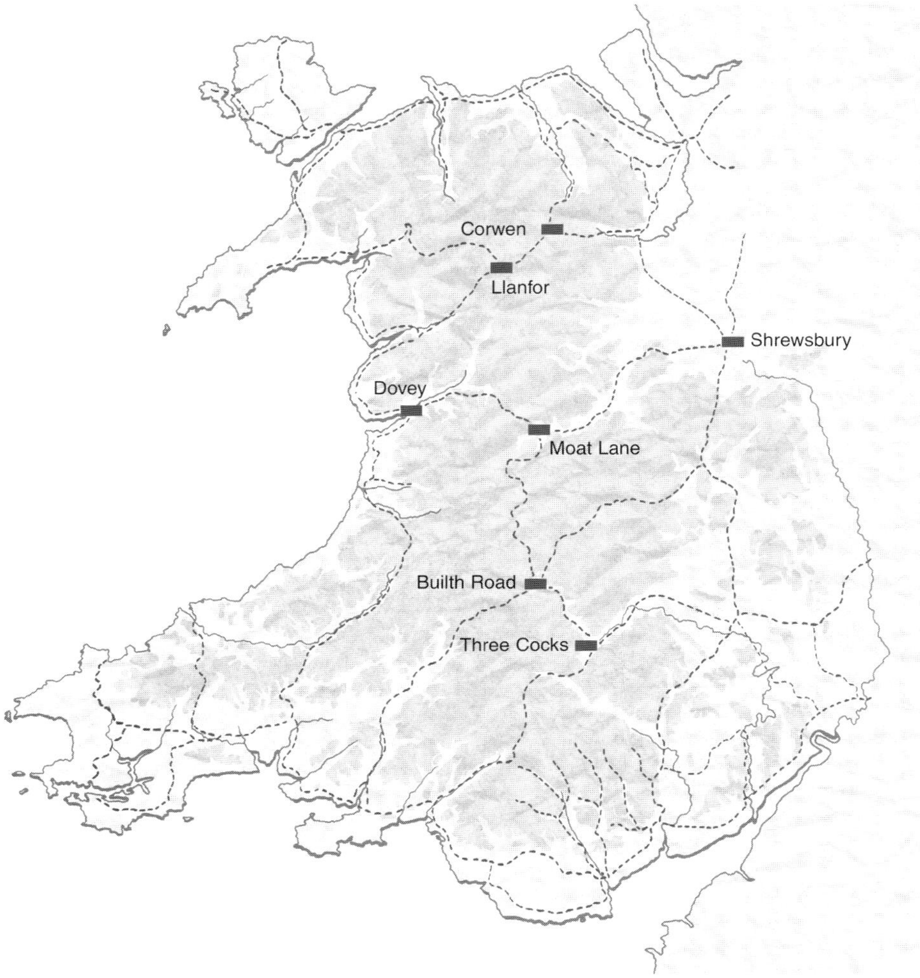

3.2 *The railways of Wales in their heyday, c 1910. Lines of purely local significance have been omitted*

Romans reached Cardiff is not clear. The small rectangular earthwork opposite Caerleon at Coed-y-caerau (Cat's Ash), if it is a fort at all, is presumably pre-Flavian – it seems unlikely to have been contemporary with Caerleon – and Chepstow has produced a little early material but no site to which it can be attributed.[43] No other temporary or permanent sites of the period have been identified on this route.[44]

Perhaps the route was not of early importance – or possibly we have not looked in the right places. That Usk and Abergavenny were occupied at much the same date as Cardiff, emphasises the importance of the Usk Valley; but movement may have been upstream, downstream or both. Approach from Gloucester might have been via Weston under Penyard and Monmouth.[45] Both have material of the right date, but Weston under Penyard (which is ripe for re-excavation) has produced no structural evidence. From Usk, a route to Cardiff might have lain via Coed-y-caerau, which has the advantage of an outlook over the coastal plain and the Severn Estuary. Boon long ago pointed to evidence for an early occupation at Sea Mills,[46] near the mouth of the Avon and 'combined operations' may have been involved in one or more of the campaigns against the Silures, but apart from Cardiff, the only coastal site with clear evidence of Roman occupation before 77 is Sudbrook, which originated as a native promontory fort. However, occupation of North Devon begins in the 50s[47] and the coastal sites there must surely suggest the presence of a fleet in the Bristol Channel and increase the chances that operations against the Silures were not entirely on land.

At least six seasons of campaigning are in question.[48] In 49 Scapula moved *legio XX* from Colchester to deal with a perceived threat from the Silures under Caratacus.[49] Part at least of the legion was probably established at Kingsholm, Gloucester; another part may have been at Clifford in the middle reaches of the Wye. The response of Caratacus was to transfer his activities to the land of the Ordovices where he was eventually defeated in 51. The attack on his fortified hill involved crossing a river sufficiently wide or deep in summer conditions for the Roman army to hesitate before crossing.[50] It is usually believed that this was the Severn, above Caersws, and that the Romans started from a base in the Shrewsbury area – probably at Leighton, for Wroxeter does not seem to have been occupied as early as this. But if Ordovician lands extended as far south as Leintwardine, the sites at Clifford and Clyro might be relevant and the river involved in 'Caratacus' Last Stand' may conceivably have been the Wye rather than the Severn although, except in flood, the Wye is hardly broad enough in its middle reaches to fit the Tacitean account, if that is accurate.[51]

However, the interest of the Romans in the area near Hay-on-Wye is clear enough. One large fort at Clifford (6.5 hectares) was probably short-lived; it is liable to flooding. It was presumably replaced by another large fort, discovered at Clock Mills, Clifford. Both were presumably abandoned when the larger fort at Clyro (10.4 hectares) was built. Clyro is the only one of the three to be excavated, albeit on a small scale; its defences were rebuilt at least once and the few finds which survived the wet and acidic soil conditions were pre-Flavian in date. While Brandon Hill, near Leintwardine and Walton, near Old Radnor were presumably initially built to deal with the Ordovices, the Clyro 'group' might have served against either the Ordovices or the Silures (or both).[52] Returning to our analogy with the railway system, this indicates several possible routes from Three Cocks (near Clyro) to the Usk Valley and we should perhaps seek another fort between Clyro and Abergavenny.

The Silures continued to oppose the Romans after Caratacus' defeat. In the guerrilla warfare of 51–2 they were fairly successful; amongst the Roman forces attacked was a legionary detachment of perhaps 2,000 men; a *praefectus castrorum* and eight centurions were amongst the casualties in an attack on troops building fortifications.[53] Late in the summer of 52 they defeated the Twentieth Legion, after the death of Scapula and before the arrival of his successor Didius Gallus.[54]

Tacitus had little time for Gallus. The governor dealt with a further Brigantian revolt, and, according to the *Annales*, merely held on to what had already been conquered; from the *Agricola* we learn that he did advance the frontier slightly, building new forts in order to gain credit for enlarging his province. The extension of territory could have been in northern England, but south and mid-Wales seem far more likely areas. Even Tacitus admits that on the arrival of Gallus the Silures were driven off. The antipathy of Tacitus is probably unfair. Gallus arrived during the campaigning season of 52, and may have had campaigns in 53 and 54; but in October 54 Claudius was succeeded by Nero. The new emperor, we are told, considered abandoning Britain, but decided against this because it would reflect on the reputation of his adoptive father Claudius; inevitably Suetonius fails to supply a date for this, but Eric Birley has shown that it must have been in the early years of the reign and that the appointment of Q. Veranius in 57 indicates that, by then, a decision to retain Britain had been made.[55] While policy was in doubt – that is during the campaigning seasons of 55 and 56 – Gallus was presumably under orders to avoid war as far as possible. The only campaign of Veranius – provoking sneers from Tacitus about 'little raids against the Silures'[56] – suggests that the tribe continued to cause problems, and that its conquest was a high priority.

The platform for 'raids' against the Silures, whatever their magnitude, must have been the fortress at Usk, founded in the mid-50s.[57] When coupled with the base, apparently of some size, at Kingsholm and with the large fort sites of Clyro and Cardiff we can see a considerable concentration of troops around the fringes of Silurian territory. Whatever the initial misgivings of the emperor, by the later 50s there can have been little doubt in the minds of all concerned that a major advance was under way.

Veranius died within a year, saying in his will that in a further two years he could have conquered the whole province. Tacitus gives the impression that *provincia* means the whole island, but it is not clear that this is what Veranius or Nero understood; policy at this stage was still tied to a Brigantian client-state in northern England, and only a year or two earlier Gallus had intervened there to support Cartimandua. In these circumstances it seems likely that Veranius was claiming that the conquest of Wales could be achieved in two further years. This is plausible enough. His successor Paulinus had two successful seasons, conquering tribes and establishing forts before he invaded Anglesey in 60.[58] In 58 Paulinus was presumably continuing action against the Silures. 59 may have been devoted to them or to fighting further north – we simply do not have the evidence to decide. If the Deceangli had not already submitted we may guess that they did so as a result of the activities of Paulinus in 59.

The invasion of Anglesey was planned in advance, for boats were built to carry the infantry; the cavalry were able to ford and swim the Menai Strait.[59] This suggests a route via Caernarfon, where it is possible to ford the Strait, rather than Bangor where it is not. Such a route must certainly have been taken by Agricola in 77, for he lacked boats even for his infantry. It may be significant that Agricola had been in Britain under Paulinus, though he was not certainly involved in the Anglesey campaign. The earliest known fort at Caernarfon was probably Agricolan; it cannot be more than a year or two earlier.[60] Neither forts nor temporary camps in the area point clearly to the route used by Paulinus. The depot at Rhyn Park or the (later) fort there (with the base and fort at Llanfor) indicate penetration along the upper Dee, but not certainly under Paulinus. The camp at Penrhos near Corwen might well relate to campaigns against the Deceangli. It is at a key junction as the nineteenth-century railway engineers knew; from Corwen there were railways to Llanfor (another nodal point) or to Ruthin and the Vale of Clwyd. The Roman site might, therefore, be of 48 or 49 (if for use against the Deceangli), rather than later (as a springboard for Anglesey). Whatever the date, the modern A5, rather than the railways, should perhaps be our guide, with advance via Cerrigydrudion to Betws-y-coed in the Conway valley.

If sites associated with Paulinus are lacking on the mainland so are they in Anglesey. Tacitus gives us a vivid description of what sounds like a primitive eisteddfod: 'The enemy lined the shore: a dense host of armed men, interspersed with women clothed in black, like the Furies, with their hair hanging down, and holding torches in their hands. Round these were the Druids, uttering dire curses and stretching out their hands towards heaven'.[61] We are told that a fort was built[62] before the campaign came to an abrupt end with the news of the Boudiccan rising. The only Roman site which might be of this date is Aberffraw.[63]

The Boudiccan rising ended not merely the Anglesey campaign, but also delayed any further advance in Wales or in England. Keith Branigan has argued for some advance in the decade 61–71, but the evidence is fairly sparse.[64] As far as Wales is concerned most of the evidence may – and probably does – relate to the 50s rather than the 60s, although the speed of advance, when it came in the mid-70s must surely indicate some earlier military activity beyond the frontier of the 60s and early 70s. Whatever, most of Wales had come to terms with Rome before 60, even if the archaeological evidence at present suggests that no permanent control pattern had been established. The system of pre-Flavian forts, so far as it is known, looks like a half-finished project; it is in marked contrast to the final dispositions of Frontinus and Agricola in Wales. This must surely be one consequence of the Boudiccan rebellion; it may also reflect the fact that Roman ideas of how to control conquered territory were still being developed at this period. Wales in the late 70s, with a network of closely spaced forts each housing 500 or 1,000 men, is radically different from Wales twenty years earlier when large sites like Rhyn Park, Clyro (Figures 3.3 and 3.4) and Usk seem to have acted as bases with some smaller forts ahead of them indicating possible lines of advance. The function of the 'large fort' is unclear, and may not have been the same for all of them. If they were to house troops they will have held far more than 1,000 men, whether these were legionary detachments or several brigaded auxiliary units (or a mixture of both). Some at least may have been depots from which the smaller forts drew supplies. It has been assumed by some that Usk was a supply depot on the basis of an apparently disproportionate number of granaries. This is probably an illusion, however, created by the random nature of the areas excavated[65] and it is more probably a reasonably standard legionary fortress.

3.3 *Rhyn Park (Shrops): fortress (c 18 ha) from the south, marked by its ditches. The west gate is visible, with a length of bank and ditch outside it. The north-west corner of the later fort is visible centre right (photograph: reproduced by permission of Cambridge University Collection of Air Photographs)*

However, both Llanfor and Llansantffraid have apparently polygonal stores-depots, which would reflect the commissariat needs of an army on campaign, travelling light and therefore needing constant supplies. One wonders if the pattern is repeated in south Wales and if more of such diagnostic sites are yet to be found there.

Other sites may reflect campaigning in a different way. In Gaul under Caesar the army campaigned during the summer then retired to 'winter-quarters', often some distance from the campaigning area. The 'winter-quarters' might be used once or over several years, and not necessarily with the same garrison every winter. We may be seeing this pattern of events or the assembly of troops immediately prior to a campaign season in the clusters of temporary camps to be found along the Welsh Marches at such sites as Wroxeter and Leintwardine.[66]

One problem which is apparent when considering this early period is the difficulty, not only of assigning specific garrisons to forts, but also of assigning the type of garrison. Even the disposition of particular legions is not entirely clear, although we may now reasonably suppose that, by the mid-50s, *legio II Augusta* was divided in some way between Exeter and Gloucester, *legio XX* was at Usk and *legio XIIII* at Wroxeter.[67] What, however, of the other large forts such as Cardiff, Clyro and Rhyn? For these some sort

3.4 *Rhyn Park (Shrops): fort (c 6 ha) from the north. The west ditches show the staggered entrance clearly. The east ditches of the earlier fortress run left of the centre of the picture (photograph: reproduced by permission of Cambridge University Collection of Air Photographs)*

of mixed garrison would seem appropriate. We may note that the deteriorating military situation at the death of Scapula involved a legionary detachment building fortifications (see above), which may be an indication that the larger forts held some legionary cohorts. They may well also have held units of other types. Cardiff, for instance, sits astride the coastal plain of south Wales, surely ideal cavalry country. It also, of course, commands a river mouth and will presumably have provided shelter for naval detachments. It seems likely that the military commanders of the Claudian and Neronian periods were more willing to divide legions and to mix detachments in single forts than were their Flavian successors.[68] We may reasonably ask if *legio II*, in particular, functioned as a divided force, in the period between the subjugation of the south-western peninsula in the late 40s and the establishment of Caerleon in the mid-70s.[69]

A fundamental problem is that historical and archaeological evidence are two different things. Tacitus can speak of campaigns against one tribe or another which may be assignable to specific years, but even with far more artefacts from much more excavation than it is reasonable to expect, archaeology cannot achieve that level of precision. By their nature temporary camps will produce few datable objects; such camps were not necessarily occupied for more than a night or two by an army travelling light. What, indeed, is a datable object in this context? Coins or inscriptions obviously carry with them a reasonably certain date of manufacture. Pottery, our main dating tool for all these sites, is only datable by association. As all students are repeatedly told, ultimately it is sites which date pottery and not *vice versa*. In the period under consideration, we are fortunate in having a number of historically attested events which will independently date certain pottery (and particularly samian) deposits. The initial Claudian conquest of Britain, the destruction of incipient Roman towns by Boudicca and the destruction of Pompeii in 79[70] provide a framework into which we can fit pottery from less well dated sites. Key events in 43, 61 and 79 do not, however, give us the sort of precision which will enable us to distinguish the pottery of one governorship from that of an immediate predecessor. We may be able to argue on stylistic grounds that specific pots are more likely to have been made nearer to one of our key events than to another. Beyond that, we are fortunate if we are not reliant upon analogies with sites dated by our historical interpretation of the conquest of western Britain. The danger of circularity, if we try to use the pottery to give precision to our historical interpretation, is obvious.

The main reason for dating many camps to the period of campaigning is their size. Large camps imply a force of suitable size for initial conquest and one so large that it was unlikely to be assembled later once Wales was conquered. Only such camps have been shown on Figure 3.5. All are 6 hectares or more in size and might provide sufficient space for 5,000 or more soldiers. Smaller camps may belong to the mid-first century, or may reflect troop movements after 77.

In Scotland it has proved possible to group camps by size and plan and to link different series of camps to specific campaigns. In Wales we have fewer camps and more campaigns – at least thirteen between 48 and 77. Nonetheless, by adding the evidence of early forts (Figure 3.6) to that of the temporary camps we can deduce some likely campaigning routes, even if we cannot date them precisely. Recent discoveries, though usually of sites which have not yet produced any dating evidence, encourage further speculation about routes – and about sites yet to be discovered.

We have already looked at some of these routes, but we should examine others. We have seen that Monmouth, recently confirmed as a pre-Flavian site, may have linked Gloucester and Weston under Penyard to the Usk Valley sites; and we have noted the emphasis on the middle Wye at Clifford and Clyro. The discovery of forts in the Monnow and Golden Valleys at Castlefield, near Kentchurch (Figure 3.7), and Abbey Dore (Figure 3.8)[71] suggests a link between Monmouth and Clyro. Kentchurch has produced Claudio-Neronian pottery. Another site between Abbey Dore and Clyro presumably awaits

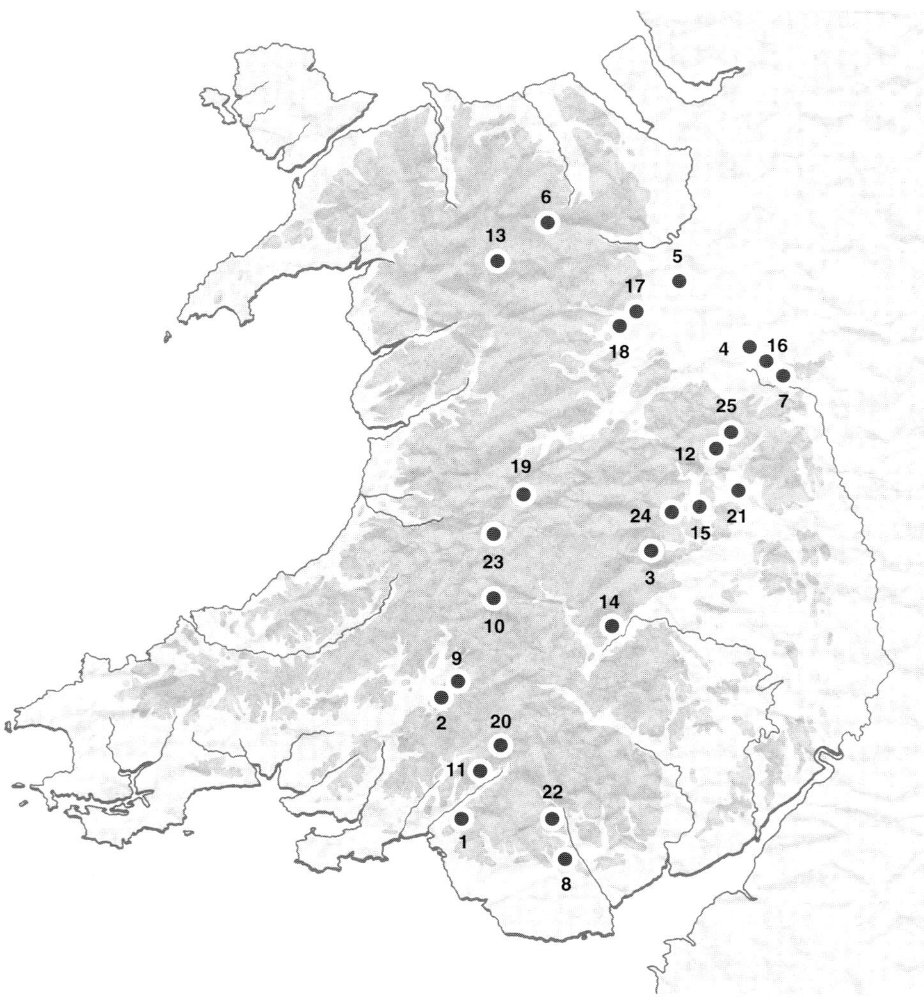

3.5 *Temporary camps, presumably of the campaigning period; all are at least 6 ha in area. (1) Blaen-cwm-bach (2) Arosfa Garreg (3) Walton (4) Uffington (5) Whittington (6) Penrhos (7) Leighton (8) Pen-y-coedcae (9) Y Pigwn (10) Beulah (11) Coelbren (12) Stretford Bridge (13) Llanfor (14) Clyro (15) Walford (16) Attingham Park (17) Abertanat (18) Llansantffraid-ym-Mechain (19) St Harmon (20) Ystradfellte (21) Bromfield (22) Twyn y Briddallt (23) Esgairperfedd (24) Brampton Bryan (25) Upper Affcot. Some sites were occupied by several camps in succession; some were apparently succeeded by more permanent forts or depots, shown on Figure 3.6*

discovery near Peterchurch or Dorstone. The complex earthworks below Snodhill Castle might repay aerial photography. This line of forts suggests that the early material from Chepstow may be a pointer to another pre-Flavian fort. Clyro may well have served as a base for further advance up the Wye, where large temporary camps are known.

The fort discovered at Canon Frome, east of Hereford, seems unlikely to be related directly to these lines of advance. It may mark progress via the fort (Figure 3.9) or the large camp at Walton to the upper Wye – much the line of the modern A44. It would also provide a point on a route to the Leintwardine area where the earliest fort (Brandon Camp) has been extensively excavated and dated *c* 55–65.[72] The succession of forts in this area, with occupation into the fourth century, indicates that the Romans attached great importance to it. Brandon Camp, in the Teme Valley, suggests the possibility of advance upstream to Knighton and on to the upper Wye near Rhyader; or a less easy route via Dolfor to the Severn Valley where the fort at Llwyn-y-brain (Figure 3.10) is surely pre-Flavian.[73]

The proximity of Llwyn-y-brain to Moat Lane Junction – by our railway analogy – suggests caution. Moat Lane was reached from Shrewsbury, the modern equivalent of Wroxeter, up the Severn Valley. From the junction, lines led south to Rhyader in the Wye Valley and westwards to Dovey Junction and the coast. Near Dovey Junction, the unexcavated Roman

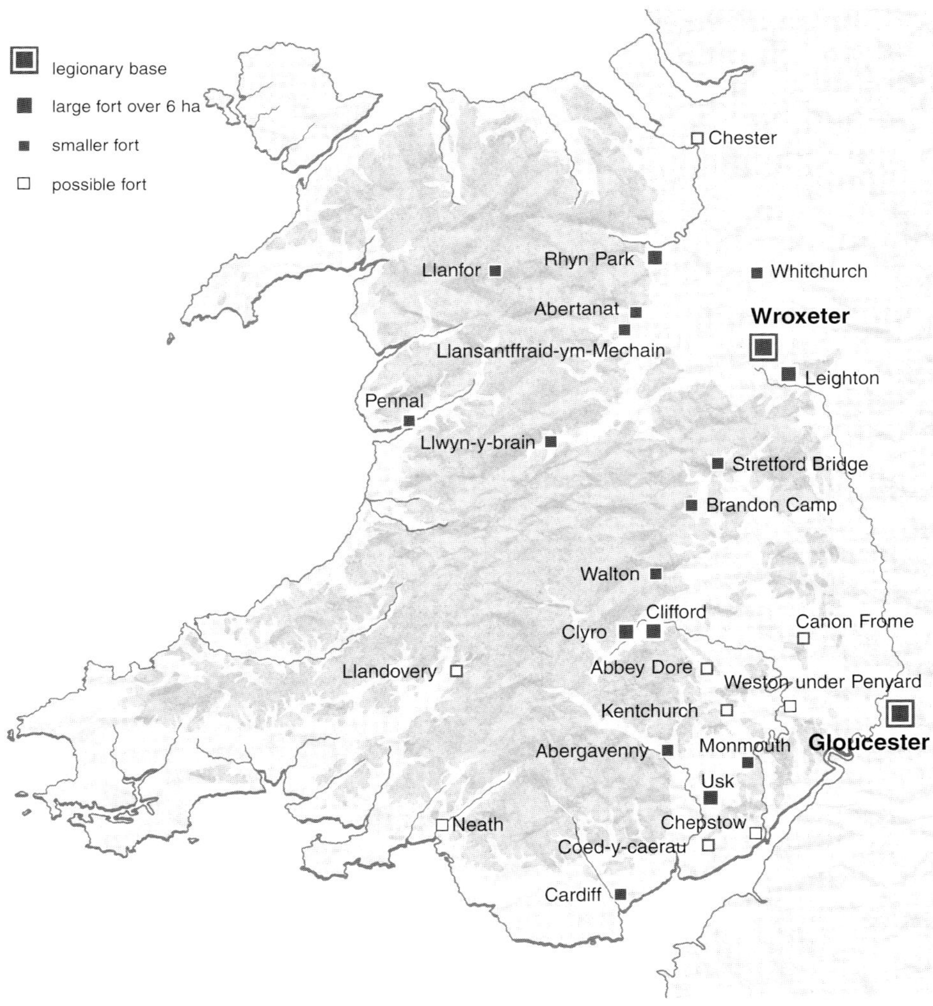

3.6 *Pre-Flavian forts and depots. Some became part of the 'permanent' pattern of control from the 70s onward*

3.7 *Castlefield, Kentchurch (Herefs): fort, possibly part of a chain from Monmouth to Clyro (photograph: reproduced by permission of the Clwyd-Powys Archaeological Trust, Ref 89-MB-898)*

3.8 *Abbey Dore (Herefs): fort in the Golden Valley (photograph: reproduced by permission of the Clwyd-Powys Archaeological Trust, Ref 89-MB-894)*

fort at Pennal has produced two bottles in Central Gaulish glazed pottery and a sherd of a pre-Flavian mortarium.[74] All would normally be regarded as evidence of pre-Flavian activity as would another glazed Central Gaulish bottle found at Caer Gai, overlooking Llyn Tegid (Bala Lake); but the latter might belong to the mid- or late 70s in deposition, for no pre-Flavian material was found in excavations at the fort. Another glazed bottle, from a cremation 350 metres from the fort, may, on the other hand, indicate an earlier undetected site. This material illustrates very well the problems of dating using pottery alone.

a b

3.9 *Walton (Rads): fort at Hindwell Farm: a revealed from the air by earthworks in winter; b by parch marks in summer conditions (photographs: reproduced by permission of Cambridge University Collection of Air Photographs)*

The *floruit* of the glazed ware is undoubtedly pre-Flavian,[75] though survivals into the Flavian period undoubtedly exist. Are we justified in using the evidence to suggest activity before rather than after 70, and the possibility of a Roman fleet operating in conjunction with land-based forces? The obvious land route to Pennal would be from Llwyn-y-brain. Boon and Brewer suggest the possibility of water-borne supplies being landed in the Mawddach estuary and taken up the Wnion Valley to the base at Llanfor (Figure 3.11). We could be seeing here some hint of activity in the period between the Boudiccan episode and the Flavian conquest, but we cannot be certain that the pottery is indicative of pre-Flavian rather than early Flavian activity. Our dating of the pottery depends in part on our interpretations of the Welsh sites. We are in danger of an argument which is, at the very least, penannular.

Wroxeter may or may not have been the base for advance up the Severn to Llwyn-y-brain, but it (or the earlier fort at Leighton, close by) was certainly important for advances further north. St Joseph had identified one possible line of camps extending between the Severn and Dee from Wall (near Lichfield) via Wroxeter to Whittington and Penrhos. That this was a route favoured by the Romans is confirmed by the absence of a major pre-Flavian site in the Chester area.

Work by the late Professor Barri Jones again points to an approach from the south-east. An important concentration of sites has been found and excavated in recent years.[76] Abertanat (camps and a depot), Clawdd Coch (2 camps) and Llansantffraid-ym-Mechain (a camp and a fort) are so close that they are unlikely to have all been held simultaneously. Slightly further north, the site at Rhyn Park (near Chirk) has produced

3.10 *Llwyn-y-brain (Mont): ditches of the fort from the south. Sometimes known as 'Caersws I' it presumably preceded the better-known fort below Caersws village, which seems to have been built in the 70s (photograph: reproduced by permission of Cambridge University Collection of Air Photographs)*

3.11 *Llanfor (Mer): ditches of the pentagonal stores compound, with fort beyond (photograph: reproduced by permission of Cambridge University Collection of Air Photographs)*

evidence for a large base of 18.6 hectares and a smaller (but still sizeable) fort of 5.7 hectares. The dating evidence is sparse but includes a brooch which is probably Neronian.[77] Rhyn Park seems likely to have preceded Chester as a forward base for campaigns; movement down the Dee Valley to the estuary, or up-river to Penrhos and the Vale of Clwyd would be relatively easy. The more southerly complex of sites around Llansantffraid surely indicates movement up the Tanat and across the Berwyns to Llanfor.

Let us stress again that even if the association of different sites and possible lines of advance is correct, the evidence will not yet enable us to say with any confidence to which tribes or campaigns specific routes relate. Here there is scope for hours of harmless speculation for each of us. The map of pre-Flavian forts (Figure 3.6), does, however, make clear the density of sites of this period in all but the northern Marches and the importance of the valleys of the Usk, Wye and Severn and their tributaries.

If the interpretation of the newly discovered sites in Herefordshire is correct we can perhaps see a pattern of control emerging.[78] From legionary fortresses at Wroxeter and Kingsholm/Gloucester lines of advance may be projected leading to larger forward bases (Rhyn Park, Clyro, Usk and Cardiff). Much work remains to be done both in dating newly discovered sites and in locating others which must exist but, in the south-east, our forward line appears to be supported by a network of smaller forts and bases 15–20 kilometres apart; a pattern remarkably similar to what we have hitherto seen as an innovation of Frontinus and Agricola in the 70s. The situation of the legionary fortress at Usk on this advanced line is of particular interest. It must surely have been intended to replace Gloucester (and Exeter?) once the Silures were subdued.[79] Is it too fanciful to see a similarity between the frontier commanded by Usk in south-east Wales in the 50s and 60s and that commanded a generation later by Inchtuthil? Both are situated on the edge of an upland block and appear to fulfil the dual function of facilitating the advance of Roman forces up river valley routes while blocking egress by the native inhabitants.

Earlier writings on the subject of Roman campaigns in Wales placed much emphasis on the upper Usk Valley. At the head of the valley, large temporary camps at Y Pigwn are only 7 kilometres from the fort at Llandovery in the Tywi Valley.[80] This suggested combined operations with a force landing in the Tywi estuary to join another advancing up the Usk. On this we have no new information except the purely negative. Extensive excavations at Carmarthen have produced no evidence of pre-Flavian occupation although, of course, other sites near the estuary may remain to be found. However, the real reason for leaving this to the last is that it enables a re-examination of the evidence for early occupation of the Llandovery fort. Its earliest defence was destroyed by fire.[81] The second defence need not be later than 77. Finds from the excavations do not necessarily indicate earlier occupation, though they include a spectacular piece of a small glass cup. Originally thought to be early, the Llandovery mosaic glass cup has now been re-evaluated by Professor Jennifer Price and shown to be Flavian or later.[82] Whatever, its high quality reduces its archaeological value. The cup is of 'heirloom' quality and could have been several decades old when it reached Llandovery. The excavated pottery appears to be Flavian. In the absence of other excavated evidence, the pre-Flavian fort at Llandovery must remain doubtful[83] – a salutary reminder of the problems of using archaeology as a source for military history.

ACKNOWLEDGEMENTS

We wish to record our thanks to all those who have assisted in the preparation of the lecture and of the original and revised publication. They include Richard Brewer, William Britnell, Dr Jeffrey Davies, Professor William Manning, John Morgan, Chris Musson, Janet Webster, David R Wilson and David Zienkiewicz. We are grateful to Tony Daly, National Museums & Galleries of Wales, for drawing the maps.

Appendix

The sites listed here are mentioned either in the text or on maps 3.5 and 3.6. Only the latest reference is usually given. *AW*=*Archaeology in Wales; JRS*=*Journal of Roman Studies; RCE*=Welfare and Swan 1995; *RFW*=Nash-Williams/Jarrett 1969 where more extensive references will be found.

A. Temporary camps

1	Blaen-cwm-bach	SS 7998	25 ha	*RFW*, 124; *AW* 10 (1970), 17; 12 (1972), 25; 14 (1974), 24–5
2	Arosfa Garreg	SN 8026	18 ha	*RFW*, 124
3	Walton	SO 2560	18 ha	*JRS* 63 (1973), 239–40
4	Uffington	SJ 5213	15 ha and 17 ha	*JRS* 67 (1977), 145; *RCE*, 164–5
5	Whittington	SJ 3530	16 ha	*JRS* 63 (1973), 236; *RCE*, 166–8
6	Penrhos	SJ 0442	16 ha	*JRS* 63 (1973), 237
7	Leighton	SJ 6005	8 ha	*JRS* 63 (1973), 234–5
8	Pen-y-coedcae	ST 0587	15 ha	*RFW*, 124
9	Y Pigwn	SN 8231	15 ha and 10 ha	*RFW*, 124; RCAHMW, *Brecknock* 1986, 150–3
10	Beulah	SN 9150	15 ha	*RFW*, 200; RCAHMW, *Brecknock* 1986,131 and 155
11	Coelbren	SN 8610	14 ha	*RFW*, 126
12	Stretford Bridge	SO 4385	14 ha	*JRS* 63 (1973), 235; *RCE*, 162–4
13	Llanfor	SH 9336	12 ha	*Britannia* 7 (1976), 296; *JRS* 67 (1977), 149–50; *Britannia*, 29 (1998), 368–9; *AW* 37 (1997), 13–20
14	Clyro	SO 2243	10 ha	*RFW*, 200
15	Walford	SO 3972	10 ha?	*RFW*, 126
16	Attingham Park and Norton	SJ 5509	9 ha and 13 ha	*JRS* 67 (1977), 145; *RCE*, 150–1, 158–9
17	Abertanat and Clawdd Coch	SJ 2421	–	See n 76; *Britannia* 23 (1992), 256–8 for general plan
18	Llansantffraid-ym-Mechain	SJ 2220	–	*Britannia* 20 (1989), 260
19	St Harmon	SN 9871	8 ha	*JRS* 59 (1969), 123
20	Ystradfellte	SN 9216	8 ha	*RFW*, 126; RCAHMW, *Brecknock* 1986, 153–4
21	Bromfield	SO 4877	8 ha	*RFW*, 126; *RCE*, 150–3
22	Twyn y Briddallt	ST 0098	6 ha	*RFW*, 126
23	Esgairperfedd	SN 9269	6 ha	*RFW*, 126
24	Brampton Bryan	SO 3672	26 ha	*JRS* 63 (1973), 235; *RCE*, 61–3
25	Upper Affcot	SO 4486	6 ha+	*RCE*, 164–6

B. Other sites

Abbey Dore	*AW* 29 (1989), 56
Abergavenny	*RFW*, 45–6; Blockley and Ashmore 1993
Abertanat	See Part A
Brandon Camp	See n 72
Caer Gai	*RFW*, 54–6
Canon Frome	*JRS* 63 (1963), 237
Cardiff	See n 41
Chepstow	See n 43
Clifford	*JRS* 63 (1973), 238; Clock Mills, *Britannia* 23 (1992), 283
Clyro	*RFW*, 77–80
Coed-y-caerau/Cat's Ash	*RFW*, 80–1
Kentchurch/Castlefield	*Britannia* 18 (1987), 323
Leighton/Eaton Constantine	*JRS* 63 (1973), 234–5
Llandovery	*RFW*, 95–6; *AW* 23 (1983), 34
Llanfor	See Part A
Llansanffraid-ym-Mechain	See Part A
Llwyn-y-brain/Caersws I	See n 73
Monmouth	*AW* 32 (1992), 1–2; see n 45
Neath	Marvell and Heywood 1992
Pennal	See n 74; *RFW*, 104–6
Rhyn Park	*Britannia* 10 (1979), 296
Sea Mills	See n 46
Stretford Bridge	*JRS* 63 (1973), 235
Sudbrook	See n 44
Usk	See n 57
Walton	*JRS* 63 (1973), 239–40; *Britannia* 8 (1977), 360
Weston under Penyard	G Webster 1958, 66–7

Notes

1 Jarrett 1964b. Also Nash-Williams/Jarrett 1969; the first chapter, 'The Invasion' (pp 1–8) is particularly relevant here.

2 Translations are most readily available in Penguin Classics: M Grant, *Tacitus: The Annals of Imperial Rome* (1956), Harmondsworth; H Mattingly, *Tacitus on Britain and Germany* (1948), Harmondsworth. More literal translations can be found in: G G Ramsay, *The Annals of Tacitus. Books XI–XVI* (1909), London and W Peterson, *Tacitus: Dialogus, Agricola, Germania*, Loeb (1920), London. Many of the key texts are gathered together, with translations, in Manning 1981, 24–6. See also: Ogilvie and Richmond 1967.

3 Tacitus, *Annales* 12.40.8: 'These events took place under the two Governors and were spread over several years; but I have related them in conjunction, fearing that they might be less remembered if told unconnectedly. I now return to the regular order of events.' (Ramsay op cit n 2).

4 Cassius Dio 60.19–22. The relevant passage is to be found in the Loeb edition (trans E Cary, *Dio's Roman History* (1924), London) vol VII, 414–23.

5 Tacitus, *Annales* 12.31.1 (Ramsay op cit n 2).

6 Tacitus, *Agricola* 17.1.

7 Tacitus, *Agricola* 14.1: 'certain states were handed over to King Cogidumnus – he has remained continuously loyal down to our own times' (Peterson op cit n 2). The traditional name of this ruler (Cogidumnus or Cogidubnus) has been prefered here despite the more recent use of 'Togidubnus'.

8 Suetonius, *Nero* 18: 'Nero felt no ambition to extend the Roman Empire, and even considered withdrawing his forces from Britain; yet kept them there because such a decision might have reflected on the glory won by his adoptive father Claudius' (trans R Graves, *Suetonius, The Twelve Caesars* (1957), Harmondsworth).

9 A winter visit to the continent might be implied in the opening of the *Agricola*, 24: 'In the fifth year of campaigning, he crossed in the first ship to make the passage' (Peterson op cit n 2), although Ogilvie and Richmond (1967, 235) take this to mean that Agricola led the fleet towards the new season's campaign. Despatches after the battle of Mons Graupius are mentioned in Tacitus, *Agricola*, 39.1. Our best guide to the close liaison between governor and emperor is, of course, Pliny's *Epistulae* to the Emperor Trajan. Hanson discusses the effect of imperial policy on Agricola's campaigning (Hanson 1987, 107 and 115).

10 This and the following sections include many references to individual sites. These are listed with references in the Appendix.

11 Jarrett and Mann 1968.

12 For the British section of the *Geographia*, see Rivet and Smith 1979, 103–47. For more recent discussion of many of the sites mentioned here, see Manning 1997.

13 Ptolemy, *Geographia* 2.3.23.

14 *Itinerarium Antonini*, 484.1. The British section is discussed by Rivet 1970, 34–68 and by Rivet and Smith 1979, 150–84. For Maridunum/Moridunum, see ibid, 422.

15 Rivet and Smith 1979, 400.

16 Information on Llandeilo from Dr J L Davies.

17 James 1990. Pending full publication of the 1980s excavations, dating evidence will be found in archive reports, Cambria Archaeology, Llandeilo.

18 *RIB* II.1, 2404.31–2, 2404.36.

19 Rhys 1892.

20 Tacitus, *Annales* 12.32.1.

21 Although there is a fort at Ruthin on the very edge of this area, see Waddelove *et al* 1990.

22 Although it may be noted that the Conway Valley might better fit the Tacitean reference as 'almost' the shore facing Ireland.

23 Ptolemy, *Geographia* 2.3.24.

24 *Itinerarium Antonini*, 484.5.

25 *Itinerarium Antonini*, 405.9; *RIB* I, 311.

26 Tacitus, *Agricola* 17.2: 'Julius Frontinus was a great man ... his arms reduced the Silures, a powerful and warlike race; he surmounted not only the valour of the enemy but also the physical difficulties of their land' (Peterson op cit n 2, 199).

27 Although Manning argues strongly for a boundary on the lower Severn, see Manning 1981, 15–23.

28 *RIB* I, 2250.

29 *RIB* I, 288.

30 Rivet and Smith 1979, 415–16.

31 Ibid, 120–1.

32 Richmond and Crawford 1949, 1–50, provides the most readily accessible version. In the list, the names as given in the *Ravenna Cosmography* are quoted first; amendments and identification by Rivet and Smith 1979 are placed in square brackets.

33 Richmond and Crawford (1949, 37) suggest this may be Forden Gaer, but this is dependant upon their identification of *Mediomano* as Caersws. Rivet and Smith suggest a reading of *Levobrinta*, but offer no identification (1979, 391).

34 Which may have been appended to *Mediolanum* by mistake, see Rivet and Smith 1979, 415.

35 Tacitus, *Agricola* 18.

36 Ptolemy, *Geographia* 2.3.18.

37 Jarrett and Mann 1968, 169; Rivet and Smith 1979, 275.
38 Richmond and Crawford 1949, 25.
39 Tacitus, *Annales* 12.33.
40 The map has been simplified by omission of many coal lines in the south and the Snowdon Mountain Railway in the north.
41 P V Webster 1990.
42 Cardiff is dated to the Neronian period by a coin list closely similar to that from Usk in that it contains many copies of Claudian bronze coinage, common up to 64 and quickly withdrawn thereafter. No fort further west betrays the same pattern. Neath (Marvell and Heywood 1992) contains a few pieces of pottery, including samian, which, if found in quantity, would indicate a pre-Flavian site. However, they do not appear in quantity and are more likely to indicate the pattern to be expected in primary levels of Flavian forts. Loughor (Owen-John and Marvell 1997) shows a similar pattern to Neath.
43 Shoesmith 1991, 92–3. Of the pottery found, no. 1 has similarities with an Usk fortress type, no. 3 in Severn Valley Ware and would best suit a mid-first century date, while no. 10 is certainly pre-85 and could well be Neronian to early Flavian. See also *Archaeol Wales* 33 (1993), 61.
44 The site at Sudbrook (Nash-Williams 1939) might be added to this list, see Manning this volume, 40. Recent re-excavation of some of Nash-Williams' trenches (S Sell for Glamorgan-Gwent Archaeological Trust) has added little except renewed doubts as to some of Nash-Williams' conclusions. One is left with the pottery, which bears a close resemblance to that from the later 'legionary' phases at Usk. As Manning points out, a military post guarding a ferry crossing of the Severn seems probable.
45 *Archaeol Wales* 32 (1992), 74. A number of early sites around Monmouth suggest military activity in the conquest period and soon after. The earliest appears to lie on the rise occupied by the modern town where pre-Flavian samian suggests early activity.
46 Boon 1949, 185–6.
47 Fox and Ravenhill 1966. See Manning this volume, 37 and n 44 above.
48 The early campaigns in south-east Wales are discussed in detail by Manning this volume. Here the aim is to give more of an overview in relation to Roman policy towards Wales as a whole.
49 'The tribe of the Silures was turned neither by brutality nor by clemency from pursuing war, requiring the encampment of legions to keep it down. To secure the desired end more quickly, a powerful colony of veterans was settled ... at Camulodunum', Tacitus, *Annales* 12.32. It is of interest that Tacitus, in the phrase *castrisque legionum premenda foret*, certainly implies more than one legion, and may imply more than one camp.
50 Tacitus, *Annales* 12.33–5.
51 The same objection can be raised to an alternative site at Llanymynech suggested by Jones (Frere 1992, 258 and Burnham 1995, 328). Llanymynech hillfort shows signs of hasty additions to the defences and Roman temporary works are known in the area (see Appendix, Abertanat and Clawdd Coch). However, it is difficult to know how much reliance to place on the geographical descriptions made by Tacitus and it would be useful to be able to test these against certain remains associated with any British battle which he describes.
52 The account of how Caratacus transferred the war northwards (n 39 above) may indicate that he feared a Roman move to isolate him in south Wales. This could have been achieved by Roman penetration of either the upper Usk or the middle Wye valleys.
53 Tacitus, *Annales* 12.38: 'They surrounded a *Praefectus Castrorum*, with the legionary cohorts which had been left behind to construct defences in the Silurian country; and had not help been quickly sent up to the beseiged men from the neighbouring forts ... they would have been cut off ...' (Ramsay op cit n 2). This shows clearly both the involvement of legionary troops and the construction of new forts.
54 Tacitus, *Annales* 12.40.
55 E Birley 1953b. Suetonius, *Nero* 18.
56 Tacitus, *Annales* 14.29.2.
57 See Manning this volume, 39; 1981; 1989.
58 Tacitus, *Agricola* 14.3.
59 Tacitus, *Annales* 14.29–30.
60 See Casey *et al* 1993, 10: 'The balance of probability indicated that the site is Agricolan and dates to 77 or shortly after'.
61 Tacitus, *Annales* 14.30.1–3.
62 Tacitus, *Annales*, 14.30.4.
63 For this possible site, see *Archaeol Wales* 13 (1973), 36–7.
64 Branigan 1977.
65 See Manning 1989, 165, also Figs 4 and 71.
66 Welfare and Swan 1995, Fig 126, 150–65 (Wroxeter area); Fig 51, 61–6 (Leintwardine area).
67 For further discussion of this point, see Manning this volume.
68 Although it might be pointed out that the Vindolanda tablets indicate that the splitting of units was by no means exclusively pre-Flavian, see R E Birley 1993a, 20.
69 But see Manning this volume for a different view.

70 Pompeii is significant, even for Britain, because it provides a *terminus ante quem* for samian found in the destroyed town and, in particular, a date for the so-called 'Pompeii Hoard' of samian found still in its crate and thus brought to the site not long before the eruption. See Atkinson 1914.

71 Frere 1987c, 323.

72 Frere 1987b.

73 This site is perhaps better known as Caersws I; see Nash-Williams/Jarrett 1969, 66–7; also St Joseph 1969, 121–3. It is presumably earlier than the fort under Caersws village (Caersws II) for which there is no reason to doubt a Flavian foundation (although some probably Neronian finds may be noted). So far, Llwyn-y-brain has not yielded diagnostic material (see *Archaeol Wales* 36 (1996), 79).

74 Boon and Brewer 1981. See also *Archaeol Wales* 23 (1983), 39–40.

75 The evidence is summarized in Greene 1979, 99–100. The flagon neck from Caerleon, Prysg Field may be noted.

76 For Abertanat, see Frere 1991, 223–4 which also cites earlier reports; Burnham 1997, 404 and for Clawdd Coch, see Burnham 1995, 326, which also cites earlier reports.

77 See J Webber 2001.

78 The argument here was, in part, anticipated by Frere 1987b, 69–71.

79 It is presumably only the 'accident' of the faulty siting of Usk in a position liable to occasional flood which led to the moving, in the mid-70s, of the main south Wales legionary base, downriver to Caerleon.

80 See RCAHMW, *Brecknock* 1986, 150–3; the map, (ibid, 126) shows how the Llandovery region could be reached from either the Usk or Wye valleys.

81 See Frere1983, 281. See also Davies and Kirby 1994, 280.

82 See Price 2002.

83 Re-examination of the pottery evidence from Llandovery (P V Webster forthcoming) does not appear to support a pre-Flavian date, despite claims to the contrary. However, the early defences do not seem to have produced datable material. The argument for pre-Frontinan military activity along the Usk–Tywi 'corridor' well in advance of the legionary base at Usk remains an attractive one but as a possible pre-Flavian fort site Llandovery has always appeared isolated.

CHAPTER 4

THE SECOND AUGUSTAN LEGION IN NORTH BRITAIN

DAVID J BREEZE

Michael Jarrett's study of *legio II Augusta* in Britain, published in 1964,[1] tackled the subject chronologically, with special attention paid, naturally, to the relationship between the legion's activities and the archaeological evidence for the occupation of Caerleon. Here a different approach is taken. Firstly, this paper is only concerned with *legio II Augusta* in the north. This can be defined as England north of the Humber–Mersey line together with Scotland; in the third century the area made up the greater part of the province of Lower Britain. Secondly, the activities of the legion in the north are examined, not chronologically, but under the following heads: fighting, building, living and dying. Unlike the early history of *legio II Augusta*,[2] there are no surviving literary sources for the history of the legion in north Britain and therefore a continuous narrative is not possible. The main evidence is provided by inscriptions.

FIGHTING

The paucity of our sources render comment on any fighting by *legio II Augusta* in the north of Britain brief. No record survives of the names of any units which took part in the great series of campaigns led by the Flavian governors of Britain from 71 to 83 or 84, when Wales, northern England and much of Scotland were conquered by Petillius Cerialis, Julius Frontinus and Julius Agricola, with the exception of a single reference to *legio VIIII Hispana*.[3] It is possible that *II Augusta*, preoccupied with its own problems in south Wales, did not supply any troops for the campaign of Cerialis against the Brigantes or those of Agricola further north.

Two points may be made in relation to Agricola's final seasons in north-eastern Scotland, the campaign which culminated in his victory over the Caledonians at Mons Graupius, fought probably somewhere in north-east Scotland. Firstly, it is very possible that the number of legionaries in his army did not exceed that of the auxiliary infantry, which we know numbered 8,000 men. The whole tenor of the discussion of the battle of Mons Graupius, during which the legionaries were kept in reserve, suggests that Agricola's army was not large: the Caledonian force of 30,000 was greatly superior to it in numbers.[4] Even an equivalent number of legionaries and auxiliary infantry would, together with the cavalry, produce a force of either 19,000 or 21,000, depending on how the ambiguity concerning the number of cavalry is read (it seems probable that the four squadrons of cavalry, 2,000 men, kept in reserve were an addition to the 3,000 cavalry mentioned earlier otherwise there would have been only one cavalry unit on each wing). A force of such a size might be thought to invalidate the phrase 'greatly superior', which may indicate a relationship of about 2 to 1. The legionary strength may therefore have been no more than about 4,000, producing a total force of 15,000 or 17,000. The 4,000 men could have been provided *in toto* by *legio VIIII Hispana*, which had certainly been with the army the previous year when Tacitus records that it had been badly mauled in the night attack on its camp.[5] As a result of this attack the legion may have been supported by one or more detachments from its sister legions in the following season. Less likely, perhaps, the 4,000 legionaries could have been made up of four equal sized detachments drawn from the four legions of the province.[6] The second point is that at this time, most probably in 83,[7] a detachment of *II Augusta*, presumably two cohorts strong, the normal size, was serving on the continent.[8] Since 1,000 soldiers were away on this duty and with the Silures only recently conquered, it may have been thought unwise to detach too many men for service on the northern frontier. Thus the two points coincide in the very real possibility that no soldiers of *II Augusta* participated in the battle of Mons Graupius.

The second century was regularly punctuated by wars and other troubles on the northern frontier. These continued from Trajan's reign, when at least one unit, and possibly two, appears to have won military distinction in Britain, through to the campaigns of the Emperor Septimius Serverus against the Maeatae and Caledonians between 208 and 211.[9] In not one of these wars can it be demonstrated that *legio II Augusta* took part. On two occasions, however, there is circumstantial evidence to call into play. In 139 and 140 the legion was at Corbridge rebuilding the fort in preparation for the reoccupation of southern Scotland, while on the successful completion of the invasion it assisted in the construction of the Antonine Wall.[10] There can thus be a strong presumption that the legion took part in the invasion itself. The second occasion was the campaigns of Septimius Severus in 208–11. Herodian records that Severus 'summoned troops from all directions and assembled a large army', while Cassius Dio states that the Romans lost 50,000 men during the campaign of 209, surely an exaggeration, but nevertheless indicating a sizeable Roman force.[11] The testimony of these two contemporary writers is supported by the exceptional size of the marching camps which are considered to date to these campaigns: 67, 52 and 26 hectares in area.[12] It seems probable that *legio II Augusta* was one of the units which made up this considerable force, and again the building activity of the legion at Severus' fortress at Carpow on the Tay, apparently the basis of his strategy for the occupation of Scotland, points to the presence of the legion during the fighting.[13] Support for the participation of the legion in the army of invasion may come from the presence in the north, possibly at Corbridge, of L. Julius Julianus, who dedicated an inscription to the Victory of the Emperor, and who has been equated with the commander of *II Augusta* of that name, and the man mentioned in a rescript of Severus and Caracalla.[14] Apart from these two occasions, however, it would be useless to speculate about the presence or otherwise of the legion in the other wars of the second century.

BUILDING

In the area of building activity we are on surer ground. This is primarily through the existence of inscriptions which record the construction of frontiers, forts and individual buildings. These demonstrate the considerable involvement of *legio II Augusta* in the two great military engineering feats of the second century, the building of Hadrian's Wall (Figure 4.1) and the Antonine Wall (Figure 4.4). This is not the place to enter into detailed consideration of the work of the legion in the construction of either frontier, about each there being both voluminous modern literature and complex arguments,[15] but the general nature of this activity must be examined.

The original plan for Hadrian's Wall seems to have entailed the division of most of the barrier into blocks of about 8 kilometres, each being assigned to a legion.[16] *Legio II Augusta* was certainly responsible for two blocks on the stone wall, a total of 18 kilometres, and there is some evidence to suggest that it also built two blocks on the turf wall, 16 kilometres in length. Within its sector each legion erected milecastles and turrets to its own distinctive plan, recording the construction of each milecastle by the erection of an inscription over each of its two gates. By chance, four of the inscriptions of *II Augusta* survive from three milecastles.[17] It is possible that each legion also placed inscriptions at the turrets which it erected, but none survive recording the work of *II Augusta*, and its turrets can only be identified by their relationship with adjacent milecastles. Each legion marked the end of its block of curtain wall by an inscription. The division of work within each block was similarly recorded by cohort stones and centurial stones. These inscriptions allow us to demonstrate the presence of seven cohorts of the legion, either in whole or part, building on Hadrian's Wall: cohorts I, II, III, VI, VII, VIII and X. The centurial stones furnish the names of as many as forty centurions of the legion participating in this building programme.[18]

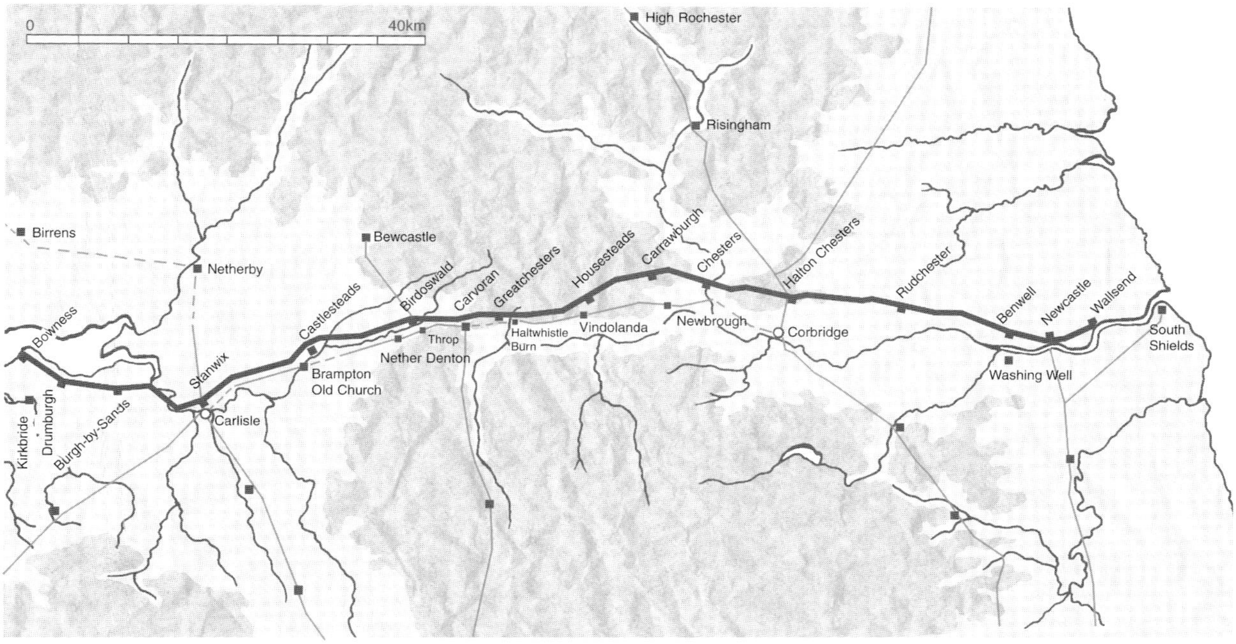

4.1 *Map of Hadrian's Wall, showing also some of the sites previously occupied on the Stanegate*

4.2 *Milecastle 42 (Cawfields), built by* legio II Augusta *(Photograph: David J Breeze)*

Legio II Augusta is also recorded building at Netherby, one of the outpost forts to Hadrian's Wall, and probably also at Birrens.[19] There is some evidence to suggest that these two forts, together with the third outpost fort, Bewcastle, were part of the original plan for the Wall.[20] It is possible that the legion also built some of the forts which were placed on Hadrian's Wall itself as part of the revised plan for the frontier: in the original plan the forts were not on the Wall, but behind it on the Stanegate. This is suggested by the similarity between the Second Legion milecastle gateways on the Wall and the fort gateways at Housesteads and Great Chesters.[21]

Modifications to Hadrian's Wall seem to have continued throughout much of Hadrian's reign and *II Augusta* may have played a part in at least one of

4.3 RIB *I, 1638 records the building of milecastle 38 (Hotbank) by soldiers of* legio II Augusta *under the governor A. Platorius Nepos in the reign of the Emperor Caesar Traianus Hadrianus Augustus (Photograph: reproduced by permission of the Museum of Antiquities, Newcastle upon Tyne)*

these, namely the rebuilding of the turf sector of the Wall in stone. This appears to have started before Hadrian's death in 138, only to be completed much later in the century. The most easterly 8 kilometres of the turf wall is all that was rebuilt before the demise of the architect of the Wall. An inscription of *II Augusta* was found in milecastle 50 on the rebuilt sector and, as this milecastle was in a different location from its turf and timber predecessor – which in any case has yielded a timber inscription – the Second Legion stone must refer to the building or a rebuilding of the stone milecastle.[22] Alas, it is not clear whether it commemorates the original building of the milecastle or a subsequent repair, for an inscription of *legio VI Victrix* has also been found at the site.[23]

The building of Hadrian's Wall and the subsequent changes to the simple original plan, through the addition of forts to the Wall and the start of the rebuilding of the turf wall in stone, resulted in soldiers of *II Augusta* staying on the northern frontier for many years from 122. The death of Hadrian brought no end to their labours, for his successor, Antoninus Pius, overthrew the policy of his predecessor and decided on a move forward in Britain.[24] Hadrian's Wall was abandoned and the army re-conquered southern Scotland as far north as the Tay. As part of the preparations for this move north we have already seen that the Second Legion was involved in rebuilding the fort at Corbridge in 139 and 140.[25] The legion also helped build the Antonine Wall, the new frontier constructed across the narrow waist of Scotland from the Firth of Forth to the River Clyde.

Unlike Hadrian's Wall, the Antonine Wall was built entirely of turf, though placed on a stone base. The construction of the Wall was divided between the three legions of the province, *II Augusta, VI Victrix* and *XX Valeria Victrix*, but, so far as we know, not in such a neat way as Hadrian's Wall. Nevertheless, as before, each legion marked both ends of its block by inscriptions, seemingly one being placed on the south side of the rampart and another on the north.[26] Within each legionary block we know of no cohort or centurial stones, though some junctions between

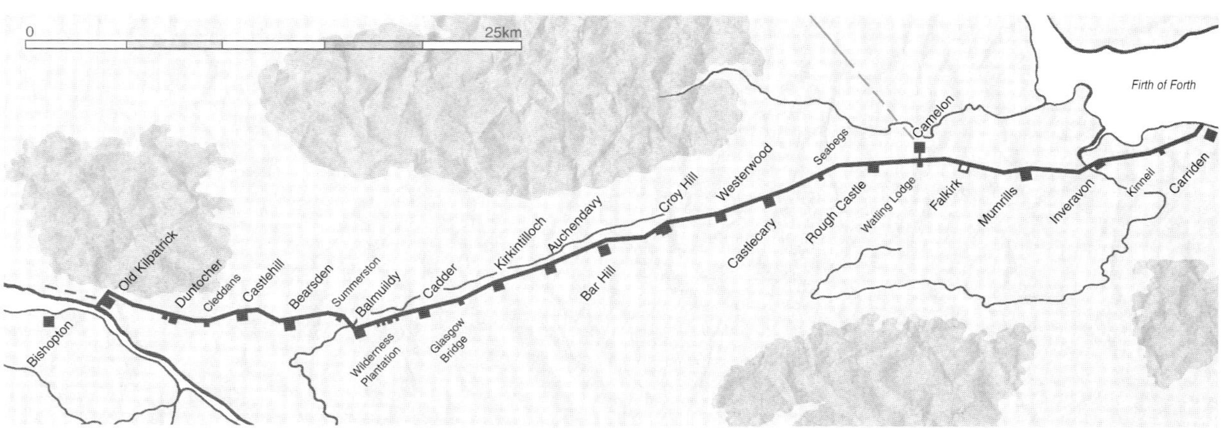

4.4 *Map of the Antonine Wall*

different gangs building the base have been recognized.[27] It may have been in order to compensate for the materials of construction, and possibly for the fewer number of epigraphic building records, when compared with Hadrian's Wall, that the legions on the Antonine Wall erected such magnificent inscriptions signalling their work. The scale of the inscriptions may also reflect that they were commemorating an extension of the Empire, the Hadrian's Wall stones marking only the continuation of the *status quo*.[28] These inscriptions are known as distance slabs because they record the length of work of each legion.[29] Twenty distance slabs survive and five of these were erected by *II Augusta*.[30] They range from the very simple stone probably erected near Cadder to the largest stone of all, the distance slab found in 1868 at Bridgeness and believed to be the eastern terminal stone (Figure 4.5). Two stones bear the symbols of *II Augusta*, the capricorn and pegasus (Figure 4.6), while the capricorn also appears on a third stone, that from Summerston, which in addition bears an eagle. Two stones carry scenes of a Roman cavalryman riding down a group of barbarians; one also bears a depiction of the ritual sacrifice or

4.5 *The Bridgeness distance slab found at Bo'ness near the eastern end of the Antonine Wall in 1868* (RIB *I, 2139). It records that for the Emperor Caesar Titus Aelius Hadrianus Antoninus Augustus Pius* pater patriae *(father of his country).* legio II Augusta *built 4,652 paces. The left-hand panel shows a Roman cavalryman riding down a group of barbarians, while on the right is a depiction of the purification ceremony which took place before the start of a military campaign (photograph: reproduced by permission of the National Museums of Scotland)*

4.6 *This is one of two simpler distance slabs of* legio II Augusta *from the Antonine Wall* (RIB *I, 2204). Found at Carleith, a mile from the western end of the Wall, before 1699, it records the construction of 3,271 feet by the legion. Both the capricorn and the pegasus appear on the stone (photograph: reproduced by permission of the Hunterian Museum, University of Glasgow)*

suovetaurilia undertaken before the commencement of the campaign (Figure 6.6) and the other a victory preparing to crown the successful cavalryman. It can be said with no exaggeration that these stones, presumably all carved by army craftsmen, are among the most important military sculpture to survive from the Roman Empire.

Amongst other things these distance slabs provide evidence about the builders of the Antonine Wall. They unequivocally demonstrate that while *legio II Augusta* was present in Scotland at full strength, only detachments of *VI Victrix* and *XX Valeria Victrix* worked on the Wall. The building of the linear barrier was divided equally between the three legions, so far as we can tell (surviving stones indicate building both in sectors of paces 4,652, 3,666½, and 3,000 long, and of much shorter lengths which were measured in feet).[31] Thus the implication is that while part of *II Augusta* equivalent in size to the detachments of the other two legions was at work on the barrier, that is the rampart and ditch of the Antonine Wall, the rest of the legion was employed elsewhere on the northern frontier. The original plan for the Antonine Wall probably called for the placing of six forts on the Wall, and one of these, Balmuildy, the only one to have produced a legionary building stone, was built by *II Augusta.*[32] Thus it seems possible that part of the legion was assigned to the construction of forts on the Wall, and perhaps elsewhere in the frontier zone.

A further point can be made about the work of the legions on the linear barrier. The discovery of temporary camps along the Wall line provides some insight into both the organization of the detachments building the Wall and their numbers.[33] There are two camps at each end of the eastern stretch of the Wall running from Bridgeness to the River Avon built by *II Augusta.* Thus, presumably this stretch of the Wall was built inwards from each end, with the work being further subdivided, one group possibly being responsible for the rampart and the other for the ditch.[34] The size of the camps varies between 1.6 to 3.2 hectares. It is not known whether materials were stored in these camps, and if so how much space was available for the men, but it seems not unreasonable to suggest that a 2 hectare camp might have been occupied by no more than a legionary cohort and therefore these four camps held between four and six cohorts in total. Thus perhaps only about half the legion was active building the rampart and ditch of the Antonine Wall, the rest being occupied by the construction of forts.

Since the whole of *legio II Augusta* moved north to build the Antonine Wall, it follows that building inscriptions from the Wall which refer to detachments of the legion must record later work. These include the stones from Auchendavy, Bar Hill and Cadder.[35] The date of such repairs within the short life of the Antonine Wall from about 142 to about 160 cannot be determined.

On the abandonment of the Antonine Wall, perhaps about 160, Hadrian's Wall once more became the northern frontier of the province of Britain. The Wall was repaired and it appears that it was now that the rebuilding of the turf wall in stone was completed. A number of inscriptions of *legio II Augusta* presumably refer to their involvement in this work.[36] The ornate stones from Benwell and Halton Chesters may also date to this time.[37] These have been dated on stylistic grounds to the Antonine period, but the style continues into the early third century.[38] While conforming generally to the 'Antonine' style the stones are very unusual, three bearing the capricorn and pegasus, and because of this it is not even possible to be certain that they fall within the above date brackets.

Legio II Augusta was involved in one final, important building operation in the north, the construction of the legionary base on the River Tay at Carpow in the early third century (Figure 4.7). There can be little doubt that this fort was designed to be the linchpin of Severus' plan for the occupation of southern Scotland. The fort (Figure 4.8) apparently had a short life, and was presumably one of those sites which, as Cassius Dio records, Caracalla abandoned after the death of his father in 211.[39] Stamped tiles record *VI Victrix* building here, while from the east gate was recovered part of an inscription of *II Augusta.* It is recognizably the work of the Second Legion by the presence of its emblems, the capricorn and the pegasus, on the stone (Figure 4.9).[40] It is uncertain, however, whether the intention was for these two legions to provide not only the builders but also the soldiers to man the fort.

Legio II Augusta left its emblems on many stones throughout the north, on Hadrian's Wall, the

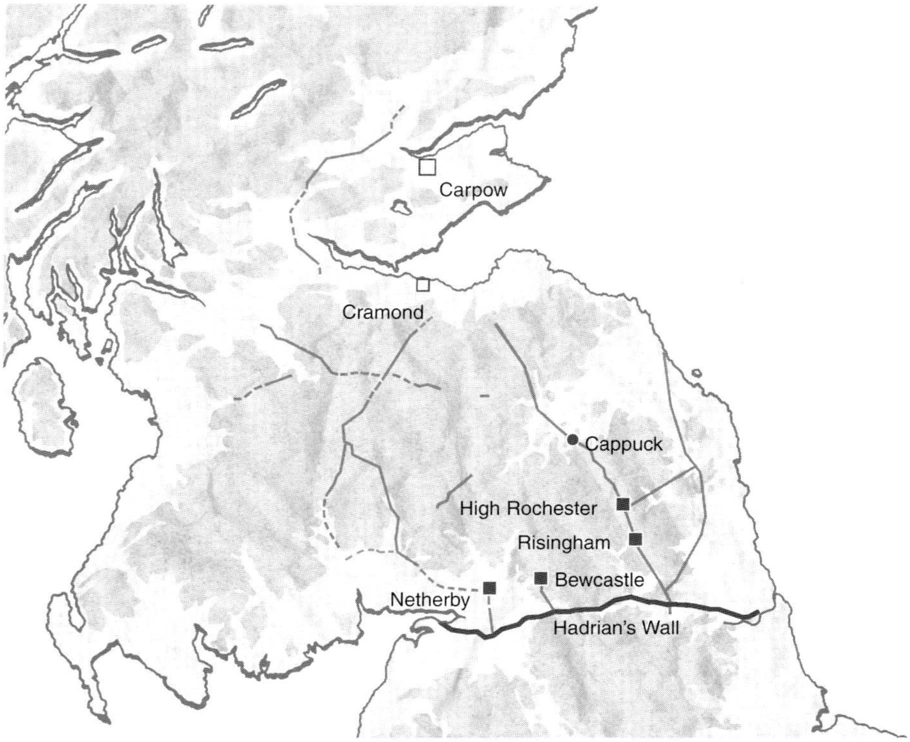

4.7 *Map of north Britain showing forts which may have been held at the end of the reign of Septimius Severus in 211*

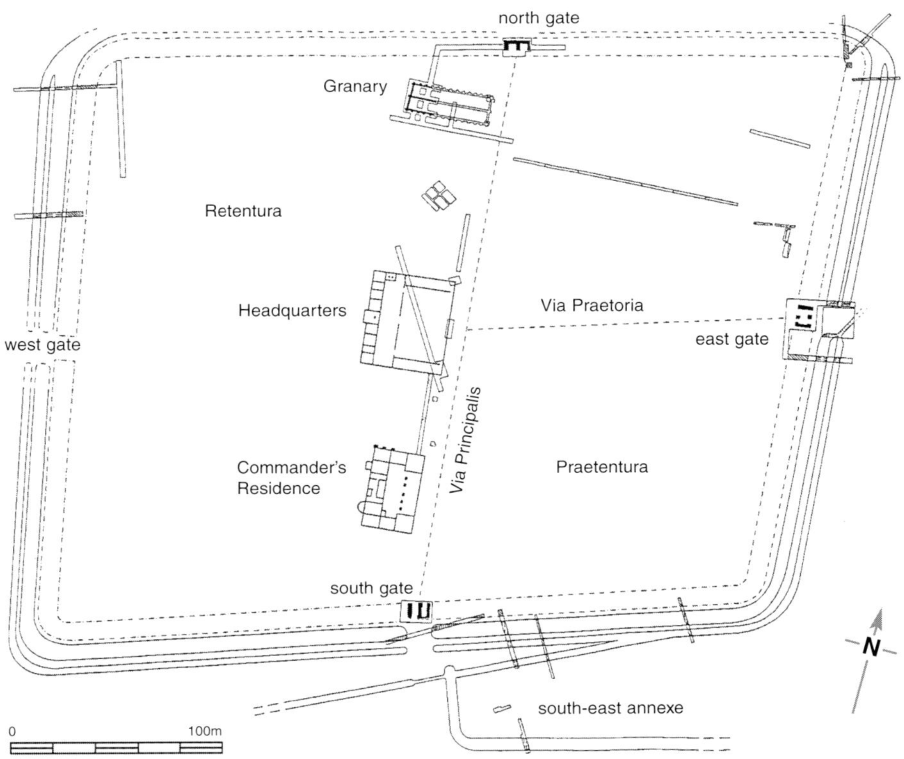

4.8 *Plan of Carpow legionary base (reproduced by permission of Professor J J Wilkes)*

4.9 *A fragment of a monumental building inscription found on the roadway in front of the east gate of the legionary base at Carpow in 1964. In the upper part of the pelta stands a Victory. The two symbols of* legio II Augusta, *the capricorn and the pegasus, also appear (photograph: reproduced by permission of Dundee Museum and Art Galleries)*

4.10 *A capricorn and a pegasus on a stone found at Castlesteads on Hadrian's Wall* (RIB *I, 2397*=CSIR *I.6,* Hadrian's Wall West, *no. 398) (photograph: reproduced by permission of Tullie House Museum, Carlisle)*

Antonine Wall and at Carpow. They survive also on a stone from Castledykes between the Walls, where the capricorn was incised on a building stone, and at Castlesteads on the southern Wall (Figure 4.10). A pegasus appears on a stone in a souterrain at Crichton, 24 kilometres south of Edinburgh, but how it got there no one knows (Figure 4.11).[41]

Finally, we should not leave building activity without a look at some evidence for the Second Legion at the quarry face. Inscriptions at a number of quarries in Cumberland record the work of its legionaries. These quarries lie at Chalk, 11 kilometres south-west of Carlisle; Cardewlees 7 kilometres south-west of Carlisle; Crowdundle near Kirkby Thore; and by the river Gelt near Brampton.[42] These inscriptions are difficult to date, but one is on the same rock-face as a second inscription dated to 207. The soldiers cutting the stones appear to have left us rare depictions of their comrades (Figure 4.12).

LIVING

While soldiers of *legio II Augusta* were heavily engaged in building operations on Hadrian's Wall and then the Antonine Wall, perhaps more or less continuously for about 25 years from 122, there is no evidence for most of that period that detachments from the legion were intended to stay permanently in the north; once their building work was completed, they would have returned to Caerleon. In the latter part of this period, however, during the reign of Antoninus Pius, this changes. There is an altar from Benwell on Hadrian's Wall, datable to the reign of this emperor.[43] This was dedicated to Jupiter Dolichenus, the deities of the emperors and *legio II Augusta* by

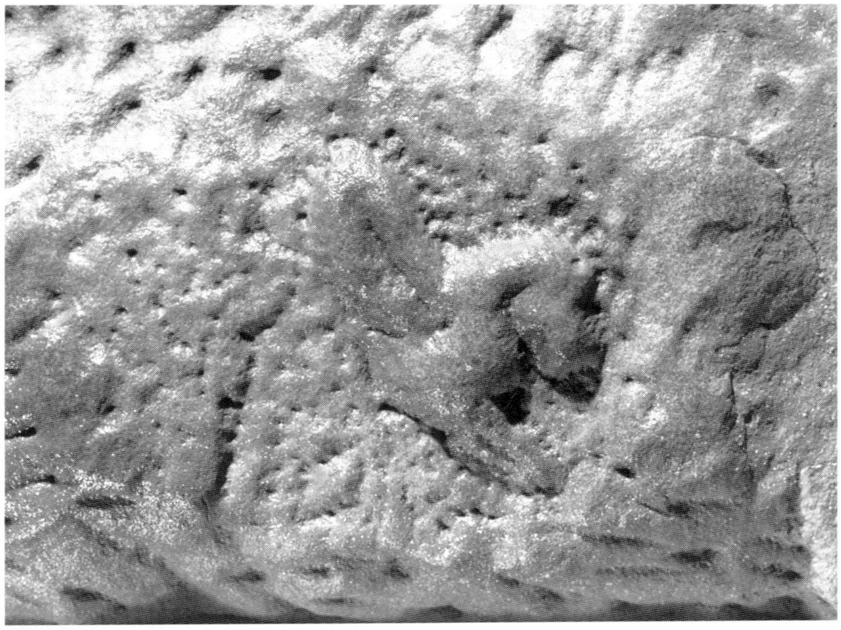

4.11 *A pegasus on one of the Roman stones used in the souterrain at Crichton, 24 km south of Edinburgh (photograph: reproduced by permission of the Royal Commission on the Ancient and Historical Monuments of Scotland)*

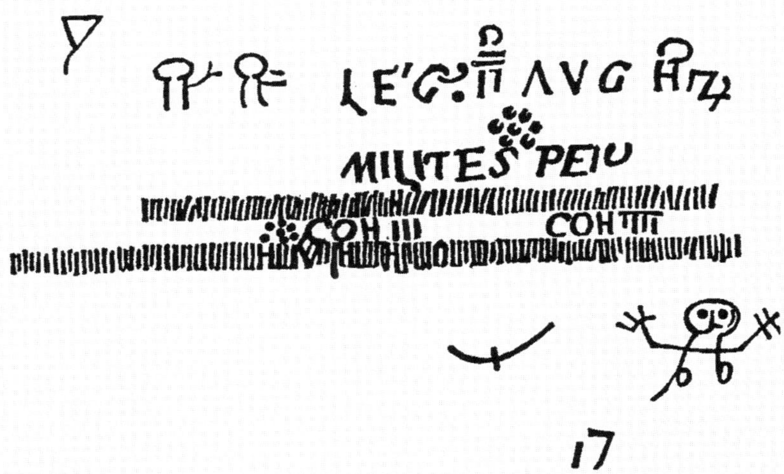

4.12 *Quarry inscriptions at Crowdundle, Cumbria* (RIB *I, 1001)*

Liburnius Fronto, a centurion of the legion. It may indicate a legionary presence at Benwell some time during the reign of Antoninus Pius, 138–61. This assumption is often supported by citing building stones of the legion which are of the style in fashion during the reign of Antoninus Pius, as discussed above. It is possible to turn the situation round, however, and suggest that if the legionaries were building in the Antonine period for an auxiliary unit, they may have made the dedication at the time, when they were in temporary residence.

If the nature of *II Augusta*'s activity on Hadrian's Wall in the reign of Antoninus Pius is problematic, we are perhaps on surer ground on the Antonine Wall.

While each fort on Hadrian's Wall, with perhaps one exception, appears to have been built for a single auxiliary unit, the position on the Antonine Wall was more complex. Each of the first series of forts constructed was of a size to hold a single auxiliary unit, but the forts added part-way through the building programme were generally smaller and many were insufficiently large to hold a complete auxiliary unit. Such a fort was Rough Castle where *cohors VI Nerviorum* is attested. This fort covered 0.75 hectares and was clearly incapable of holding even the six centuries of this 500–strong cohort. The splitting of auxiliary units between forts along the Wall may have been accompanied by the introduction of legionaries to certain forts, though scholarly opinion has long been divided on this question.

An inscription to the goddess Fortuna in the bathhouse at Castlecary by detachments of *II Augusta* and *VI Victrix* offers the probability that these soldiers were based here at some time during the life of this fort.[44] A second inscription at Castlecary may refer to the same detachment(s) while a further two were dedications by soldiers of *legio VI Victrix*.[45] One records the erection of a shrine and statuette to Mercury and has been dated to the period 175–90, some time after the date of abandonment of the Antonine Wall as suggested by the ceramic evidence.[46] Castlecary, on the watershed between the Forth and Clyde river systems, has produced the latest dating evidence of any fort in central Scotland at the end of both the late first century and the late second century periods of occupation.[47] Further, the units based here are significant. It is the only fort on the Antonine Wall which has furnished evidence of the presence of two thousand-strong infantry cohorts, though both would not have been in residence at the same time.[48] In fact there is an embarrassment of different units and detachments attested at this site. It may be that small detachments of legionaries were posted here while the auxiliary units were in residence. It is perhaps more likely, especially if the late date of the dedication to Mercury is accepted, that the legionaries were here at a different time, presumably when the rest of the Antonine Wall was abandoned, and Castlecary served as a kind of northern outpost. The fact that the dedication to Fortuna by the soldiers of *II Augusta* and *VI Victrix* was left in the bathhouse when the fort was abandoned, may suggest that these detachments were the last group of soldiers to reside at the fort. Some would argue that this evidence would support occupation of the Antonine Wall continuing later into the second century than the generally preferred date of about 160.

The most interesting collection of legionary inscriptions was found at Auchendavy. Four inscriptions of *legio II Augusta* were recovered from a pit to the south-west of the fort in 1771 during the construction of the Forth-Clyde canal. The inscriptions are dedications by the centurion Marcus Cocceius Firmus to a total of eleven deities (Figure 4.13).[49] There is also a dedication by a soldier of the legion and the tombstone of another soldier, Flavius Lucianus.[50]

Marcus Cocceius Firmus has been the subject of an in-depth examination by Professor Eric Birley.[51] He drew attention to the range of deities dedicated to by Firmus: Jupiter, Victorious Victory, Diana and Apollo, the genius of the land of Britain, Mars, Minerva, the Campestres, Hercules, Epona and Victory. Birley was able to demonstrate that these dedications revealed that Firmus had seen previous service in the *equites singulares Augusti*, the emperor's mounted bodyguard in Rome. Most probably Firmus had served in the guard as a decurion and had been promoted thence to a centurion in *II Augusta*. Further, the dedications to Diana and Apollo suggest that Firmus came originally from the lower Danube. An altar of 169 at Histria on the Black Sea was erected under the care of local officers, one of whom was a Cocceius Firmus, and Birley suggested that this was possibly the same man, returned to his homeland on retirement. Birley also suggested an identification with the centurion Cocceius Firmus who was the subject of a legal ruling concerning the refunding of money by the Imperial Treasury. The case cited in Justinian's *Digest of Roman Law* dates to the period Hadrian to Marcus Aurelius, roughly 120 to 180, and describes how a woman condemned for a crime to hard labour in the salt-works, was subsequently captured by bandits from beyond the Empire; in the course of lawful trade she was sold, and by repurchase returned to her original condition; the purchase-price had to be refunded from the Imperial Treasury to the centurion Cocceius Firmus. Birley pointed out that the name, rank and date were compatible and that there was a high degree of

4.13 RIB *I, 2176, found at Auchendavy in 1771, is a dedication to Jupiter Best and Greatest and Victorious Victory for the welfare of the Emperor and the welfare of himself and his family by M. Cocceius Firmus, centurion of the Second Augustan Legion (photograph: reproduced by permission of the Hunterian Museum, University of Glasgow)*

probability that the centurion at Auchendavy was the same as the centurion of the *Digest.* The salt-works may have lain in Fife, where modern salt-works are known, an area adjacent to the frontier. Birley's stimulating and detailed study thus offers the possibility of the identification of three references to a Cocceius Firmus relating to the same man: a recruit from the lower Danube, who served in the emperor's bodyguard in Rome and then in *legio II Augusta* on the Antonine Wall, finally retiring back to the Black Sea coast.

It remains to be considered whether these inscriptions suggest that legionaries were stationed on the Antonine Wall some time during its life, or whether they were erected by soldiers present at these sites only during brief building operations. It is, as a result of the nature of the evidence, impossible to be certain, yet to balance the single building stone of the Second Legion at Auchendavy there are four altars, a possible fifth,[52] and a tombstone. These suggest a longer stay than would be necessary to build the fort and would receive support from Birley's identification of Marcus Cocceius Firmus with the centurion in the *Digest,* if correct.

In summary, it is impossible to be certain about the significance of the legionary stones from the Antonine Wall, and indeed it is possible that they do not all indicate the same situation at each site. So far as *legio II Augusta* is concerned there must be a strong presumption that a detachment of the unit was outposted to Auchendavy on the Antonine Wall and also a possibility that further soldiers were stationed at Castlecary for a time.

Two inscriptions on Hadrian's Wall, one from Housesteads mentioning soldiers in garrison, and the other a dedication to Mars Cocidius at milescastle 52, point to other groups of soldiers from the legion being outposted to the north some time in either the second or third century.[53]

The final area of activity which I would like to examine concerns the role of *II Augusta* in the northern province of Lower Britain in the third century. Under the Emperor Septimius Severus the island province was divided into two, though it may not have achieved its final form until the sole reign of his son, Caracalla.[54] The army was unequally divided between the two provinces. Upper Britain, the southern part of the island, contained legions *II* and *XX* together with a handful of auxiliary units, while Lower Britain has the remaining legion, *VI,* and fifty or more auxiliary units. The regimental commanding officers were responsible to the provincial governor. Each unit would normally serve within its own province and could only move outside the province with specific permission from Rome; indeed the governor lost his authority on stepping outside his province. This is not to say that no units and no governors strayed over their provincial boundaries. Of particular significance are the regular arrangements made in certain provinces for the governor's staff to be provided by the legions in neighbouring provinces. The best recorded example is Dalmatia, largely modern Croatia. Seven legions from four provinces at different times furnished legionaries for this governor's staff.

It seems that some such arrangement must have been made in Britain, for there are several examples of soldiers of both legions *II* and *XX*, based in Upper Britain, operating in Lower Britain. These include centurions of *II Augusta* acting as temporary commanders of auxiliary units, presumably when the prefect or tribune was incapacitated. Julius Honoratus is thus attested at Wallsend and Julius Marcellinus at Birdoswald.[55] Neither inscription is dated, but both inscriptions ought to date to after about 180, and the likelihood is that both are third century. Certainly of that date, in fact 255–9, is an inscription from Cardewlees near Carlisle which, although fragmentary, is probably another dedication by a centurion of *II Augusta* dedicating in his capacity as a temporary auxiliary commander.[56] A centurion of *legio II Augusta* in a temporary position of command appears on an inscription found 20 years ago at Piercebridge.[57] This is a dedication to Jupiter Best and Greatest Dolichenus by a detachment of *VI Victrix* and soldiers from the army of the two Germanies under the temporary command of Marcus Lollius Venator, centurion of *II Augusta*. The inscription has been dated to the reign of Caracalla (211–17) by Eric Birley.[58] Vindolanda (Chesterholm) has produced an inscription of a *beneficiarius,* a staff officer, of the governor of Upper Britain, but drawn from the ranks of *II Augusta*.[59]

The connection between *legio II Augusta* and Corbridge is well known, primarily perhaps through the discovery of the altar dedicated to the Discipline of the Emperors within the strong-room of the headquarters building of the west compound (Figures 4.14 and 4.15).[60] This is not the only connection. We have already noted that the legion was building here in 139 and 140, and a further four building stones of the legion survive as does a second altar, a tombstone, and an item of sculpture.[61] The role of the compounds was thoroughly examined by the late Sir Ian Richmond in a justifiably well-known paper, 'Roman legionaries at Corbridge, their supply-

4.14 *The strong-room in the headquarters building in the Second Legion's compound at Corbridge. The altar to the Discipline of the Emperors was found on the steps of the strong-room (photograph: David J Breeze)*

4.15 *Altar dedicated to the Discipline of the Emperors by* legio II Augusta. *Found on the steps of the underground strong-room of the headquarters building at Corbridge (photograph: reproduced by permission of English Heritage)*

base, temples and religious cults', published in 1943. This paper was the culmination of six year's work on this part of the Roman site at Corbridge, mostly published in conjunction with Eric Birley.[62]

Richmond and Birley defined the two compounds, described the headquarters building, drawing attention to the unusual features which could be explained by its use by a legion rather than by an auxiliary unit, and examined the sculpture found there. This included the altar to Discipline, a sculptural panel showing Hercules attacking the Hydra, and a statue of Jupiter (Figure 4.16).[63] In his summary of the results of the work on the compounds Richmond suggested that each compound was designed for legionaries, the west for *II Augusta*, the east for an unknown unit, each with a different set of buildings as so far examined. It so happens that the east compound has yielded mainly living accommodation, while the west was mainly composed of workshops, of which nine are known. The four workshops excavated in 1938 and 1939 produced evidence for iron-working, and the objects found there included heads for arrows or darts and nails. The wider significance of this is not clear. There are too many workshops for the legionary detachment to have been merely servicing its own soldiers. Thus it is usually assumed that *II Augusta*'s compound at Corbridge acted as a military supply depot for Hadrian's Wall; and we know that the army had factories producing weapons and armour elsewhere in the Empire. Unfortunately as the objects made at Corbridge were not stamped, and therefore cannot be traced elsewhere, it is not possible to assess the wider role of the legion's work in the frontier area.

Richmond and Birley were in no doubt about the date of the compounds. They carefully examined the available evidence and suggested that they were constructed in the early third century, probably in the aftermath of the Severan campaigns into Scotland.[64] They were led to this conclusion in part by the archaeological evidence, but also by the epigraphic material. There is an inscription recording the building of the granary by an unknown legion during the first decade of the third century.[65] This was presumably in connection with Severus' campaigns against the Caledones and Maeatae. These campaigns are presumably the reason for the presence in the area of L. Julius Julianus, the legate of the legion, as we have seen. The Second Augustan Legion's dedication in its headquarters building at Corbridge is to the Discipline of two, or more, emperors and the most likely emperors are the Severi, there being two emperors from 198–209 and three from 209–11.[66] While the building inscription and the presence of the legionary legate may relate primarily to the Severan campaigns in Scotland, archaeological evidence suggests that the granaries and compounds are contemporary and form part of the same plan for the centre of the Roman town. Thus we seem to have here a relic of Severus' plans for the north continuing after the wholesale abandonment of those plans by Caracalla.

4.16 *a Fragmentary statue of Jupiter; b part of a sculptural panel showing Hercules, holding a club, attacking the Hydra; both found in the Second Legion's headquarters building at Corbridge (photographs: reproduced by permission of English Heritage)*

Another aspect of *legio II Augusta* in the north was metalworking. Among the lead seals found at Brough-under-Stainmore are thirteen of the legion. Richmond convincingly argues that Brough was a central collecting and sorting depot for metals, most probably lead and silver.[67] Here consignments were repacked, resulting in the dumping of the original seals. Eight auxiliary units are recorded on these seals and two legions, *VI* and *II*. Only one seal survives of *legio VI*, but the thirteen of *II Augusta* are the third most numerous collection, after the forty-six of *cohors VII Thracum* and seventeen of *cohors II Nerviorum*. The latter unit was stationed close to Brough at Whitley Castle, a fort situated beside the later lead mines at Alston. Richmond considered that most of the units recorded on these seals were based in north-west England in the third century. But one unit was not, *cohors I Batavorum*; this was at Carrawburgh. If one unit from the South Tyne Valley was represented, it is equally possible that the *II Augusta* seals refer to that detachment of the legion based at Corbridge only 15 kilometres from Carrawburgh. There is thus another industrial connection here and a hint at the range of activity of the legion. It is not impossible, though, that the seals emanated from Housesteads where soldiers of the legion were possibly in garrison some time in the third century, as we have seen.

Finally, there are a number of building inscriptions erected by detachments of the Second and Twentieth Legions in the third century in north Britain. These have been found at Netherby, where it is dated to about 219, and also possibly Bewcastle, the stone here having been re-read by Eric Birley to refer to the Emperor Trajan Decius, 249–51, and not the Emperor Trajan Hadrian.[68] Jarrett has noted the difficulty in dating such stones, for one building inscription erected by detachments of the Second and Twentieth Legions at Bar Hill on the Antonine Wall surely dates to the second century, before the division of Britain, though without knowledge of the findspot one would have been tempted to offer a third century date.[69] This is simply because it is in the third century that detachments of the Second and Twentieth, the legions of Upper Britain, are likely to have been operating together in Lower Britain. Before that date other combinations are recorded, for example *II* and *VI* or *VI* and *XX*,[70] but the division of the island into two provinces created a situation when detachments of either of the legions of Upper Britain, *II* and *XX*, were most unlikely to operate with the legion of Lower Britain, *VI*. Thus the combination of *II* and *XX* is more likely to date to the third century, though the possibility of an earlier date cannot be ruled out. Eric Birley has seen the combination of detachments, presumably each about 1,000 men strong, from the two legions of a province like Upper Britain as a step towards the creation of new mobile field armies,[71] in an attempt to break out of the straight-jacket produced by static frontiers and a static army.

Evidence of a different, and perhaps more definite nature for *II Augusta* building on the northern frontier in the third century comes from the quarry known as the Written Rock of Gelt in Cumbria. Here worked a detachment of the Second Legion under the *optio* Agricola, leaving their record on the same rock face as a second inscription dated to 207. At Crowdundle near Kirkby Thore in Cumbria, *II Augusta* was associated with *XX Valeria Victrix* on the rock face.[72]

Thus *legio II Augusta* in the third century provided individual officers, groups of soldiers on detached duty and soldiers for building operations to the neighbouring province of Lower Britain.

DYING

It is not surprising that all this activity by *legio II Augusta* in northern Britain should have resulted in several soldiers leaving their bones in the north. At Ilkley there is the tombstone of Pudens, a *tesserarius*, the junior officer who carried the password.[73] An unknown soldier was buried at Corbridge.[74] The most northerly known tombstone is that of Flavius Lucianus at Auchendavy on the Antonine Wall.[75]

CONCLUSIONS

Each legion carried its own engineering corps and legionaries are most frequently attested in north Britain building, in particular on both Hadrian's Wall and the Antonine Wall. As a result of these two projects many soldiers must have been absent from Caerleon for years. In addition smaller groups of soldiers stayed even longer, on outpost duty at various sites, including Corbridge, Housesteads on Hadrian's Wall, and probably Auchendavy and Castlecary on the Antonine Wall. Individual soldiers operated in northern Britain in a variety of capacities, as centurions temporarily commanding auxiliary units or as staff officers. Possibly even a field army was created in the third century drawn in part on *legio II Augusta*.

Once south Wales had been subdued, the continuing presence of the Second Augustan Legion at Caerleon was an anachronism. The forces of inertia led to the legion remaining in south Wales, but the main theatre of military activity lay further north. It was simply this continuing military activity on the northern frontier that drew soldiers of *II Augusta* away so often from their base at Caerleon.

ACKNOWLEDGEMENTS

I am pleased to acknowledge the help I have received from many friends and colleagues in the preparation of the lecture and this paper, Dr Brian Dobson, Professor Lawrence Keppie and the late Professor John Mann kindly read and commented upon the text. Mr P S Austen; The British Museum; Tullie House Museum, Carlisle; Dundee Museum; English Heritage; the Hunterian Museum, University of Glasgow; Newcastle Museum of Antiquities; the National Museums of Scotland; Professor John Wilkes, all generously provided slides and/or photographs for the lecture and the publication.

Notes

1 Jarrett 1964a.
2 Manning this volume.
3 Tacitus, *Agricola* 26.
4 Tacitus, *Agricola* 29.35–70.
5 Tacitus, *Agricola* 16.
6 Mann 1985, 23–4; Breeze 1986–7, 7–22.
7 Dobson 1978, 216–17; *pace* Kennedy 1985.
8 *ILS* 9200.
9 Breeze and Dobson 2000, 14, 88–90, 117–42.
10 *RIB* I, 1147, 1148 (Corbridge); 2191 (Balmuildy).
11 Herodian 3.14.3; Cassius Dio 76.12. 2.
12 St Joseph 1969, 114–17; 1973, 230–1.
13 R E Birley 1962–3, 196–9; Leach and Wilkes 1977, 47–59; Wright 1963–4.
14 *RIB* I, 1138; A R Birley 1981, 265–6; *CIL* XI, 4182.
15 Breeze and Dobson 2000; Hanson and Maxwell 1986.
16 Breeze and Dobson 2000, 25–87.
17 *RIB* I, 1964 (MC 37); 1637, 1638 (MC 38); 1666 (MC 42).
18 Stevens 1966, 101.
19 *RIB* I, 974 (Netherby); 996 with E Birley 1959–60, 142–4.
20 Breeze and Dobson 2000, 46.
21 Breeze and Dobson 1969, 32, citing a suggestion by E Birley.
22 *RIB* I, 1932 (MC 50 SW); 1935 (MC 50 TW).
23 *RIB* I, 1934; Professor J C Mann has pointed out to me the restoration of *[SIL* as *vex]sil(latio)* on *RIB* I, 1933 will not do.
24 *SHA, Antoninus Pius* 5. 4.
25 *RIB* I, 1147, 1148.
26 Steer and Cormack 1968–9, 125.
27 Keppie and Breeze 1981, 245.
28 I owe this suggestion to Prof L J F Keppie.
29 See Keppie 1979; 1998.
30 *RIB* I, 2139, 2186, 2193, 2203, 2204.
31 Keppie 1979, 6.
32 *RIB* I, 2191.
33 Hanson and Maxwell 1986, 117–36; Breeze and Dobson 2000, 98–9.
34 Hanson and Maxwell 1986, 117–18; 129–31.
35 *RIB* I, 2180, 2171, 2187.
36 *RIB* I, 2011, 2012, 2054. A building stone recording work by *legio II Augusta* and *legio XX* at Maryport (*RIB* I 852) may date to this time, although Jarrett prefers a date in the early third century (Jarrett 1964a, 58).
37 *RIB* I, 1341–1344 (Benwell); *RIB* I 1428 (Halton Chesters).
38 Swinbank 1953, 391 (Antonine); Thompson 1968 (early third century).
39 Cassius Dio 77.1.1.
40 See n 13.
41 *CSIR* I.4, *Scotland*, nos 41 and 58; *CSIR* I.6, *Hadrian's Wall West*, no. 398.
42 *RIB* I, 998, 999, 1001, 1008; see Davies 1968.
43 *RIB* I, 1330.
44 *RIB* I, 2146.
45 *RIB* I, 2147, 2148, 2151.
46 Mann 1963.
47 Hartley 1972, 14 and 28–9.
48 *RIB* I, 2149, 2155.
49 *RIB* I, 2174–2177; Keppie 1998, nos 33–6.
50 *RIB* I, 2179, 2181; Keppie and Walker 1985, 33–55.
51 E Birley 1936.
52 *RIB* I, 2174–2178; 2179 and Davies 1976.
53 *RIB* I, 1583, 1955.
54 Herodian 3.8.2; Mann and Jarrett 1967.
55 *RIB* I, 1299, 1880.
56 *RIB* I, 913.
57 Wright 1967, 205, no. 16.
58 E Birley 1967, 103–7.
59 *RIB* I, 1696; note also *RIB* I, 745 from Greta Bridge, which records a soldier from Upper Britain and thus possibly from *legio II Augusta.*
60 *RIB* I, 1127.
61 *RIB* I, 1154–1158, 1177; *CSIR* I.1, *Hadrian's Wall East*, no. 102.
62 Richmond 1943; Birley and Richmond 1938; Richmond and Birley 1940.
63 *CSIR* I.1, *Hadrian's Wall East*, nos 6 and 9.
64 Birley and Richmond 1938, 262–4; Richmond and Birley 1940, 115.
65 *RIB* I, 1151.
66 *RIB* I, 1127. See n 14. For the hint that the legion was preparing to leave Isca about 200, see Zienkiewicz 1986a, 47–9.
67 Richmond 1936.
68 *RIB* I, 980, 995 with E Birley, *in litt* to Jarrett, cited in Jarrett 1968, 86; *RIB* I, 852 at Maryport may date to this time.
69 Jarrett 1964a, 58; 1968, 5.
70 *RIB* I, 2146, 1148.
71 E Birley, *in litt* to Jarrett cited in Jarrett 1968, 86.
72 *RIB* I, 1008, 1009.
73 *RIB* I, 638.
74 *RIB* I, 1177.
75 *RIB* I, 2181.

Chapter 5

The Second Augustan Legion in the west of Britain

Michael G Fulford

This paper covers the history of the legion and its activities in south Wales and the west of Britain from the late first century onwards. There are two vital matters in which this topic has not received the attention it deserves: the first is very clear, what functions did the legion perform from its base at Caerleon when all the action, almost from the foundation of the fortress onwards, seems to have been in the north? Secondly, what impact did the legion have on provincial society in Britain, given that it continued to discharge a steady stream of veterans throughout its history? In any study of Caerleon, George Boon's *Isca* (1972) remains a pivotal work, but the history of the legion and its fortress is not our concern here; there is no point in unnecessary duplication![1]

The continuing presence of *legio II Augusta* at Caerleon after the conquest of northern Britain remains an enigma. With the organization of the *civitates* of the Silures and the Demetae in the second century, the fortress at Caerleon appears as an island of military activity in the midst of a civilian sea. Numerous inscriptions from the line of Hadrian's Wall and, later, the Antonine Wall as well as from their respective hinterlands attest to the involvement of *II Augusta* in the affairs of the north certainly up to the early third century and the peace of Caracalla. The maintenance of the legion at Caerleon has sometimes been described as an anachronism reflecting inertia on the part of the provincial government to make alternative arrangements. Equally, however, the costs of building a new, permanent fortress in the north have to be acknowledged.[2] Certainly, Caerleon in its surroundings of south-east Wales contrast with that of the legionary fortress at Chester and the north of Wales which saw no comparable civil development to parallel that in the south; there is no equivalent to a Caerwent within a few miles of the fortress, nor a parallel to the villas of the Vale of Glamorgan in the fertile lands of Anglesey or the Cheshire Plain. The situation in south Wales compares with that in the north-east, where the legionary fortress at York was also retained while the *civitates* of the Brigantes and the Parisi flourished around it. Like Caerleon, York was also close to areas which continued to pose difficulties and required the presence of auxiliary garrisons. Just as forts in south Wales remained in occupation (Figure 5.1) – some like Brecon and Castell Collen into the late Roman period – so too did similar sites in the Pennines and the north-east. We should not, therefore, underestimate how the threat of the mountainous hinterland beyond the lowlands of south Wales continued to be perceived. This, rather than inertia, may have been the greater influence which deterred the establishment of a full legionary presence at Carlisle, for example, or Corbridge where there is plentiful evidence to show that detachments from all three legions were stationed during the second and third centuries.[3]

Within Wales we can draw on epigraphic evidence to define the respective commands of *II Augusta* and *XX Valeria Victrix*. There is not much to go on, but the dedication slab from Castell Collen, believed to commemorate work undertaken by *II Augusta* and of probable Antonine date, seems to mark the furthest point north of its influence.[4] Conveniently, brick-stamps of *XX Valeria Victrix* from Caersws in the headwaters of the Severn may attest the southern limits of that legion's command.[5] Tentatively, we may

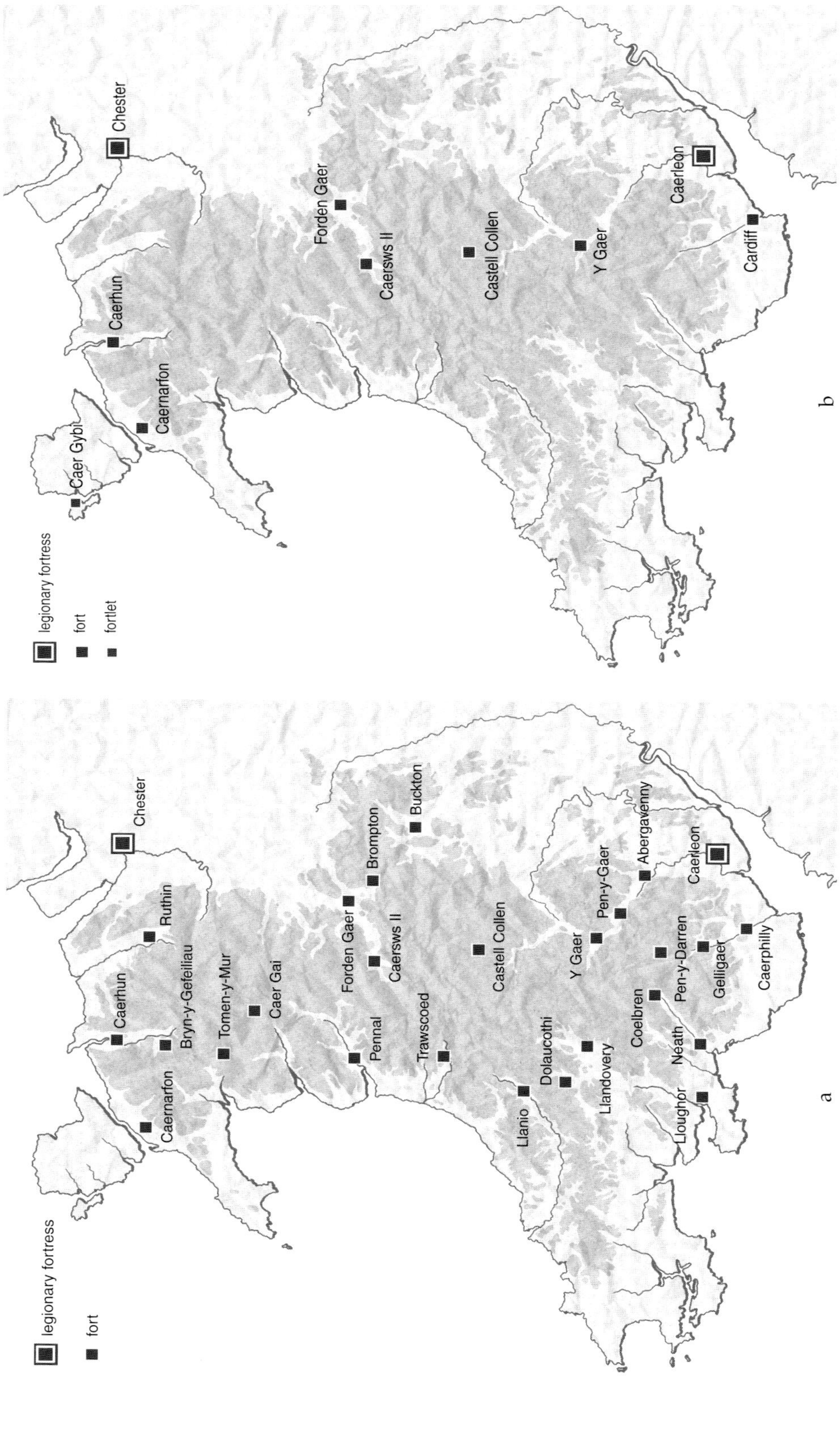

5.1 *a Wales: the garrison in the early second century; b Wales: the garrison in the fourth century*

go further and suggest that the road and associated forts running west up the Severn through Caersws and over to Pennal (where an early third century tile-stamp of the legion has been reported)[6] and the Dovey may at some time, if not through the lifetime of the two legions, have marked the dividing line between their commands in Wales. Closer to home, the distribution of Caerleon-type stamps of *II Augusta* may indicate the auxiliary forts with which the parent legion had the most contact (Figure 5.2).[7]

Locally, there is little evidence to define the extent of the legion's *territorium*. With the creation of the *civitas* of the Silures, the eastern limit must have fallen some way short of Caerwent, while to the west it is likely that the lead mines at Machen and Draethen, if only as islands of territory under military control, would have been incorporated.[8] Whether the settlement about 2 kilometres to the east at Great Bulmore, which has produced several tombstones (Figure 5.3), possibly including one of a serving soldier, lay within the territory is uncertain, but seems likely, if only due to its proximity.[9] The same may be true of Usk to the north, which as the base of *legio XX* in the mid-first century had certainly been legionary *territorium*. There a serving legionary of *II Augusta* had a tombstone erected for his son, but, by then this may simply have been the home of a family which had chosen to settle on its own land relatively near the fortress.[10] To the south, firmer evidence for a boundary is provided by the Goldcliff stone

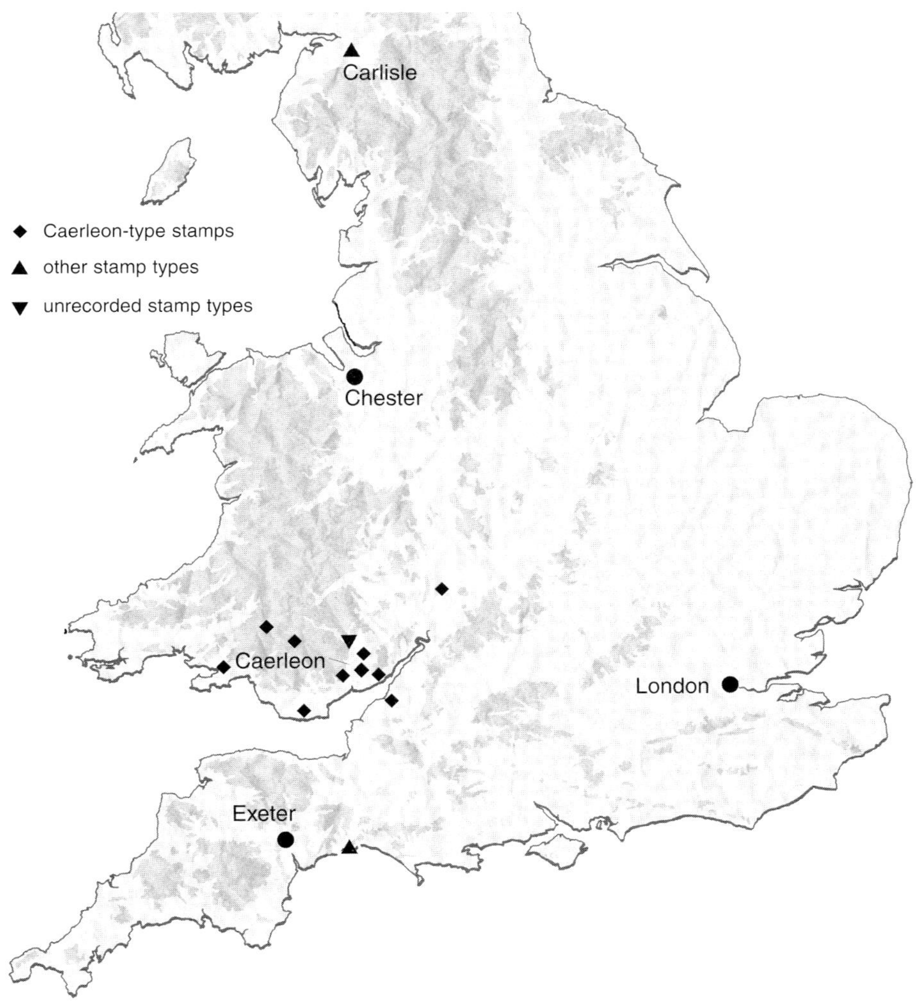

5.2 *Distribution of stamped tiles of* legio II Augusta

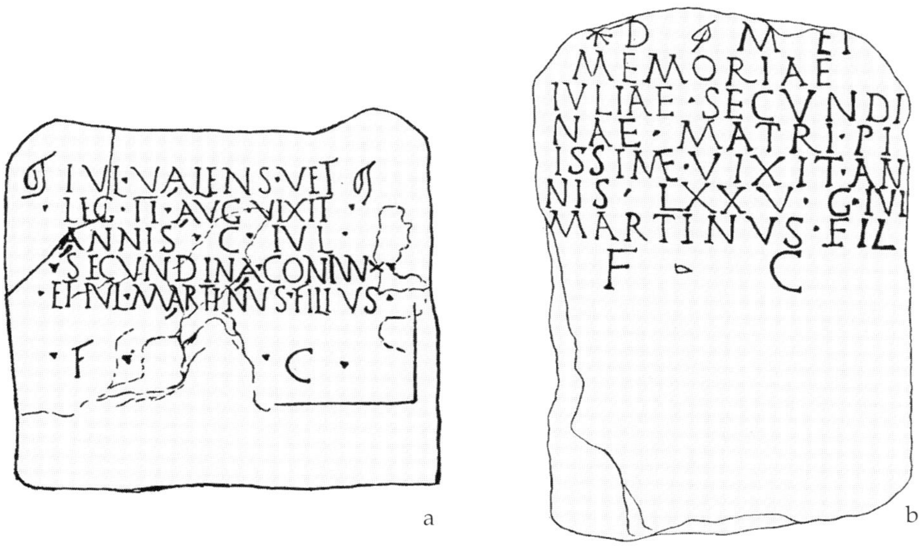

a b

5.3 *Tombstones from Great Bulmore, near Caerleon: a of a veteran, Julius Valens, of* legio II Augusta *(RIB I, 363); b his wife, Julia Secundina (RIB I, 373)*

(Figure 5.4) which records the construction of a length of seabank or drainage dyke, probably in connection with the reclamation of some of the tidal saltmarshes of the Caldicot Level east of the River Usk.[11] Further evidence of reclamation of Roman date and on a scale which implies a legionary involvement comes from the Wentlooge Level between the Usk and Rhymney rivers (Figure 5.5). These two areas of reclaimed wetlands would have provided excellent grazing for horses and cattle, but there is also some evidence for their cultivation.[12]

Although clear boundaries would have defined the legal limits of the legion's territory from the outset, and particularly in the face of competing demands as rural settlement developed from the second century onwards, in other respects the distinction between the legionary and civilian developments is likely to have become blurred. Tombstones from Caerleon and Bulmore reveal that veterans settled in the *canabae* around the fortress and that some of their descendants served in the legion;[13] the Usk tombstone implies that other veterans or serving soldiers put down roots a little further away. Apart from memorials to serving soldiers from

5.4 *Stone recording the construction of 33½ paces of seabank (?) from Goldcliff, near Newport (*RIB *I, 395) (photograph: National Museum of Wales)*

5.5 *A reclaimed saltmarsh: the Wentlooge Level, south Wales. The present-day pattern of field ditches enshrines a Roman layout of which elements have been excavated on the foreshore*

London and the north of Britain, we have to look overseas for evidence of others who served in *II Augusta*; but there are precious few of these. What happened to other veterans of the legion; how many settled in south Wales? Each year the legion discharged two hundred or so veterans; that number might be doubled if we take account of the possible number of auxiliary regiments associated with the legion. Numbers will have fluctuated according to the effects of campaigning, the incidence of disease etc, but too little account has been given to the steady stream of veterans released from the army. Along with his savings, each soldier received land and/or a donative of 3,000 *denarii* on retirement;[14] altogether a substantial sum, part of which could be used to invest in property and land. In general we can be sure that, as local recruitment replaced that from Italy and well established provinces in Gaul and Spain, the proportion of veterans settling in Britain would have increased.[15] Some will have chosen to retire to the *coloniae* as they were established and, in the case of *II Augusta*, the former base at Gloucester was a likely destination from the end of the first century. However, like Orange (founded by Octavian with veterans of the Second Legion), it has produced no memorials of veterans of *II Augusta*.[16] Indeed, Gloucester shows no evidence that it developed disproportionately in comparison with Colchester or Lincoln, its direct contemporary, or with other *civitas* capitals; indeed in comparison with the latter Gloucester seems quite modest.

Some evidence from Caerwent may give a further clue as to the local destination of veterans. The celebrated Paulinus statue base seems to commemorate some act of patronage which was deeply appreciated by the *ordo* of the *civitas* of the Silures (Figure 6.11).[17] Tiberius Claudius Paulinus had served as *legatus* (commander) of *II Augusta*, probably during the reign of Caracalla, *c* 211–14, but the stone was erected just before 220, after he had held the proconsulship of Narbonensis and governorship of Lugdunensis and before he became governor of Lower Britain. What Paulinus did for the Silures is unknown, but the discovery in the town of a lead ingot and tiles stamped by *II Augusta*, may give a clue to the kinds of assistance given.[18] Even if Paulinus carried out this benevolent act after he had left Caerleon, the relationship with the *ordo* is likely to have begun earlier. We can only speculate, but a lobby of individuals, whether veterans themselves or from families of military origin, would have been well placed to act, particularly if Paulinus had to be pursued after he left Caerleon. Evidence of the military, however, whether serving or retired, is limited at Caerwent. The altar dedicated to Mars Ocelus by Aelius Augustinus, *optio* (centurion's second-in-command), is unequivocal (Figure 5.6); and that by a Roman citizen, M. Nonius Romanus in

5.6 *Altar from Caerwent dedicated to Mars Ocelus by Aelius Augustinus,* optio *(RIB I, 310) (photograph: National Museum of Wales)*

152 to Mars Lenus or Ocelus Vellaunus is suggestive.[19] While the cult of Lenus Mars may have originated in Trier, the military associations of this cult in Britain are strengthened by a dedication to Mars Ocelus and the Deity of the Emperor Alexander and Julia Mamaea at Carlisle, and to Lenus Mars and Ancamna at Trier by an individual from Chester, home of *XX Valeria Victrix*.[20] More tentatively, the tile marked by Bellicianus at Caerwent recalls the tombstones erected by a Belicianus at Caerleon, and for a Bellicianus at Chester.[21] Wacher has drawn attention to what he describes as a distinct 'foreign' element in the houses of Caerwent. Though probably of third or fourth century date, House XVI.3s with its compact, peristyle plan is seen to be most representative.[22] Such houses are also to be found earlier in the *coloniae* of Colchester and Gloucester. The wealth of Caerwent in comparison with towns like Caistor-by-Norwich, Exeter or Brough-on-Humber is also striking, inviting the thought that it attracted comparatively wealthy veterans more than other cities elsewhere in Britain. Given its later date of foundation and the even later date when it appears to take off as a town, can it possibly be regarded as a *de facto colonia*? As we have observed already, the fact that it has produced no tombstones of veterans should not occasion much surprise; only two (respectively of *VI Victrix* and *XX Valeria Victrix*) are recorded from the British *coloniae.* Although proof is elusive, one suspects that veteran settlement in south Wales (and elsewhere in southern Britain) was significant; and the influence of *II Augusta* all pervasive.

If that influence developed from a policy which regarded the security of south Wales as the decisive factor in retaining *II Augusta* at Caerleon, there are further aspects of the legion to be considered which give it a unique character amongst the legions of the western Empire. These, too, extended its influence beyond south Wales in several directions. To begin with we should recall that there were imperial interests within the civil zone for which, either continuously, or intermittently, the army had responsibility (Figure 5.7). In the south of Britain and south Wales there was a range of minerals whose exploitation is attested during the Roman period. In the case of Mendip lead we have the authority of two stamped pigs for the involvement of *II Augusta* in that enterprise: one undated, the other of the reign of Nero (Figure 5.8).[23] Although there is evidence for the involvement of lessees in the Mendip field during the reign of both Nero and Vespasian, the later pigs of Hadrian, Antoninus Pius and the joint reign of Aurelius and Verus carry no indication of the organizations involved in production.[24] The fact that there is parallel evidence from Nero's reign of both the legion's involvement and a probable lessee, C. Nipius Ascanius, does not preclude a continuing military supervision, particularly in the second century when the pigs are silent on the question of organization.[25]

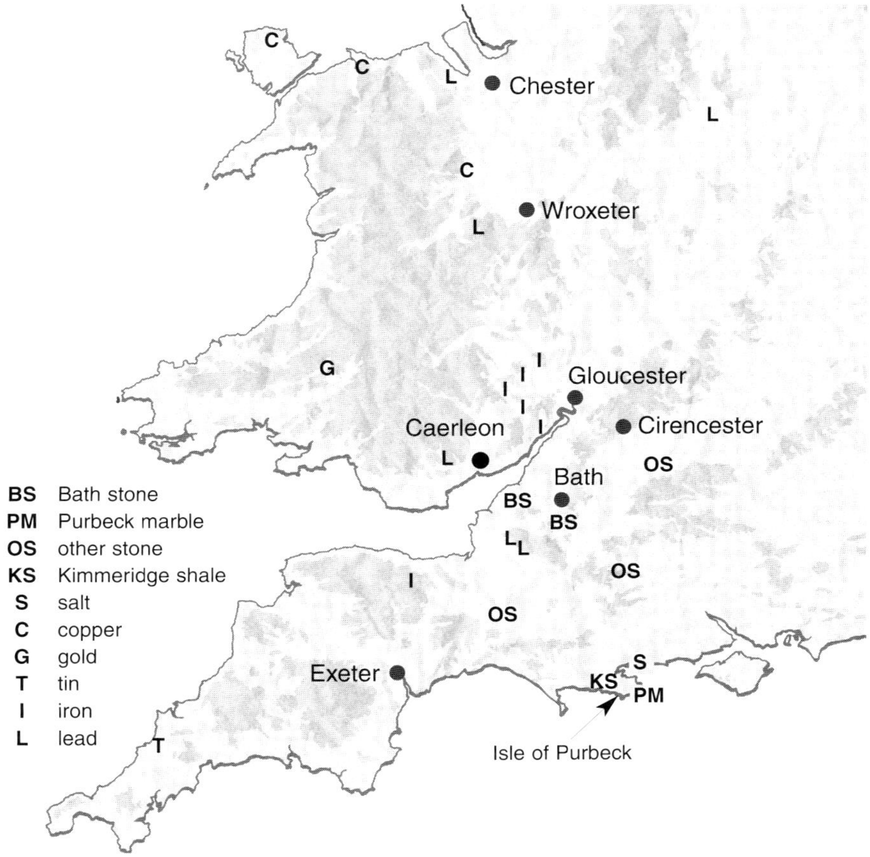

5.7 *Stone and mineral resources in the west of Britain*

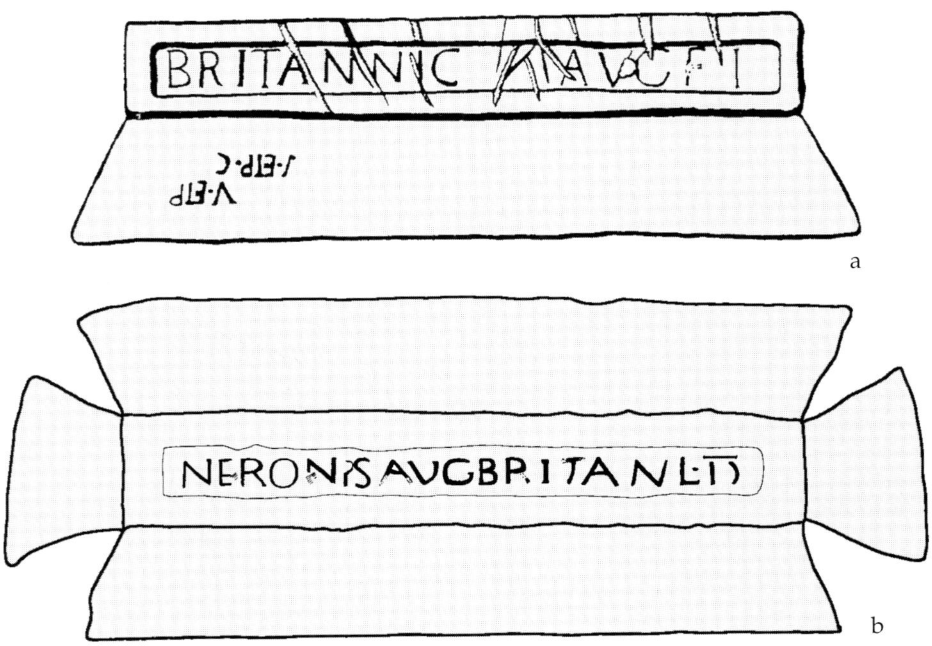

5.8 *Lead pigs from the Mendips produced by* legio II: *a from Blagdon, Avon* (RIB II.1, 2404.2); *b from St Valéry sur Somme, France of the reign of Nero* (RIB II.1, 2404.24)

Support for military supervision of an area close to, and perhaps including Bath in the early third century is implied by the inscription found in the centre of the city recording a *centurio regionarius* ('district officer'), Gaius Severius Emeritus, restoring a *locus religiosus* (Figure 5.9a).[26] The *regio* concerned could have embraced both the nearby Mendip lead field and the Bath stone quarries. Stone from the latter was used both locally and in distant locations for military and public building from the reign of Nero onwards.[27] Celebrated examples include the temple and spa complex at Bath itself, the first-century baths and second-century *forum-basilica* at Silchester and the legionary fortress at Caerleon itself. At the latter the oolite was supplemented by the local, but inferior Triassic Sudbrook sandstone, which was the principal freestone used at Caerwent. Close to Bath at Combe Down was found the inscription recording the restoration of a ruined *principia* by Naevius, procurator's assistant (Figure 5.9b), probably in the reign of Caracalla.[28] In being tempted to see this as the headquarters where Gaius Severius Emeritus might have served, these inscriptions also raise the nature of the relationship between the army and the procurator's office. The evidence of the lead pigs suggests that the procurator could call on the services of the army to assist in the supervision and management of imperial interests in the province. Setting aside their military skills, the army also represented the greatest source of technical expertise as well as literacy in the formative province. We should not forget that need for skilled manpower extended down to the running of the *cursus publicus* (imperial posting-service); who, for example, did the procurator call on to man the *mansiones, mutationes* and *praetoria*?

As we have seen, it is likely that *II Augusta* retained responsibility for overseeing the lead mines at Draethen, Machen and Risca, some 10–12 kilometres west of Caerleon. In addition to lead there was the exploitation of gold at Dolaucothi in Carmarthenshire and of tin in Cornwall. While we have no evidence for the organizations responsible for the production of Cornish tin, the proximity of an auxiliary fort at Pumsaint close to the gold mine points to military oversight there. That leaves the supervision of iron production in the Forest of Dean. Although more evidence for military involvement can be assigned a third/fourth rather than a first/second century date, there is some evidence for the latter from Weston under Penyard (Ariconium) in Herefordshire (see below).[29]

One other type of stone remains to be mentioned where a military involvement in its exploitation is probable in the first and second centuries. Like Bath oolite, Purbeck marble was also worked early. It was used abundantly in the Neronian legionary fortress at Exeter, as in the Neronian and Flavian palaces at Fishbourne and it provided the principal source of stone for inscriptions across southern Britain in Colchester, London, Verulamium, Silchester, Chichester and Dorchester. It was also used quite extensively in

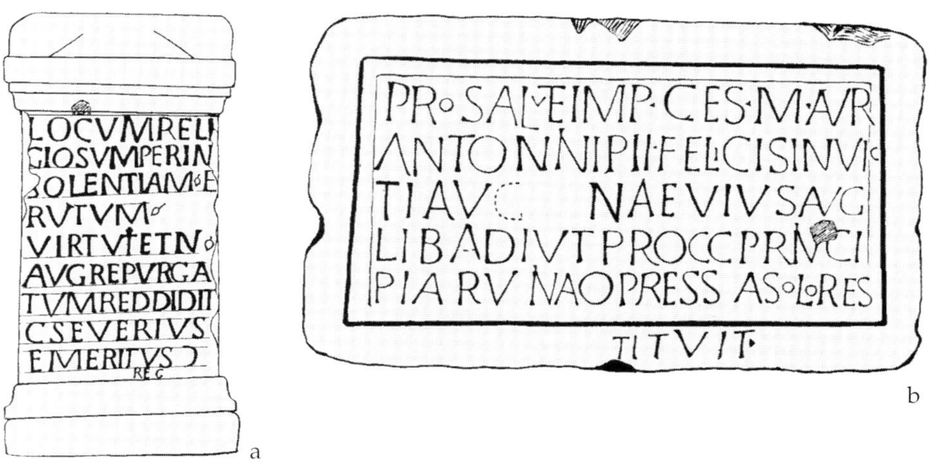

5.9 *a Altar from Bath commemorating the restoration of a holy place by Severius Emeritus,* centurio regionarius *(RIB I, 1520); b dedication stone from Combe Down, near Bath which records the restoration of a ruined* principia *by the freedman Naevius, procurator's assistant* (RIB I, 179)

the legionary fortress at Caerleon and, to a lesser degree, at Chester from *c* 75.[30] The material continued to be used for the adornment of public buildings in London and the south of Britain, as at Silchester, through the second century. Marble, however, was not the only resource to be extracted from the Isle of Purbeck (see below).

There are two other groups of inscriptions from southern England (London and Bath) which refer to *II Augusta* and which require comment here (Figure 5.10). London attracted individuals and detachments from the legions and auxiliary regiments, presumably to serve on the staff of the governor or the procurator and to man the Cripplegate fort. Along with *II Augusta*, which is represented by three inscriptions, *VI Victrix* and *XX Valeria Victrix* are also recorded. With the exception of a dedication to Mithras by Ulpius Silvanus, *emeritus* (veteran) of *II Augusta*, all are inscribed on tombstones.[31]

The three longest-serving of the legions stationed in Britain, are also represented at Bath, along with tombstones of a *miles* (soldier) of *II Adiutrix* and of an *eques* (horseman) of the *ala Vettonum*. All the inscriptions relating to *II Augusta* and *VI Victrix* are dedications on altars by centurions and an *imaginifer*, and represent offerings to Sulis for a safe recovery (Figure 5.11). *Legio XX Valeria Victrix* did not fare so well; two of the inscriptions are on tombstones of serving soldiers, while the third is of one recently retired (aged 45).[32] Although the sample is small, it is clear that the military formed a major constituency of those who enjoyed the waters and other services that the spa at Bath had to offer (Figure 5.12). This raises the question for whom the spa and temple complex was principally intended, and who paid for the work. The evidence points to construction work beginning in the Neronian/early Flavian period,[33] a time when *II Augusta*, certainly, and *XX Valeria Victrix*, possibly,

5.10 *Distribution of inscriptions on stone of* legio II Augusta *from the west and south of Britain*

5.11 *Altars from Bath dedicated to Sulis Minerva: a by Gaius Curiatius Saturninus, centurion of* legio II Augusta *(*RIB *I, 146); b for the welfare of Gaius Javolenus Saturnalis, imaginifer of* legio II Augusta *by Lucius Manius Dionisias, his freedman (*RIB *I, 147)*

were based in Wales and the south-west, with the principal base of *II Augusta* at Exeter, and that of *XX Valeria Victrix* at Usk or Gloucester (Kingsholm). It is difficult to imagine that the spa was the initiative of anybody but the army and, perhaps, the procurator's office and, on grounds of proximity alone, *II Augusta* and, perhaps, *XX Valeria Victrix* were likely to gain the most benefit at the time work started.[34] However, if *II Augusta* were responsible for the new fortress at Gloucester from the mid-60s,[35] the initiative at Bath may have rested with it from the outset. Certainly in the longer term with the spa virtually on its doorstep, the interest and advantage lay with *II Augusta* at Caerleon; it is difficult to see how over time it did not benefit the most. To a cynical observer, Bath may have been a powerful, if sybaritic, reason for the legion staying put at Caerleon. It is interesting to speculate how many veterans might have chosen to retire in or near Bath.

Before leaving the south, it is appropriate to return to Purbeck where, as we have seen, there is a strong case for legionary/procuratorial involvement in the quarrying of the marble, perhaps from as early as 49. One of the most distinctive products of that area, from the shores of Poole Harbour, is the Durotrigan pottery, which found favour with the army during the conquest of the south-west in the 40s and 50s. The developed products of that native industry reached an enormous provincial market from the early second century and that transformation of form and production is marked by a change of terminology on our part – Durotrigan becomes black-burnished ware 1 (BB1). Even during the Neronian period this pottery was reaching out beyond its native consumers to Exeter and the south-west, and across the Bristol Channel to Usk and the pre-Flavian garrisons of south Wales.[36] There may well be pre-Roman antecedents, but the Roman conquest of these two areas certainly marks a change of tempo.

Although it has long been established that BB1 is well represented on the northern frontier – Hadrian's Wall, the Antonine Wall and hinterland forts – as well as elsewhere in Britain, it has never received a wide-ranging, quantitative assessment of its distribution.[37] Although a cursory glance at recent literature reveals that it is much more abundant in the west of Britain

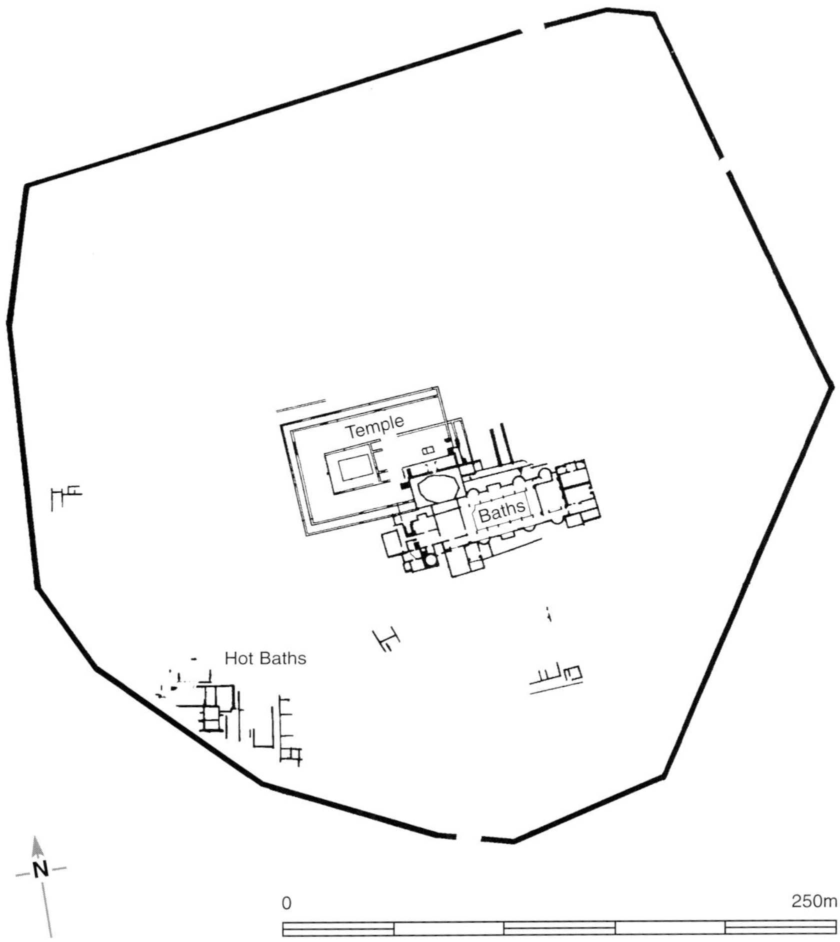

5.12 *Bath (Aquae Sulis): plan of the walled area with the temple precinct and baths*

than the east, it is possible to go much further in the analysis of its distribution. Figure 5.13 shows just such a study of BB1 in Wales and the south-west during the main period of production and distribution between the early second and the mid-fourth centuries; the contours are at logarithmic intervals.[38] Although the distribution extends significantly northwards and eastwards of the study area, the latter reveals some interesting patterns. Apart from the local heartland, high ratios of BB1 extend northwards across the Bristol Channel into south Wales and the Forest of Dean. High spots occur around the Welsh coast to Caernarfon and Chester. In the south-west the lines of the major roads exert an important influence, particularly the Fosse Way towards Cirencester, but also the Portway to Silchester and London. It is a curious picture with higher ratios at military and civilian sites on the north shores of the Bristol Channel and the Severn Estuary than on the south, except at the mouth of the River Parrett; indeed the representation on sites in south Wales and the Forest of Dean is greater than along the English Channel coast.

What has BB1 to do with *II Augusta*? Although the supply of this pottery to the northern frontier has been described in terms of military contracts – and there is no doubt that the military is privileged in the north of Britain – little attempt has been made to describe how this supply was organized. *Negotiatores* (businessmen) working on contract for the army or the procurator's office are one possible explanation, but there is no evidence from the west of Britain. At first glance, the same appears true for a direct military involvement as the lack of evidence for the presence

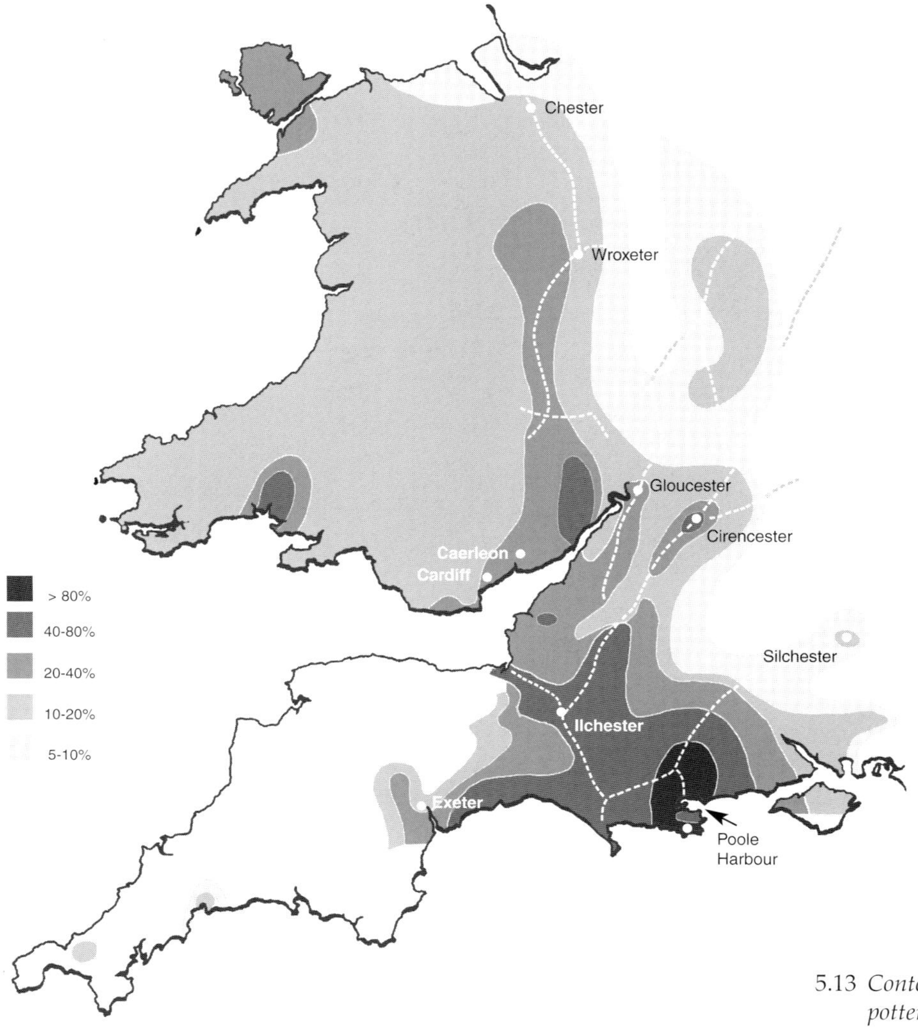

5.13 *Contoured distribution of BB1 pottery in the west of Britain*

of the fleet, the *Classis Britannica,* in the west of Britain is well known. In fact, the circumstantial evidence for the involvement of the army in matters of supply around the western shores of Britain, and of *II Augusta* in particular, is substantial. If we take BB1 there is, firstly, the general, northward skew in the distribution. Secondly, the discrepancy between its representation on the north and south sides of the Bristol Channel and the Severn Estuary invites further comment. If the distribution of BB1 was in civilian hands, we might expect equal ratios on north and south shores, but this is emphatically not the case. If there was no channelling of the distribution, it is unlikely that the New Forest industry in Hampshire would have developed in such close proximity. But why go to such lengths over pottery when other, more accessible sources, such as Caerleon Ware, could be – and were – organized? The importance of Purbeck for its marble has already been commented on; shale whose production long pre-dates the Roman conquest was another commodity that was exploited in this area for furniture, *tesserae,* articles of personal decoration, etc. More important from a military point of view was salt whose production around Poole Harbour is also attested from the pre-Roman Iron Age. Shellfish, particularly oysters, are likely to have been a much appreciated commodity. So a number of factors lie behind the preference for BB1 and its distinctive pattern of distribution in which a direct military involvement at the hands of *II Augusta* seems at present the most satisfactory explanation. Of course the supply of forts in Wales and the north would have involved a much greater range of goods than those derived from the Isle of Purbeck, and it is possible that commodities such as minerals, hides and cattle were brought in return. In respect of the operation of the system of supply, it is relevant to recall buildings on the coast, other than forts, such as the third-century building at Cold Knap, Barry, Vale of Glamorgan, interpreted as a *mansio* (lodging for officials).[39] It may have been intended partly to store cereals and other goods from neighbouring estates for onward transmission.

Legio II Augusta was heavily involved in the north from the reign of Hadrian onwards into the third century; the latest dated inscription is from Netherby where *II Augusta* and *XX Valeria Victrix* were engaged in rebuilding in 219.[40] Although this involvement was concentrated first on Hadrian's Wall and, secondly, on the Antonine Wall, it extended throughout the north-west. Just as there are few inscriptions of *legio VI* west of the Pennines and south of Hadrian's Wall, so too evidence of *II Augusta* off the line of Hadrian's Wall in the north-east is limited (Figure 5.14).[41] There was also an important presence of the legion at Corbridge and Carlisle.[42] Even though the number of closely datable inscriptions is small and is spread thinly over the period, the scale of commitments, the consequences of changes of policy, as well as active campaigning, are likely to have kept *II Augusta* continuously in the north up to and beyond 219. In the north-west certain responsibilities seem to have been shared with *XX Valeria Victrix* and, off the line of the Walls, there are a number of sites – Bewcastle, Netherby, Maryport and the Cumberland Quarries where detachments of the two legions worked together and made joint dedications (Figure 5.15).[43] The production of tiles by both legions, perhaps at Scalesceugh, in the vicinity of Carlisle suggests that they worked together at that site where there is evidence of a legionary presence.[44] At Chester itself there is a tombstone of a soldier of *II Augusta* who died there, probably in the reign of Caracalla.[45] Conversely, joint dedications with *VI Victrix* either by *II Augusta* or *XX Valeria Victrix* are rare, and there is no evidence that the latter worked on building projects in partnership with *VI Victrix* (although all three worked beside each other on the

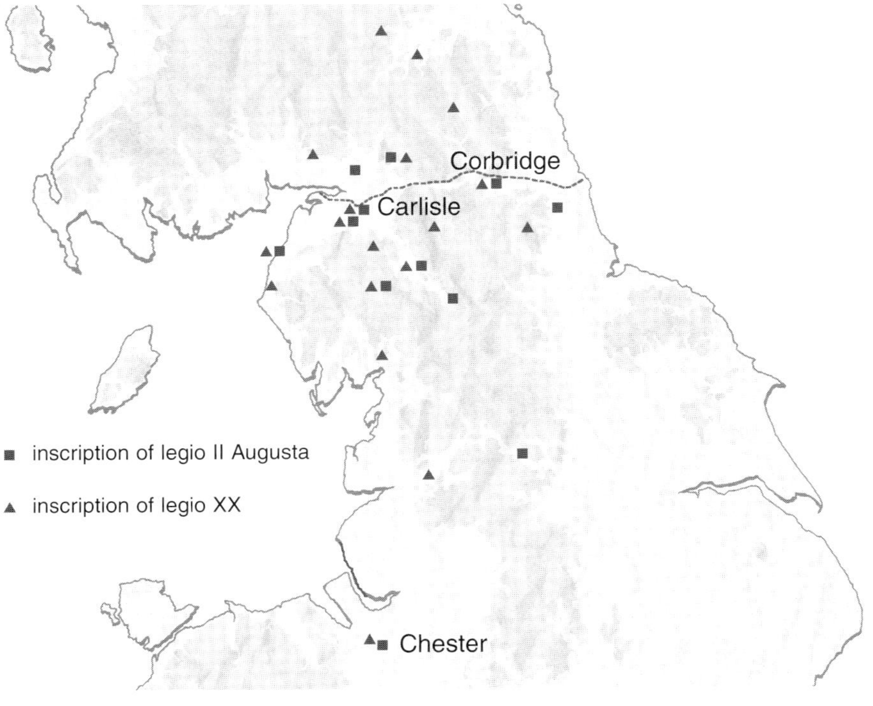

5.14 *Distribution of inscriptions on stone of* legio II Augusta *and* legio XX Valeria Victrix *in the north of Britain (excluding the Antonine Wall and Hadrian's Wall)*

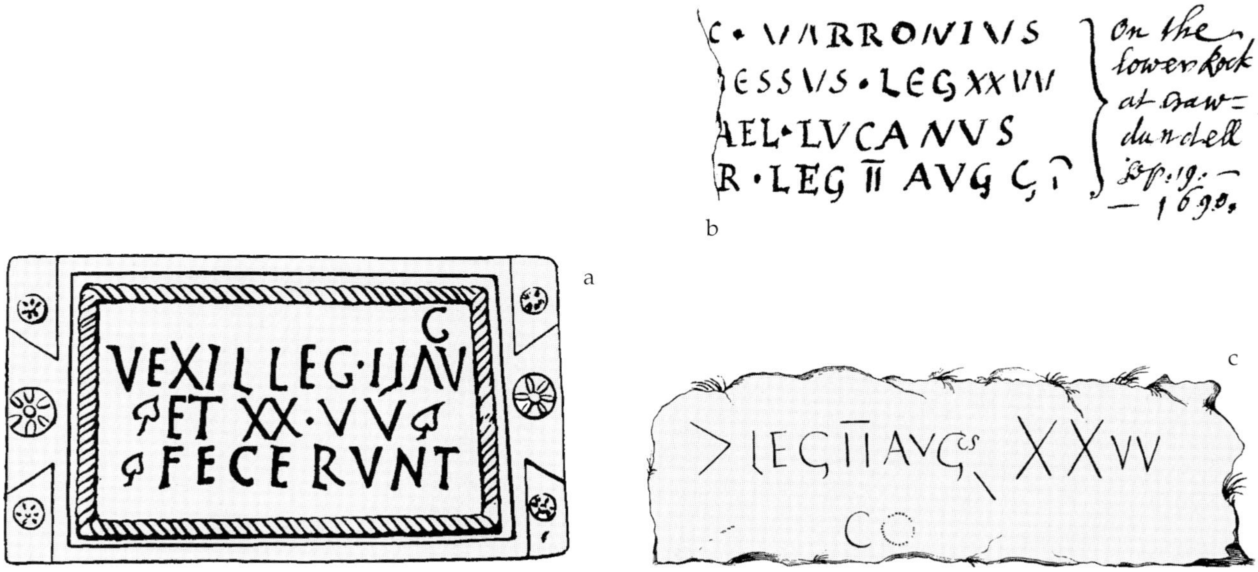

5.15 *A building stone and quarry inscriptions recording the joint activities of* legio II Augusta *and* legio XX Valeria Victrix: *a from Maryport, Cumbria* (RIB *I, 852); b part of a quarry inscription recorded in 1690 at Crowdundle, Cumbria* (RIB *I, 998); c quarry inscription also from Crowdundle* (RIB *I, 999)*

two Walls). At Corbridge where detachments of all three legions served in the second and third centuries there are joint dedications to Concord and Jupiter by *VI Victrix* and *XX Valeria Victrix;* the surviving record shows that *II Augusta* made its dedications alone.[46] Uniquely as far as *II Augusta* and *VI Victrix* are concerned there is a joint dedication to Fortuna at Castlecary on the Antonine Wall.[47] A bronze roundel found in Gaul and probably dating to the third century shows soldiers from vexillations of *II Augusta* and *XX Valeria Victrix* (Figure 9.1).[48]

The distribution of BB1 reinforces this sense of interdependency of the two legions, because it was supplied not only to Chester and north Wales forts such as Caernarfon, but to all sites in the north-west, irrespective of their garrison. If we are right to attribute a major role to *II Augusta* in the supply of the north, with BB1 being one of the principal tracers in the archaeological record, the idea gains support from the twenty lead sealings (possibly from bales of merchandise or official stores) of the legion found at Brough-under-Stainmore; there is one tag of *VI Victrix* from the same site.[49] Including unprovenanced examples, there are twice as many sealings (26) of *II Augusta* as there are from *VI Victrix* and *XX Valeria Victrix* together.[50]

Despite the lack of supporting epigraphic material for the role advocated for the Second Legion, we should recall the altar erected at York by M. Minucius Audens, *gubernator* (helmsman or river pilot) of *VI Victrix* (Figure 5.16a), attesting that, even in the second or third centuries when the evidence for the *Classis Britannica* is most abundant, the legions had access to their own craft and crews.[51] In the west we should recall the *optio*, probably of *XX Valeria Victrix,* but conceivably of *II Augusta,* who perished in a shipwreck (Figure 5.16b).[52] Although this is a self-fulfilling prophecy, if the role of supply to the northern frontier is placed in the hands of *II Augusta,* it would account for the lack of epigraphic material referring to the *Classis Britannica.* Physically, it is likely that there were at least two fleets in Britain: navigation around Land's End and along the north Cornish coast is hazardous and there is little evidence that it was undertaken regularly. Indeed the distribution of BB1 shows that the land route was preferred for the transhipment of goods across the peninsula. The sphere of operations of the *Classis*

5.16 *a Altar from York dedicated to the African, Gallic and Italian Mother Goddesses by Marcus Minucius Audens,* gubernator *of* legio VI Victrix (RIB *I, 653); b tombstone from Chester of an* optio *who died by shipwreck* (RIB *I, 544)*

Britannica was in the Channel and the North Sea; *II Augusta*, perhaps with the assistance of others, looked after the west. The ratios of BB1 from sites around the coast of Wales imply transport by sea, and the later Roman development of forts at Cardiff and Caer Gybi at Holyhead imply the continuing existence of some kind of naval unit. For ships returning in ballast we have the hard-standings behind the wharves at Caerleon which were, to a noticeable extent, composed of chips of slate from the Preseli Mountains.[53] Purbeck marble has already been mentioned in connection with Caerleon; it is also interesting to record its use as far north as Chester for an official inscription of 79.[54] Quixotically, perhaps, there appears to be a greater incidence of dolphins and other sea beasts at Caerleon than either Chester or York, or anywhere else in Britain. These occur in a variety of contexts, both unofficial such as tombstones (where the dolphin may take on another significance), or official like antefixes (Figure 5.17a) or the decoration of the baths (Figure 5.17b).[55] Indeed the adoption of the capricorn (half goat/half sea beast) as the badge of the Second Legion, which is not attested in direct association before the early second century, may allude as much to the mix of marine and terrestrial activities as to the association with Augustus who adopted it as his astrological sign.[56]

The history of the legion has been tied closely to the surviving epigraphy. We have already noted the latest closely dated inscription from the north of 219, others could be later. From Caerleon itself there are the inscriptions of Valerian and Gallienus of 255–60 recording the rebuilding of the barracks of the seventh cohort, and of Aurelian of 270–5 of uncertain purpose; a third inscription on a tile might be attributable to 269–71.[57] Although *II Augusta* occurs on the coinage of Carausius, the next locational piece of evidence is the listing of the legion at Richborough in the *Notitia Dignitatum* which dates to the end of the fourth century.[58] However, the inclination has been to assume the posting of that detachment to Richborough under Carausius, since he may have been responsible for the construction of the late Roman fort.[59] That leaves a number of problems: firstly, despite the undoubted robbing or demolition of some buildings from as early as the late second century, there is also evidence of continuity of occupation at Caerleon to the late fourth century or later;[60] secondly, the lack of epigraphic evidence both at Caerleon and in the north is also not necessarily significant – late Roman inscriptions generally are rare; thirdly, BB1 continues to be distributed as extensively as before until about the middle of the fourth century. The continuing use of the barrack

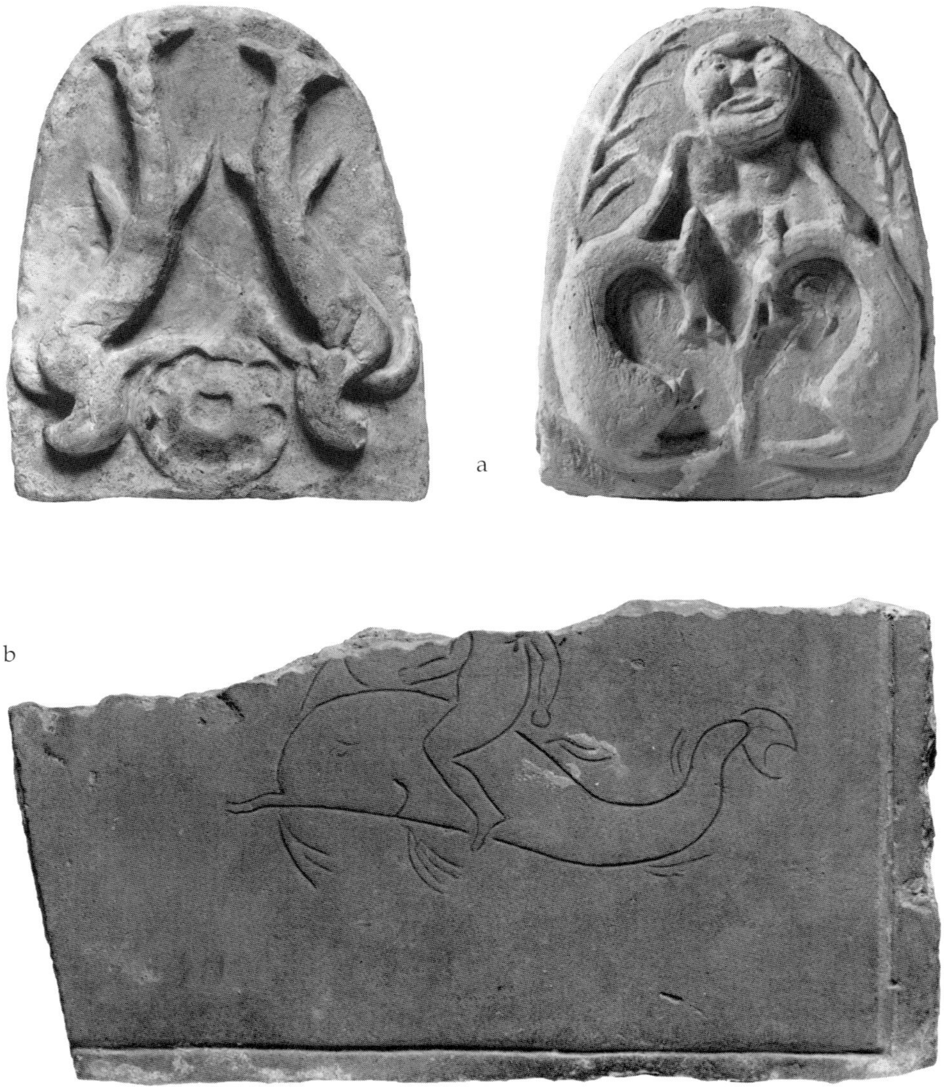

5.17 *a Tile antefixes of* legio II Augusta *from Caerleon; b slab from the 'Castle' Baths, Caerleon inscribed with a cupid astride a dolphin (photographs: National Museum of Wales)*

blocks at the Roman Gates site, Caerleon is very suggestive, but features which distinguish military from civilian assemblages are extremely difficult to characterise in the Late Empire. The evidence points towards the continuation of military occupation at Caerleon until the late fourth century, but the evidence is such that we cannot preclude a partial or total civilian presence.

However, a fortress the size of Caerleon had become redundant for the needs of a legion by the mid-to-late third century. Legionary detachments were constantly in demand elsewhere, and where fortresses were built for legions *de novo* in the fourth century they embraced a fraction of the space. The most striking, single, military development in south Wales in the later Roman period is the building of the coastal fort at Cardiff.[61] Although the latter remains to be dated, comparable forts in the south-east (Pevensey, Portchester, Richborough) have recently been assigned to the usurpation of Carausius and Allectus.[62] Given the history of its maritime involvement, it makes very good sense for *II Augusta* to have been stationed at Richborough, but we have no evidence that this transfer took place before the late fourth century. It is, therefore, proposed that the legion was first assigned in the late third century to Cardiff where it could carry out the maritime element of its activities more effectively and that it remained there until the late fourth century. The site is more accessible to the Severn Estuary than Caerleon and, at 3.57 hectares, the size of the fort would seem to be closer to what a late Roman legion might require than the vast (20.5 hectares), derelict and indefensible wastes of Caerleon (Figure 5.18). A move eastward to Richborough would coincide with the evidence for the run-down of traffic along the western seaboard, as indicated by the marked decline or absence of BB1 in the north from about the third quarter of the fourth century, a run-down often attributed to the effects of the 367 disaster, or the subsequent reorganizations by Count Theodosius.[63] Except at Caerwent, Valentinianic issues are the latest to be represented with any frequency in south Wales, and they are the latest to have been found at Cardiff.[64]

Further evidence for the existence of a fleet in the west comes from Lydney where a mosaic floor (Figure 5.19) in the temple carries the inscription (reconstructed), which Collingwood read as: 'To the god

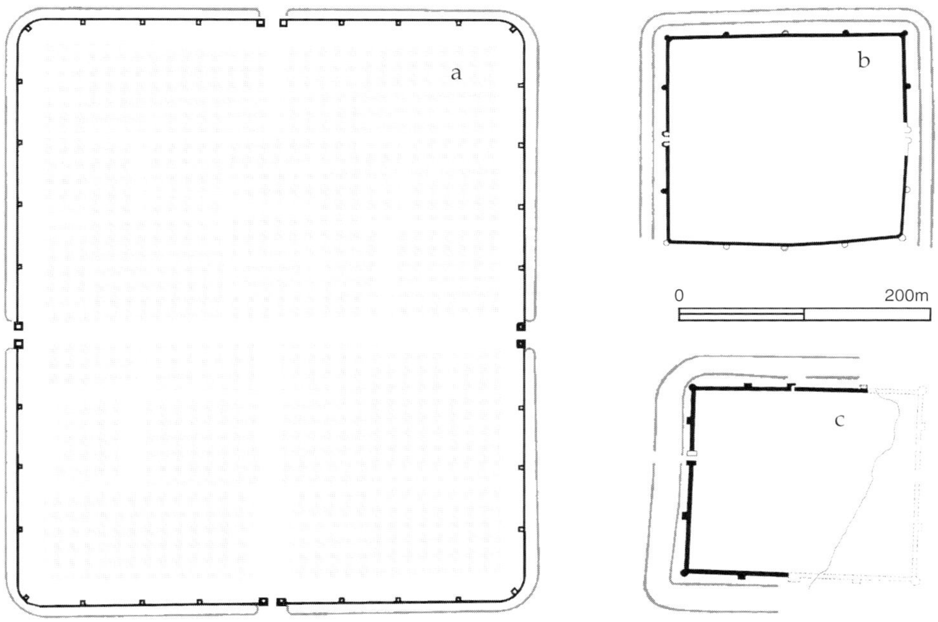

5.18 *Outline plans of: a the late first-century legionary fortress, Caerleon; b the late Roman coastal fort at Cardiff; c the late third-century coastal fort at Richborough, Kent*

5.19 *Lydney: mosaic pavement from the* cella *of the temple*

Nodens, Titus Flavius Senilis, *praepositus reliquationis* (officer in charge of the supply depot of the fleet), laid this pavement out of money offerings (*ex stipibus*); the work being in charge of Victorinus, interpreter on the governor's staff'.[65] Recently, Wright and Hassall have read *pr rel* as *praepositus religionis* (superintendent of cult) and *inter....* as *interpretiante* (interpreter of dreams).[66] Part of the reason for preferring a religious dedication is that the site is believed to have provided accommodation for pilgrims visiting the temple which was dedicated to Nodens who is thought to be a minor god of healing; taken in immediate context, but out of a wider setting, the new interpretation seems eminently sensible even though there is no parallel for *praepositus religionis*. However, Lydney has produced another, certainly military inscription with a dedication to Nodens by Flavius Blandinus, *armatura* (weapon instructor).[67] Besides the inscriptions there is the dedication of the temple itself to Mars Nodens which, interestingly, is only paralleled in the north-west at Cockersand Moss in Lancashire where two statuettes of Mars dedicated to Mars Nodons were found before 1718.[68] Among the other finds we can point to the incidence of crossbow brooches,[69] which is greater in number than at any other site in the south apart from Richborough, and the high ratio of BB1 which seems also to be significant (Figure 5.13). With its proximity to the forest and supplies of timber and iron (whose exploitation could be supervised), and to the largest river draining into the upper estuary of the Severn, Lydney is an obvious place to serve as a supply depot and to build and repair ships; functions it has served in the early modern period. Interestingly, below the inscription on the mosaic pavement is a frieze decorated with sea monsters and fish.[70] What is known of Roman Lydney is likely to represent only a small part of a settlement whose role could have embraced overseeing the production of iron as well as that of a fleet depot; the buildings surrounding the temple could form part of a late Roman headquarters complex rather than accommodation for pilgrims (Figure 5.20) – the Guest House becomes a *principia* or the prefect's residence, the Long Building or Abaton becomes accommodation for officers! Whichever interpretation is chosen, it is clear that Lydney was frequented by soldiers. Above all, as we have argued above, there is once again a naval/military context in which to place Lydney.

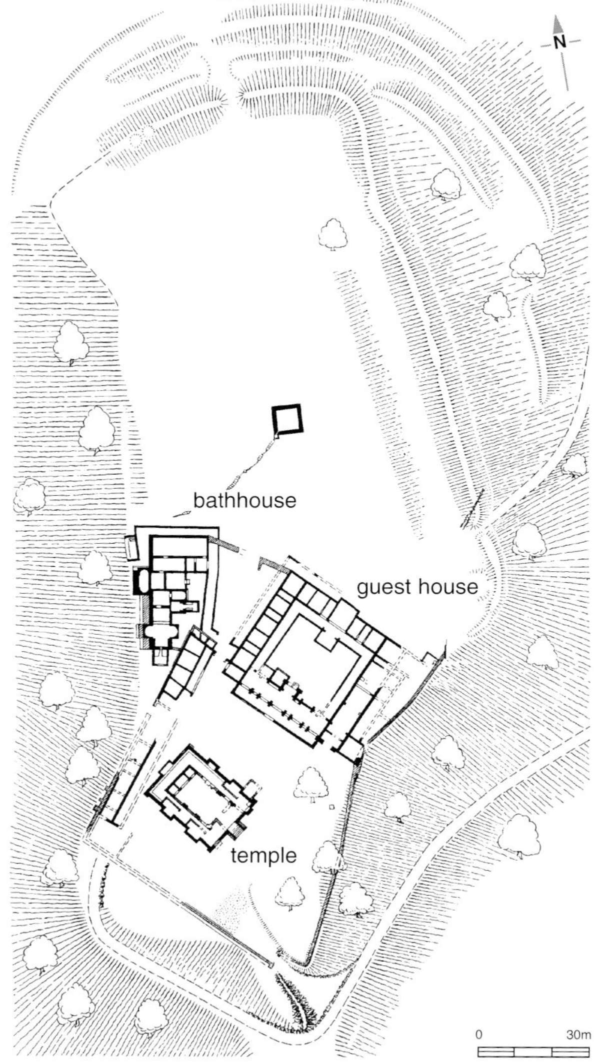

5.20 *Lydney: plan of the temple and associated buildings*

This essay has tried to develop a theme which does justice to those aspects of *II Augusta* which were not concerned with its role as a fighting unit. It seems clear that it had a major role to play in the supply of Wales, the north-west, where its activities were closely related to those of *XX Valeria Victrix*, and the north as a whole. That role continued, with part of the legion probably based at Cardiff, until the late fourth century when that element was moved to Richborough. The presence and influence of the legion were all pervasive in south

Wales, but a range of responsibilities and involvement elsewhere in the south of Britain meant that these extended much more widely than we have been inclined to believe in the past.

ACKNOWLEDGEMENTS

Several people have very kindly helped me with the preparation of this paper. I thank Steve Allen (University of Reading) and Tony Daly (National Museums & Galleries of Wales) for preparing the illustrations; Professor Sheppard Frere, Francis Grew, Professor Lawrence Keppie and the late Dr Tim Potter for their help with the text and further illustrations. I particularly single out Richard Brewer without whose help this would never have happened!

Notes

1 Boon 1972.
2 Breeze this volume, 81; Zienkiewiecz 1990, 33.
3 Richmond 1943; *RIB* I, 1120–1175. For legionaries of *II Augusta* and *XX Valeria Victrix* at Carlisle, see Hassall and Tomlin 1986, 437, no. 11; Hassall and Tomlin 1989, 331, no. 5.
4 *CSIR* I.5, *Wales*, no. 36.
5 *RIB* II.4, 2463.7(i), 2463.44(v).
6 Pennal, *RIB* II.4, 2459.54(vii). Doubt has, however, been cast on the provenance of this tile-stamp, see White 1978, 62, n 18.
7 Boon1984; specifically, for the Caerleon types, *RIB* II.4, 2459.4, 2459.6–13, 2459.17, 2459.21 and 2459.36.
8 Boon 1972, 17; 1987, 17–24; Jones and Mattingly 1990, 185.
9 *RIB* I, 359, 363, 371–375, 377.
10 *RIB* I, 396.
11 *RIB* I, 395.
12 Allen and Fulford 1986; Fulford *et al* 1994.
13 Eg *RIB* I, 396.
14 Le Bohec 1994, 223–4; Watson 1969, 147–53.
15 Mann 1983.
16 There is, however, one tombstone of a veteran of *XX Valeria Victrix* from Gloucester. It is dated to the second half of the second century or later. Hassall and Tomlin 1984, 333.
17 *RIB* I, 311.
18 *RIB* II.1, 2404.25; *RIB* II.4, 2459.4 (v–vii), 2459.21(i).
19 *RIB* I, 310, 309.
20 *RIB* I, 949; *AE* 1915, no. 70.
21 *Bel(l)icianus, RIB* II.5, 2491.80 (Caerwent); *RIB* I, 375 (Caerleon); 495 (Chester).
22 Wacher 1995, 389.
23 *RIB* II.1, 2404.2 (Blagdon); 2404.24 (St Valéry sur Somme).
24 *RIB* II.1, 2404.14–22.
25 *RIB* II.1, 2404.3.
26 *RIB* I, 152.
27 *RIB* I, 200, 201.
28 *RIB* I, 179.
29 For two possible fortlets, see Walters and Walters 1989.
30 Bidwell 1979; Cunliffe 1971b; *RIB* I, *passim.*
31 *RIB* I, 3 (Ulpius Silvanus), 17, 19.
32 *RIB* I, 139–160, *passim.*
33 Blagg 1979.
34 Von Petrikovits suggests that the *thermae* at Aquae Iasae in Pannonia, Aquae Granni and, probably, Aquae Mattiacae in Germania were primarily for use by the army, 'Aquae Iasae', von Petrikovits 1976, 479–83; 1980a, 122.
35 Hurst 1988.
36 Bidwell 1979; Greene 1993, especially 64–6.
37 Gillam and Greene 1981.
38 Allen and Fulford 1996.
39 Evans *et al* 1985.
40 *RIB* I, 980.
41 Eg *legio II* at Chester-le-Street (*RIB* I, 1050); *legio VI* at Manchester and Ribchester (*RIB* I, 575, 583, 589, 591).
42 See n 3.
43 *RIB* I, 995, 980, 852, 998, 999.
44 See n 3 and *RIB* II.4, 2459.1–2, 2463.1–3.
45 *RIB* I, 488.
46 *RIB* I, 1125, 1130 (*VI Victrix* and *XX Valeria Victrix);* see 1127 (*II Augusta*).
47 *RIB* I, 2146.
48 Boon 1972, 65–6, Fig 37; *RIB* II.3, 2427.26.
49 *RIB* II.1, 2411.42, 2411.44–50, 2411.59–62, 2411.64.
50 *RIB* II.1, 2411.42–67, 2411.68–75, 2411.76–80.
51 *RIB* I, 653.
52 *RIB* I, 544.
53 Boon 1972, 52; 1978.
54 *RIB* I, 463.
55 *RIB* I, 375, *CSIR* I.5, *Wales*, nos 7, 23, 57, 58, 59, Boon 1984, 3–4, 10 (Pl), which documents the occurrence of *antefixa* decorated with dolphins (and made in the same mould as those from Caerleon) from the time of the construction of the legionary *thermae* at Exeter, *c* 55. The marine component in sculpture associated with *II Augusta* is such that it is reasonable to reassert the latter's responsibility for the splendid, but fragmentary (?) distance slab from Hag Knowe on the line of the Antonine Wall, see *CSIR* I.4, *Scotland*, no. 84.
56 Keppie this volume, 13–16.
57 *RIB* I, 334; Hassall 1992; *RIB* II.4, 2459.64.
58 *Not Dig Occ* 28.19.
59 Boon 1972, 65–6.
60 Ibid, 66–9; Hassall 1992.
61 Nash-Williams/Jarrett 1969, 70–3, Fig 32; P V Webster 1984, 305–7.
62 Fulford and Tyers 1995.
63 Gillam 1973, 61–2; 1976, 59; P V Webster 1993, 252–3.
64 Robinson 1988, vii–xxiv; for Cardiff, see n 61.
65 *RIB* II.4, 2448.3; Collingwood 1932, 102–4.
66 Hassall 1980, 82; Wright 1985.
67 *RIB* I, 305.
68 *RIB* I, 616, 617.
69 Wheeler and Wheeler 1932, 78, Fig 13.
70 Ibid, Pl XIX.

Chapter 6

Officers of the Second Augustan Legion in Britain

Anthony R Birley

'Vettius Adiutor aquilifer leg. II Aug. Cassio Saeculari fraterclo suo plurimam [salutem]': 'Vettius Adiutor eagle-bearer of the Second Augustan Legion to Cassius Saecularis his little brother very many [greetings]' (Tab Vindol Inv 88/940=*Tab Vindol II*, 214).

It was a delightful coincidence that not long after I received the invitation to contribute to the Annual Caerleon Lecture series *'In honorem aquilae'*, and had offered the subject 'Officers of the Second Augustan Legion in Britain', I saw the newly taken photograph of this writing-tablet from Vindolanda, found in August 1988. Only the initial greeting is preserved, but it is the longest such opening in any Vindolanda letter (Figure 6.1). We now have the first recorded *aquilifer* of *II Augusta*, manifestly an auspicious matter for this series.[1]

By 'officer' in the Roman army I understand men with the rank of centurion and upwards, in other words, what we might call 'commissioned officers'. In that case the *aquilifer* may be regarded as a senior 'non-commissioned officer', receiving, according to Domaszewski, three times the pay of an ordinary legionary and being eligible for a centurion's commission like other leading *principales*.[2] A valuable article by M P Speidel, 'Eagle-bearer and Trumpeter', provides full coverage of the *aquiliferi* and their standards.[3] He was able to list thirty-three such non-commissioned officers, none of them, as it happens, from the army of Britain. While referring to the legionary eagle in this prologue I must mention also the instructive study by P Herz, *'Honos aquilae'*, which *inter alia* illuminates precisely the Caerleon dedications which prompted these lectures.[4]

I cannot leave our *aquilifer* of *II Augusta* without a little further comment, necessarily rather speculative. His names are at first sight not very informative. 'Vettius' is a common *gentilicium*, both in Italy and elsewhere, and 'Adiutor' is a *cognomen* of which I Kajanto in his admirable handbook found over 200 epigraphic instances.[5] Still, we can note that Géza Alföldy pointed out that 'Adiutor', in common with a string of other ostensibly Latin names found in the Celtic province of Noricum, is a latinisation of a native original.[6] He had earlier reported, in his study of the nomenclature of Dalmatia, that 'Adiutor' was widespread everywhere, especially in Northern Italy, Gaul and Noricum; for Dalmatia itself he could list

6.1 *The letter sent by Adiutor, eagle-bearer of* II Augusta, *to Vindolanda (photograph: reproduced by permission of the Vindolanda Trust)*

seven specimens.[7] Hence one could legitimately regard Vettius Adiutor as deriving from the Celtic part of the Empire. There is, however, another consideration. Adiutor writes to his Vindolanda correspondent Cassius Saecularis as *'fraterclo suo'*, his 'little brother'. In a good many of the Vindolanda letters, conforming to normal Roman practice, the writers call one another *'frater'*, *'domine frater'*, *'frater karissime'*, or indeed, in the case of Claudia Severa to Sulpicia Lepidina, *'soror karissima'*. In such cases the inference must be, not that the correspondents were actual brothers or sisters, but close friends of about the same age and rank. But what about *'fraterc(u)lus'*, 'little brother'? Cassius Saecularis is known from another Vindolanda letter: in Tab Vindol Inv 865 (=*Tab Vindol II*, 213) he is written to by Curtius Super, all that survives being the words *'ut interpreteris et ut hordeum commercium habeant a te'*, 'that you may explain and that they may have barley as commercial goods from you'. But from this he seems to be a person of some consequence, and we had taken him to be a prefect. But could a legionary non-commissioned officer, however senior, call an equestrian officer his *'fraterculus'*? Might it be better to regard Cassius Saecularis as, for example, a former legionary of *II Augusta*, now promoted to centurion, in charge of a working party there, or even acting commander of the garrison? What about the name 'Saecularis'? It is by no means so common as 'Adiutor'.[8] At Klis in Croatia, between Salonae and neighbouring Epetium, a lady was buried on land adjoining that of a family of Cassii, specified as Atiutor, S(a)ecularis and Fidelis.[9] Since there are Vettii attested at the same place, one of them a legionary soldier,[10] it is at least legitimate to suppose that we have here a later generation from the family of our *aquilifer* Vettius Adiutor and his 'little brother' Cassius Saecularis. In other words, the two men had the same mother, married first to a Vettius then to a Cassius. So much by way of prologue.

* * * * * * *

I turn now to the commissioned officers of *legio II Augusta* in Britain. We are dealing with a period of just over two hundred years, from the conquest in AD 43 up till the 250s, when our evidence runs out. For this period we have the names of a dozen legionary legates, a bare seven *tribuni laticlavii*, eleven *tribuni angusticlavii*, five *praefecti castrorum*, and about two hundred centurions (many of whom, it must be added, can only conjecturally be assigned to *II Augusta*).[11] If, as seems to be the case, the average tenure of command for a legionary legate was between two and three years, nearly ninety men must have commanded *II Augusta* between AD 43 and 260. So we know rather less than 15 per cent of the legates. With the lower-ranking officers the picture is even less favourable. Nonetheless, what we do have in the way of evidence is quite well distributed chronologically, and I hope will prove instructive.

Since the man who led *II Augusta* to Britain became the Emperor Vespasian (Figure 6.2), we naturally know more about him than about any other legionary legate in the British army.[12] He was born in the evening of 17 November AD 9, at Falacrinae on the Via Salaria, north-east of Rome, close to Reate, which counted as his home town. Hence he was aged 33 at the time of the invasion. He had already been commanding *II Augusta* at its previous base, Strasbourg (Argentorate) in Upper Germany, so had become legate soon after his praetorship, datable to AD 39 or 40. This was to be the standard pattern followed, with a bare handful of exceptions, from the time of his accession in AD 69 until the ending of senatorial military service by Gallienus in AD 260. Under the Julio-Claudians, as it happens, it was

6.2 *Silver* denarius *of the Emperor Vespasian (69–79). He commanded the Second Augustan Legion with distinction during the early days of the conquest of Britain (photograph: National Musem of Wales)*

common enough for senators to become legate of a legion before the praetorship, when still in their twenties. This was the case, for example, with Vespasian's son Titus, given command of *XV Apollinaris* in AD 66, aged 26.[13] We need not pursue Vespasian's career here in any detail. But we may note that he owed his appointment to the powerful freedman *ab epistulis* (Chief Secretary) Narcissus, and that he probably commanded the legion for more than four years, until AD 47, when he presumably received his *ornamenta triumphalia* (honorary triumph) at the time of Aulus Plautius' *ovatio* (minor triumph).

We are fortunate in having the names of two of his subordinate officers, both of whom had previously served in Upper Germany. P. Anicius Maximus, from the Augustan colony of Antioch towards Pisidia, had previously been chief centurion, *primus pilus*, of the eastern legion *XII Fulminata* (Figure 6.3). His assignment to *II Augusta* as camp prefect was evidently while it was still at Strasbourg, a few years before the invasion, for he was decorated by an unnamed emperor for service in an expedition which ought to be the eccentric campaign of Caligula in AD 39, as well as by Claudius *'ob bellum Britannicum'*. Anicius Maximus went on to be 'prefect of the army in Egypt', which led the city of Alexandria to honour him with a statue in his home town, the base of which supplies us with his *cursus*. The other officer was one of the five equestrian *tribuni angusticlavii*, M. Stlaccius Coranus, from a family prominent at Ostia. Stlaccius had previously served as staff officer – *praefectus fabrum* – to some high official and as a juryman at Rome before beginning his *tres militiae* as prefect of *cohors V Bracaraugustanorum* in Upper Germany, from which he was promoted to *II Augusta*, perhaps on the eve of the invasion. In Britain he was promoted further, to prefect of cavalry in command of an *ala Hispanorum*, and was duly decorated.

The next officer of *II Augusta* whom we can identify was long known from a *cursus* inscription at Urvinum Mataurense (Urbino), his home, L. Vettius Statura. No obvious dating indications are supplied. His common *gentilicium*, which we have just been discussing, is offset by his rare *cognomen*, otherwise known only in the case of a Trajanic centurion and his son from nearby Tifernum. A recently published inscription from Xanthus in Lycia allows us to date

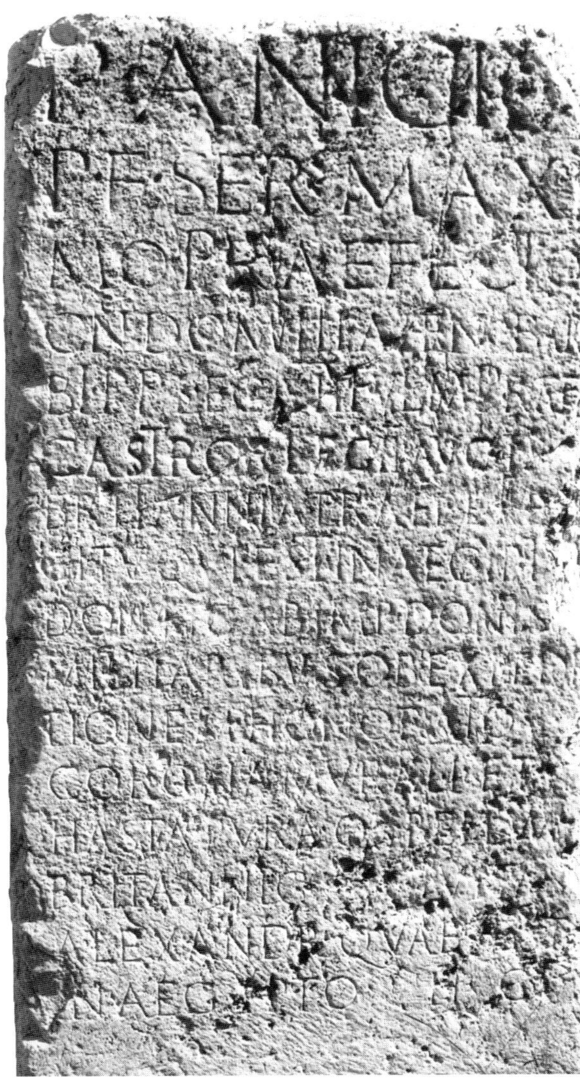

6.3 *Statue base of P. Anicius Maximus, camp prefect of* II Augusta. *Yalvaç, Turkey (CIL III 6809) (photograph: reproduced by permission of Professor S Mitchell)*

Vettius Statura to the time of Claudius or Nero. The name of the honorand is missing, but the career details match exactly, with the additional information that after the praetorship he was legate of Nero in Syria, presumably as a subordinate of Corbulo or one of his colleagues.[14]

Only Tacitus supplies us with the story of the camp prefect at the time of Boudicca's rebellion, Poenius Postumus, who took his own life from shame after failing to respond to Paullinus' call for help.[15] As has been observed,[16] the fact that the camp prefect was evidently the senior officer at the legion's base allows the inference that not only the legate but also the *tribunus laticlavius,* his second in command, were absent, presumably already with Paullinus. Since we know that Julius Agricola was attached to the governor's staff, perhaps he was the senatorial tribune of *II Augusta* at the time of the great revolt. But no certainty is possible. We do at any rate know another senatorial tribune at the time of the next crisis to affect Britain, the great upheaval following Nero's downfall. M. Trebellius Maximus, governor since AD 63, was expelled from the province by his own army in AD 69, the lead being taken by the legate of the Twentieth, M. Roscius Coelius. The legionary legates then shared the government of the province, but Roscius, says Tacitus, was 'the more powerful through his daring', *'audendo potentior'*. Since the comparative is used one might infer that there was only one other legionary legate at the time, and an inscription from Pisidian Antioch gives a further clue, suggesting that *II Augusta* was temporarily under the command of its *tribunus laticlavius* in AD 69. It is the famous stone giving the decree of L. Antistius Rusticus, governor of Cappadocia at a time of famine in the year 90 – the famine of which the author of *Revelation* speaks (6.6): 'A measure of wheat for a penny, and three measures of barley for a penny; and the oil and wine hurt thou not.' Rusticus clamped down on hoarding and profiteering and was honoured with a statue and was chosen as the colony's patron, *'quod [ind]ustrie prospexit annon.'*, 'because he diligently looked after the food supply'. The statue base sets out his career: after the vigintivirate (as *Xvir stlitibus iudicandis),* he was *'trib. mil. leg. II [A]ug.'* and decorated by Vespasian and Titus with *dona* appropriate to an ex-praetor. Furthermore, he was allowed to omit quaestorship and tribunate of the plebs (or aedileship), being adlected *inter praetorios.* Tacitus tells us that *II Augusta* played an important role in swinging Britain round to Vespasian's side in AD 69.[17] Rusticus may have played a key part, as acting commander, in bringing this about.[18] He died in office in his insalubrious eastern province, to be commemorated by the Spanish poet Martial. He was himself from the peninsula, as a recent paper by Sir Ronald Syme reminds us: 'Antistius Rusticus: a Consular from Corduba'.[19]

II Augusta was well disposed to its old legate, Vespasian, Tacitus says in connection with its conduct in AD 69.[20] A remarkable fact, seeing that he left the legion twenty-two years before. The answer no doubt lies with the centurions. These officers, unlike any other branch of the armed forces, could serve for life, and we know a fair number who went on for forty, fifty, or even sixty years.[21] Many centurions of course were in the ranks for a long time before being commissioned, others for a short time or indeed not at all, for direct commissions could be obtained. It is true that a great many inscriptions show us centurions moving from legion to legion and province to province. Still there is no difficulty in supposing that there were centurions of *II Augusta* in AD 69 who had served under Vespasian in the 40s. It is another matter to pinpoint any of these men in our list of centurions, most of whom belong to the second century. At best we may note that T. Julius Celer, buried at Asseria in Dalmatia, is probably a centurion from the Julio-Claudian period (but may only have been a *miles*). L. Arnius Bassus of Trieste began as a soldier in *XV Apollinaris* (then on the Danube), moved to the praetorian guard, held an auxiliary centurionate in Germany and then became a centurion, successively with *XIIII Gemina, II Augusta* and *VI Victrix;* but his dating is very uncertain. Blandius Latinus, buried at Geneva, held centurionates in three British legions, *VIIII Hispana* and *XX Valeria Victrix* as well as *II Augusta,* and also served in *I Italica,* which was formed in the 60s.

We can at any rate assign several officers firmly to the Flavian period. A man from Verona, L. Bellicius Sollers Ti. Claudius Alpinus by his full names, served his *tres militiae* in the 80s: as prefect of a cohort in Germany, he was decorated for the campaign of AD 83; then went to *II Augusta;* and commanded the *ala Augusta* in Syria. We must note that Alpinus rather than his father Augustanus (as generally supposed) in due course became procurator of Britain.[22] A word is called for on the names 'Ti. Claudius'. In almost all such cases this derives from a grant of citizenship under Claudius or Nero. However, given the origin and date of this father and son, it may be suggested that their citizenship goes back to the campaign in the Alps by Augustus' stepsons Tiberius and Drusus in 15 BC.[23] Alpinus was adopted by a man from Vicetia and changed his name to Bellicius Sollers; and later became a senator. From about the same period we now have a man of uncertain rank, but surely at least a centurion if not a tribune, Ofillius, named on a writing-tablet from Caerleon, with one or more colleagues, in charge of a detachment *'[ad opin]ionem peten[dam]'*, 'to get the pay estimates' (Figure 6.4). The *gentilicium* is uncommon, but there is too little evidence to link this man to the procurator of an imperial estate in Africa, L. Ofillius Felix, or to any other known Ofillius.[24]

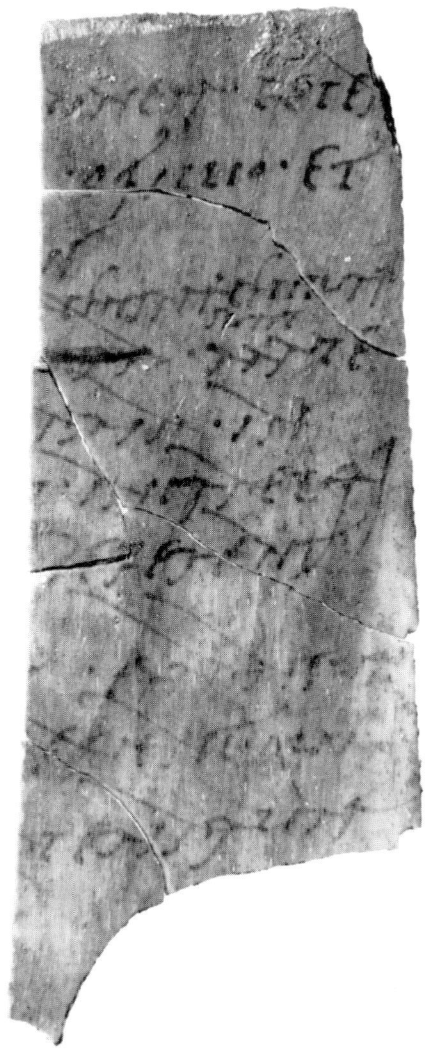

6.4 *Part of a wooden writing tablet referring to soldiers' duties. Ofillius, of uncertain rank, was placed in charge of a detachment sent to collect pay. Caerleon, 1985 (photograph: National Museum of Wales)*

We also know a chief centurion of the legion from this time, a man with a resplendent set of names, Cn. Pompeius Sex. f. Qui. Homullus Aelius Gracilis Cassianus Longus, probably a Roman from Spain, commemorated by his heirs at Rome after an impressive career. The initial stages are omitted, except that the military *dona* he won from an unnamed emperor, presumably Domitian, should belong to his previous period as a centurion, on the Rhine or Danube. The primipilate of *II Augusta* is the first post listed. Homullus went on to be tribune in the three units of the Rome garrison, and to a second primipilate attached to *legio X Fretensis* in Judaea, before returning to Britain as procurator, later becoming procurator in Lugdunensis and Aquitania and, finally, *a rationibus* (Minister of Finance).

I have already indicated that there is a long gap between Vespasian and the next legate of *II Augusta*. But I cannot resist referring to the slim possibility that we have a legate from the late 80s or early 90s on another Vindolanda writing-tablet. A strength report from period I (Tab Vindol Inv 88/841=*Tab Vindol II*, 154) gives details of the *cohors I Tungrorum* under its prefect Julius Verecundus. Well over half the unit is listed under *'absentes'*, including, at the heading of the list, forty-six men serving as *'singulares leg. officio Ferocis'*, which I take to be 'guards of the (legionary) legate in the *officium* of Ferox'. Only two senatorial bearers of this *cognomen* are known, both from precisely this period, Cn. Pompeius Ferox, consul suffect in AD 98, and Ti. Julius Ferox, consul designate in AD 99 when Pliny mentions his contribution to a famous senatorial debate calling him *'vir rectus et sanctus'*, 'an upright and honourable man'.[25] If either of these two is our man, I have a slight preference for the latter, for he certainly later governed a military province.[26] But this is by no means decisive and in any case it is not certain that *'officio Ferocis'* in the tablet goes with *'singulares leg.'* in the preceding line; and even if this is so, the legate's legion is unspecified.

Let us turn instead to facts. Two inscriptions from Numidia attest the legateship of A. Larcius Priscus, who went on from Caerleon to command the army there. The *cursus honorum* that they reveal has a highly unusual feature. Larcius Priscus, a native of Italian Antium (Anzio), and son of a man who had been an early supporter of Vespasian and commanded a legion under Titus in Judaea, began conventionally enough as *Xvir stlitibus iudicandis,* omitted a military tribunate and went on to be quaestor of Asia. This was evidently in the year AD 97. Before the end of the year his course changed dramatically. The new Emperor Nerva was far from secure. Among other problems, the governor of Syria was behaving in a threatening fashion. In October, Nerva solved the crisis by adopting the governor of Upper Germany as his son and Caesar. The Syrian governor and at least two of his legionary legates were sacked. Larcius Priscus became legate of *legio IIII Scythica* and acting governor of Syria.[27] After this startling – and probably very brief – episode, Priscus' career reverted to normal: he was tribune of the plebs, praetor, legate to a proconsul of Baetica and *praefectus frumenti dandi* (prefect in charge of the corn-dole distribution) – these two latter being undistinguished 'fill-in' posts – before taking up his command at Caerleon. His stay can be dated reasonably closely, for his immediate predecessor in Numidia is attested there in AD 105 and was consul in AD 106, when Priscus no doubt took over. This gives us the years *c* AD 104–6 for Priscus' legateship of *II Augusta.* His later career, apart from a proconsulship, in Narbonensis, and the consulship, is unknown. We have one other legate from the end of Trajan's reign and the beginning of Hadrian's, a Spaniard called Calpurnius Flaccus; but it is not quite certain that his legion was *II Augusta* – *VIII Augusta* is also possible.

The junior officers of the legion are better attested from this period. We have two *tribuni laticlavii* datable to Hadrian's reign, L. Annius Fabianus, consul at the beginning of the 140s after governing Dacia Superior, and C. Fabius Agrippinus, from a well-known Ostian family, consul in AD 148. An equestrian tribune from the time of Trajan or Hadrian is L. Aemilius Arcanus of Narbo in the south of France, presumably son of the poet Martial's friend Arcanus from that colony. He was tribune in three successive legions, the first perhaps *VII Gemina* in Tarraconensis (it is wrongly inscribed as *'XI Gem.'*), followed by *I Minervia,* normally at Bonn, and finally *II Augusta.* He was then made a senator by Hadrian, held the quaestorship and tribunate of the plebs, but died as praetor designate. From about the same time we have another L. Aemilius who was chief centurion of the legion, L. Aemilius Paternus, evidently a Spaniard from Tarraconensis. He was a Roman knight but after brief equestrian service, as *praefectus fabrum,* clearly preferred the guarantee of a lifelong career offered by the centurionate, serving first in *VII Gemina* and then in *I Minervia,* like the tribune Arcanus, then in two Danubian legions before being promoted to the Rome garrison. He was decorated by Trajan for service in both Dacian Wars and in the Parthian War, and was then transferred to *II Augusta* as *centurio trecenarius* (third in rank of the centurions) before achieving the position of *primus pilus.* His widow Atilia Vera, who commemorated him at Aeso, was herself, it seems, the grand-daughter of a chief centurion, indeed of one whose valiant attempt to protect the *aquila* of the newly formed *VII Galbiana* at the battle of Cremona deserves registering today.[28] An exact or near contemporary was L. Decrius Longinus, buried by his son, also a centurion, outside Naples (not their home: their tribe 'Sergia' points rather to Spain).[29] Like Aemilius Paternus, Longinus had begun as *praefectus fabrum,* but accepted a direct commission as centurion, in his case in *II Augusta.* He went on to *VII Gemina* in Spain and *XXII Deiotariana,* of which he became chief centurion. This eastern legion did not survive Hadrian's reign; and by coincidence Longinus' final posting was as camp prefect of the ill-starred Ninth (which, however, is now thought to have survived until AD 161).

Aemilius Paternus and Decrius Longinus might well have been involved in the building of Hadrian's Wall, from which we have the names of so many centurions of the British legions. Unfortunately a bare five only, Julius Tertullianus (Figure 6.5), M. Liburnius Fronto, Valerius Flavus, Volusius and Aelianus, can be assigned definitely to *II Augusta* – and Liburnius Fronto was actually in the Twentieth while the Wall was being built, although he turns up later, when Antoninus Pius was already emperor, dedicating an altar at Benwell, by then in the Second. However, study of the structures of the Wall, of which the most ingenious example is the monograph by C E Stevens, allows us to add the names of over thirty others, listed in the appendix as 'HW' with a question-mark before their names.[30] This is an appropriate moment to make some general comments about the nomenclature and origins of *II Augusta*'s centurions. By far the commonest *nomen* is 'Julius', with twelve specimens, reflecting the probable

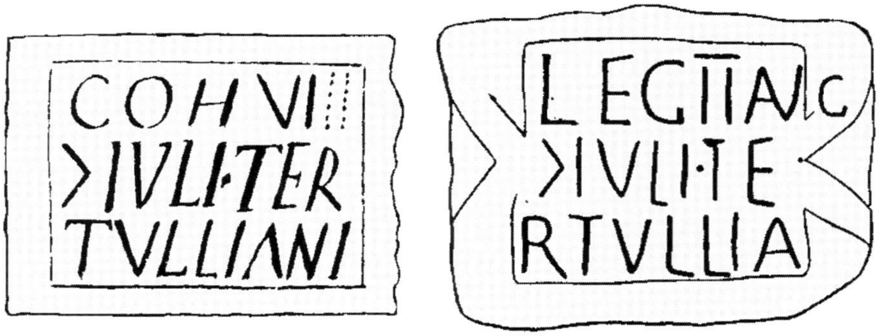

6.5 *Stones recording building work by the century of Julius Tertullianus of* II Augusta *on Hadrian's Wall* (RIB *I, 1970 now lost and 2016)*

origins of these men in the Caesarian and Augustan colonial foundations, an origin which they shared with three or four governors of Britain: Agricola, Frontinus (?), Julius Severus and Julius Verus. There are three Claudii, whose citizenship therefore goes back to Claudius or Nero, five Flavii, one Cocceius, one Ulpius and one Aelius – but no Aurelii or Septimii. Of the other commoner *gentilicia*, sometimes called 'colonial' because they reflect the activities in the western provinces of certain great families of the later Republic, we may note the four or five Pompeii, three or four Valerii, an Aemilius (already discussed) and a Cornelius, two Junii, a Licinius and a Marius. Licinius Nerva has a high-sounding name, that of a noble family with *consules ordinarii* (ie consuls after whom the year was named) in AD 7 and 65. His parents were pretentious, we may infer,[31] as were perhaps those of Cari(us) or Cari(sius) Scipio – his *cognomen* is almost wholly confined to the famous senatorial family. Three have rare or indeed otherwise unrecorded *gentilicia*, Congaonius being in the latter category while Audac(ilius) and Savius are uncommon. There are a few so-called 'fabricated' *gentilicia* which point to an origin in the Celtic north-west: Blandius, Secundinius, Severius, Tertinius, the last of whom is indeed attested at Lugdunum. Two have 'native'-sounding *cognomina*, Commidus (if that is the correct reading) and Hisavus; there is only one Greek name, Fenius Alexander. Most of the *cognomina* are standard enough, with men from North Africa being suitably equipped with the past participle forms there favoured: Fortunatus, Honoratus, Quadratus. Three have nicely military *cognomina*, hinting that they were soldiers' sons: Quintinius Aquila, Savius (or Sadius) Tiro, Severius Emeritus. One *cognomen* is apparently unexampled elsewhere, Subsequens. More could be said about the origin of these men, but we will shortly look at a few more in some detail so these remarks must suffice.[32]

With the accession of Antoninus our attention moves further north still, to the new frontier in Scotland, and we can place another known legate with confidence at the time of Lollius Urbicus' campaign and the building of the Antonine Wall. He is a surprising figure to find engaged in warfare on Rome's most northerly frontier, A. Claudius Charax, whose career inscription from his native Pergamum in Asia was first published thirty years ago. It is the base of a statue set up to him by the city of Patrae in Greece. Claudius Charax was already known to students of literature as the author of a lost forty book *Hellenica*. The inscription supplied his *praenomen* – a surprise in itself, for scarcely any Claudius was hitherto known to have been called Aulus (suggesting that he may really have been A. Julius Ti. Claudius Charax – his grandson was A. Julius Charax) – and, above all, his *cursus*. After listing his offices in descending order the people of Patrae added: 'the historian'. There is no mention of any preliminary post, either as *vigintivir* or military tribune. He began, perhaps a late entrant, with the quaestorship of Sicily, followed – I think the text requires emendation here – by the charge of the senatorial records and adlection to the rank of ex-aedile; then came the praetorship and the curatorship of the Via Latina, followed by command over *II Augusta*. It is rather puzzling to find a man with no previous military experience and no service in a western province (for Sicily was largely Greek) commanding the legion at this very time. The post can be readily dated, for Charax was consul in AD 147, having in the meantime governed Cilicia. Hence he should have commanded *II Augusta c* AD 141–3 and should have participated in Urbicus' campaign and supervised the legion's part in erecting the Antonine Wall. Perhaps he is indeed the man shown sacrificing on the Bridgeness distance slab that *II Augusta* put up (Figure 6.6).[33]

It is possible to detect two potential successors to Charax from this period, both recorded at Tibur (Tivoli) near Rome. One inscription is very fragmentary and not much can be said about it except that it records a legate of *II Augusta* under Antoninus. The other commemorates T. Marcius Clemens, whose career cannot be very precisely dated; his career up till *II Augusta*, his latest post, was conventional enough except that he omitted the vigintivirate; and his tribe 'Falerna' points to Italian origin.

We can assign with confidence to the 160s the altar to Jupiter Dolichenus, now lost, which is the first record so far of a legate at Caerleon itself, dedicated by a man called, among other names, Aemilianus, Calpurnius and Rufilianus (Figure 6.7). His title, *'legatus Augustorum'*, written out in full, surely indicates that it was still a novelty to have joint emperors, as was the case first from AD 161–9 under Marcus and Verus. Certain elements in Rufilianus' names are thought to hint at African origin. However this may be, we can now ascribe such a home with certainty to the man recorded by another lost

6.6 *Scene from the Bridgeness distance slab found at Bo'ness near the eastern end of the Antonine Wall in 1868. The man shown sacrificing may possibly be Claudius Charax, legate of* II Augusta *(*RIB *I, 2139) (photograph: reproduced by permission of the National Museums of Scotland)*

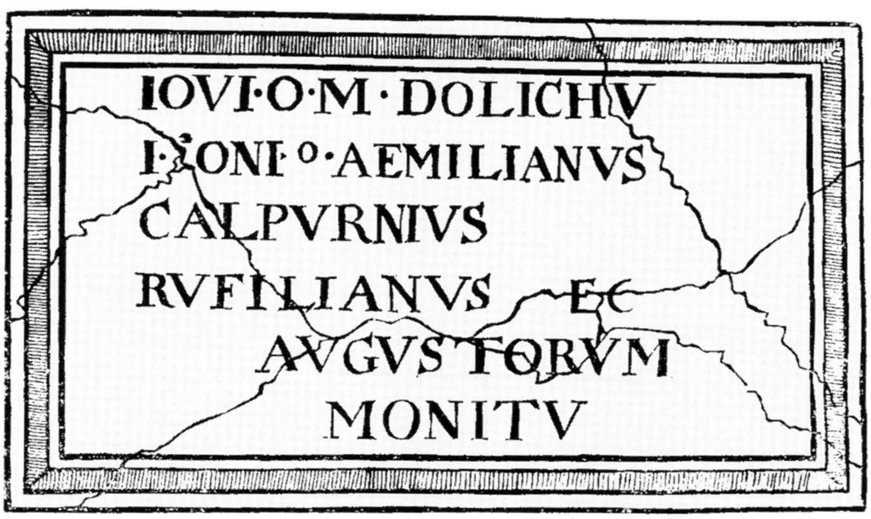

6.7 *Altar to Jupiter Dolichenus dedicated by Rufilianus, legate of* II Augusta. *Caerleon, 1653, now lost. From Gibson's Camden,* Britannia, *1695, 604 (*RIB *I, 320)*

Caerleon inscription, which registered not indeed his legionary command but the governorship of Cilicia, to which he clearly proceeded direct from the legionary legateship, as was the case with Charax. It is one of a number of examples of 'Inscriptions indicative of impending or recent movements', to use the title of an article by Eric Birley.[34] The drawing in Camden on which we rely gives us only 'Haterianus' as a definite name (Figure 6.8). But several of the others may now be restored with a strong degree of probability, since Ginette di Vita-Evrard has identified him with a member of an influential Lepcis Magna family, the Silii Plautii, where a fragmentary inscription gives his career up to the governorship of Cilicia. His quaestorship can also be dated from an inscription in neighbouring Cyrenaica, where he held it, to AD 165–6, making it probable that he came to Caerleon five or six years later, *c* AD 170–1.[35] One may also wonder if he was instrumental in securing a tribunate in *II Augusta* for a young man from Lepcis, P. Septimius Geta, whose tenure of this post was revealed by his *cursus*-inscription found in the 1940s. Unfortunately we do not know whether Geta was the elder or younger brother of the future emperor Septimius Severus. On the whole it is perhaps more probable that Geta served at Caerleon in the 160s. However, there was another African Roman who probably served with Silius Plautius Haterianus, a young man from Bulla Regia at the opposite end of Africa Proconsularis, C. Memmius Fidus Julius Albius.

This is an appropriate point to mention some of the North African centurions of our legion. Two inscriptions give us details of men who were directly commissioned. M. Julius Quadratus from Castellum Arsacalitanum in Numidia had served on the jury panels at Rome and was a recipient of the 'public horse' which denoted equestrian rank, before being commissioned as '*7 leg. XIII Gem. in Dacia*' then '*7 leg. III Aug. in Afr.*' and finally '*7 leg. II Aug. Britta.*', where he died on active service at the age of 38: '*def. Brittaniae in procinctu* ('died in Britain at the front') *v.a. XXXVIII h.s.e.*'. He cannot be exactly dated, but the Hadrianic–Antonine period looks probable. C. Octavius Honoratus, another Roman knight who chose the centurionate, was specifically described on his tombstone at Thuburnica in Africa as '*7 adlecto ex eq. R. a divo Pio in leg. II Aug.*', going on to legions in Moesia Superior, Syria and Pannonia Superior. Another African centurion of *II Augusta* who died in Britain was M. Petronius Fortunatus of Cillium after only six years service, first in the Upper German *XXII*

6.8 *Altar dedicated by Haterianus. He was probably legate of* II Augusta, *and on his appointment to the governorship of Cilicia set up this dedication without specifying the recent office. Caerleon, 1602, now lost. From Camden,* Britannia, *1607, 490* (RIB *I, 335)*

Primigenia, then in *II Augusta*. It is a pity that I cannot also accept as a centurion of our legion Fortunatus' remarkable father of the same names, whose career spanned fifty years, forty-six as a centurion, in a total of thirteen legions, beginning with *I Italica* in Moesia Inferior and ending with *I Adiutrix* in Pannonia. To be sure, his fifth legion is generally restored to read *'II A[ug.]'*, but I feel confident that it was *'II A[di.]'*, for he had previously served in the Syrian *VI Ferrata*, then in *I Minervia* and *X Gemina*, both normally on the northern frontiers but in the 160s temporarily transferred east along with *II Adiutrix*, for the duration of the Parthian War, in which Fortunatus was decorated.[36]

However, if I have removed one long-serving centurion from the list I can offer another as a substitute. M. Sabidius Maximus, who was in the army for forty years, twenty of them in the ranks, was centurion of a string of legions, according to his epitaph from Macedonia, including one that could be restored as *I[I Aug.]*. Since 'Sabidius' is rather an uncommon *gentilicium*, I suggest that this centurion could be the Sabidius Maximus who dedicated an altar to Silvanus at Cirencester. We have no clues as to why this Sabidius Maximus was at Cirencester, incidentally; he could have been on leave, and engaged in hunting; or on his way elsewhere, for example to Bath, where we meet C. Curiatius Saturninus, centurion of the Second, probably there merely to take the waters. I have included in the list C. Severius Emeritus, *'7 regionarius'*, even though his legion is unspecified, since I find it hard to believe that any other legion than *II Augusta* would have supplied officers and men to police the Bath *regio* in the second or third centuries. A third centurion on duty elsewhere was Vivius Marcianus, who died at London, although he is not credited with his rank in *RIB*; however, a centurial sign can readily be discerned before *'leg. II Aug.'* and he is actually portrayed holding the *vitis*, his officer's baton or swagger-stick (Figure 6.9).

You will not think it out of order if I refrain from detailed examination of the centurion M. Cocceius Firmus, the justly renowned dedicator of the five Auchendavy altars (Figure 4.13), and refer you to Eric Birley's article of 1936, republished in his *Roman Britain and the Roman Army*.[37] It is enough to register the fact that Firmus seems to derive from the lower Danube area, from the province of Moesia Inferior. From the province of Moesia Superior, specifically from Viminacium, came T. Vitellius Atillianus, who served a total of forty-eight years, with ten legionary

6.9 *Tombstone of the centurion Vivius Marcianus found in Ludgate Hill, London, 1669* (RIB *I, 17*) *(photograph: reproduced by permission of the Museum of London)*

centurionates, including one in *II Augusta*, and, after a spell back on the Danube, one in *VI Victrix*. Atillianus was buried at Lambaesis, where he ended up, as did a man from Cologne, C. Julius Maritimus, whose final post was also in *III Augusta*. Maritimus, however, had previously served in succession in each of the three British legions, *VI Victrix*, *XX Valeria Victrix* and *II Augusta*. One might conjecture that he had joined the Sixth while it was still in Lower Germany and that he moved with it to Britain. He might perfectly well be the centurion *'Marit'* who played a part in building Hadrian's Wall.

For a change we may turn to a centurion who gives his home as 'Roma', Ti. Claudius Fatalis, who began in *II Augusta*, had a spell in the Twentieth and then returned to *II Augusta* before moving to the Danube armies, to Cappadocia and finally to Judaea where he died at Jerusalem at the age of 42 after twenty-three years service, and was commemorated by his freed-woman and heir Cleonice. Claudius Fatalis cannot be dated very closely. Eric Birley has assigned him to the Hadrianic–Antonine period in general terms.[38] You will bear with me if I raise the possibility that our man may be the Fatalis mentioned in one of the most interesting Vindolanda letters, the four page, forty-five line long screed directed to one Candidus at Vindolanda (the address VINDOL is written across one corner of the back of page 4: Tab Vindol Inv 88/946=*Tab Vindol II*, 343) by Octavius. The letter concerns Octavius' dealings in supplies of corn and hides, and he is desperate for money. After appealing to Candidus to send him at least 500 *denarii* to bail him out, he remembers the relatively trifling sum of 8½ *denarii*. Candidus is to get on to Tertius about this money, which he received from Fatalis – 'he has not credited it to my account'. Apart from these four names, another seven men are mentioned, two of whom, Firmus and Spectatus, who are sent greetings and are thus at Vindolanda with Candidus, are mentioned along with Candidus in an account for corn, a *ratio frumenti* from the same level (Tab Vindol Inv 88/943=*Tab Vindol II*, 180), where *frumentum* is distributed by their orders, and hence they should be officers; 'legionary soldiers' are among those assigned rations. I am inclined to identify Octavius, Candidus, Firmus and Spectatus as legionary centurions. The tablets concerned are from the later, if not the latest, levels (ie period IV). The question arises whether they can be matched by the Hadrianic centurial stones or other evidence on stone from the frontier area. It remains very speculative, but Candidus might be Congaonius Candidus on our list or alternatively the Julius Candidus of *legio XX*.[39] Octavius could be the Octavius Sebanus responsible apparently for work on the vallum.[40] Tertius could be the centurion of that name on our list, and why not Fatalis also? There is even a faint chance that Firmus could be the celebrated M. Cocceius Firmus; and another name in the Octavius letter, that of Marinus, might be identifiable with the Mari[ ] of *RIB* I, 1650. I forebear from inflicting on you further conjectures about other persons mentioned in the Vindolanda tablets, although there is a possible link in the case of another centurion of *II Augusta* whose home, like Fatalis', seems to have been at Rome itself. This is M. Cornelius Saturninus. He and his brother buried their 82 year old father there. The puzzle is that the father is called 'M. Julius Hiero', while the brothers are both 'M. Cornelius Ti. f.'. Perhaps Hiero was actually the stepfather; but even so, Ti. goes with 'Julius' or 'Claudius', hardly with 'Cornelius'. On the whole it seems unlikely that this Cornelius Saturninus is the same as the chief centurion of that name, Pannonian by origin, whose son Cornelius Victor, *s(ingularis) c(onsularis)*, (member of the governor's guards), was buried at Vindolanda.[41]

A splendid character from central Italy served in *II Augusta* in the second century, C. Caesius Silvester, who began as a praetorian guardsman and was decorated in Trajan's Dacian Wars, was *beneficiarius* of a Guard Prefect and *evocatus Augusti* ('Emperor's Veteran', in an élite group of ex-praetorians with special duties) before being commissioned in *II Augusta*. He served in four other legions, including *XX Valeria Victrix*, before achieving the primipilate with *IIII Flavia* at Singidunum (Belgrade). He then retired to his home town, Tuficum in Umbria, where no fewer than fifteen inscriptions reveal him as a local magnate and benefactor of some distinction.

There are several more centurions who deserve a mention, but there is no more space to refer to others from the second century. We must now return to the higher ranks, and first of all to a legate from the time of Commodus. This was a troubled period for the army of Britain, beginning with an invasion in the north when a legate was killed, followed by a bitter war under the martinet Ulpius Marcellus. Shortly after his victory in AD 184 Marcellus was recalled, and the legionary legates were dismissed and replaced with equestrian prefects, a foretaste of what was to happen seventy-five years later. What prompted this move, ordered by the Guard Prefect Perennis, is unknown. However, we may note that a legionary legate called Priscus was actually hailed as emperor by his men in opposition to Commodus, which may have provoked wholesale dismissals. Shortly afterwards, a detachment of 1,500 men from the army of Britain turned up at Rome in mysterious circumstances and, after denouncing Perennis, were allowed to lynch him.[42] An inscription from Mainz may shed further light on this affair. It is a dedication to Liber and Apollo for the welfare of Commodus by Q. Aurel(ius) Polus Terentianus, legate of the Mainz legion *XXII Primigenia*, and of *II Augusta*. It is another of those 'inscriptions indicative of recent or impending movements' of which we have already seen an example. Further, we may note that it was only in unusual circumstances that a man commanded two legions; and that Polus Terentianus was later, in AD 193, consular governor of the Three Dacias, so that this dedication should be datable to *c* AD 185. He was presumably chosen to deal with an especially difficult mob, as *II Augusta* may well have been regarded at this time; perhaps indeed the legate Priscus was their commander and it was they who had tried to overthrow Commodus. Since Polus was not only legate of Dacia in AD 193, when Severus began his bid for power, but was later proconsul of Asia, he clearly supported the right side in the civil wars of AD 193–7. We have already noticed that Severus' brother Geta had served with *II Augusta*. Two former equestrian officers of the Second also served on the winning side in those wars. One, T. Cornasidius Sabinus, may well have been under the orders of Polus Terentianus *c* AD 185; he was later to govern one of the tiny Alpine provinces at the time of the showdown with Albinus in AD 196–7. The other, Ti. Claudius Candidus, had been with *II Augusta* in the mid-170s. Shortly after that he held a special supply post in the Marcomannic Wars and went on to a minor procuratorship before gaining senatorial rank. For reasons which escape us he was picked by Severus to command the Illyrian expeditionary corps formed from the Pannonian legions which, as the *exercitus Illyricus*, fought under him in all Severus' wars between AD 193 and 197.

We cannot even speculate about the officers who served in *II Augusta* in those years. The senior among them may well have lost their lives in AD 197 even if they survived the battle of Lugdunum. Transfers probably took place at the centurion level, of which a possible case is T. Flavius Virilis. He died at the age of 70, after forty-five years service, and was buried at Lambaesis in Numidia by his widow Lollia Bodicca, having had centurionates in *II Augusta*, *XX Valeria Victrix* and *VI Victrix*, then in the Lambaesis legion *III Augusta* and finally in the newly raised *III Parthica*. Lollia Bodicca was clearly British: her *cognomen* is another version of 'Boudicca', and one may surmise that an ancestor was enfranchised through the good offices of Lollius Urbicus. Virilis too was very probably a local boy, who joined his local legion and rose to centurion.

Britain may have had a short breathing-space after AD 197, apart from 'mopping up operations'. This is the period when the camp prefect P. Sallienius Thalamus from Hadria in eastern Italy made his two dedications for the welfare of Severus and his sons (Figure 6.10). Before long the legion was on the march again, this time back in the north. Its legate L. Julius Julianus made a dedication to imperial Victory at or near Corbridge, perhaps *c* AD 207 during the campaigns of Alfenus Senecio which preceded the imperial expedition of AD 208–11. Julianus is also known from a statue base giving part of his career, at Interamna in central Italy, of which he had been curator after his praetorship and where he probably had an estate. He went on from that post to be proconsul of Achaia before commanding *II Augusta*; and after his legionary command he proceeded to the governorship of Aquitania and the consulship. He might be the descendant of a freedman, to judge from his tribe, the 'Palatina'. Interamna was presumably his home, since his former *officiales* from Aquitania honoured him there, but he perhaps derived from nearby Ocriculum where a municipal worthy of the same name is recorded.

A few years later another man with equally commonplace names, who might derive from anywhere in the Empire, Ti. Claudius Paulinus, commanded *II Augusta*. The particular interest attaching to this man is owed to two factors. First, he is the

6.10 *Altar to Salus Regina dedicated by P. Sallienius Thalamus, prefect of* II Augusta, *and his two sons. Caerleon, 1845 (*RIB *I, 324) (photograph: National Museum of Wales)*

6.11 *Statue base inscribed by the Silurian local authority at Caerwent in honour of Tiberius Claudius Paulinus, legate of* II Augusta, *subsequently a provincial governor in Gaul, and in Britain AD 220. Caerwent, 1903 (*RIB *I, 311) (photograph: National Museum of Wales)*

honorand of the sole *cursus*-inscription surviving in Britain, the statue base at Caerwent erected in his honour by the *civitas Silurum* after he had moved on to higher things, the proconsulship of Narbonensis and the governorship of Lugdunensis (Figure 6.11). That he was a man whose patronage was worth cultivating is attested by the remarkable monument, erected over twenty years later in northern Gaul for Paulinus' former client T. Sennius Sollemnis, the 'marbre de Thorigny' to which H-G Pflaum devoted a monograph. This refers to a later stage in Paulinus' career, when he returned to Britain, now divided,[43] to command *VI Victrix* and at the same time govern Lower Britain – a post he was holding in the year AD 220, as a stone from High Rochester attests. Sollemnis had defended Paulinus successfully against a vote of censure at the *concilium Galliarum* and received his reward, with effusive letters, reproduced at Thorigny, one of which shows him to have been appointed *assessor* at York and to have received valuable presents.

We leap forward a quarter of a century to an inscription of especial interest today, set up on 23 September AD 244 (Figure 6.12). A dedication was made then to the *numina* of the emperors – unnamed: they were Philip the Arab and his son – and the *genius* of the legion, *'in honorem [aquilae]'*, by the chief centurion. His names are omitted in the text printed in *RIB*, but as Peter Herz points out, Manby's drawings allows us to restore them in part: *M. Va[ ] Fe[ ]*, followed perhaps by further names. He was

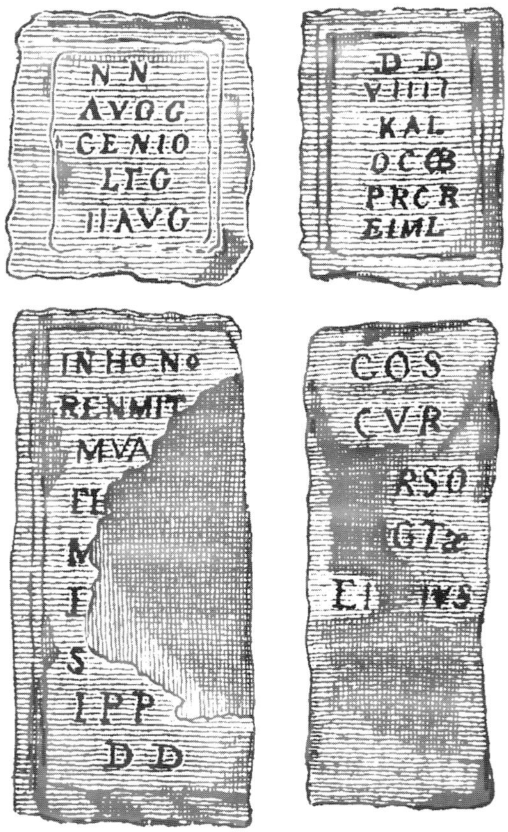

6.12 *Inscription set up in the headquarters building at Caerleon by the chief centurion in 'honour of the Eagle' on 23 September 244. Found 1800, now lost. From G W Manby,* An Historic and Picturesque Guide from Clifton through the Counties of Monmouth, Glamorgan, and Brecknock, *1802, 57, pl facing p 55* (RIB *I, 327)*

probably called *M. Va[lerius] Fe[lix]*, but could have been *M. Va[rius] Fe[stus]* or a variety of other possibilities.[44]

Finally we reach the 250s and it is then, we may presume, that the legate T. Flavius Postumius Varus, probably from a family whose home was at Cirta in Numidia and already senatorial in the Antonine era, restored a temple of Diana at Caerleon (Figure 6.13). A few years later, *c* AD 255–8, the barracks of the seventh cohort were rebuilt by the authority of the governor – of Upper Britain – Desticius Juba, a man from Concordia in northern Italy, and of the legate of *II Augusta* Vitulasius Laetinianus (Figure 6.14). The camp prefect Domitius Potentinus supervised the work. Neither Laetinianus nor Potentinus can be identified. Both *cognomina*, especially the former, are exceedingly rare; and 'Vitulasius' is scarcely found. He might be a descendant of the consul of AD 78, Sex. Vitulasius Nepos, and if so was probably Italian. Vitulasius Laetinianus has the melancholy distinction of being the latest legate of a legion on record anywhere in the Empire. In AD 260 Gallienus barred senators from military service, ending what we can fairly call a thousand year old tradition that Rome's citizen soldiers were commanded by the landholding élite. The new equestrian generals who took over were not even from the old style landed gentry who had supplied the equestrian officers of former times: they were tough hard-bitten ex-rankers of peasant origin.

It is difficult to find a single other officer of *II Augusta* after the 250s. We may note a late centurion, a man from Lugdunum, Tertinius Severianus, who commemorated his sister there with an elaborate funerary monument that is unmistakably later third century in its wording: *'memoriae perenni quieti aeternae Tertiniae Victorinae feminae rarissimae stolatae quondam spirito incomparabili'*, 'in perennial memory, and to the eternal rest, of the late Tertinia Victorina, most rare and Honourable lady, an incomparable spirit', with exhortations in Greek at the side (*'stolata'*, 'Honourable', was a title of rank, indicating membership of the councillor, curial, class). Victorina herself had buried her own husband Exomnius Paternianus – a splendid Celtic pseudo-*gentilicium* – with an epitaph of similar phraseology, in which she calls him *'quondam centurionis legionarii'*, legion unspecified. Perhaps he was also in *II Augusta* and married a fellow-officer's sister.

By the 250s changes were already in train which would lead to the transformation of the army, not merely of its officer-corps. Elements of *II Augusta* were sent to the Rhine and Danube in vexillations, which the establishment of the breakaway *imperium Galliarum* prevented from returning: they probably became the nucleus of new units in the later third century. One such 'field-service brigade' is immortalised in an unusual way, on the badge of its presumed commander Aurelius Cervianus, preserved in the Cabinet de France (Figure 9.1).[45] Two rows of legionaries, five in each, face one another, above the *vexilla*,

6.13 *Tablet recording the restoration of the Temple of Diana by T. Flavius Postumius Varus, c AD 250. Caerleon, 1603 (RIB I, 316) (photograph: National Museum of Wales)*

6.14 *Inscription recording the rebuilding of barracks for the seventh cohort at Caerleon c AD 255–8. The work was authorised by Desticius Juba, governor of Upper Britain and by the legate Vitulasius Laetinianus, and supervised by the camp prefect Domitius Potentinus. Found 1845 (RIB I, 334) (photograph: National Museum of Wales)*

flag-standards, of *'leg. XX V.V.'* on the left, with its wild boar, and *'leg. secunda Augus.'* on the right with its capricorn. Below the soldiers are the words *'utere felix'* and an assortment of animals, two peacocks, one dog chasing a hare, another a stag – neatly echoing the name of Cervianus – with a lion waiting to pounce beyond it. At the top, between the *vexilla,* is an *aquila*: an appropriate point at which to conclude.

ACKNOWLEDGEMENTS

I am happy to record my gratitude for the courtesy and hospitality shown to me by the staff of the National Museum of Wales, and by others, during my visit to Caerleon and Cardiff, and, in particular, to Richard Brewer for his help in preparing the Lecture for the press. [He has kindly allowed me to make revisions for this volume; see especially notes 10, 22, 26 and 40].

Appendix

Legati legionis II Augustae			*Fasti of Roman Britain*[46]
	T.	Flavius T. f. Qui. Vespasianus	pp 225–8
	A.	Larcius A. f. Quir. Priscus	235–7
	[C.	Calpurnius C. f.] Quir. Flaccus (?)	237
	A.	Claudius Charax	250–1
	ignotus Inscr It IV 143, Tibur		256
	T.	Marcius T. f. Fal. Cle[mens]	263
		...oni…Aemilianus...Calpurnius...Rufilianus	258
+	[?	Am]icus Cl[audius S]ilius Q. P[lautius] Haterianus	256–7
	Q.	Aurelius Polus Terentianus	261–3
	L.	Julius L. f. Pal. Julianus	265–6
	Ti.	Claudius Paulinus	189–90
	T.	Flavius Postumius Varus	266–7
		Vitulasius Laetinianus	267

Tribuni laticlavii			
+	L.	Vettius L. f. Stel. Statura	281
	L.	Antistius L. f. Gal. Rusticus	269–70
	L.	Annius Fabianus	272–3
	C.	Fabius C. f. Vot. Agrippinus	276
	P.	Septimius P. f. Qui. Geta	278
	C.	Memmius C. f. Qui. Fidus Julius Albius	278
		Rubrenus	280–1
	ignotus CIL XIV, 182, Ostia		282–3
	ignotus CIL X, 525, Salernum		284
	ignotus CIL XIV, 2926, Praeneste (?)		284
		Julius T. f. Insteius Paulinus (?)	284

Tribuni angusticlavii			*Devijver no*[47]
	L.	Aemilius L. f. Pap. Arcanus	A 74
		Attius Tuticanus	A 190
	M.	Aurelius Lucius	A 240
+	Ti.	Claudius Ti. f. Quir. Alpinus	C 122
	Ti.	Claudius Candidus	C 128
	T.	Cornasidius T. f. Fab. Sabinus	C 225
	L.	Domitius Proclus	D 29
	P.	Gavius Balbus	G 7
	L.	Marcius Optatus (?)	M 30 + Add. (vols 4–5)
*	[L.]	Marcius L. f. Ter. Sulla	M 31
	M.	Stlaccius C. f. Col. Coranus	S 81
	ignotus CIL II, 1086		*incertus* 3
	ignotus CIL XIV, 182		*incertus* 247
	ignotus CIL XIV, 4129		*incertus* 251
	ignotus CIL XII, 4186 (?)		*incertus* 227
	ignotus Rendic. Lincei 31 (1976) 84 (?)		*incertus* 126 bis

+ revision of the version in the *Fasti* is offered in this paper
* normally regarded as *'[prim. p]il.'*, but Devijver reads *'[trib. m]il.'*

Praefecti castrorum

P.	Anicius P. f. Ser. Maximus	*CIL* III, 6809
	Domitius Potentinus	*RIB* I, 334
	[J]ulius [Ba]ssus	*RIB* I, 317
	Poenius Postumus	Tacitus, *Annales* 14.37.3
P.	Sallienius P. f. Maec. Thalamus	*RIB* I, 324, 326

Praepositus vexillationi (?)

	Aurelius Cervianus	*CIL* XV, 7164

Centurions

		Aelius Romulus	*JRS* 1929=*RIB* II.8, 2503.116	Caerleon
	L.	Aemilius L. f. Gal. Paternus *(p.p.)*	*CIL* II, 4461=*ILS* 2661	Aeso
	Q.	Aquilius Lucius	*CIL* III, 261, cf. *CIL* VII, 689	Ancyra
	L.	Arnius L. f. Pup. Bassus	*CIL* V, 522	Tergeste
?		Arrius	*RIB* I, 1345–6, 1402	HW
?		Artius	*RIB* I, 409–10	Llanio
?		Atilius Natalis coh. VII	*JRS* 1959	HW
?		Atisius	*RIB* I, 1367	HW
		Audac. Romanus	*RIB* I, 1779	Carvoran
		Blandius C. f. Vol. Latinus	*CIL* XII, 2601	Geneva
	C.	Caesius C. f. Ouf. Silvester	*CIL* XI, 5696	Tuficum
?		Cari. Scipio	*RIB* I, 1936, *JRS* 1959	HW
		Cassius Priscus coh. VI	*RIB* 1415, 1869, *JRS* 1963	HW
		Claudius Cel[	*JRS* 1956	Caerleon
		Claudius Cup(itus)	*RIB* I, 344	Caerleon
	Ti.	Claudius Ti. f. Po[1.] Fatalis	*AE* 1939, 157	Jerusalem
	M.	Cocceius Firmus	*RIB* I, 2174–7	Auchendavy
?		Congaonius Candidus	*RIB* I, 1917	HW
	M.	Cornelius Ti. f. Saturninus	*CIL* VI, 3585	Rome
	C.	Curiatius Saturninus	*RIB* I, 146	Bath
	L.	Decrius L. f. Ser. Longinus	*AE* 1913, 22	Thermae Anianae
?		Eppius Constans coh. VI	*JRS* 1958, 1967	HW
?		Fenius Alexander coh. VI	*JRS* 1956	HW
?		Flavius Basus coh. VIII	*JRS* 1958	HW
		Flavius Julinus coh. X	*RIB* I, 343	Caerleon
?		Flavius Latinus coh. VIII	*RIB* I, 1409	HW
	T.	Flavius T. f. Pup. Rufus	*CIL* XI, 20	Ravenna
	T.	Flavius Virilis	*CIL* VIII, 2877=*ILS* 2653	Lambaesis
		Ful(vius) Macer	*RIB* I, 345	Caerleon
		Ful[vius] Potitus	*JRS* 1940=*RIB* II.3, 2427.13	Caerleon
		M F S	*RIB* II.1, 2411.65	Brough under Stainmore
?		Hellenius	*RIB* I, 1515	HW
?		Hos(tilius) Lupus	*RIB* I, 1410	HW
?		Humanius	*RIB* I, 1413	HW
	C.	Julius Caecinianus	*RIB* I, 346	Caerleon
?	T.	Julius T. f. Cla. C[e]ller	*CIL* III, 15024	Asseria
?		Julius Commidus coh. X	*RIB* I, 1514	HW
		Julius Gemellus coh. VIII	*JRS* 1961	Caerleon
		Julius Honoratus	*RIB* I, 1299	Wallsend
		Julius Marcellinus	*RIB* I, 1880	Birdoswald
	C.	Julius C. f. Cla. Maritimus Ara	*CIL* VIII, 2907, cf *RIB* I, 1656	Lambaesis

	Julius Maximus	*JRS* 1933	Caerleon
?	Julius Primus coh. VIII	*RIB* I, 1369, *JRS* 1958	HW
	M. Julius C. f. Quir. Quadratus	*AE* 1957, 249	Castellum Arsacalitanum
	Julius Subsequens	*JRS* 1933=*RIB* II.1, 2409.5	Caerleon
	Julius Tertullianus coh. VIII	*RIB* I, 1970, 2016	HW
	Junius M[ ] coh. V[ ]	*Brit* 1971	Caerleon
	Junius Nepos	*Brit* 1977	Caerleon
?	Juv(entius)	*RIB* 1407	HW
	M. Liburnius Fronto	*RIB* I, 1330	Benwell
	Licinius Nerva	*RIB* I, 347	Caerleon
	Livius	*RIB* I, 336	Caerleon
	M. Lollius Venator	*JRS* 1967	Piercebridge
?	Marcius Rufus coh. VIIII	*RIB* I, 1943, *JRS* 1959	HW
	Marius	*CIL* XII, 2355	nr Vienne
	C. Octavius Q. f. Cornel. Honoratus	*CIL* VIII, 14698=*ILS* 2655	Thuburnica
?	Pedius Qui( ) coh. IIII	*RIB* I, 1400	HW
	(M. Petronius Fortunatus pater)	*CIL* VIII, 217=*ILS* 2658+add.	Cillium
	M. Petronius Fortunatus filius	ibid	ibid
?	Pompeius coh. VII	*RIB* I, 1649	HW
?	Pompeius Aemilianus	*JRS* 1959	HW
?	Pompeius Albinus coh. VI	*JRS* 1961	HW
	Cn. Pompeius Sex. f. Qui. Homullus Aelius Gracilis Cassianus Longus *(p.p.)*	*CIL* VI, 1626	Rome
?	Pompeius Rufus	*RIB* I, 1447	HW
	Quintinius Aquila	*JRS* 1927, *RIB* I, 349=*RIB* II.1, 2409.7	Caerleon
	Roesius Moderatus coh. VI hast. prio.	*RIB* I, 341	Caerleon
?	Rom. Pro( )	*RIB* I, 1519	HW
	Rufinius Primus coh. III	*RIB* I, 339	Caerleon
?	M. Sabidius Maximus	*RIB* I, 104, *AE* 1937, 101	Cirencester, Macedonia
	Savius Tiro	*RIB* I, 350	Caerleon
?	Secundinius Verullus	*JRS* 1958	HW
?	C. Severius Emeritus	*RIB* I, 152	Bath
	Statorius Maximus coh. I	*RIB* I, 395	Caerleon
?	Terentius Cantaber coh. I	*RIB* I, 1568	HW
	Tertinius Severianus	*CIL* XIII, 1898	Lugdunum
?	Turrianius Priscus	*RIB* I, 1416	HW
?	Ulpius Paullus	*JRS* 1958	HW
	M. Va[ ] Fe[ ] *(p.p.)*	*RIB* I, 327	Caerleon
?	Valerius Flavinus	*RIB* I, 416	Castell Collen
	Valerius Flavus coh. II	*RIB* I, 337, 1362–3	Caerleon, HW
	Valerius Maxsimus coh. VIII	*RIB* I, 351–2	Caerleon
	Vecilius	*RIB* I, 353	Caerleon
	Vibius Proculus	*RIB* I, 354, *JRS* 1928=*RIB* II.1, 2410.4	Caerleon
	Vibius Severus	*JRS* 1929=*RIB* II.1, 2409.10–11	Caerleon
	Vinuleius Super	*JRS* 1927=*RIB* II.1, 2410.5	Caerleon
	T. Vitellius T. f. Atillianus Viminaci	*CIL* VIII, 3001	Lambaesis
	Vivius Marcianus	*RIB* I, 17	London
?	Voconius Co[	*RIB* I, 1412	HW
	Volusius	*RIB* I, 1441, 1965	HW
	]arinius Aureli( )	*RIB* I, 913	Cardewlees
?	]isius Verus	*RIB* I, 1408	HW

	Aelianus	*RIB* I, 2024, 1847	nr M/C 65, HW
?	Alexander	*RIB* I, 1554	HW
?	Aprilis coh. VI	*RIB* I, 1401	HW
?	Dentio	*RIB* I, 400	Gelligaer
	Ge(r)manus	*Brit* 1971	Caerleon
	Hisavus	*JRS* 1956	Caerleon
?	Marcus	*RIB* I, 415	Castell Collen
	Paetinus coh. V	*RIB* I, 340	Caerleon
?	Peregrinus	*RIB* I, 401	Tretower
?	Probus	*RIB* I, 1868	HW
?	Pro(culus?)	*RIB* I, 1364	HW
	Rufinus	*JRS* 1957	Caerleon
	Sanctus	*RIB* I, 2024	nr M/C 65
	Secundinus	ibid	ibid
?	Tertius	*JRS* 1957	HW
?	Valens	*RIB* I, 402	Tretower
?	Verio	*RIB* I, 411	Llanio
?	Vic[tor]	*JRS* 1937=*RIB* II.7, 2501.1	Caerleon
	]ellinus [coh.] II	*RIB* I, 338	Caerleon
	Pian[	*RIB* I, 348	Caerleon
?	I[	*RIB* I, 1361	HW
?	Imi[	*RIB* I, 1406	HW
?	]i inana coh. VII	*JRS* 1960	HW
	Er[ ]	*JRS* 1960=*RIB* II.6, 2494.126	Caerleon
	Cu[ ]	*JRS* 1940=*RIB* II.3, 2427.25	Caerleon
	S( ) A( ) coh. IV	*RIB* I, 2137	Cramond
	(Exomnius Paternianus)	*CIL* XIII, 1854	Lugdunum

Rank uncertain

	Ofillius	*Brit* 1986	Caerleon

Glossary

Aquilifer: eagle-bearer
Beneficiarius: literally 'recipient of a favour', a non-commisssioned officer who served as aide to a senior officer
Cognomen: the Roman third name
Cursus honorum: literally 'passage of honours', ie career
Gentilicium: the Roman second, or family name
Miles: soldier
Nomen: also called *gentilicium,* q v
Praefectus castrorum: prefect of the camp
Praefectus fabrum: literally 'prefect of engineers', a post which later became a kind of senior staff officer
Praenomen: the Roman forename
Primus Pilus: chief centurion of the legion
Principales: senior non-commissioned officers receiving pay-and-a-half or double pay
Tres Militiae: the three stages of military service for equestrian officers
Tribunus angusticlavius: 'narrow stripe' tribune, ie equestrian military tribune
Tribunus laticlavius: 'broad stripe' tribune, ie senatorial military tribune
Vigintiviri: literally 'the twenty men', a group of pre-senatorial junior magistrates at Rome
Xviri stlitibus iudicandis: 'the ten men for judging lawsuits', who formed half of the *vigintiviri* each year

Notes

1 Jarrett 1964a remains of great value; as does the section on *II Augusta* in the monumental article by Ritterling 1924/5, cols 1457–66.

2 von Domaszewski/Dobson 1967, 41; 71 f.

3 Speidel 1976.

4 Herz 1975.

5 Kajanto 1965, 360.

6 Alföldy 1974, 135.

7 Alföldy 1969, 141 f.

8 Kajanto 1965, 220; see Alföldy 1969, 286 for the Dalmatian examples; also Alföldy 1967, 130.

9 *CIL* III, 2386.

10 *CIL* III, 14703. The editors prefer to read the *aquilifer*'s *gentilicium* as 'Vittius' rather than 'Vettius' in *Tab Vindol II*, 214. This is certainly possible, but there appears to be a cross-stroke (which they think, however, 'is not ink') and the letter I elsewhere, for example in 'Adiutor' and *'aquilifer'*, is markedly different. (The apparent serif at the top left of this E or I could well have been a continuation of the right-hand stroke of the V.) I happily accept their reading of 865=*Tab Vindol II*, 213 and have amended my text accordingly. They also identify two other letters (*Tab Vindol II*, 215–16) as addressed to Cassius Saecularis.

11 A R Birley 1981, 225 ff; 269 ff discusses the *legati* and *tribuni laticlavii* (some revisions are referred to in the notes, below). The equestrian officers are handled by Devijver in 5 vols, 1976–93. Dobson 1978, lists the *praefecti castrorum* and *primi pili*, with discussion of several of them. There is no up to date list of the centurions. Ritterling 1924/5, 1465 f could produce some forty names (a few of these belonging to the period before AD 43). The Index to *RIB* I (index published 1983) gives only thirty-one names of centurions of *II Augusta* attested in Britain, avoiding conjectural attributions (referred to in n 30 below); there are a few more in *RIB* II.

12 Since Vespasian and the other persons listed in the Appendix to this paper are furnished with basic references there, I refrain from inflating the annotation unless new information is to hand. For Vespasian it is a pleasure to be able to refer to Wiseman 1981.

13 *PIR*^{2} F 399.

14 Balland 1981, no. 48.

15 Tacitus, *Annales* 14.37.

16 Syme 1958, 764 f.

17 Tacitus, *Historiae* 3.44.

18 E Birley 1978.

19 Syme 1983, 359–74.

20 Tacitus, *Historiae* 3.44.

21 E Birley 1963–64; see esp his appendix, 32 f.

22 *CIL* V, 3337 (Verona); discussed by A R Birley 1981, 289 ff. Salomies 1992, 45 ff, has convinced me that in *CIL* V, 3337, *[Ti]b. Claudio Tib. f. Quir. Augustano patri Bellici Sollertis proc. Aug. prov. Britain. Claudia Ti. f. Marcellina socero optimo, proc.* should be understood as *proc(uratoris)*, ie referring to Bellicius Sollers, and not as *proc(uratori)*, taken with his father Augustanus. The identity of Alpinus with Bellicius Sollers is guaranteed by *CIL* V, 3356=*ILS* 2710, also dedicated by his wife, which gives his career as an equestrian officer, including the tribunate of *II Augusta*. Salomies points out that 'it is best to assume that at least two lines are missing' from the beginning of this stone and that it 'originally began with the adoptive items of our man's nomenclature'.

23 Cf remarks of Syme 1977, 138.

24 *PIR*^{2} 0 85, cf 83–4, 86–90.

25 Pliny, *Epistulae* 2.11.5.

26 Pliny, *Epistulae* 10.87.3. M A Speidel 1995, argues that only governors should normally have had *singulares*, but that Ferox might have been a legionary legate who became acting-governor after the execution of Sallustius Lucullus (Suetonius, *Domitian* 10.3). If this is correct, it would perhaps slightly strengthen the possibility that he was legate of *II Augusta*, the legion nearest to London.

27 Syme 1958, 631 f.; and elsewhere.

28 Tacitus, *Historiae* 3.22.

29 Dobson 1978, 232, suggests the Paelignian part of central Italy as *origo*, on the grounds of the *nomen* and tribe. But the tribe 'Sergia' is much commoner in Spain; and names like 'Decrius' are also common there.

30 Stevens 1966, esp 101, 138. I have also included centurions from Castell Collen, Gelligaer, Tretower and Llanio, who might of course have been auxiliaries; these too are marked with a query.

31 See some examples from elsewhere: A R Birley 1988, 12 f.

32 Perhaps I may refer to A R Birley 1979, 14 ff; 72 ff, for discussion of Roman nomenclature in general and of the centurions who served in Britain.

33 *RIB* I, 2139: his face, alas, is missing

34 E Birley 1979.

35 di Vita-Evrard 1982.

36 A R Birley 1979, 79; for a different view, E Birley 1963–64, 23 f.

37 E Birley 1936.

38 E Birley 1941, 55.

39 *RIB* I, 1632, 1646, 1674.

40 *RIB* I, 2082; the name 'Seranus' (read by Hübner) is perhaps more plausible. It is quite common, whereas 'Sebanus' is unmatched. The editors of *Tab Vindol II* have identified another Vindolanda letter, no. 349, also from period 4, like no. 343, as being (as the address side shows) from a man named Fatalis, of whose *gentilicium* only the last two letters, *-io,* are fully legible, the traces of the previous one being, in their view unlikely to be a D. They do not publish a photograph. That taken by Alison Rutherford (Neg no. K/195147/8, taken on 5 December 1987, now in the Vindolanda Museum) shows only the faintest of marks before the *-io,* so no firm decision is possible. They do not report further faint traces of lettering below the name (and not written on an upward slant, as the name is), which might be taken as *.en..ri..* , perhaps *[c]en[tu]ri[one]*?

41 *RIB* I, 1713.

42 A R Birley 1981, 140 ff; 260 f.

43 I continue to regard the year AD 214 as the likeliest for the first division of Britain, as argued in A R Birley 1981, 168 ff. Had space permitted, I would have liked at this point to discuss the centurion of *II Augusta* M. Lollius Venator, in charge of a detachment of *VI Victrix* and of men from both Germanies at Piercebridge. E Birley 1967, dates this to *c* AD 217. Cf also Jarrett 1964a, 58 ff, for evidence of men from *II Augusta* in the Lower province after the division.

44 Hertz 1975, 193 f. I hesitate to mention the fact that Herz here prefers the reading *'in honorem mil[it]'*, based on Manby's drawing, rather than *'in honorem [aquilae?]'* as in *RIB*.

45 See the remarks of Jarrett 1968, 88 f.

46 A R Birley 1981.

47 Devijver 1976–93.

CHAPTER 7

THE FRAMEWORK OF AN IMPERIAL LEGION

MICHAEL P SPEIDEL

INTRODUCTION

Isca, now Caerleon, is a thought-provoking place. It stands out as one of the very few well-preserved and well-excavated legionary fortresses, although there once were more than thirty legions, all of which changed their base several times over a period of 400 years. As one walks through the fortress at Caerleon with its barracks, baths, and training-grounds, or as one studies a plan of the site, questions are bound to arise. Can we learn the strength and structure of a legion from the layout of its base? Do the discoveries made at the fortress tell us how the legion fought?

Some answers to these questions may be found in the remains of the buildings, either at Caerleon or, for instance, at the fortress at Inchtuthil in Scotland. But in order to understand the strength and function of the legions and its sub-units we can turn also to the literary sources, and to what Rome's military technicians and historians have to say about these matters. And when their reports get sketchy and confusing – as they often do – help may come from inscriptions set on buildings, or carved on altars and gravestones.

The archaeological evidence is gathered in some very useful books. For Caerleon we have Boon's *Isca*; for Inchtuthil there is a fine excavation report; and, to name but one more, we have von Petrikovits' comprehensive survey of the interior buildings in legionary fortresses throughout the Empire. The state of our knowledge is still patchy, however, and further excavations at Caerleon and other fortresses will certainly teach us much that is new about the framework and the life of the legions.[1]

The literary sources have been known for centuries, but they are not all trustworthy. We have to check them against archaeological evidence and against inscriptions before we can say to what historical period they refer and how reliable they are. Only for Caesar's time are we well informed, because of his own reports on the Gallic and the Civil Wars. For the time of the Empire our knowledge of the tactics of the legions is still surprisingly poor and chaotic. Only a few islands of certainty have emerged from an unruly sea of guesswork and surmise as to what cohorts and *centuriae* really did. Even von Domaszewski, the master of Roman army studies, who was seldom at a loss for a hypothesis, thought we would perhaps never learn how the imperial legions fought, so inadequate are the literary sources.[2] Tacitus, for one, offers a rousing tale of the battle on Mons Graupius, but without telling us anything of how the legions were arrayed in battle-lines. Small wonder that for decades scholars have argued over the structure and the tactics of the legion with such fact-starved and complicated opinions that today one might fear to tread in this minefield.

Yet there is progress and profit in such studies, for excavations are going on in many legionary fortresses, and inscriptions keep coming to light at a steady rate each year. Among these inscriptions there is, every now and then, one that can establish a point once and for all. Or else, a series of similar inscriptions accrues over time, reaching a 'critical mass' that reveals a pattern. In this way, archaeology and inscriptions allow us new insight into how the legions were structured for housing, work, and fighting. The history of warfare, like any other field of history, holds out the promise of bringing the past alive. Each year our growing evidence brings us a step closer to our goal, and one may claim that we now have a far better understanding of the order in which the imperial legions fought.

THE STRENGTH AND STRUCTURE OF THE LEGION

A legion of the Early Empire, like *II Augusta* that came in AD 74 or 75 to establish the fortress at Isca, comprised some 6,000 men in ten cohorts. This was its book-strength, however, and its actual strength was perhaps much less. Yet even the book-strength of a legion, its standard number of soldiers, and its detailed structure, have always been a matter of controversy among scholars. By far our most reliable literary source for this is Hyginus' essay on 'How to lay out a camp'. Writing at the end of the first century AD, Hyginus states that a cohort had 480 men and that the first cohort was of double strength. Hence all ten cohorts together would amount to 5,280 men for the legion in the field. If one adds the *remansores,* who guarded the fortress and the relevant frontier sector, one comes to some 6,000 men.[3]

Hyginus' statement that the first cohort was of double strength has been confirmed for the Flavian period by excavations at Caerleon (Figure 7.1), Inchtuthil and Nijmegen.[4] At other legionary fortresses, however, the situation is uncertain, for some evidently held less than a full legion, while in others the barracks of the first cohort are hard to trace. It has also been suggested that if we knew the layout of the original timber barrack blocks at Caerleon, they might demonstrate that the first cohort had shrunk somewhat between AD 74 and the time the barracks were rebuilt in stone in the late Flavian period. This seems to be the case at Nijmegen, for during this period some double barrack blocks of the first cohort gave way to single-room blocks of the kind found also at Caerleon. Excavations, however, have yet to prove that the first cohort lost all its additional strength after the Flavian period. And since three discharge lists of the years AD 134, 157, and 195, each time show the first cohort to have dismissed about twice as many veterans as any of the other nine cohorts, it might well be that the first cohort was stronger, if not twice as strong as the others, during much of the first two centuries of the Empire.[5]

During the early Republic the legion had three main battle-lines, the *pilani, principes,* and *hastati.* The front ranks of each line were the *priores,* the rear ranks the *posteriores.* When Marius, in the second century BC, divided the legion into ten cohorts, each cohort

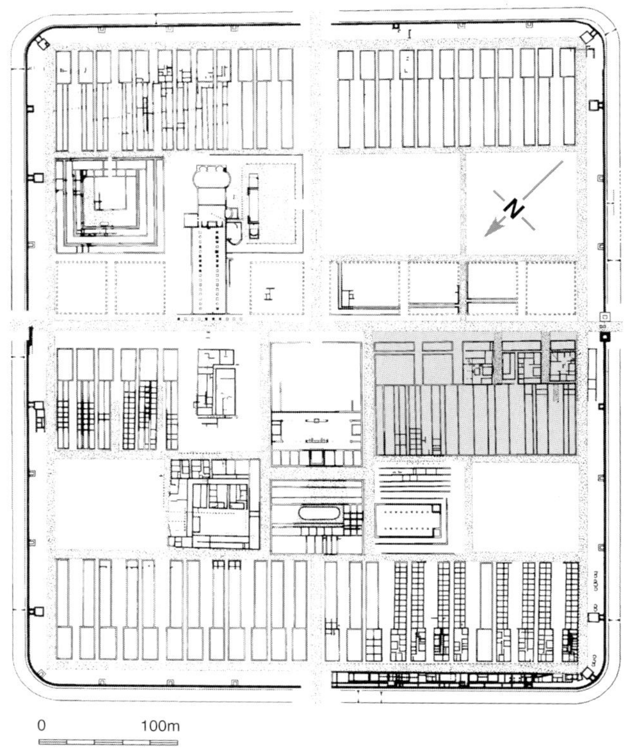

7.1 *Plan of the legionary fortress at Isca–Caerleon. The barracks of the first cohort are highlighted*

kept its one-tenth of the three lines. This remained so even during the Empire, for a regular cohort then had six *centuriae* named after the old battle-lines:

pilus prior
pilus posterior

princeps prior
princeps posterior

hastatus prior
hastatus posterior

The fact that a cohort had six *centuriae* is known from Hyginus' treatise and from the layout of the barracks at excavated legionary fortresses. The first cohort, however, although it was twice as strong, may at times have had only five *centuriae* and only five regular centurions. Though scholars by no means agree on this number, only five (double) *centuriae* of the first cohort are known at Nijmegen and Inchtuthil, where their barrack blocks have been found, together with five peristyle houses for the five centurions. Evidence for five centurions in the first cohort also comes from Caerleon (Figure 7.1), where three centurions' houses have been excavated and there is room for only two more. The number of five centurions in the first cohort seemed also to be confirmed by an inscription unearthed at Lambaesis, the fortress of the African legion. That text, carved about AD 200 and brought up-to-date in 253, mentions on both occasions only five centurions of the first cohort. Also, among the many inscriptions telling of the centurions of the first cohort, there was until recently none with the rank of *pilus posterior.* Now, however, one has come to light and we may assume that the first cohort was standardised at some time in the second century.[6]

Assuming a depth of four and a width of twenty men per *centuria,* one may thus envisage the structure of the legion as in Figure 7.2.

Other aspects of the structure of the legion have also become somewhat better understood, among them the role of the maniple. During the Republic, the three groups of *centuriae* – the *pili, principes* and *hastati* – were arrayed in pairs, the so-called maniples. These were thought by some scholars to have retained a role in the administration of the legion during the first and second centuries AD. Maniples, however, are not mentioned in the inscriptions and papyri of the Early Empire, not even in the Julio-Claudian period, and as a consequence they are unlikely to have played any administrative role. As for tactics, one might suppose that in the battle-line the *posteriores* backed up the *priores,* but proof is hard to come by. In the legionary fortresses barrack blocks are usually arranged in facing pairs, but this alone is a weak argument for the existence of maniples, all the more since at Caerleon and in Hyginus' layout for a camp the *centuriae* at times are not paired. On the other hand a good, but not conclusive, argument for the existence of maniples exists in two inscriptions that mention *priores* and *posteriores* as paired *centuriae.*[7]

By contrast, the presence of the 120 legionary horsemen at all times is no longer in any doubt. Surprisingly Hyginus does not mention them, perhaps because in the field they stayed with the legionary commanders, whose bodyguards they were. An inscription from Lambaesis, hitherto overlooked, suggests that they were housed together as a unit, although their barracks cannot be positively identified at Inchtuthil, Nijmegen, or Caerleon. Scholars, noting the absence of the legionary horse in Hyginus, have suggested that they were abolished under Vespasian, and then re-instituted by Hadrian. Not long ago, however, an inscription was found recording the presence of the legionary horse in the middle of that very period, and we may conclude, with some confidence, that they existed throughout the first three centuries of the Empire.[8]

The structure of the legion and of the cohorts is illuminated by the sixty ranks of the centurionate, the famous *Rangordnung.* But that, too, is hotly debated. One theory maintains that only the centurions of the first cohort, the so-called *primi ordines,* had different ranks, while the centurions of cohorts II–X all ranked equally.[9] The opposing theory holds that all sixty centurions differed in rank, and that hence any transfer was, in effect, a promotion; even within a cohort one could rise five steps from the lowly *hastatus posterior* to the lofty *pilus prior.*[10] The latter theory is undoubtedly right, for in the inscriptions

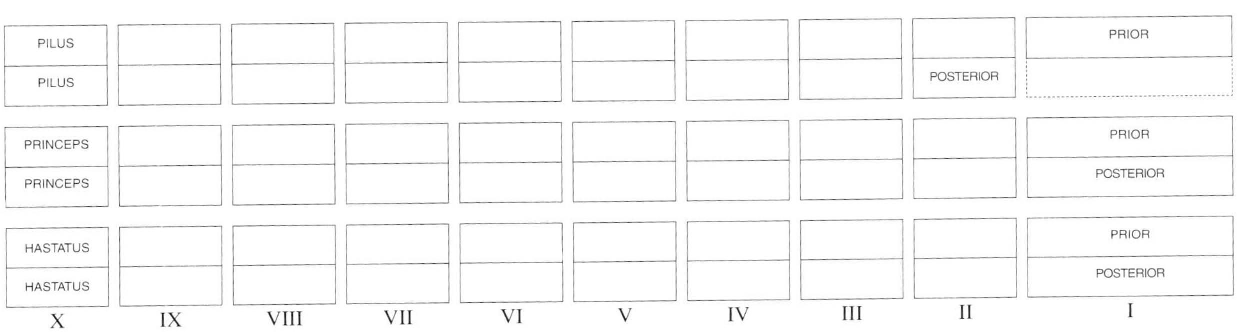

7.2 *The ten cohorts and their* centuriae

one so transferred is called *promotus,* and the force of the word is such that a promotion in rank must be meant.[11]

We may, therefore, see the hierarchy of the centurions as sixty positions all differing in rank. A higher rank in this sense need not have meant higher pay, nor did the centurions' houses in the legionary fortresses differ at all in size for cohorts II–X. Rank, rather than seniority, seems best to describe the difference between the sixty centurions, for they had different titles. Higher rank, then, meant mainly getting closer to promotion into the outstanding positions of the first cohort.[12] Unfortunately, we do not yet know how much the six ranks inside a cohort counted towards promotion to the next cohort, but certainly highly qualified men could leap-frog many of the positions. There are also compelling reasons to believe that this *Rangordnung* remained the same throughout the first three centuries of the Empire.

What matters greatly, however, is that not only were the centurions marked by these ranks, but the *centuriae* also – that is the men themselves. This is known from Egyptian papyri, where it is fully spelled out,[13] and nearer at home from building inscriptions of *legio II Augusta.* Thus, a stone from Caerleon (Figure 7.3) reads:

> *C(o)hor(tis) VI (sextae) hast(atus) prio(r),*
> *7(centuria) Roesi(i) Modera(ti)*
> The *hastatus prior* of the sixth cohort,
> the *centuria* of Roesius Moderatus (built this)

The meaning of this inscription has not been properly understood. In the *Roman Inscriptions of Britain,* the term *hastatus prior* is taken to mean the rank of the centurion himself. Yet *hastatus prior* here cannot refer to the centurion or his rank, for if it did, the text would have to begin with the sign for a centurion or with the centurion's name. Clearly, the men themselves are meant, and they are that part of the sixth cohort which belonged to the *hastatus prior.*[14] The same mistake was made about three further building inscriptions (Figure 7.4), very likely also of *legio II Augusta,* from Hadrian's Wall. There, too, the rank is mentioned but not the centurion, as is quite clear from the word order: it describes the men themselves. The first two inscriptions are to be read *Coh(ortis) (quartae) [has]ta(tus) pos(terior) [c(enturia) Mar]ciana* (Figure 7.4a) and *Coh(ortis) (quartae) pr(inceps) pos(terior) c(enturia) Iul(i) Vitalis* (Figure 7.4b). In the first of these two, the centurion, indicated in the adjectival form, is not even the commander of the unit any longer. In the third example, the two *hastati centuriae* sign together: *Coh(ortis) (quartae) hastati* (Figure 7.4c).[15]

Many other examples are known of *centuriae* which are described by their position rather than by the name of their centurion, particularly from the second and third centuries, and some from as late as the Philippi emperors.[16] It is, therefore, certainly false to say that 'the differentiation of troops by reference to their projected position in the line of battle became pointless', or that 'the names *hastati, principes,* and *pilani* were retained simply for distinguishing the rank of the sixty *(sic)* centurions in a legion'.[17] Quite the opposite: it is safe to say that the identification of the men by the position of their *centuria* survived throughout the first three centuries of the Empire.

But why is a *centuria* sometimes identified by its position rather than simply by the name of its commander? As indicated above, these positions –

7.3 *A building inscription from Caerleon* (RIB *I, 341) (photograph: National Museum of Wales)*

7.4 *Three building inscriptions from Hadrian's Wall: a Castlesteads* (RIB I, 2001)*; b Drawdikes Castle, near Stanwix* (RIB I, 2023)*; c Carlisle* (RIB I, 2032)

the same as the ranks of the centurions – were originally places in the battle-lines. Could it be that they still signify projected positions in battle? If so, they would help us solve that great riddle of the Roman imperial legions: its order of battle.

WEAPON SPECIALISTS

Although the literary sources reveal next to nothing of the imperial legion's battle-order, several very helpful inscriptions have been found over the years. At the beginning of the last century the store-rooms for weapons in the fortress of *legio III Augusta* at Lambaesis yielded several inscriptions mentioning:

Arma antesignana XXX
Arma postsignana XIV

The wording, which may be understood to mean 'weapons for those who fight before the standards' and 'weapons for those who fight behind the standards', may be old-fashioned and thus may tell us little about the battlefield positions of men fighting before and behind the standards in imperial times. But this much is certain: under Trajan, when the fortress at Lambaesis was built, or at some time thereafter, certain ranks of the legion were armed differently from others. Since then, a gravestone has been found of a soldier who had belonged to *legio VIII Augusta* at Strasbourg in the years after AD 70 and who had served *armis antesignanis,* as he proudly says; thereby betraying a difference in weapons among legionaries. A further *antesignanus* has become known from Syria, datable to the year AD 172. From Caesar and Vegetius we learn that *antesignani* were men with slightly lighter arms who could rush into the no-man's land between two armies to occupy a hill (as shown on Trajan's Column, scene LXXII, hitherto misunderstood), or who could fight beside the cavalry. From the evidence available it is clear that the imperial legion of the first and second centuries was not one body of men all uniformly equipped and trained: instead, some of its ranks were armed – and trained – differently, for specific tasks on the battlefield.[18] Unfortunately, we do not know whether the *antesignani* formed *centuriae* of their own.

As time progresses we find an ever growing differentiation in the weapons and tactics of the legion. Arrian, in his famous 'Battle-order against the Alani' of AD 135, had his legions arrayed in one block, eight ranks deep. The first four ranks – the first line – were armed with a long, heavy *pilum*, good for throwing at a short distance and for using as a pike in case the Alani horse dared a shock attack. The *pilum* was traditionally the Roman soldier's main weapon, but in Arrian's battle-order the four rear ranks – the second line – had *lanciae* instead, which they were to hurl over the heads of those before them. Such *lanciae*, good for throwing from afar, have now become known from the third-century gravestone of a soldier of *legio II Parthica* buried at Apamea in Syria. That soldier, according to the inscription, had the rank of *discens lanciarium* and is shown holding five dart-like javelins, light enough to be thrown from very far. Hence, from AD 135, at the latest, the legions had no less than two differently-equipped and trained battle-lines, one in front, armed with the *pilum*, and one in the rear, armed with javelins.[19]

Legionary *lanciarii*, however, can be found as early as the first century AD. The gravestone of Flavoleius Cordus from Mainz (Figure 7.5) shows a soldier of *legio XIIII Gemina* holding a lance. Most of the weapon is broken away, but one can still see that the man's right index finger held a thong fastened to the shaft. Such a spear with a thong, to believe Isidore, is a *lancia*. *Lanciarii* thus were part of the legions as early as AD 43. Moreover, the base of a column, apparently from the headquarters building of the legionary fortress at Mainz (Figure 7.6b) shows a soldier forging ahead holding in his left hand an oval shield and a handful of javelins, much like the third-century Syrian *lanciarius* mentioned above. *Lanciarii* with the short, thongless lance would thus appear to have been part of the legions as early as the Flavian period; the time when *legio II Augusta* came to Caerleon. The lancers' equipment, especially their oval shield, was lighter and hence better suited to soldiers who held and hurled several short spears rather than one heavy *pilum*.

There is no reason to believe that the lancers gradually gave up their oval shield for the better-known curved, rectangular one, nor indeed that there was any trend in the legions towards uniformity in weapons. At Caerleon, the leather cover of an oval shield has been found, datable, it seems, to the second century (Figure 7.7). If it belonged to a legionary then very likely he was an *antesignanus* or a *lanciarius* also.[20]

7.5 *Gravestone of Flavoleius Cordus from Mainz (photograph: reproduced by permission of the Mittelrheinisches Landesmuseum)*

The oval shield of the *lanciarius* was not only lighter, but was designed for fighting in open ranks against lightly-armed enemies, while the well-known curved, rectangular shield was better suited for sword-fighters in closed ranks – the two tactics are neatly contrasted in the reliefs from the headquarters-building in Mainz (Figure 7.6). By the mid-third century the differentiation had grown so strong that the function of *lanciarius* had become a rank in itself. Later the *lanciarii* went so far as to form units of their own.[21]

7.6 *Two reliefs from the first-century legionary headquarters-building at Mainz: a heavily-armed legionaries fighting in close ranks; b lightly-armed legionary with several* lanciae, *fighting in open ranks (photographs: reproduced by permission of the Mittelrheinisches Landesmuseum)*

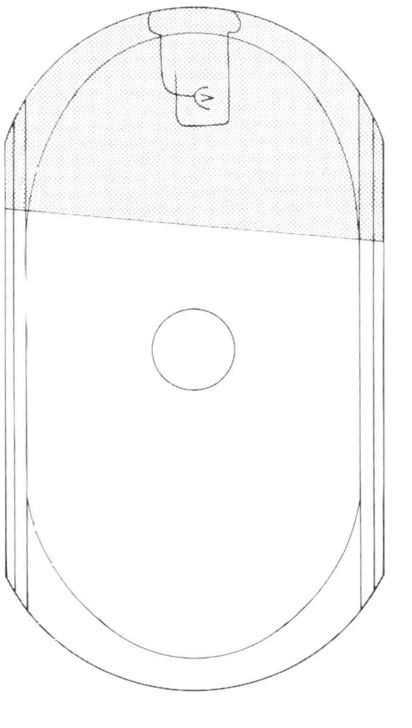

Every third or fourth legionary learned how to shoot with bow and arrow, if for no other reason than to defend a wall. By the third century, however, legionaries could specialize as bowmen, rising to the rank of *sagittarius*. On the battlefield they were in earlier times mixed in with the *centuriae*, but later they had tasks of their own. At Caerleon, antler laths for bows have been found in a third-century workshop, indicating the presence of bowmen in *legio II Augusta*.[22]

From Apamea and *legio II Parthica* comes a third-century gravestone of a *discens phalangarium*, a soldier who was trained to fight in close-knit phalanx formation. A more highly-trained phalanx-line had become necessary in the Orient since Roman turncoats had taught the Parthians how to oppose such a line. The *phalangarii*, too, must have had a pre-planned place in the battle-order, for in pitched

7.7 *Oval leather shield-cover from Caerleon (after C van Driel-Murray)*

battles like the one envisaged by Arrian, the front ranks no doubt regularly fought as a phalanx, while the rear ranks, serving as *lanciarii*, overshot them. Hence, they, too, were specialized legionary ranks on the battlefield.[23]

Weapon specialists of *legio II Augusta* were part of a force of 1,500 'spearmen' whom the three British legions chose in AD 185 from among their ranks and sent to Rome to 'lobby' Commodus.[24] We do not know for certain whether the Greek term 'spearman' means *lanciarii, pilani*, or *hastati*, but it seems the men were picked for their special weapons.

Another group of legionary specialists tied to a battle-line were the *triarii*. Inscriptions of the late third century speak of them – using this very old term from the time of the Republic – as equivalent to the *pilani*. It once denoted the older men who formed the third line and who stayed in the rear of battle, sitting down until they had to swing into action. If in the third century AD, the term came into use again, as a rank and even as a special unit, we must acknowledge once more a differentiation – men who specialize in rear battle-line fighting (older men, perhaps, or veterans).[25]

The many specialists within the legion itself and its steadily growing cavalry show Rome's skill of adapting to the fighting techniques of its foes. Rome and its legions thus were far nimbler than H G Wells dreamt when he wrote, somewhat rashly, in his 'Outline of History':

> 'The Romans had been held at the Euphrates by an array of mounted archers. It was clear that as the legion was organized it was useless in wide open country, and it should have been equally clear that sooner or later the mounted nomads of east Germany, south Russia or Parthia were bound to try conclusions with the Empire. But the Romans, two hundred years after Caesar's time, were still marching about, the same drilled and clanking cohorts they had always been, easily ridden round and shot to pieces. The Empire had learnt nothing even from Carrhae.'[26]

BATTLE-LINES

How did all these specialists fit into the existing framework of the legion? Were whole *centuriae* chosen to arm and train as *lanciarii, phalangarii, or sagittarii?* Inscriptions show that this was not so. The specialists, like the legionary horsemen, stayed in their *centuriae*, and while they could be pulled out for special tasks (and even organized into new *centuriae* – like subunits for the purpose), they mainly stayed and fought with their own *centuria*.[27] Despite all specialization, the *centuriae* and cohorts still made up the main battle-lines, as they had done for centuries (Figure 7.8).

Inscriptions support this. In AD 128 the Emperor Hadrian inspected the manoeuvres of *III Augusta* at Lambaesis in Africa. His manoeuvre critique, addressed to the troops and afterwards inscribed on a stone monument in the middle of their training-ground, opens with the emperor's words *At pilos*. These *pili* were thought to have been the twenty centurions of the first line.[28] Yet the remarks that follow are all directed at bodies of troops. The *pili* to whom Hadrian spoke seem to be not just the centurions but the *centuriae*, that is the men themselves, as we have seen above. It does not matter much for our argument, whether Hadrian meant the

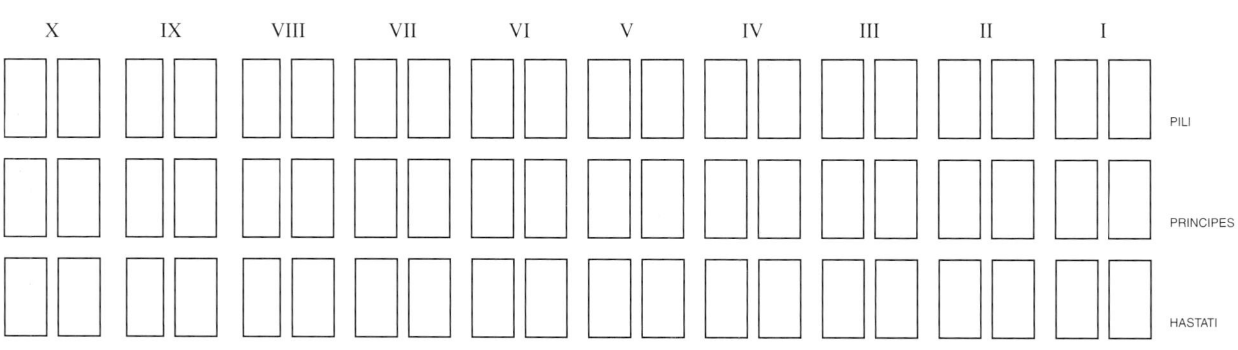

7.8 *The cohorts in manipular lines*

pili-centurions or the *pili-centuriae,* for, either way, he addressed them as having shown their skills in a manoeuvre. The *pili,* therefore, were in Hadrian's time a battle-line that could manoeuvre on its own, and more or less independently of the *principes* and *hastati.* Two further inscriptions from Lambaesis define the standard-bearers of the *pili* as an *ordo.* Whether *ordo* is taken to mean a battle-line or merely a group, it is hard to see what else the *pilani* standard-bearers could have in common save that they directed the same battle-line.[29]

If indeed the *pilani, principes* and *hastati,* down to the mid-third century, took their allotted places in the battle-order according to the *Rangordnung,* the *pilani,* belonging to the highest ranking *centuriae* – and the ones first to be addressed by Hadrian – stood in front, whereas earlier they had been the third-line reserves. Fittingly, the excavated barrack blocks show that during the Empire the *pilani* had the same number of men as the *principes* and *hastati,* while before they had been only half as strong. Already under Caesar the *pilani* led the attack.[30]

Roman literary sources may not tell us much about the legion's battle-order, but a Byzantine officer's handbook does. Maurice's *Strategikon,* written in the early sixth century, contains a chapter on the infantry, that reveals the traditional way the legions fought: in files sixteen deep. These files consisted of two groups (*contubernia*) of eight men each, who lived and ate together, one group was called *primi,* the other *secundi.*[31] Mess-mates and tent-mates fighting together is such a basic principle that it surely also applied to the legions of the Early Empire.[32] Hence the *priores* together with the *posteriores* of the *pili, principes* and *hastati* each made up a double file, with a single file being eight deep. If lines needed to be longer than files of sixteen allowed, their depth could be halved as ordered by Arrian in AD 135 against the Alani and Constantine in AD 311 during the battle of Verona. So as not to be outflanked, each gave up the tried and trusted double file (*acies duplex*) for a risky single file (*acies simplex*) only eight deep.[33]

The basic battle-order of the legion – and of the cohort – was in three lines: *pili, princepes* and *hastati,* each having double files of sixteen. Originally one group would have stood behind the other as reserves, but during the battles of the Empire more often than not they stood besides each other. That they still existed is beyond doubt, and on the parade ground very likely they still stood one behind the other. This explains why *centuriae* named after the three battle-lines occur so often in inscriptions.[34] It also explains why, as we saw in Figure 7.4c, inscriptions sometimes mention maniples of *priores* and *posteriores* together.

Centuriae named by their rank are found particularly often on inscriptions of the second and third centuries, especially when on campaigns. This was the time when, instead of whole legions, mainly detachments took to the field. Since such detachments were raised from many legions and had to be moulded into battle-lines, it mattered very much where one could place them. It is possible that their place in the ranking order marked their fighting quality. In the two new legions that were raised from such detachments, *legio II Traiana* and *legio II Parthica,* the *centuriae* retained the habit of being named not after the centurions but after their place in the battle-array – just as must have been the case with the detachments from which they were drawn.[35]

Despite the rise of weapon specialists in the legion, it would appear that the battle-order changed very little. On Trajan's Column (Figure 7.9) the *signa*-standards of the *centuriae* (or maniples) still dominate, and hence we may assume that battle tactics were still based on *centuriae* (and maniples), for in battle soldiers followed the standards.[36] In the late second and the early third centuries things are not so clear, for it has not yet been researched to what extent the traditional legionary *signum* (standard) held its own during the time when the *vexillum* (flag), used by composite units, became prominent. Even if the *signa* lost some of their importance, the new *vexilla,* too, may stand for *centuria*-like sub-units.[37] If so, battle-lines were still built of *centuriae,* and there would be no need to assume an abrupt mid second-century break in battle tactics.

Detachments sent away on campaigns under their *vexilla* are one thing, while training at the home fortresses is quite another. Vegetius says that units exercised at their home bases 'in the order in which the soldiers are listed in the rosters' *(secundum matriculae ordinem in aciem dirigendi).* Since the way soldiers were listed in the rosters was by *centuriae,* it follows, that they were also trained by *centuriae.*[38]

We may conclude that from Marius to Trajan, and very likely down to the mid-third century – as long as

7.9 *Two legionary* centuria-*standards and a flag on Trajan's Column*

a legion still comprised some 6,000 men – the three battle-lines of *pili, principes* and *hastati* continued to exist and also to function.[39] Throughout that time they never quite gave way before the cohorts, the main tactical bodies of the legions. A compelling reason for this has yet to be found. Though it is possible that battle-line position was seen as a yardstick for a *centuria*'s fighting quality or for a soldier's prospect of promotion.

GOADING THE SOLDIERS INTO BATTLE: THE OPTIO AND HIS HASTILE-STAFF

Battle-lines were four, eight, or sixteen ranks deep; less than four was too weak, more than sixteen made the rear ranks useless, as we learn from Maurice's sixth-century handbook on tactics. Although dealing with a period two or three hundred years later than the time with which we are concerned, Maurice reveals much about the Roman imperial army, for the basic conditions of fighting had not changed – and the early Byzantines followed ancient tradition as doggedly as the Romans. Arrian's legionary battle-line likewise was eight deep. The *centuria* of eighty men thus stood normally ten wide and eight deep, with the centurion standing, no doubt, in front to the right, and the *optio* to the left in the rear.[40]

On altars and gravestones the *optio* is often shown holding a long staff (Figure 7.10), the name and function of which has hitherto been a mystery. But for enlightenment one may again turn to Maurice, whose

7.10 *Gravestone from Chester, showing an* optio *and his staff* (RIB *I, 492) (photograph: reproduced by permission of the Grosvenor Museum, Chester)*

work brings home so graphically what it was like to stand there, awaiting the enemy:[41]

> 'There must be absolute quiet in the battle array and the *optiones* of each line must be told that if they hear a noise from someone in their group to poke him with the shaft *(hastile)* of their spear. During the fight they are to goad those before them, so as to keep any laggards from hanging back.'

Hastile is the shaft of a spear, and to use it against soldiers shying from battle was an age-old practice. Thus, in the battle of Mutina in 193 BC the Gallic officers with their *hastilia* beat their men back into line if they tried to flee. The humane thing about the staff of the *optio* is that it had no blade at all, while in Maurice's time the butt of a spear was used – in case of need such a spear could be turned around to inflict serious wounds. In the legions of the Early Empire, in peacetime, discipline was such that one did not reckon with soldiers openly defying the *optio*. That these were indeed considerations of the Roman high command can be seen from the fact that the Emperor's own bodyguard, the *speculatores,* until Trajan's time carried dangerous lances with a reinforced butt on one end, and a sharp blade on the other. In the milder regime of Hadrian the *speculatores* and their lances were replaced by *hastiliarii* who carried mere staffs without blades, perhaps as a concession to the soldiers. The staff of the *optio* thus reflects the state of discipline in the army during the Early Empire, indicating a careful treatment of the soldiers, a trend that was to be reversed only with the decline of discipline in the later Roman army.[42]

The gravestone of an *optio* in Budapest shows the *hastile* as long as a spear. It had to be this long so that the *optio* could reach the men in all the ranks before him. An altar of *legio II Augusta,* found on Hadrian's Wall (Figure 7.11), illustrates the importance of the *optio*'s function: in the growing number of field detachments the most important officer after the commander, and the one most often mentioned, came to be the *optio,* surely in his role as sergeant. The *tesserarius* and the *armorum custos,* and very likely other under officers too, also had such staffs, for they also had the right to beat the soldiers.[43]

It is a great pity that we have no Maurice for the Early Empire. Excavations, inscriptions, and reliefs, however, bring us ever closer, step by step, to a comparably rich and lifelike picture of the imperial army even when the literary sources leave us in the dark.

7.11 *Altar from Hadrian's Wall, set up by a detachment from two* centuriae *of* legio II Augusta *(RIB I, 2024)*

'To Mars Cocidius the soldiers of legio II Augusta, *from the Sanctian century and from the century of Secundinus, with this gift fulfilled their vow under the command of the centurion Aelianus; Oppius Felix,* optio, *had charge of the task.'*

THE LATER ROMAN LEGION AND THE ROLE OF THE COHORTS

The Empire during the first three centuries AD had thirty-three legions, while the late Roman government handbook of the *Notitia Dignitatum* lists 174. From all we know, the strength of the late Roman army was nearly the same as that of the Early Empire. Since there were now five or six times as many legions, it follows that they were only one fifth or one sixth of their former size. The late Roman legion, therefore, was little more that 1,000 men strong – albeit that an exact figure is nowhere spelled out.[44] Such a small legion could very well have been divided into ten cohorts but hardly into sixty *centuriae* also. One would, therefore, expect the *centuriae* to vanish, and indeed they did. By the fourth century, mention of the *centuriae* has largely gone from inscriptions.

This leads us to consider the fate of the cohorts. Ever since Marius, they had been tactical sub-units, big chunks of a legion, that could be moved around on the battlefield. Caesar was the grand master of cohort tactics. Cohorts not only camped together, but also played a role in the selection of detachments. Several inscriptions list outposted legionaries cohort by cohort. It seems that the legionary commander, when choosing the men for outposting, watched over the relative strength of each cohort at home so as to keep a balanced order of battle, but those who asked for the men may also have specified from what cohorts they should come. Cohorts, like battle-line positions, may have been yardsticks for fighting quality.[45]

At any rate, by Diocletian's time we find detachments of the legions subdivided into cohorts. Sundry gravestones and a dedication have come to light where men are described as belonging to a cohort rather than to a *centuria*.[46] These stones, all from the period of Diocletian or Constantine, establish that the late Roman legion was still subdivided into cohorts, a point that has been much disputed.[47] Twice men of two different cohorts occur together. In the first case, cohorts X and VII of *legio II Herculia* join in setting up a religious dedication. During the Early Empire not even full cohorts were wont to set up dedications, a fact which reveals a new feeling of belonging together as a group, analogous to that of the former *centuria*. In the second case, cohorts I and II of *legio III Italica* share a standard-bearer and hence are clearly not full cohorts, but rather detachments on campaigns.[48]

The brigading together of men from two cohorts under a single command reminds one of the joint detachments of two *centuriae* of *legio II Augusta* which appear a hundred years earlier on Hadrian's Wall, best illustrated by the altar found near Stanwix, set up by men of two *centuriae* under the command of an *optio* (Figure 7.11).[49]

The principle of joining men from two *centuriae* or two cohorts is the same as the principle of joining field detachments from two legions, such as the men of *II Augusta* and *XX Valeria Victrix* depicted on the famous bronze roundel found in France (Figure 9.1).[50] The reason why Roman commanders preferred to brigade men from two units rather than take them from one or from three units was to stimulate competition such as went on among Agricola's units. Vegetius, too, states that well-trained troops 'if they come together from different units will surely want to outdo each other in gallantry and thus prefer battle over being idle'.[51] The principle of the brigaded double-unit has been called 'the key to understanding the creation and development of the whole Roman army from Diocletian on'. If we are right in seeing this principle at work in the brigading of *centuriae* and of cohorts, then it cannot have originated from the situation of provinces increasingly having two legions. Indeed the opposite might be true, namely that increasingly each frontier province was given two legions so that it could furnish such *Doppeltruppen*-detachments for its own defence and for the emperor's field army.[52]

The cohorts in the legionary detachments (or new legions) of Diocletian's time may also reveal a tactical feature. Theoretically one could have called up a certain number of soldiers from an old legion and made new sub-units of them, say of 100 men each – as was obviously done when *centenarii* were appointed as leaders. But the sub-units of the new field-army legions were cohorts, not simply *centenaria*. These cohorts still functioned as tactical sub-units by the turn of the fifth century, for Vegetius says of his own time that legionary cohorts carried a dragon-standard into battle. Cohorts as sub-units allowed the new, much smaller, field-army legion some internal flexibility, enabling it, by replacing or reinforcing its front ranks, to outlast their foes.[53]

At the turn of the fourth century the frontier legions, too, betray a new emphasis on the cohort: it is now often outposted as a whole unit.[54] An inscription from Caerleon, dated about AD 255, should be seen in this context, for it records the rebuilding of the barracks for the seventh cohort from the ground up (Figure 6.14). The cohort may have been away for some length of time, be it on a campaign or at an outpost.[55]

From the late third century on, the legions dissolve into small, and increasingly independent units. Shrunken frontier legions such as *legio II Augusta* at Caerleon[56] split into outposted cohorts, field-army legions of 1,000 men, or specialist units such as the *lanciarii, triarii, ballistarii,* and *promoti.* To be sure, a field commander could place such smaller units in the battle-lines where it suited him best, but Vegetius did not approve. He much preferred the large legion of 6,000 men, for he found that if they all belonged to one interconnected legion, the various groups would better get along with each other. He had a point, for brawls between army units were always rife.[57]

Vegetius also points out that having trained together, the various parts of a legion would fight together with much more precision. However, in this Vegetius was hopelessly romantic, for the Empire had lost the initiative, and the never-ending need to rush troops to a hydra of trouble-spots effectively tore the legion up. Even the need for precision in training and fighting had gone, for the equipment had become standardized again. Nearly all legionaries now carried round shields and two spears (Figure 7.12) and fought from afar, in open ranks, without armour – just like the tribes beyond the borders from which they were recruited.[58]

7.12 *Legionary from the turn of the fourth century, equipped with two spears and a round shield for fighting in open ranks* (CIL V, *944 from Aquileia) (photograph: reproduced by permission of Hanns Ubl, Vienna)*

The large, intricate, highly-trained, and well-disciplined legion of the first century befitted an Empire towering over its enemies. By contrast, the many small units of the fourth century best answered the needs of an Empire beset on all sides and whose troops, often enough, had to seek shelter behind walls.[59]

The reader having come this far, will forgive being reminded only now of Vegetius' cheerful words, written 1600 years ago, but still handy:[60]

> 'I have set forth the framework of the ancient legion, in line with army usage. If the account seems somewhat foggy and uneven, blame it on the tough subject matter, not on me. Read it carefully several times, then mind and memory will grasp it.'

APPENDIX

Vegetius' antiqua ordinatio *and the first cohort*

The only detailed description we have of a legion is that by Vegetius *(Epitoma rei militaris),* written at the end of the fourth century or in the first half of the fifth century. By his time the legion had shrunk in size, numbering no more than 1,000 or 2,000 men. Yet Vegetius wanted to restore the days when the legions dominated the battlefields and vanquished all enemies. He, therefore, drew up a memo for the emperor, setting forth, as he understood it, how the old legions of some 6,000 men had been structured and how they had functioned, suggesting that the legions of his own day should be restored along these lines. According to Vegetius, the legion of old – he calls its framework the *antiqua ordinatio* – had ten cohorts. There is nothing extraordinary about the number of cohorts, but when Vegetius (2.6) goes into detail, setting forth the strength of each cohort and *centuria,* he gives very unusual numbers (Figure 7.13).

The arithmetic has gone astray. There are four horsemen and five centurions too many in the total. More bothersome still are the puzzling figures for the strength of the cohorts, 1,105 men in the first cohort

Unit	Foot	Horse	Centurions
First cohort	1105	132	5
2nd-10th cohort	555	66	5
Legion total	6100	730	55

7.13 *Vegetius'* antiqua ordinatio

and 555 in each of the others. However, two paragraphs further on (2.8), Vegetius gives the strength of the first cohort as 1,000 men, which is much more likely. Clearly, the figure of 1,105 reflects some additions. But what has been added? Some scholars have suggested the eleven men working the field gun *(carroballista)* of each *centuria*.[61] But why should the gunners not be part of the regular strength of the legion? To count them as extra was a desperate expedient to make sense of Vegetius' numbers and no more convincing than if any other specialists had been singled out for arbitrary later addition to the figure of 1,000.

How then did Vegetius reach the figures of 1,105 for the first cohort and 555 for the other cohorts? One need not look far, since he says that for every ten men there was a *decanus* (2.8), and also that a centurion commanded 110 men (2.14). Ten *decani* thus were added to each *centuria* of 100. If one includes, as one must, the centurion himself, the full strength of the *centuria* rises to 111 men. Since Vegetius reckons only five *centuriae* to a cohort, the figure of 555 is thereby reached. The first cohort, twice as strong, had ten times 110 men, but only five centurions, which brings us to Vegetius' figure of 1,105.

It is an unusual way of reckoning to state first the strength of a unit and then to add afterwards under-officers and officers for a new higher total. Roman army records known from papyri regularly include officers in the total, and when they refer to the officers they do so with the phrase 'among these....', ie among the total. Likewise Hyginus (16) when explaining the strength of an *ala milliaria*, counts the *decuriones*, *duplicarii*, and *sesquiplicarii* among the 1,000 *(in numerum computantur)*. Obviously Vegetius, or his source, are here very peculiar. What is more, the same way of reckoning is apparent in Vegetius' figures for the legionary horse, which matter needs now to be considered.

A regular squadron *(turma)* of horsemen in the Roman army consisted of thirty men.[62] Vegetius, however, counted thirty-two men in a *turma* (2.14). He must have reached that figure by adding the two cavalry under-officers of *duplicarius* and *sesquiplicarius* to the total of thirty. That he added under-officers and officers to the cavalry *turmae* in the same way as he added them to the infantry *centuriae*, is proven by his figure for the legionary horse; the sixty-six horsemen for cohorts II–X are obviously two *turmae*, each consisting of thirty-two men and one decurion, while the 132 horsemen of the first cohort represent four such *turmae* with their decurions.

Vegetius thus reached his detailed figures for legionary foot and horse in exactly the same way, a parallelism that proves this was indeed his way of reckoning. Even the mistake in the totals may now be explained. The exact parallel for foot and horse shows that he mistakenly counted the five centurions and four decurions of the first cohort twice, mindful, perhaps, to double the strength of the first cohort. There is no more need, therefore, to reckon with added field-gunners etc.[63] Indeed, as Baatz pointed out, Vegetius may have known no more than three facts: (1) that an ancient legion had about 6,000 men; (2) that the first cohort was milliary; and (3) that it had five centurions.[64] From the word *centurio*, so similar to the *centenarius* of his own day (2.8), he inferred that a *centuria* had 100 men. From this all the other figures follow and are his own, unwarranted reconstruction – especially the division of cohorts II–X into five rather than six *centuriae* which, though necessary for his computation, clashes with our evidence from both excavations and inscriptions.

About the legionary horse, Vegetius may have known that each cohort had two *turmae* of thirty men. If so, his ancient legion had 600 horsemen (or 660 if the first cohort had twice the standard number). But even this is altogether unreliable. Formerly a legion had 120 horse and Vegetius could have taken those as the four *turmae* of the first cohort, inferring that cohorts II–X should have half as many. Although it will be wise to keep an eye out for other evidence indicating a body of 600 or 660 legionary horse in twenty or twenty-two *turmae* at some time during the later third century, Vegetius' figures in themselves constitute no proof and should be discounted unless confirmed by other sources.[65]

Vegetius' reconstructed figures of strength for the *antiqua ordinatio,* therefore, cannot teach us anything about the legions and run counter to the rest of our knowledge. Not wanting to let go of a precious piece of 'evidence', scholars have fallen over each other to assign Vegetius' ancient legion to the time from Gallienus to Diocletian, the dark decades about which we know the least and which are, therefore, least likely to contradict fanciful theories. Vegetius' figures must now be struck from the historical record.

No heed need be paid either to Vegetius' much debated account of the first cohort, whose centurions he reports as having led 400, 200, 150, and 100 men respectively – figures that have been accepted, astonishingly, by the very best scholars.[66] Excavations, however, at Caerleon, Inchtuthil and elsewhere, have shown that the barrack blocks of the first cohort were all the same size (the double *centuria* of the *primus pilus* merely had twice as many blocks). Besides, how could a *centuria* of 400 men have fitted into a battle-line? When all ten cohorts stood next to each other (Figure 7.2), the double strength of the first cohort did not disturb the line, for as it stood on the right wing, it merely extended the lines somewhat to the right. But if a single *centuria* were 400 strong, then who would have filled the space behind it in the next line?[67]

Vegetius, it must be admitted, does not help us much with the framework of the legion. Yet in setting him aside we are, at least, no longer beholden to his views and thus can have a fresh look at what other evidence there is.

ACKNOWLEDGEMENTS

For many years, indeed decades, Dietwulf Baatz has freely shared with me his rich expertise of the archaeology of the Roman army. In this paper there is much that I have learned from him on visits to sites, in discussions and letters, and from his written work.

The great support and courtesy granted me by Richard Brewer and David Zienkiewicz (formerly of the Roman Legionary Museum) made my visit to Caerleon and south Wales a pleasure.

I dedicate this lecture to the late George Boon, *antesignanus* of scholarly work on Caerleon.

Glossary

Antesignanus: élite legionary
Ballistarius: gunner
Centenarius: leader of 100 men
Centuria: company of eighty men
Centurion: leader of eighty men
Cohort: regiment of 480 men, sub-unit of a legion
Contubernium: mess-unit of eight men
Decanus: leader of ten men
Decurio: leader of a cavalry squadron *(turma)* of thirty men
Duplicarius: second-in-command to a *decurio*
Hastatus/hastati: third battle-line
Lanciarius: wielder of a throwing-spear *(lancia)*
Maniple: a pair of two *centuriae*
Optio: second-in-command to a centurion
Phalangarius: heavily-armed legionary in a phalanx
Pilus/pilani: first battle-line
Primi ordines: highest-ranking centurions
Princeps/principes: second battle-line
Promotus: late Roman legionary horseman
Rangordnung: hierarchy of ranks
Remansores: a caretaker force
Sagittarius: bowman
Sesquiplicarius: third-in-command to a *decurio*
Triarii: third battle-line; a late Roman unit
Turma: cavalry squadron of thirty men

Notes

1 Caerleon: Boon 1972 and 1987. Inchtuthil: Pitts and St Joseph 1985. Internal buildings: von Petrikovits 1975 and Baatz 1977. The new inscriptions and reliefs from Apamea, Syria (*AE* 1993, 1571–1597) set this revised version of my essay right in many ways.

2 von Domaszewski 1885, 1.

3 Roth 1994; he prefers to count not those who stayed behind but the slaves. *Remansores:* Speidel 1994b, 80 f. Soldiers, not slaves, counted as *homines* in army calculations, see ibid, 33.

4 Hyginus: Lenoir 1979. For the likely Flavian date of the rebuilt stone barracks at Caerleon, see Zienkiewicz 1990. Inchtuthil: Pitts and St Joseph 1985. Nijmegen: Davidson 1989, 52 f (with the review by Haalebos 1992).

5 First-cohort barracks: von Petrikovits 1975, 38 ff as reviewed by Baatz 1977; also Baatz 1987, review of Pitts and St Joseph 1985. Discharge lists: *CIL* III, 6178=*ISM* V, 137 (Troesmis, AD 134); *AE* 1969–70, 633 (Nicopolis, AD 157); *CIL* III, 14507=*IMS* II, 53 (Viminacium, AD 195). There is no evidence that soldiers with long years of service were promoted unusually often to this cohort, but it remains possible that part of the extra strength of the first cohort was owing to the veterans who served on, see Keppie 1984, 176 and the *reliqui veterani* of *CIL* III, 6178. For the larger size of the first cohort, or at least its first *centuria*, under Caesar, see *de Bello Civili* 3.91 where the *primus pilus* Crastinus of the Tenth Legion is said to have dashed forward with 120 volunteers from his *centuria*. For the discussion, see also Davidson 1989, 52 ff.

6 Lambaesis-inscription: *CIL* VIII, 18072; *pilus posterior* lacking: Speidel 1983a. Wegeleben 1913, 38 f rightly objected to both these arguments. The new *primus pilus posterior: AE* 1993, 1588. Standardised: E Birley 1952a, 232. See also von Domaszewski/Dobson 1967, XXIV; von Domaszewski (97) makes much of the supposedly five extra centurions in the first cohort, but *CIL* XIII, 6801 on which this is based must be read differently, see Speidel 1986, 329. The *Rangordnung* of the centurions is known, under the Empire, as early as AD 8 (*AE* 1975, 626).

7 Maniple: Speidel 1983b. The maniple is seen as important for tactics by Domaszewski 1885, 22 f; and as important for the administration by Parker 1932, esp p 130; see also von Petrikovits 1975, 132 f. Keppie 1984, 173 f, sees the maniple as inconsequential during the time of the Empire, while Le Bohec 1994, 142 sees it as the most important tactical unit. At Caerleon two of the barrack blocks near the *porta principalis sinistra* were reversed in certain phases and thus no longer paired, see Zienkiewicz 1986a, fig 1. Hyginus: Lenoir 1979, 119; Davidson 1989, 45 f. Inscriptions: *RIB* I, 2032 (below, Fig 4c); *IDR* II, 327=Speidel 1978.

8 120 horse: Josephus, *Bellum Iudaicum* 3.120; Breeze 1969; Speidel 1987a. A camp of their own: *AE* 1957, 85 in the 'Camp of 81' for which see Le Bohec 1989, 407, its use for horsemen confirmed by *AE* 1957, 122=*AE* 1971, 507. Horsemen at Inchtuthil are discussed by Pitts and St Joseph 1985, 169 f. An inscription showing that the legionary horse existed: *AE* 1969–70, 583; Le Bohec 1989, 188, citing Hyginus, suggests that they were suppressed by Trajan and restored by Hadrian.

9 Wegeleben 1913, adopted by E Birley 1963–64 and by Le Bohec 1994, 43.

10 Domaszewski/Dobson 1967, 90–7 and XXII–XXV; adopted by Strobel 1987. Strobel 1988a, suggests further that the *priores* centurions ranked as a class above all *posteriores*, but this is true only if Caesius Verus' career (Strobel 1988b, 176 f, no. 12) is indeed ascending; see Bruun 1988.

11 Especially the careers of Ti. Claudius Vitalis, *CIL* VI, 3586=*ILS* 2656 and of M. Sabidius Maximus, *AE* 1937, 101.

12 This is apparent from the phrase *militavit usqu(e) in IV (quartum) hast(atum) post(eriorem)*, *IGLS* 9187, line 11.

13 Worp 1983; Speidel 1990; 1989b, 359. For *hastatus prior* etc meaning the *centuria* itself see the examples gathered by Marquardt 1884, 369.

14 *RIB* I, 341 reads *c(o)hor(tis) VI hast(ati) prio(ris) c(enturia) Roesi Modera(ti)* and translates 'From the sixth cohort the century of Roesius Moderatus, hastatus prior, (built this)'. I owe to Roger Tomlin the suggestion to expand *hast(...) pri(...)* in the plural.

15 See also *RIB* I, 1391 and 1571. For two *centuriae* together see eg *RIB* I, 1774, 1915, 2024, 2077. It remains a riddle why so many centuries of the fourth cohort but no others insisted on indicating their position.

16 Speidel 1983a. For Britain see also *RIB* I, 1391, 1571. Philippi emperors: *CIL* III, 8047=*IDR* II, 328=Speidel 1983a, 52; *AE* 1939, 28=*IDR* II, 327=Speidel 1983a, 57 (both from Romula in Dacia).

17 Thus Parker 1928, 31 for the time of Marius. If by nothing else, this would be refuted by the inscriptions *h(astati)* and *p(rincipes)* on Mark Antony's standards (von Domaszewski 1885, 22).

18 Lambaesis: Le Bohec 1989, 188 (with bibliography); see also Veith 1928, esp 408; von Nischer 1928, esp 494 and 522 f. Gravestones: *AE* 1978, 471; *IGLS* 2132.

Caesar: *de Bello Civili* 1.43–46, 1.57.1, 3.75.5 *(expeditos antesignanos)*; 3.84.3. Caesar's *antesignani* are 400 and led by the *hastatus prior*, from which Sander 1952, esp 82 infers that they account for the double size of the first cohort. Vegetius, *Epit* also mentions *antesignani*: 2.2, 2.7, 2.16 (with small cuirasses). Frontinus (*Strategemata*, 2.3.17) sees in them the first battle-line, in the *postsignani* the second battle-line – perhaps rightly so not only for the time of Sulla, but also for part of the first century AD. Goldsworthy 1996, 18 wrongly claims I implied they were skirmishers.

19 Perhaps the men of the third line, if such existed, were left at base, which would explain why Arrian's legionaries march four abreast while those with Vespasian in Palestine marched six abreast (Josephus, *Bellum Iudaicum* 3.124) – but this is speculative, as it is to deduce from Arrian's marching-column (no strength given) a whole new legionary organization (Wheeler 1979, esp 313). Apamea *lanciarius:* Balty 1988, Pl XIV.

20 Isidore, *Origines* 18.7.5; *lancea est hasta amentum habens in medio; dicta autem lancea, quia aequa lance, id est aequali ammento, ponderata vibratur*; likewise Silius Italicus, *Punica*, 318. Flavoleius: Keppie 1984, pl 19d with p 233; there is no need to assume a growing uniformity (Keppie 1984, 173; Le Bohec 1994, 122). Lancers with their lighter weapons may have served as *antesignani* or in the commander's guard, see Josephus, *Bellum Iudaicum* 3.95 and Ritterling 1919, 9–34. For the Mainz reliefs, see Selzer 1988, 54 and 104, and nos 266 and 271. Shield from Caerleon: van Driel-Murray 1988. Other early *lanciarii* on gravestones: *CIL* III, 14349 (Budapest); *CIL* V, 5196 (Bergamo, see Franzoni 1987, pl XXVII).

21 Units: Hoffman 1969–70, 218–22.

22 Learning: Vegetius, *Epit* 1.15, 3.9. Caerleon: Nash-Williams 1932, 94–6. *Sagittarius: CIL* VI, 37262 and Balty 1988, 101. In the *centuriae:* Vegetius, *Epit* 1.15 (time of the Republic), 2.2; independent tasks for infantry bowmen: Hoffmann 1969–70, 240 f (fourth century AD); also Vegetius, *Epit* 2.15.4.

23 *Discens phalangarium:* Balty 1988. Phalanx: Wheeler 1979. Refugees: Herodian 3.4; for the need already under Caracalla, see Cassius Dio, 77.7 and 18; also *ILS* 8878.

24 Brunt 1973.

25 Rank: *AE* 1981, 777; unit: *CIL* VI, 37281.

26 Wells 1921, 468.

27 *AE* 1993, 1575 (Apamae) has a *lanciarius* in *centuria VIIII pili prioris.*

28 *ILS* 9133, with commentary. Le Bohec, who is working on a new edition of the monument, warns that Dessau's text may not stand up to scrutiny.

29 *CIL* VII, 18073 and 18088 (printed upside down). For the sign denoting *pilus*, see Speidel 1986, 328.

30 See n 5 above.

31 Maurice's, *Strategikon*: Dennis 1981, 12, B, 8; Dennis 1984, XVIII and 140–2. Similarly the sixth-century Anonymous, *de re strategica*, 127 (Dennis 1985, 85). A depth of four as in Maurice, 12, B, 16 is for élite troops.

32 See Wheeler 1979, 312.

33 Arrian, *Ectaxis*, 15 ff; Constantine: *Paneg Lat* 12.9. Wheeler 1979, 317 is right in that Arrian's *Ectaxis* is our best source in this.

34 Speidel 1983a; 1986, add *AE* 1993, 1572, 1575, 1579, 1588 and *AE* 1994 (Julius Julianus).

35 *Legio II Traiana* and *legio II Parthica:* Speidel 1983a, 47 f; 1986, 328.

36 von Domaszewski 1885. For the later legionary horsemen, see n 65 below.

37 For such composite units see below, p 135 ff.

38 Vegetius, *Epit* 1.26. See the discussion by Fink 1971, 2 f.

39 Contra: Sander 1939.

40 Maurice: Dennis 1981, 12, B, 16. That the *optio* stood in the rear follows from his Greek title *ouragos* (Polybius 6.24.2).

41 The staff of the *optio* as the specific weapon of this rank was first recognized by Ubl 1969, 434 f. Maurice: Dennis 1981, 12, B, 17.

42 Mutina: Livy 35.5.10. Lances of *speculatores:* Trajan's Column, scene V and *AE* 1955, 24=Bonanome in Giuliano 1984, 189, *Hastiliarii* by AD 135: *CIL* VI, 31143=Speidel 1992b, no. 7, depicted on the Aurelian Column, scene 74. Trend: adopted even by the Severan legate's guard at Lambaesis (*CIL* VIII, 2562=18051).

43 Budapest: *CIL* III, 3530=Schober 1923, 157. Speidel 1985a. *Tesserarius: AE* 1993, 1585. *Armorum Custos: CIL* V, 5196 (above n 20). Right to beat: Justinian, *Digest* 49.16.13: *etiam a principali coercendus est.*

44 See Casey this volume, 170 ff.

45 Speidel 1982, 855 f; *AE* 1990, 893. Saxer 1967, 102; 128. Fighting quality of cohorts: Vegetius, *Epit* 2.6.

46 Speidel 1982; (ibid, n 40, shows a Silvanus *centuriae*, not *cohortis*). Scheithauer and Wesch-Klein 1990. Perhaps *IGLS* 741 belongs here, too, for the *primus pilus* is absent, as usual after Gallienus.

47 No cohorts: Grosse 1920, 37; Passerini 1949, esp 623. Cohorts: Sander 1932.

48 If, as in earlier times there was one standard bearer for eighty men, then each cohort supplied here some forty soldiers and the detachment was some 400 men strong; see also Casey this volume, 171. Cassius Dio's (75.12) 550 men at Hatra are a comparable

detachment, unless they are a regular cohort as suggested by E Birley 1952a, 234.

49 Detachments from two *centuriae:* see n 15 above. For *RIB* 2024, see also E Birley 1952b, 69 ff.

50 *CIL* XV, 7164. See also *RIB* I, 2075, 2171, 2146 and Hassall and Tomlin 1989, 331, no. 4.

51 Tacitus, *Agricola,* 26.2; *Historiae* 3.27 and 29; Aristides, *Roman Or,* 85; Josephus, *Bellum Iudaicum,* 3.485, 3.496, 5.502, 6.142; Arrian, *Ectaxis* 22 f; Vegetius, *Epit* 3.4; see also 1.23; Speidel 1994a, 219.

52 *Doppeltruppe,* key to understanding, owing to provinces with two legions: Ritterling 1924/5, 1350. See also Hoffmann 1969–70, 11–15; E Birley 1980, 81; 1952c, 184.

53 Vegetius, *Epit* 2.13, 2.15. For continued tactical sophistication of the later Roman army units, see Speidel 1985b.

54 See eg Sarnowski 1985; *AE* 1981, 719; Speidel 1987b. Cohorts, of course, could be outposted even earlier: *P Mich* 466 (see Speidel 1977, 694); *CIL* VIII, 18042.

55 See eg Davies 1991, 53.

56 Ibid, 53.

57 See *RIB* I, 1125 with Richmond's commentary (add Hassall and Tomlin 1989, 331); *CIL* III, 4832=*ILS* 2528; Tacitus, *Annales* 1.27; *Historiae* 2.72 and 88, etc. Vegetius, *Epit* 2.21.

58 Fighting together: Vegetius, *Epit* 2.2. Lightly armed: ibid, 2.15, *'levis armatura – sicut nunc prope omnes milites videntur armati'.*

59 Libanius, *Orationes* 18.37.

60 Vegetius, *Epit* 2.4.

61 Nischer 1928, 492 ff. Parker 1932, 147; *Carroballista:* Vegetius, *Epit* 2.25.

62 Hyginus 16; Lenoir 1979, 71.

63 Nischer 1928, 494. Sander 1952, 92 saw in the five extra centurions those whom von Domaszewski/Dobson (1967), misreading *CIL* XIII, 6801, added to the first cohort.

64 Vegetius, *Epit* l.17 and 2.6.

65 Domaszewski/Dobson 1967, 49 accept Vegetius' figures for the horse as *durchaus glaubwürdig. P Col* VII, 188 shows eight centurions in *legio II Traiana;* if each of them commanded a full *centuria* of *equites promoti,* the legion would have had 640 horsemen; if they commanded horsemen, though, their units, more likely, were *turmae* of thirty men.

66 By Mommsen 1912, 360–84; Domaszewski/Dobson 1967, 28 f; von Petrikovits 1975, 123, though not by Pitts and St Joseph 1985, 166.

67 My table (Figure 7.2) shows a gap at the *primus pilus posterior* position. E Birley 1952a, 232 suggested Hadrian gave each legion two *centuriae primipili* (see *CIL* VIII, 18065 of AD 161 and *CIL* XVI, p 146, no. 13 of AD 150; and the discussion in Domaszewski/Dobson 1967, XXIV, and Dobson 1978, 64 f) so as to increase the supply of *primipilares*-officers. Perhaps the intent was also to even out the newly important battle-lines, giving the *pili* of the first cohort the same depth as the other *pili.*

Chapter 8

Soldier and Civilian: Life beyond the Ramparts

Valerie A Maxfield

The other papers in this volume focus primarily on matters strictly military, examining the legion, its history, structure and function. Individuals are considered, but as serving soldiers and as officers. Here, I wish to consider them as people, as sons and brothers, as husbands and fathers; in short, to examine the non-military side of the life of a soldier and the links between the members of the army, their families and the civilians who lived within the military orbit.

The range of evidence which has a bearing on this theme is diverse and widely-scattered, taking us far beyond the area of operations of *legio II Augusta*. But our starting-point is close to home – a fine family tombstone from the collection in the Roman Legionary Museum Caerleon – a tombstone which names Tadius Exuperatus, a soldier who was presumably serving with *II Augusta* when he died, aged 37, while on a German expedition (Figure 8.1).[1] The memorial names, in prime position on the stone, Exuperatus' mother, Tadia Vallaunius; it is essentially her tombstone. His name follows. Having died in Germany he presumably was not actually buried at Caerleon, but is being commemorated, along with his mother, by his sister, Tadia Exuperata. Further, we are told that the memorial was erected beside the father's tomb. So here we have a complete family, father and mother, brother and sister, only this last now alive. It is a remarkably 'unmilitary' memorial for a soldier; only the mention of the German expedition, and the findspot, outside a legionary fortress, betray the fact that Exuperatus was a soldier. Unit, rank, origin, all are missing, though the first and last of these may be deduced. Exuperatus is the one certain case from Britain of a phenomenon attested quite frequently elsewhere in the Empire, of a soldier born *castris*: that is to say born in a settlement outside a legionary base. As such, he serves as an example of the increasing

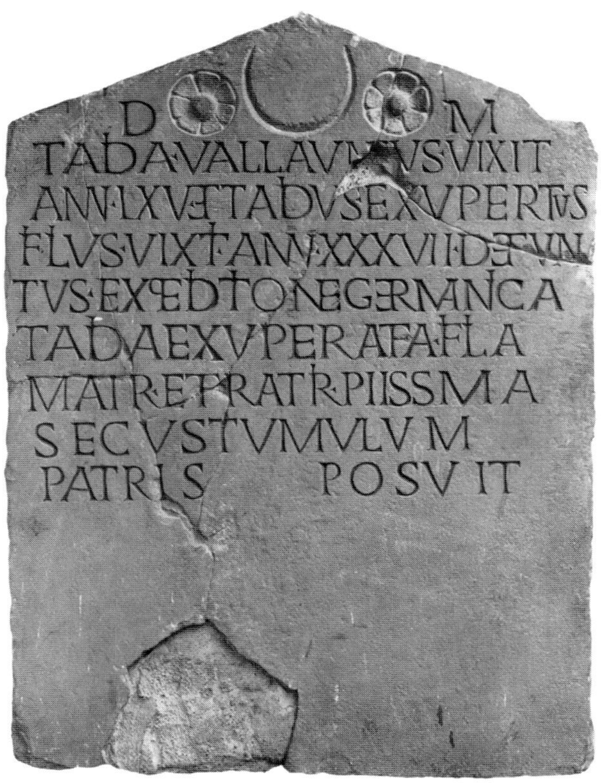

8.1 *The tombstone of Tadia Vallaunius and her son, Tadius Exuperatus, soldier of* legio II Augusta, *who died while on a German expedition. Caerleon* (RIB *I, 369*) *(photograph: National Museum of Wales)*

trend to local recruitment in the Roman army, and emphasizes the consequent change which this practice wrought in the nature of that army – what originated as an alien, invading, conquering force is piecemeal transformed into an establishment with close links with the local community.

The developing relationship between the army and the civil population is linked to the increasing immobility of military bases. As new provinces ceased to be won, as the frontiers congealed, so complete units gradually ceased to be moved about. Detachments would be sent out as required and then return to their parent unit. This is well illustrated by the case of Caerleon which remained the home base for *II Augusta* from its foundation in the context of the Flavian conquest of Wales until the army reforms of the late third century, although during this time substantial detachments were absent for considerable periods of time, operating elsewhere in the province (campaigning in Scotland, building Hadrian's Wall and then the Antonine Wall for example) or indeed overseas.[2] This situation contrasts markedly with the years of the Early Empire when *II Augusta,* in common with the army as a whole, was fully mobile, occupying some half a dozen different bases in Spain, Gaul, the Rhineland and southern Britain, expropriating land for its military bases and bringing with it a substantial complement of civilians, but one which was totally alien and totally dependent on the military for its continuing existence.

The civilian settlements which developed outside military bases had their nuclei in the substantial civilian tail which followed the army. Even an army on campaign into new and hostile territory had its band of camp-followers, and if the evidence of Tacitus is to be trusted, the non-military personnel who followed the army could, on occasion, outnumber the strictly military, constituting a very considerable problem in terms of housing and feeding.[3] The burden of the civilian train is very neatly pointed up by Quintilian in his *Orationes,* in which he likens the excessive use of epithets in a sentence to an army with a large number of camp-followers: 'It (the sentence) becomes long-winded and cumbrous, in fact you might compare it to an army with as many camp-followers as soldiers, an army, that is to say, doubled in numbers without doubling its strength'.[4]

This tail comprised camp servants, slaves, merchants, prostitutes and entertainers of various sorts, as well as the women who chose to follow their menfolk to an uncertain future, rather than risk losing them. While these camp-followers would commonly be left to their own ingenuity to provide themselves with food and shelter on the march, some might, on occasion, be taken inside the protection of the camp itself. For example, during operations in north-eastern Gaul (in Caesar's Gallic campaigns), stores had been concentrated at Cicero's base camp at Aduatuca (Tongres); menaced by the Germans, Cicero had confined to camp, not only the army itself but also the camp-followers, allowing not a single one to venture beyond the rampart.[5] Clearly then, part of the civilian following had been allowed within the defences, unlike the merchants who are singled out as having remained outside, camped, as we are told 'close under the rampart', where they had no chance of retreating when the Germans did eventually attack. Again, in Germany, in AD 9, the army which was annihilated under Varus was accompanied by a large civilian train. As Dio says of Varus' column: 'They had with them many waggons and many beasts of burden as in time of peace; moreover, not a few women and children and a large retinue of servants were following them.'[6] Arminius and his men go on to attack and then to attempt to starve out a Roman fort where there was again a large concentration of civilians: 'the soldiers were but few, the unarmed many.' Some of the Roman garrison attempt to escape the siege under cover of darkness: 'They succeeded in getting past the foe's first and second lines, but when they reached the third they were discovered, for the women and children, by reason of their fatigue and fear, as well as on account of the darkness and cold, kept calling to the warriors to come back.' [7]

The problems which could be caused by the presence of civilians both on the march and concentrated about a camp are illustrated all too clearly in this episode, and the bad effect which the proliferation of camp-followers had on military discipline is a theme often taken up by army reformers. Scipio, restoring discipline to the army encamped before Numantia, is said to have 'expelled all traders and harlots, also the soothsayers and diviners whom the soldiers were continually consulting ... those who had servants to bathe and anoint them were ridiculed by Scipio'.[8] Metellus, taking over the army campaigning against Jugurtha in Africa, found it in a run-down state, 'spiritless and unwarlike ... Neither had the camp been fortified nor the watches kept, according to military usage; everyone had been allowed to leave his post when he pleased. The camp-followers mingled with the soldiers, wandering about day and night, ravaging the country, robbing the houses and vying with one another in carrying off cattle and slaves which they exchanged with traders for foreign wine and other luxuries ... (Metellus') first measure was to remove incentives to idleness, by a general order that ... no sutlers should follow the army; and that no common soldier should have a servant or beast of burden either in the camp or on the march.'[9]

In practice, of course, while the worst abuses which arose from the presence of civilians in a military context might be removed, the civilians themselves remained a fact of life. And whatever disciplinarians such as Scipio and Metellus might say, it remained common practice for soldiers to have with them, particularly in the relatively settled conditions of the more permanent winter bases, slaves or freedmen who acted as personal servants and attendants. The best evidence for them is on inscriptions, occasionally commemorated in their own right, but more commonly featuring as incidental players on the gravestones of their masters. The slaves are most often attested as *liberti*, freedmen (freed in their master's will if not before), and are frequently named as the person responsible for the setting up of the tombstone. One of the best-known of British military tombstones, that of Marcus Favonius Facilis from Colchester, was erected by his *liberti*, Verecundus and Novicius, who will have accompanied him in the invasion of Britain in AD 43.[10] In contrast, the freedmen of Marcus Caelius, killed in the Varus disaster, almost certainly died with their master.[11] They are not recorded as having been responsible for setting up the memorial. Rather, their busts (identified by name) flank that of Caelius on his funerary monument which was erected outside the camp on the Fürstenburg at Xanten where his legion, *XVIII*, had been based (Figure 8.2). The text of the stone indicates that permission was granted for their bones to be interred beside his.[12]

The practice of *liberti* taking responsibility for the erection of soldiers' tombstones is one which is particularly prevalent in the first century, gradually dying out thereafter. The clear inference from this is that no family member was present to take on the responsibility, a situation which changes with the stabilisation of the army and the growth of soldier families.

Occasionally, though much less commonly, slaves and freedmen are commemorated in their own right by the soldiers whom they served. A particularly fine example is the stone set up at South Shields by Numerianus, a cavalryman serving in a Spanish *ala*, to Victor, his Moorish freedman (Figure 8.3).[13] This is a lavish and hence expensive piece of work, indicative both of the soldier's wealth and of the care he felt for his ex-slave whom he had clearly manumitted quite young, before he reached the age of 20, the age at which he died.

While some of the slaves present in the army train were personal slaves, privately owned, belonging to individual soldiers, others were officially attached to the army itself and thus presumably owned by the state.[14] Many of these fulfilled a pseudo-military role. We encounter them being used to forage, to fetch supplies, to drive the mules and wagons and to help defend the baggage train. Moreover, both Josephus in the first century and Vegetius in the fourth indicate that they had some military training. Josephus is specific on the point: 'Servants ... may properly be included in the category of combatants, whose military training they shared; for taking part in peacetime in all their masters' training and in wartime in their dangers, they yielded to none but them in skill and prowess. One cannot but admire the forethought shown in this particular by the Romans, in making their servants useful to them not only for ordinary life but also for war.'[15] Vegetius notes that the most able and experienced were called *galearii*, a term which derives from the word *galea*, a helmet.[16] Such servants appear not infrequently on military tombstones, specifically those of cavalrymen. They are depicted in two main ways. One type of scene shows the servant walking behind a riderless horse, which is held on a long rein (Figure 8.4). The servant wears a tunic and a helmet, and a pair of spears rests across his shoulder.[17] In another common type of scene the cavalryman appears on a prancing horse. In this case,

8.2 *The tombstone of Marcus Caelius, killed in the Varan disaster. To either side of Caelius are the busts of his freedmen, Marcus Caelius Privatus and Marcus Caelius Thiaminus. Xanten (photograph: reproduced by permission of the Landesmuseum, Bonn)*

the servant, standing behind horse and rider and holding a pair of spears (or, in the case of a mounted archer, a quiver full of arrows), is unhelmeted (Figure 8.5).[18] The almost invariable association with cavalrymen (in both *alae* and equitate cohorts) suggests a role as grooms; this is consistent with the evidence of Vegetius who states that the *galearii* were taught to swim along with the cavalry and their horses.[19] No actual reference is ever made to these men in the text of the tombstone on which they appear. They feature neither by name nor function, hence their status is uncertain: free-men, freedmen or slaves? Perhaps they are to be subsumed within the general category of slaves and freedmen, discussed above, who frequently saw to the setting up of their master's tombstone, for no servant or groom is ever named as such in this capacity.

Where these various, and apparently very numerous, personal and unit slaves and servants were housed in the military base, inside or out, is an intriguing if unanswerable question, but one which has important ramifications for our understanding of space allocation within military bases. Given the tasks which they performed, it is probable that they were accommodated close by their masters and, where appropriate, their horses. The other elements of the train, the merchants, cooks, prostitutes and players will have set up outside the ramparts; in a make-shift encampment initially, then in the simple timber barrack-like accommodation which gave the name *canabae* to the settlements which they formed – humble beginnings from which ultimately developed some very sophisticated urban settlements. While the presence of *canabae* are attested outside the two successive bases of *II Augusta* in Britain, of the camp-followers themselves we know very little. Perhaps to be numbered among them, in the days before the legion came to Britain, is Polla Matidia, 'otherwise

8.3 *The tombstone of Victor, a Moor, freedman of Numerianus, a cavalryman in the* ala I Asturum, *who had the stone erected. South Shields (photograph: reproduced by permission of Tyne and Wear Museums)*

8.4 *The tombstone of Longinus, cavalryman in the* ala Sulpicia. *His servant, clad in a tunic and wearing a helmet, walks behind his riderless horse, a pair of spears across his shoulder. Cologne (photograph: V A Maxfield)*

known as Olympia', a dancer or actress, whose tombstone was set up at Asciburgium (Asberg) in the northern Rhineland by a veteran of the legion, at his own expense; evidence of a relationship formed some time in the early years of the first century.[20]

Not surprisingly, women, and therefore children, feature in and around the camps, in either an official or unofficial capacity, from the earliest days of campaigning. Reference has already been made to the unfortunates whom Cassius Dio tells us were in the hapless army of the governor Varus. At the higher echelons of military society, it was common practice for a general, from the imperial family downwards, to be accompanied on campaign by his wife and children, though they would normally stay behind at base. For example, Germanicus took his wife Agrippina and his son, Gaius, to Germany with him when sent there to launch punitive campaigns against the followers of Arminius. They were based at the two-legion camp at Cologne, and it is here that Gaius acquired his nickname, *Caligula*, 'bootikins', given to him by the soldiery on account of his wearing little military boots, *caligae*.[21] Moreover, his sister, Agrippina the Younger, was born here in AD 15, and the veteran colony which subsequently came to replace the fortress was named in her honour by her then husband, Claudius – *Colonia Claudia Ara Agrippinensium*.[22] Julia Domna accompanied her

8.5 *Tombstone of Maris, a cavalryman in the* ala Parthorum et Araborum. *His servant walks behind, carrying a quiver full of arrows. Mainz (photograph: V A Maxfield)*

husband Septimius Severus to Syria, and her presence there was officially recognized by the title *Mater Castrorum* (mother of the camp) bestowed on her in AD 195. Later, in AD 208, she accompanied Severus to Britain, where her presence is attested thanks to an anecdote recorded by Dio, in which she is said to have had a conversation with the wife of a Caledonian chieftan about the relative merits of Roman and Caledonian sexual practices.[23] Though it is nowhere explicitly stated, it may be inferred that Julius Agricola brought his wife with him to Britain, since Tacitus records that his young son, born during his sixth season in Britain, died at the start of the seventh.[24]

The practice of taking wives to the provinces was not one which was universally approved of; its propriety was discussed in the Senate at Rome in AD 21 in the context of a debate over allocation to the proconsulships of Asia and Africa.[25] In the course of the debate Caecina Severus moved that no magistrate, who had been allotted a province, should be accompanied by his wife. He explained beforehand at some length that although he had a wife and six children, they had never accompanied him to any of his forty campaigns in the provinces. 'There was point in the old regulation which prohibited the dragging of women to the provinces or foreign countries: in a retinue of ladies there were elements apt, by luxury or by timidity, to retard the business of peace or war and to transmute a Roman march into something resembling an eastern procession. Weakness and a lack of endurance were not the only failings of the sex: give them scope and they turned hard, intriguing, ambitious. They paraded among the soldiers; they had the centurions at beck and call. Recently a woman had presided at the exercises of the cohorts and the manoeuvres of the legions.[26] Let the audience reflect that, whenever a magistrate was on trial for professional misconduct, the majority of the charges were levelled against his wife. It was to the wife that the basest of the provincials attached themselves; it was the wife who took in hand and transacted business. There were two potentates to salute in the streets; two government houses; and the more headstrong and autocratic orders came from the women, who ... had now cast their chains and ruled supreme in the home, the courts, and by now the army itself.' But Valerius Messalinus spoke against the motion: '... it was unjust that through the weakness of one or two, married men in general should be torn from their partners ... while at the same time a sex, frail by nature, was left alone, exposed to its own voluptuousness and the appetites of others.'

The motion failed. For better or worse governors continued to take their wives to the provinces. How Caecina Severus would have disapproved of the wife of Calvisius Sabinus, an example of just the sort of woman who 'paraded among the soldiers', an 'unchaste woman' according to Plutarch.[27] When Sabinus was serving as governor of Pannonia, his wife decided she wanted to see inside the camp. Dio tells us rather blandly that she had 'made the rounds of the sentries and had watched the soldiers at drill'. Tacitus and Plutarch are more specific. Aided and abetted by the military tribune, Titus Vinius, she had disguised herself as a soldier and entered the camp by night. There she interfered with the guard and the other soldiers on duty and committed adultery with Vinius in the *principia*.[28]

Further down the scale of command, we find legionary legates, too, accompanied by their wives and families, who would be accommodated most comfortably in the spacious house provided within the legionary base. To take just one example from Britain, Sosia Juncina, the wife of Quintus Antonius Isauricus, legate of *legio VI* at York some time in the mid-Hadrianic period, set up a dedication to Fortuna in the public baths of the settlement across the river from the fortress: why, one wonders, was she frequenting these baths when she had her own private suite in the legate's palace?[29]

Auxiliary commanders, too, were accompanied by their wives, a fact vividly illustrated by the famous birthday invitation received by Sulpicia Lepidina, wife of Flavius Cerialis, prefect of the ninth cohort of Batavians at Vindolanda (Figure 8.6).[30] It was sent to her by another prefect's wife, Claudia Severa, married to Aelius Brocchus who commanded a unit at Briga, a place of uncertain identity. This invitation is not the only piece of correspondence between these two women. A letter from Severa to Lepidina informs us that she had asked her husband's permission to visit Lepidina; permission was duly granted.[31] The two women were clearly friends. This correspondence only serves to highlight the social isolation of the women who accompanied their husbands to the frontiers of the remoter provinces. In the context of the legionary camp, there would be several women of not-dissimilar (if not exactly like) status – wives of those who were, or were destined to be, senators (the wife of the governor in the case of a one-legion province, the legionary legate's wife, the senior tribune's wife), and the wives of members of the equestrian aristocracy (the junior tribunes and those of the centurions who had obtained their posts by direct commission). The wife of the auxiliary unit commander (normally a member of the equestrian aristocracy)[32] was alone in the fort in terms of social standing. Her social equals would be found only among the wives of other unit commanders – hence friendships such as that between Severa and Lepidina. Both women had children. The birthday invitation mentions Severa's little son, and the material finds from the Vindolanda *praetorium* included childrens' shoes.[33] The writing lesson preserved on another of the Vindolanda tablets is perhaps the work of Lepidina's offspring. The exercise in question is a line from Virgil's *Aeneid*, unfortunately marked as being 'sloppy work'![34]

Notable among the inscriptions which refer to the wives and children of auxiliary commanders in Britain are two which commemorate foster-children or foundlings, *alumni*. Ylas, *alumnus karissimus* of Claudius Severus, tribune at Old Penrith (in Cumbria), was only 13 when he died; the age of Hermagoras, *alumnus* of Honoratus, tribune at High Rochester, north of Hadrian's Wall, is not recorded.[35] Among the higher echelons of the legionary officers at Caerleon, Sallienius Thalamus, camp prefect of *II*

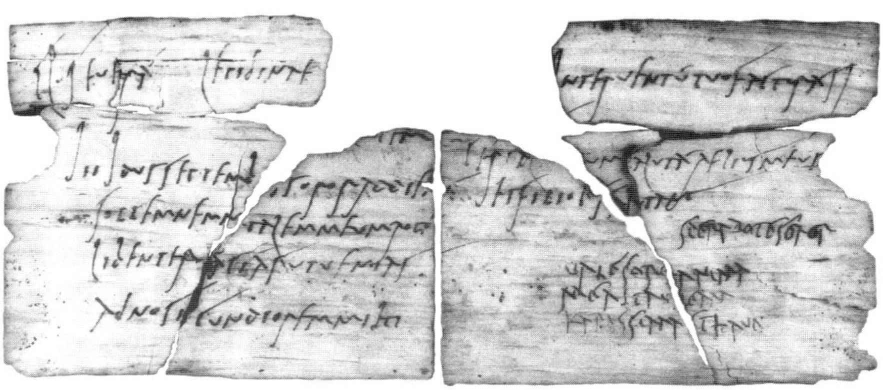

8.6 *The birthday invitation sent by Claudia Severa to Sulpicia Lepidina, wife of a commanding officer at Vindolanda (photograph: reproduced by permission of the Vindolanda Trust)*

Augusta in the late second or early third century, associated his two sons with him in two dedications which he set up – one an altar to Salus the Queen, the other an inscribed slab dedicated to the welfare of Severus, Caracalla and Geta.[36]

The majority of these officer-families will have stayed no more than about three years in any one posting; they will then have moved on, in some cases back to a civilian life, in others to another military command. The situation was very different for the common soldiery, under the colours for twenty-five unbroken years. And yet the ordinary soldier was legally forbidden to marry.[37] For the whole of his young manhood and into middle age he was to remain a bachelor! The reason for this, viewed from the standpoint of the Roman high command, is not far to seek. The army was envisaged as a mobile campaigning army, moving between summer and winter camps, moving on as the military situation developed. To permit a soldier to marry would be tacitly to accept some sort of responsibility for the soldier's dependents. Not only this, the encumbrance caused by an 'official' civilian tail would be even greater than that caused by the spontaneous army of camp-followers. All of the reservations expressed in the context of the officers' wives would be greatly magnified.

However, the context against which the ban on marriage should be viewed changed radically as the army settled down into relatively permanent bases and a man might pass his whole period of service within a single province, if not at a single station. By the time Severus relaxed the law and gave soldiers permission to contract a legal marriage (assuming this is what he did) he was probably doing no more than regularising an existing situation and making legal relationships which had already been established. The precise nature of the Severan concession has been disputed. The words used by Herodian, the one extant historical source specifically to record it, are ambiguous; while they can mean that permission was granted 'to live in wedlock with their wives', they can also mean no more than that the soldiers were now permitted 'to cohabit with their women'.[38] This, however, would be nothing very new. There is plentiful evidence, if evidence be needed, of soldiers' wives, common-law wives that is, long before the law was changed. Indeed it is very possible that our Tadius Exuperatus was the offspring of just such a relationship.

Indeed, the dichotomy which existed between principle and practice is set out very nicely in the certificate of privileges which was awarded to the auxiliary soldier on completion of twenty-five years' service. These privileges were those of Roman citizenship and *conubium*. The citizenship was bestowed not just upon the soldier in question but, at least until *c* AD 140, upon any children he might already have, as well as upon those born subsequently. The second privilege received, that of *conubium*, the right to contract a legal marriage with a non-Roman woman, was a necessary requirement for a Roman citizen. In the terminology of the diploma this right was awarded 'with the wives they had at the time when citizenship was granted to them, or if they were single, with the wives they married afterwards, provided that each took only one wife.' This legal document is thus specifically acknowledging and regularising what had until then been an illegal relationship and illegitimate children.

In the case of such existing relationships the women and children involved are named on the document. It has been calculated that just under half of the soldiers name wives and/or children.[39] What of the half who did not? Was termination of service a convenient moment at which to escape from the prospect of full-time family responsibility? While this may have been the case for some, such an interpretation of the evidence is at variance with the growing tendency for soldiers to settle where they had served. A closer examination of the figures shows that the practice of acknowledging an existing family is one which increases after the stabilisation of the frontiers in the Hadrianic period.[40] Thus it shows exactly what might be anticipated – the increasing practicability of stable relationships when the army ceases to move. That is not to say that a 'wife', albeit an unofficial one, might not be prepared to follow her man half way across the Empire. One such case is that of M. Ulpius Fronto.[41] He was a Batavian (from the Low Countries) and acknowledges a Batavian wife, as well as three daughters. He was a member of *cohors I Batavorum*. He probably started his period of service with the unit either in Britain or as it passed through the Low Countries *en route* from here to the Danube area where it was transferred under Domitian, seeing service in the Dacian Wars and later becoming part of the army of Pannonia Superior. The family probably settled on the Danube when Fronto left the service, for the diploma was found in the civil settlement outside the fort at Regensburg-Kümpfmühl, in the province of Raetia.[42]

Another possible case of a woman following her husband is that of the wife of Lucco, a Britain from the Cirencester area.[43] He was a footsoldier in *cohors I Britannica* which, at the time of his retirement in AD 105, formed part of the army of Moesia. However, he retired to Brigetio which is in Pannonia Superior. His wife is an Azalian woman, a native of the Brigetio area, and he had probably formed a liaison with her at an earlier stage in his career when his unit had been stationed in Pannonia from where she presumably followed him to Moesia. Either that, or the relationship was sufficiently stable for it to survive a separation, and for him to return to her when he received his discharge. A son and two daughters are named on the diploma.

That the irregular relationships contracted by serving soldiers could make for actual or potential legal complications, is clearly indicated by documentation surviving from Egypt. The births of the illegitimate children of these unions could not be formally registered. However, a record of their birth might be regarded as desirable for future purposes when they were legitimised on the discharge of their fathers. Accordingly, Lucretius Clemens, a cavalryman serving in an auxiliary cohort in the Thebaid, made an *attestatio*, that is a formal declaration, of the birth of his son, swearing that 'while in military service he had become the father, by Octavia Tamusta, of a natural son, Serenus ... and he stated that he made this attestation on account of the restriction imposed by military service, so as to be able to have proof at his certification of [citizen] status after his discharge that he (Serenus) is his natural son.'[44] Further and worse complications could arise in the case of the death of the soldier while still in service. There might, for example, be problems with inheritance. Lucia Macrina claimed a deposit from the property of the deceased soldier Antonius Germanus. Her case appeared before the prefect of Egypt who declared: 'We assume that such deposits are dowries. I do not grant a trial for such causes since a soldier is not permitted to marry; and if you claim a dowry and I do grant a trial, I shall give the appearance of believing that the marriage is legal ...'.[45] But of course the marriage was not legal in Roman eyes. Men could not contract a legal marriage during service and it is most probable that any existing marriage was deemed to be dissolved.[46] Any dowry not promptly claimed back, was regarded simply as part of the man's savings. If a couple wished to remain true to one another and for the man to keep the dowry and to retain control over the family finances in such a way that the woman would get the money back if her husband died in service, some legally recognized arrangement had to be made. It is this which best explains a rather problematic document concerning a dowry and a soldier 'who had been married before'.[47] Demetria had been married to Valerius Gemellus; they have two sons, one aged 14, the other 10 at the time the document is drawn up. Gemellus joins the Alexandrian fleet so the marriage is legally dissolved, the boys made illegitimate. The money which Demetria is recorded as paying to Gemellus has been ingeniously interpreted as being not a dowry made on marriage but a betrothal pledge: as such, if the marriage (that is to say the remarriage) never took place (if, for example, Gemellus died in service) Demetria would be entitled to her money back. Thus *he* retains the money but *her* interest in it is safeguarded. She will not lose it in the way that Lucia Macrina lost hers.

Likewise, soldiers' children who were born during their fathers' terms of service, being deemed illegitimate, had no claim on the property of their fathers if they died intestate. A letter from Hadrian to the prefect of Egypt was posted in the camp of the legions in Alexandria: 'I am aware, my dear Rammius, that those whom their parents acknowledged as their offspring during the period of military service have been debarred from succession to parental property, and this was not considered harsh, since the parents had acted contrary to military discipline. But for my own part I am very glad to introduce a precedent for interpreting more liberally the rather stern rule established by the emperors before me.' He goes on to grant that, although the children cannot be regarded as legal heirs they can claim an inheritance as blood relatives.[48] If Hadrian sought, by sympathetic interpretation of the law, to ameliorate the situation of the soldier family, Severus removed the problem by his simple expedient of legitimising the existing unofficial marriages.[49]

Tombstone as well as documentary evidence testifies to the existence of the soldier family long before it became a legal entity. There are, in fact, probably many more cases than have been acknowledged; it is often very difficult to distinguish later second-century epitaphs from those of the third, and there has always been a tendency to assume, in the absence of any positive evidence to the contrary, that a serving soldier's tombstone, if set up by a 'wife', post-dates the Severan change in the law. There is little justification for such an assumption as can be shown, for example, by the evidence from Carnuntum on the Danube. A fine collection of military tombstones from this site includes a group which relates to soldiers of *legio XV Apollinaris.* This legion was based at Carnuntum from the early Claudian period until late in the reign of Trajan, with just a short break under Nero: it moved east in connection with Trajan's Parthian War and never returned, being stationed thereafter on the eastern frontier, at Satala in Cappadocia. And yet the tombstones set up to or by serving soldiers include several with family connections. One is set up by a wife, another by a wife and son.[50] One soldier commemorates his 5-year-old daughter, another his 5-year-old son, while a mother, a father and several brothers (in these cases genuine brothers, as their names indicate) commemorate their sons and siblings.[51] One veteran commemorated by his wife and children survived to the age of only 40 years.[52] He can only just have been discharged before his death, so that the liaison must logically predate his return to civilian status. All of these cases can, on the evidence of the legion's known movements, date no later than the second decade of the second century, and some indeed have the phraseology of first-century stones, indicating a very early development of a civilian community outside the fortress.

These well-dated stones provide good specific evidence. What can also be observed very clearly in the tombstone evidence in general, is a trend away from dedication by a freedman, an unspecified heir, or an heir who is designated a brother (but brother soldier in this context, not a blood relative), extremely common in the first century, towards dedication by a wife and/or other family member. Compare the stone of Tadius Exuperatus with two first-century examples commemorating men who died in service, away from their homes and parental families. Largennius served in *II Augusta* at its Strasbourg base before it came to Britain: he was recruited at Lucca in northern Italy: neither family nor heir are named (Figure 1.7).[53] Later in the first century is the case of C. Valerius Victor, a native of Lugdunum (Lyon) who died in Caerleon, where his stone was erected by his heir, Annius Perpetuus.[54] Of the eleven recorded soldiers who died in service in *II Augusta* prior to its transfer to Britain (a good clear chronological divide) not one is commemorated by a wife. Six mention freedmen (or women) and/or heirs. One of these, that relating to Tiberius Babuleius Garrulus, native of Milan, is an unusual and interesting case for a secondary text commemorates family members – not a wife, but his father, mother and sister. Their epitaph was erected by a freedman and heir.[55] Had the whole family decamped with him to Germany where he died, at Strasbourg, three years before discharge?

Prior to coming to Britain, *II Augusta* appears to have received all of its recruits from northern Italy, southern Gaul and Spain and for at least the next half century after moving to Britain, the legion continued to recruit from these same areas, plus central Gaul and the Rhineland. The one man, T. Flavius Candidus, from this last source is the latest proven non-British recruit; he is recorded as coming from Ulpia Traiana, a veteran colony founded, as its name implies, by Trajan, in fact very early in his reign at the close of the first century AD.[56] Of these foreign recruits, just two chose to remain in Britain after retirement. At least three, and perhaps as many as five, returned home. The other three known died in service. These figures are far too small to have any overall statistical significance, but they do raise an interesting problem. To what extent might it be possible for a soldier who was serving well away from his parental home, to maintain contact with his family?

The one province from which we have any substantial evidence having a bearing on this subject is Egypt where significant quantities of soldiers' letters are included among the papyri retrieved from the towns of the Fayum, notably Karanis. Here we see the workings of an informal postal system with friends, colleagues and relatives being used to carry not only letters but substantial quantities of assorted goods between home and camp (Figure 8.7).

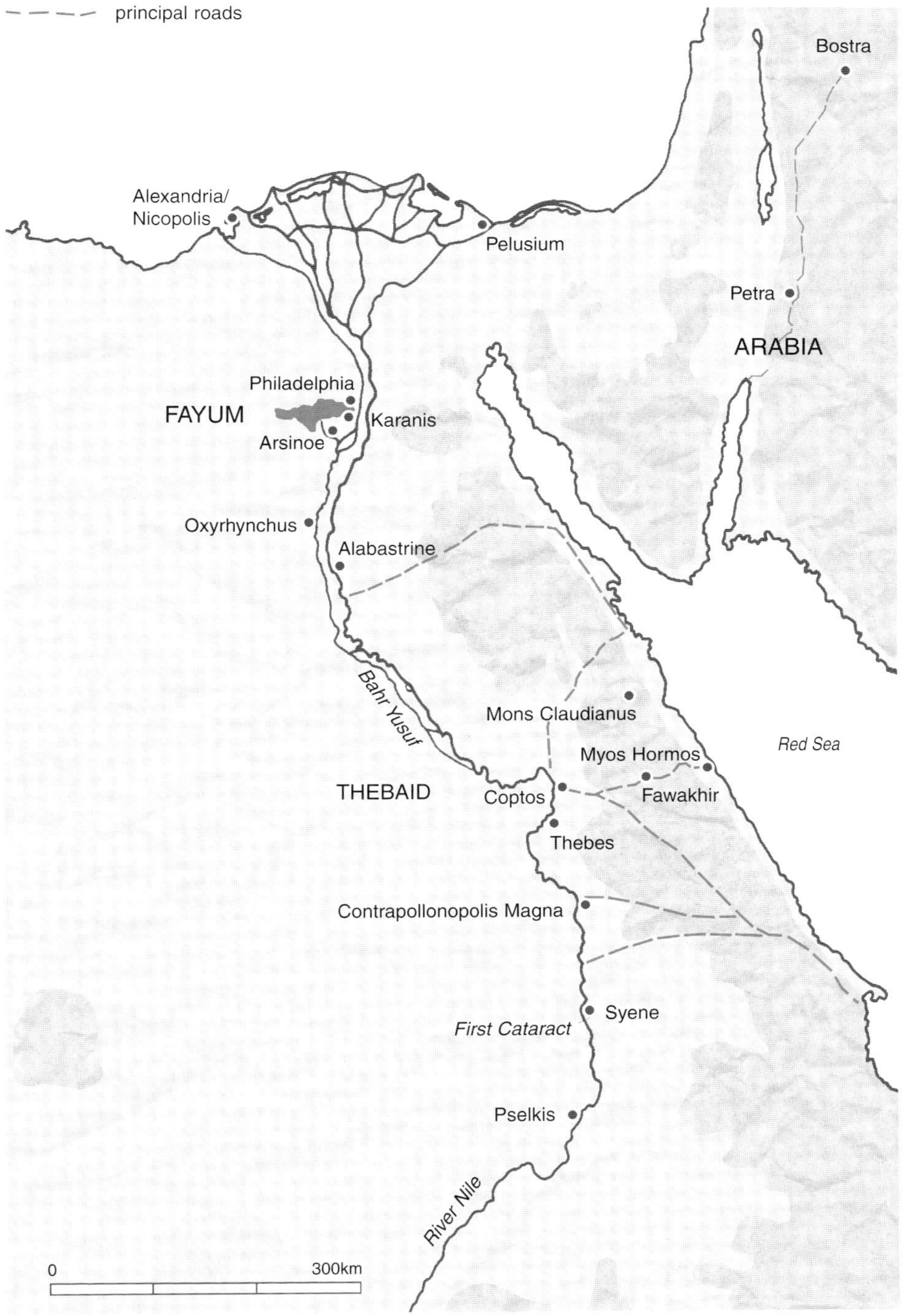

8.7 *Map of Egypt, showing the sites referred to in the text (drawing: Seán Goddard)*

The address on the back of a letter from Apion (alias Antonius Maximus) a soldier in the Misene fleet, stationed in southern Italy in the Bay of Naples, to his father Epimachus who lived in Lower Egypt, in the area of the Fayum, is particularly informative.[57] It reads: 'To Philadelphia, to Epimachus from Apion his son.' Then is added: 'Deliver at [the camp of] *cohors I Apamenorum* to Julianus, *librarius*, this letter from

Apion, to be forwarded to his father Epimachus.' Unfortunately we have no direct independent evidence as to where *I Apamenorum* was stationed at this time. In the Late Empire it was in Upper Egypt, in the Thebaid, but such a location would be a very roundabout way of reaching Philadelphia. However, a number of second-century references associate the unit with the general area of the Arsinoite nome (to which Philadelphia belongs), so it may be suspected that this is the region where it lay. Incidentally another letter from Apion, in this case to his sister, requests that greetings be conveyed to his wife and son (the latter about to celebrate his birthday), indicating that both had remained home rather than accompanying him on his posting to Italy.[58] The correspondence was two-way, for Apion refers to having received a letter from a friend at home in Philadelphia.

Another recruit to the Misene fleet, Apollinarius from Karanis, a short distance to the south-west of Philadelphia, was able to carry on a regular correspondence with his mother back home, using various intermediaries: he sent his first missive from Cyrene, while *en route* to Italy – 'finding a man who was coming to you'; he penned the next one when he got to Portus (the port of Rome, at Ostia), followed quickly by another in which he promises his mother: 'I'll write you a letter, too, if I find someone. I will not be slow to write.' And he urges her to write to him: 'And you for your part don't be slow to write about your health and that of my brothers. If you don't find anyone coming to me, write to Socrates, and he'll forward it to me.' [59]

While relatives, friends and colleagues might be called upon to carry letters and goods if they happened to be going in the right direction, a letter written from Raima, somewhere in the Eastern Desert, makes reference to a more formal postal-service; the writer noted that he was 'waiting for the post-camels'.[60] Fleet personnel, based as they were at a major Italian port, had little trouble in finding someone to carry letters for them. But neither apparently did another native of Karanis, this time a legionary soldier, C. Julius Apollinarius, whose unit was based at Bostra in the province of Arabia but who at the time of writing appears to have been in a detachment at Petra, an eight-day journey to the south. A letter to his father requests that linen garments be sent via a contact with Pelusium, from where, as he indicates, merchants regularly travelled to the legionary base. To his mother he makes a request for coarse linen, the intermediary in this case being a friend of his in Alexandria.[61]

A later letter which Apollinarius wrote concerned the leasing out of grain-bearing lands and olive-groves which he owned at five different locations in the Fayum.[62] It is an important reminder to us that, despite a long-term commitment to the army, our soldiers might retain business as well as personal links with the area from which they came. Such links might ultimately be the deciding factor in causing them to return to their roots in preference to settlement in the province where they served, assuming that the two are different. Another Egyptian legionary, Valerius Paulinus, owned a house and field in his home village (again Karanis), this despite the fact that soldiers were not supposed to own land in the province where they served – yet another of those prohibitions which became increasingly meaningless and unenforceable with the development of local recruiting. Paulinus proposed renting out his land to a fellow-soldier, Terentianus, who was due to retire from the army the year before him.[63] He writes to his brother back home: '... I ask you to receive with my recommendation the discharged soldier, Terentianus, who brings you the letter, and to let him know what sort of village people we have, in case he gets into trouble. Since he is a man of means and wants to settle down there, I urged him to give me a rental for my house for the current and coming year of 60 drachmas, and for the coming year, 137, to have my field on lease for 60 drachmas...'. Terentianus apparently did not want to return to his own home nor to settle in Alexandria where he had served. Instead he is to see how he likes it in his friend's village.[64]

The correspondence between camp and home is, not unnaturally, particularly prolific in the case of soldiers serving in their native province, though even here not inconsiderable distances may be involved. Another category of correspondence that survives is between soldiers on outpost duty and their base camps. In Egypt many such letters were written, not on the familiar papyrus, but on ostraca, broken potsherds, a cheap and readily-available alternative.[65] They attest correspondence on a wide variety of matters of private life, a mixture of family affairs and business concerns.

For example, Maximus reproaches his sister (given that this is Egypt, what is probably meant is his wife) for not letting him know when her baby was due. He tells her that when he knows, he will come in the provisions boat.[66] She was presumably living at the place where the text was found, which is thought to be Contrapollonopolis Magna, on the Upper Nile, the site of a military base.[67] Where Maximus was stationed, up- or downstream from here, we do not know.

Terentianus writes from Alexandria to his father about acquiring a wife for whom he is to seek his father's approval, while a standard-bearer in a cavalry unit based in Alexandria makes a loan (with interest) to a priest of the temples of Apollo and Isis in Alabastrine.[68] The link between the soldier and the priest was probably established when a detachment of the unit was posted south to supervise work in the alabaster quarries. This loan is a reminder of the relative affluence of the regularly-paid soldier, although elsewhere another cavalryman has had to borrow from his village, and is concerned to make repayment.[69] Another soldier who is expecting soon to be sent on an eighteen-month outposting is Saturnilus who writes to his mother Aphrodous at Karanis to tell her that he has just got another baby boy.[70] He is based at Pselkis (modern Dakke) in the south of Upper Egypt where he is accompanied by his wife and other children. He is a good correspondent: his letter indicates that he had written to her three times that month. He hopes to come to visit her before he is sent on outpost duty – most likely to one of the road or quarry sites of the eastern desert. He talks of sending his wife and children to his mother's, which suggests that they were not to remain at base during his absence nor to accompany him to his outpost. That families did sometimes accompany soldiers on their desert outpostings is suggested by both written and archaeological evidence from the desert quarry site at Mons Claudianus (Figure 8.8), while the ostraca from Wâdi Fawâkhir attest the presence of both women and children, very possibly soldiers' families.[71] That soldiers' women travelled the road on which Fawâkhir lay is indicated by an entry in the Coptos Tariff. This is a list of tolls imposed on various categories of people and goods which travelled the route eastwards from Coptos to the Red Sea coast.[72] It includes a payment of 20 *drachmae* for a soldier's woman (or wife, the Greek word can mean either), 20 for a sailor's woman, and a substantial 108 *drachmae* for a prostitute (far the most expensive entry in the list) – perhaps heading

8.8 *The fort, animal lines and store building at the heart of the quarry complex at Mons Claudianus (photograph: Seán Goddard)*

for the military outposts along the road, or for rich pickings at the major port of Myos Hormos at its terminus?[73]

Closer to home, and in a much more comfortable posting, it would appear that the wife of Vivius Marcianus, a centurion in *legio II Augusta,* followed her husband from his base at Caerleon to London, where he had presumably been seconded onto the governor's staff, accommodated in the Cripplegate fort, outside the north-west corner of the city. He died there and it is she who set up his tombstone (Figure 6.9).[74]

Returning to Wâdi Fawâkhir, the correspondence received (and presumably also sent) by the soldiers at that site is, in general, dominated by one subject – food – hardly surprising in this bleak desert posting. Indeed this topic is a very frequent one in letters home. Despite the generally high quality of the Roman military diet, requests are sent home for such basic commodities as loaves, lemons, oil, olives and also for meat. This last is an interesting one. The myth of the vegetarian diet of the Roman soldier is one which dies hard, despite the mass of archaeological evidence (at least from the northern and western parts of the Empire) for a wide range of meats.[75] A Mediterranean bias away from meats is perhaps to be anticipated in the hotter parts of the Empire, and yet a number of the Egyptian texts refer to it. Two of the ostraca from Contrapollonopolis Magna in the south of the province, record a failure to procure meat (clearly implying that it was wanted), while a soldier in Alexandria berates his mother because he had been sent nothing when his friend's mother had sent him a whole range of goods including 'a basket of meat'.[76] Several ostraca from Mons Claudianus, too, make references to meat, including suckling pigs and liver.[77]

The family is expected not only to top up the soldier's diet, but to furnish him with a wide range of other goods. Money features not infrequently – indeed one soldier asked his mother for 200 drachmas, which is the equivalent of two months basic legionary pay – and we have already heard of Julius Apollinarius' requests for linens.[78] Other clothing asked for includes trousers, a pair of leggings, a tunic with a belt, a pair of belts, a woollen cloak, leather coats, low leather boots and a pair of felt slippers.[79] To this Egyptian chronicle of clothing wants can now be added the famous Vindolanda underwear. The very first of the Vindolanda tablets to be found recorded the dispatch to an unknown soldier of '... (so many) pairs of socks, two pairs of sandals and two pairs of underpants'.[80] Tantalisingly we do not know who sent these things and from where. Is this the earliest example of knitting socks for our men at the front?

Interestingly this traffic in goods between military base and home is by no means one-way. Many of the letters record soldiers sending supplies back to their families, mostly modest gifts. The most notable is a letter sent to his father by Claudius Terentianus, serving in the fleet at Alexandria. It chronicles a fascinating collection of goods: 'I send you, father, by Martialis, a bag sewn together, in which you have a pair of capes, a pair of cloaks, a pair of towels, a pair of socks, a little wooden camp-bed. I had bought this, plus a mattress and a pillow, and while I was lying ill on board ship, they were stolen from me. You have also in the bag a cloak of single thickness; my mother sent this to you. Receive also a chicken-coop, in which you have sets of glassware, a pair of bowls of quinarius size, a dozen goblets, two papyrus rolls for school use, ink for use on the papyrus, and twenty Alexandrian loaves. I ask you father, to be content with that. If only I'd not been ill, I was hoping to send you more, and again I hope to do so, if I live.'[81]

Depending on where they were posted, the soldiers might have better access to a wider range of consumer goods than did their families. A soldier in Alexandria would have at his disposal merchants and traders from all around the Mediterranean basin not to mention the fine Alexandrian glasswares recalled by Terentianus' gift to his father. As Julius Apollinarius wrote to his mother: 'fine garments, ebony, pearls and unguents are brought here (that is Petra) in large quantities'.[82] A legionary at Carnuntum on the Danube was serving at the point where one of the major north–south European trade routes – the great Amber Road from the Baltic to the Mediterranean at Aquileia – crossed the frontier into the Empire. And major cities, some of them provincial capitals, lay immediately adjacent to very many legionary bases, Mainz, for example, capital of Upper Germany, Aquincum (Budapest) capital of Pannonia Inferior. Even in Britain where two of the three legionary bases lay a long way from a major city, legionaries would be detached from time to time to serve on the staffs of the governor and procurator in London. So too the auxiliaries who might see periods of service in the provincial governor's bodyguard. There they could exploit the range of goods being traded into Britain's premier port. Even the soldier who was never posted to an entrepôt of any significance could still benefit from the traders who swarmed around the camps to acquire goods not so readily available to families who lived in the countryside.

Very many of the letters indicate an earnest concern for the health and welfare of their distant families. From time to time the hope is expressed of a visit home. Even Julius Apollinarius, at Bostra in Arabia plans a visit: 'I shall take steps, immediately the commander begins to grant leave, to come to you immediately', while Terentianus at Alexandria urges his father to come to him when he has been ill. A subsequent letter indicates that the father did come.[83]

Leave of absence such as that sought by Apollinarius, long enough to visit another province (albeit, in this case, an adjacent one), is unlikely to have been at all common, at least not in the case of ordinary soldiers. For officers it might be possible to obtain, as is implied by a statement in Suetonius' *Life of Augustus,* that the emperor 'grudged even his generals home leave and granted this only during the winter'.[84] The only specific evidence we have for the length of a grant of leave comes from Contrapollonopolis Magna, where a soldier is granted ten days plus an extra two to return.[85] Another possible case of a leave of ten days duration (if not more) is recorded on a duty roster of *legio III Cyrenaica* at Nicopolis (by Alexandria), which lists the tasks assigned to thirty-six named soldiers. The man in question has no duties assigned him for the first eight days in a ten-day record. What happened on the last two days is unclear for the document is defective at this point.[86] Another soldier on the same document has at least two days leave, the last two on the roster, granted 'by permission of the prefect', presumably the prefect in charge of the two-legion camp at Nicopolis.[87] What these two men had planned for their time off we do not know. That the duration of leave was carefully specified is clear also from an analysis of the duties of *cohors XX Palmyrenorum* at Dura Europos in AD 219 in which it is noted that two men 'overstayed leave'.[88] Given the context, there is no indication of the permitted duration or of the purpose for which the leave was to be taken. Vegetius, in his description of the legion in the 'old days' (the *antiqua legio*) states that '... when and for how many days anyone received leave was written down in the records. For at that time little leave was given and only for the most just and approved reasons'.[89] This, if true, implies that leave was not received as a matter of course, but was given in response to a request for a specific purpose. Out of twelve requests for leave – all of them unfortunately fragmentary – from the Vindolanda archive, one indicates that the applicant wishes to go to Coria (identified as Corbridge which is about 22 kilometres or one day's journey distant) and another to Ulucium, a place we cannot identify.[90] Unfortunately, in neither case is the reason for the visit preserved, while a third tablet breaks off just at the point where this information is to be given '... so that I might ...'.[91] Not surprisingly, leave might not always be forthcoming as and when wanted. Valerius Palmas, writing to Valerius Longus, a cavalryman in the *ala Apriana* at Mons Claudianus, regrets that 'no-one has given me leave' (Figure 8.9), while extension of leave to fit in a family visit was not allowed in the case of a soldier who was being transferred (at his own request) from the legion in Alexandria to a cavalry unit at Coptos.[92] On the way south to join his new unit, the soldier passed by his parental home at Oxyrhynchus; his uncle, who had intervened to help effect the transfer and was accompanying the boy to Coptos, wrote to his brother (the boy's father): 'I wanted to pay you a visit on the voyage up, we were limited by the leave granted to the boy by the most illustrious prefect, and for that reason I did not manage to visit you'. The prefect in this case, where two units were involved, one legionary, one auxiliary, will presumably have been the provincial governor, the *praefectus Aegypti.*

Apart from family visits, soldiers are known to have spent their leave in a variety of activities, some more elevated than others. Spa complexes were popular. The army of Upper Germany favoured Wiesbaden *(Aquae Mattiacorum)* not far from the legionary fortress at Mainz, and Baden-Baden *(Aquae)* north-east of Strasbourg.[93] For the soldiers of *II Augusta* at Caerleon (as also for other units from the army in Britain) the popular venue was the religious and therapeutic complex at Bath. A centurion and an

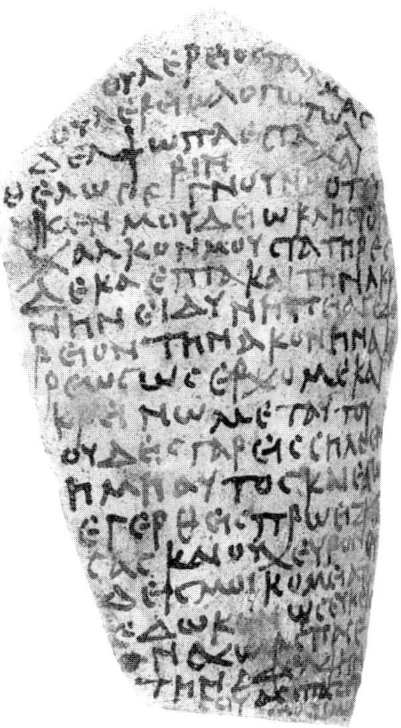

8.9 *Ostracon from Mons Claudianus, a military-controlled quarry complex in the Eastern Desert of Egypt. It alludes to the writer's failure to get leave (photograph: A Bülow-Jacobsen)*

imaginifer of the legion were among those who set up dedications there.[94] For those serving at Caerleon it was only a couple of days' journey at most, but for those from *legio VI* based at York, two of whom (one *miles* and one centurion) set up altars there, more like ten days. Three serving soldiers, including a native Briton from the *civitas Belgarum* (as well as one veteran) are known to have died there: were they perhaps on sick leave and hoping – in vain as it turned out – for a cure ?

In Egypt a popular tourist spot (then as now) was Thebes – modern Luxor – where a visit was made to the Colossi to hear Memnon sing. The graffiti on the feet of the northernmost of the two statues attest the presence, among others, of three auxiliary unit commanders, one of whom was accompanied by his wife and son, a legionary tribune, a camp prefect and several centurions.[95] All of these had travelled only within Egypt itself, but even so it is a journey of well over 800 kilometres from the legionary base at Alexandria. The prefect of the Alexandrian fleet, who visited in March 134, would presumably have had no trouble finding transportation up the Nile.[96] Indeed, he might have stopped off while on an official visit to the Thebaid, for the fleet operated as far south as the first cataract at Syene (Aswan), well upstream of Thebes. A military tribune from *legio III Augusta*, based in Numidia, had come even further to visit the tombs of the kings where he had inscribed his name in the tomb of Rameses V – how old do graffiti have to be no longer to be regarded as vandalism? – though in this case he could have been *en route* to his home in Syria at the end of his period of command, or possibly on his way to his next posting, rather than being on leave.[97] A less cultural way of spending some of one's leave is attested at Pompeii, where a soldier from the emperor's bodyguard, is among those who recorded a visit to a brothel.[98]

The theme of this paper has dwelt on the non-military aspects of a soldier's life, on the civilian contacts which he made and developed in and around the camp, and indeed well beyond it. On retirement the soldier would return to and become part of that civilian community. But just as, during his years in service, he kept his stake in the world beyond the ramparts, so as a veteran, a civilian, he very often opted to retain his contacts with the army, with that military environment in which he had passed the best years of his life. The units of the Roman army, like any army, will have developed within them a strong *esprit de corps*. Such a spirit is essential among a body of men who live together, in very close proximity, who train together and must fight together, and who are to a considerable degree dependent upon one another for their lives. This communal spirit was nurtured through into retirement by the establishment of veteran colonies where discharged legionaries, comrades in arms, might settle together. The establishment of these colonies in newly-won provinces (often in abandoned legionary fortresses) had the additional bonus of providing fertile recruiting-grounds for the army – sons of soldiers have ever been attracted to the military life – thus fostering the practice of local recruitment.[99] But the colonies filled up, the frontiers ceased to advance, the legions remained in their established bases and the supply of abandoned legionary fortresses dried up.

But as the military bases acquired permanency, so too did the settlements which had developed outside them, settlements, still within a military milieu, but where a soldier might find a wife or to which his existing family might follow him. Some soldiers, settled on discharge in a colony, might even chose to return to these military townships, these *canabae*, in preference to remaining in the city to which they had been sent. This appears to have happened, for example, in the case of veterans of the *legio XV* from Carnuntum who had been settled at Savaria, a city which lies about 120 kilometres along the road leading to the south, but had come back to live (and die) outside the fortress where they had served.[100] Given the crucial trading position occupied by Carnuntum this might have been financial astuteness, but it is as likely to be tied with the desire to continue living in a military milieu. A considerable township developed at Carnuntum and numerous veterans and their families are recorded here.

At Carnuntum, in common with the majority of the fortress sites on the Rhine and Danube frontiers, a major city lay a short distance from the military base. Many of these sites were those of existing pre-Roman settlements, and many were the sites of provincial capitals – Carnuntum, for example, was the capital of Pannonia Superior – and developed as such, often rising to the status of *municipium* and ultimately to that of *colonia*. But the *canabae* remained separate, not just physically, but constitutionally, from these nearby cities, having their own separate existence, with their own magistrates.[101] They can be regarded as an integral part of the military establishment as a whole – witness the inscription from Apulum in Dacia which refers to the magistrates 'of the *canabae* of legion *XIII Gemina*' or the dedication from Aquincum set up by 'the veterans and Roman citizens living at legion *II Adiutrix*'.[102] Soldier and civilian were intermingled. Buildings which were essentially military – the parade-ground, the amphitheatre, the bathhouse – lay within the area of the *canabae*, as well as the houses, shops and workshops of the *canabenses*. Recruits born in these townships could give no 'city' of origin: they were born 'at the camp' *castris*.

This, then, is the milieu to which Tadius Exuperatus belonged. Father, mother, sister and, no doubt, had he lived long enough, wife and family, all settled outside his home fortress. It is a development which we see foreshadowed many years earlier in the context of the army of Syria in AD 69. A threatened transfer to Germany was welcomed by neither soldiers nor civilians, as Tacitus observes: '... the provincials were accustomed to live with the soldiers, and enjoyed association with them; in fact, many civilians were bound to the soldiers by ties of friendship and of marriage, and the soldiers from their long service had come to love their old familiar camps as their very hearths and homes.' Family life no longer so sharply divided from army life: a home life that was not at all far 'beyond the ramparts'.[103]

ACKNOWLEDGEMENTS

I am most grateful to Drs D J Breeze, B Dobson and M M Roxan who have all made useful comments on this text at various stages during its preparation. Several of the translations of papyri are the work of the late Dr R W Davies. My thanks, too, to Seán Goddard who drew the map which appears as Figure 8.7, and to the following who helped in providing photographs: P T Bidwell, Figure 8.3; Mr R E Birley, Figure 8.6; and Dr A Bülow-Jacobsen, Figure 8.9. My thanks, too, to Richard Brewer and David Zienkiewicz (formerly of the Roman Legionary Museum) for looking after me so well during a most enjoyable visit to Caerleon.

Notes

1 *RIB* I, 369. *D(is) M(anibus) / Tadia Vallaun[i]us vixit / ann(os) LXV et Tadius Exuper(a)tus / filius vixit ann(os) XXXVII defun(c)tus expeditione Germanica / Tadia Exuperata filia / ma[t]ri et fratri piiss(i)ma / secus tumulum / patris posuit.*
2 Breeze this volume.
3 Tacitus, *Historiae* 2.87, 3.33.
4 Quintillian, *Orationes* 8.6.42.
5 Caesar, *de Bello Gallico* 6.36–7, 40.
6 Cassius Dio 56.20.2–5.
7 Cassius Dio 56.22.1.
8 Appian, *Iberica* 85 (134 BC).
9 Sallust, *Bellum Iugurthinum* 44–5.
10 *RIB* I, 200. This is more likely than the alternative, that they were Britons enslaved in the invasion.
11 *CIL* XIII, 8648.
12 That is, should the bones of any of them have been retrieved. In practice, those who died in the battle of the Teutoburger Wald in AD 9 remained unburied until some years later when a search party, led by Germanicus, collected together and buried, under one mound at the site of the battle, such scattered remains as could be found (Suetonius, *Gaius* 3–4).
13 *RIB* I, 1064.
14 *SHA, Hadriani* 13.7; '… he (Hadrian) received slaves from the Cappadocians for service in the camp'. Josephus, *Bellum Iudaicum* 3.124, describing the order of march of Vespasian's army, notes that '... behind the infantry the servants attached to each legion followed in a body, conducting the mules and other beasts of burden which carried the soldiers' baggage.' Of Titus' march into Judaea he notes that 'the servants attached to each legion followed in a body preceded by the baggage train', *Bellum Iudaicum* 5.49. For a recent discussion of soldiers' servants, see Speidel 1989a.
15 Josephus, *Bellum Iudaicum* 3.69–70.
16 Vegetius, *Epit* 3.6.
17 Eg *CIL* XIII, 8303=*ILS* 2508: Lucius, *eques* of the *ala Afrorum; CIL* XIII, 8312: Longinus, *eques* of the *ala Sulpicia,* both from Cologne. In this type of tombstone the deceased themselves are depicted in a separate funerary banquet scene.
18 *CIL* XIII, 8308=*ILS* 2512 add: T. Flavius Bassus, *eques* in the *ala Noricorum* from Cologne (spears); Nesselhauf and Lieb, 1959, 186–7, no. 169=*AE* 1959, 188 and *AE* 1967, 339: Maris *eques* in the *ala Parthorum et Araborum* (quiver full of arrows).
19 Vegetius, *Epit* 1.10.
20 *CIL* XIII, 12075. von Petrikovits 1980b.
21 Suetonius, *Gaius* 8–9.
22 Tacitus, *Annales* 12.27.
23 Cassius Dio 76.16.5.
24 Tacitus, *Agricola* 29.
25 Tacitus, *Annales* 3.33–4.
26 An allusion to Piso's wife, Plancina: Tacitus, *Annales* 2.55.
27 Plutarch, *Galba* 12.1.
28 Cassius Dio 59.18.4; Tacitus, *Historiae* 1.48; Plutarch, *Galba* 12.1–2.
29 *RIB* I, 644. Antonius Isauricus commanded *II Augusta* some time in the late Hadrianic period. See A R Birley 1981, 247.
30 *Tab Vindol II,* 291.
31 *Tab Vindol II,* 292. The fragmentary text 293 is probably between the same two correspondents.
32 According to Tacitus, *Historiae* 4.12, the Batavian units were commanded by their own nobles; Flavius Cerealis is probably a case in point. His *cognomen* suggests a connection with Petillius Cerialis who led the suppression of the Batavian rebellion in AD 69, while his *praenomen,* Flavius, points to his (or his father's) enfranchisement in the Flavian period. See *Tab. Vindol II,* 25.
33 R E Birley 1993b, 45–6.
34 *Tab Vindol II,* 118. *Tab Vindol II,* 119 and 120 may also be writing exercises; see Bowman 1994, 91–2 with n 22.
35 Ylas, *RIB* I, 937; Hermagoras, *RIB* I, 1291.
36 *RIB* I, 324, 326.
37 Cassius Dio 60.24.3; Mitteis and Wilcken 1912, no. 372 for papyrological evidence from the reigns of Trajan and Hadrian.
38 Herodian 3.8.4–5. Garnsey 1970, argues in favour of the view that there was no change under Severus in the legal position regarding marriage; Campbell 1978, puts the opposite view. The relevant legal codes are quoted (and differently interpreted) by these two authors.
39 Roxan 1991, esp 465.
40 Roxan 1981, esp 276–7.
41 *RMD II*, no. 86.
42 The findspot of the diploma does not necessarily indicate the exact place where the family settled, for the document (precisely dated to 16 December, AD 113) was found in a later second-century context, suggesting that it had been retained as an heirloom.
43 *CIL* XVI, 49.
44 Bell 1937; Schubert 1990, no. 1.
45 Mitteis and Wilcken 1912, no. 372; extract of AD 117.
46 Campbell 1978; *contra* Garnsey 1970.
47 Discussed by Fink 1966.
48 *BGU* 140=*Sel Pap* II.213.

49 Herodian 3.8.4–5.
50 *AE* 1954, 119=Vorbeck 1980, no. 200, wife; ibid, no. 184, wife and son.
51 Vorbeck 1980, no. 170 (5-year-old daughter); *AE* 1936, 67=Vorbeck 1980, no. 191 (5-year-old son); *AE* 1934, 266=Vorbeck 1980, no. 198 (a soldier commemorated by his mother and brother); *CIL* III, 13484=Vorbeck 1980, no. 195 (a father commemorates his soldier son); *CIL* III, 14358^{15a}=Vorbeck 1980, nos 169, 199 and 212 (in each case a soldier commemorated by his brother); Vorbeck 1980, no. 207 (two soldiers, who are brothers, and their mother are commemorated by their apparently unrelated heir).
52 *AE* 1929, 199=Vorbeck 1980, no. 224.
53 *CIL* XIII, 5978.
54 *RIB* I, 365.
55 *CIL* XIII, 5976.
56 *RIB* I, 357. The brother who set up the stone was almost certainly a brother-soldier.
57 *BGU* II, 423.
58 *BGU* II, 632.
59 *P Mich* VIII, 490–1. Socrates appears to have been a near neighbour to the mother, Taesis: see van Minnen 1994, esp 243–4.
60 *O Claud* 142.
61 *P Mich* VIII, 465.
62 *P Mich* IX, 562: AD 119.
63 *SB* 9636 (AD 136).
64 Since the letters sent by Terentianus to his family (*P Mich* VIII, 467–81) were found at Karanis which, on the evidence of the Paulinus letter, was not his parental home, Terentianus must have taken the family records and papers with him to his place of retirement. See Lewis 1959.
65 While particularly characteristic of Egypt, ostraca have also been found in other arid contexts, notably the recently-published collection from Bu Njem in Libya: Marichal 1992.
66 *O Flor* 14.
67 The editor of the *Florida ostraca* attributes them to the military base at Contrapollonopolis Magna on the strength of a note accompanying them, which named Edfu (Apollonopolis Magna) as the provenance of the collection, together with the fact that the texts mentioned cavalrymen – the unit at Contrapollonopolis was an equitate cohort, the *cohors I Augusta Praetoria Lusitanorum;* see *O Flor,* 22–3. In a review of the publication, Gilliam (1979) challenged this attribution, preferring an association with the *ala Vocontiorum,* based about 150 km to the north at Coptos.
68 *P Mich* VIII, 476; *P Mich* Inv 256 (AD 205), published by Priest 1983. Priest assumes that the whole unit was transferred south to Alabastrine from its base at Alexandria, where it is attested in AD 199 (*CIL* III, 6581).
69 *O Flor* 4.
70 *P Mich* III, 203.
71 *O Claud* 127, 137, 146 (a daughter); these probably relate to soldiers' women, but given the mixed nature of the community at Mons Claudianus, it is not always possible to be certain whether an individual is soldier or civilian. Guéraud 1942, nos 12, 31 (includes children) and 35.
72 *IGRR* I, 1183.
73 For the identification of Quseir as Myos Hormos, see Peacock 1993.
74 *RIB* I, 17.
75 See for example, Davies 1971.
76 *O Flor* 15, 17; *BGU* III, 814.
77 *O Claud* 139, 140, 145, 159 (meat); 148 (pigs); 162 (liver).
78 *BGU* III, 814, 200 drachmas; *P Mich* VIII, 465, 466, linens.
79 *P Mich* 467, tunic with belt and trousers; *P Mich* 468, boots and slippers; *BGU* III, 814, leggings, pair of belts, cloak and coats.
80 *Tab Vindol* 38, 346.
81 *P Mich* VIII, 468.
82 *P Mich* VIII, 465.
83 *P Mich* VIII, 466, 477, 478.
84 Suetonius, *Augustus* 24.1.
85 *O Flor* 1.
86 *P Gen Lat* 1=Fink 1971, 9.
87 The legions in Egypt had no legates in command, as senators were banned from the province. For the *praefectus castrorum Aegypti,* see Dobson 1982.
88 *P Dura,* 82.2.20=Fink 1971, 47.
89 Vegetius, *Epit* 2.12.
90 *Tab Vindol* 175, 174.
91 *Tab Vindol* 176.
92 *O Claud* 137; *P Oxy* 1666=*Sel Pap* I.149.
93 Eg *CIL* XIII, 7564, 7570, 7575 etc (Wiesbaden); XIII, 6304 (Baden-Baden).
94 Nine legionary inscriptions are known from the site: *RIB* I, 139, 143, 144, 146 (centurion of *leg II*), 147 (*imaginifer* of *leg II*), 156, 157, 158, 160.
95 *CIL* III, 50, 59, 49, 60, 33, 36, 42, 56, 57, 58.
96 *CIL* III, 43.
97 *CIL* III, 67=*ILS* 8760.
98 *CIL* IV, 2145.
99 For the trends in recruiting, see Mann 1983.
100 The point is made by Mócsy 1974, 77.
101 Eg *CIL* III, 1100: *decuriones canabarum leg. XIII G.* (Apulum); *CIL* III, 1214: ... *dec kanabarum* (Brigetio).
102 *CIL* III, 1100; ... *consistentes ad leg. II Ad.*: *CIL* III, 3505.
103 Tacitus, *Historiae* 2.80.

CHAPTER 9

THE LEGIONS IN THE LATER ROMAN EMPIRE

JOHN CASEY

Flavius Vegetius Renatus, writing either at the end of the fourth or in the first half of the fifth century, addressed a work to the Emperor in which he lamented the state of the army in his own day and advocated a return to the military practices and principles of the Early Empire.[1] That Vegetius' cures for the ills of the state, as he perceived them, were entirely impractical given the social and political changes which had swept the Roman world since the decades of imperial expansion, does not detract from the interest of what he says. On one point Vegetius is specific – the Roman legion had declined, was declining and should be restored to its original state:[2]

> 'The name of the legion remains indeed to this day in our armies, but its strength and substance are gone, since by the neglect of our predecessors, honours and preferments, which were formerly the recompenses of merit and long services, were to be obtained only by interest and favour. Care is no longer taken to replace the soldiers, who after serving their full time, have received their discharges. The vacancies continually happening by sickness, discharges, desertion and various other casualties, if not supplied every year or even every month, must in time disable the most numerous army. Another cause of the weakness of our legions is that in them the soldiers find the duty hard, the arms heavy, the rewards distant and the discipline severe. To avoid these inconveniences, the young men enlist in the auxiliaries, where the service is less laborious and they have reason to expect more speedy recompense.'

Vegetius' exhortations probably referred to the late imperial Palatine Legions rather than to the frontier forces, but whichever it was they went unregarded and within a short time of the date at which he was probably writing the legion as an entity had been extinguished in the western half of the Roman Empire. In the East, in name at least, the legions had nearly another two centuries of existence.

The legion in the late Roman world was a very different body from that with which we are familiar in the early imperial period. How did this change come about? In its classic form the legion consisted of between 5,500 and 6,000 effectives, all infantry, except for a small cavalry component. Heavily armoured and heavily armed, the legion was a slow moving force capable of independent military deployment or, in combination with auxiliary troops and other legions, of forming an expeditionary or punitive force sufficiently powerful to overthrow states and nations. After the defeat of the Macedonian *phalanx* no military formation existed in the ancient world which could stand up to the legion properly led. It is true that, when badly led, disasters could occur, as in the Teutoburger Forest where Arminius the German leader caught a Roman army on the march and slaughtered three legions. Indeed in Wales a similar incident took place when a *praefectus castrorum* and eight centurions, and thus presumably some 600 legionary soldiers, were defeated and killed by the Silures in 51 or 52. But normally, until the end of the second century, the legionary army dominated an area stretching from Britain to the eastern frontier on the Euphrates.

However, deployment on fixed frontiers of what had been forged as an army of mobility and conquest created problems. It is axiomatic that generals and governments refight their last war and make little provision for changing circumstances. In the European provinces the stationing of legions, whilst not strategically haphazard, seems to have come about by military accident in that they stood where the imperial policy of conquest had ground to a halt; effectively on the line of the Rhine and the Danube. Having no long linear frontier the legions of Britain were stationed where the last effective threat had been felt, in north and south Wales and in the middle of Brigantia. In the East, the Parthian kingdom, though often the scene of expeditions which reinforced the status of military minded emperors such as Trajan, does not, in retrospect, seem to have posed a serious threat to Rome. Nonetheless, the threat of Parthia could be deployed as a useful factor in Roman military politics. In any event the expeditionary routes into and from Parthia through Roman territory were historically well established, being determined by the topography, the presence of deserts and mountain ranges, and the adequacy of water and food resources to maintain campaign armies and their animals. These routes could be protected at relatively little cost by the strategic placement of individual legions.

But once installed in a conquered province what was to be the function of legions? They could be engaged in a succession of 'one off' displacement activities, furnishing fortresses with stone walls and internal buildings, building roads, constructing forts for the auxiliary garrisons or adding to the frontiers such defences as Hadrian's Wall. They could also take part in manoeuvres, and sites such as Woden Law (Roxburghshire) show the training grounds where the legions could be kept busy practising siege warfare. But keeping troops, who had no military problem to confront them, occupied and in battle-ready condition is always difficult. Rome learned this when the under-employed eastern legions were called upon to campaign in Armenia in the reign of Nero and they had to be hardened-up by Corbulo, their martinet commander.

Of course grave problems did arise, and in the second century Britain saw campaigns in the reign of Hadrian, fierce fighting at least once in that of Antoninus Pius and something of a disaster in the reign of Commodus. At the end of the second century the army of Britain fought a civil war which was followed by a period of frontier turmoil brought to an end by the personal intervention of Septimius Severus. This litany of activity notwithstanding, and we are here dealing with only five campaigns in a century, there is every reason to think that in many provinces a legionary might go through an entire military career without ever throwing a *pilum* in anger. In effect the legions represented an army in waiting since most day-to-day defence of the frontiers and policing of the provincial hinterland was in the hands of the auxiliaries, normally deployed as cavalry or infantry in regiments 500 strong.

The Roman strategist faced a dilemma. The legions acted as the central reserve of forces in the provinces, their presence ensured that should the frontiers fall or revolt arise and the auxiliaries fail to hold the line, a loyal force which could meet all eventualities was available. This force could repel invasion, campaign in enemy territory or deliver a retributive strike. But not all frontiers were equally threatened. How could legionary forces be moved to reinforce threatened areas without leaving a strategic gap in their own provinces? The answer was to detach elements from the parent legion which could operate independently or in union with similar detachments from other legions. Thus no province was left bereft of a legionary force. These vexillations – detachments which followed their own standard, the *vexillum* – are normally thought to have been about 1,000 strong, consisting of two 480-strong cohorts.

If we look at the activities of *legio II Augusta*, as assembled from epigraphic evidence, we can see the sort of places where detachments were deployed in the later second and early third centuries.[3] After the construction of Hadrian's Wall, its forts and outpost works, the legion fought in Pius' conquest of the lowlands of Scotland and was employed in the building of the Antonine Wall. A vexillation was rebuilding this Wall late in the reign of Pius or in that of Marcus Aurelius. At various times centurions from the legion were detached to command auxiliary forces, and legionary soldiers may also have served as garrisons of auxiliary forts in the later Antonine period. A vexillation may have fought in the East under Lucius Verus (161–9), and troops from the legion appear in Gaul in the reign of Commodus (181–92). In the third century, after service on the wrong side in the conflict between Clodius Albinus, the governor of Britain, and Septimius Severus, elements of the legion are found in Scotland and in northern Britain in the reign of Caracalla (211–17). In the same reign a unit may have served in Germany. A badge from Gaul depicting detachments of *II Augusta* and *XX Valeria Victrix* parading together is, presumably, evidence for part of the legion being abroad, perhaps in the middle of the third century (Figure 9.1). These soldiers may be the very troops whose return occasioned the rebuilding at Caerleon, from the ground up as the inscription states (Figure 6.14), of the barracks of the seventh cohort in the joint reign of Valerian and Gallienus (255–60).[4] If so, they got home just before the shake-up which was to change fundamentally the nature of the Roman legion.

The permanent depletion of the legion at Isca in the late second century is attested by archaeological evidence from excavations of a barrack block in the Prysg Field series, in the *retentura* of the fortress. Here the timber barracks were replaced by stone structures in the Antonine period, but this new accommodation was demolished by the end of the second century. This suggests that the garrison might be expected to be more or less permanently diminished by at least two full cohorts, or, in other terms, a vexillation.[5]

This cumulative evidence from a single legion demonstrates how the tactical use of fragments of legions became a military norm. Nonetheless new legions were raised to reinforce the army in specific instances. Two were added by Marcus Aurelius (*II* and *III Italica*) to assist in the long war against the Marcomanni on the Danubian frontier and a further three by Septimius Severus (*I, II* and *III Parthica*): two to police his conquests in the East and the third, *legio II Parthica*, to be stationed outside Rome and travel, when needed, with the emperor. But as the third century progressed there was almost certainly a shortage of legionary soldiers.

Two important factors contributed to this situation. Firstly, Caracalla granted citizenship to all freeborn inhabitants of the Empire, thus abolishing the essential distinction between citizen legionaries and non-citizen auxiliaries and opening a much less taxing career to all in the *auxilia*; just the trend noted

9.1 *A bronze roundel, possibly an officer's badge, depicting soldiers of vexillations of* legio II Augusta *and* legio XX Valeria Victrix *parading with their* vexilla. *The badge, of third century date, was found in France and may be evidence of the presence of troops from the legions of Britain in Gaul*

later, but under very different circumstances, by Vegetius. Secondly, the century was distinguished by the rule of a succession of short lived emperors, twenty between 211 and 284, who depended for their elevation on a series of bloody civil wars fought with the provincial Roman armies. Especially active in these events were the legions of the Rhine and Danube.

On the frontiers matters changed dramatically. In the German sector, attacks across the Rhine by the Franks and the Alamanni culminated in the creation of the separatist regime of the Gallic Empire (258–73). In the East, the Parthian Arsacid dynasty collapsed to be replaced by the Sassanid Persians whose imperial ambitions were founded on a policy of extending their control over the Persian Empire as it had existed under Cyrus the Great or Darius; effectively the whole of the Roman eastern provinces. In turn, the new dynasty defeated imperial armies led by the emperors Gordian III (238–44), Philip (244–9) and Valerian (253–60). Gordian was probably killed whilst on campaign, Valerian captured and never released (Figure 9.2). The extinction of large elements of the eastern Roman army can be traced in the fact that few units known to be in the East at the time can be traced in the fourth-century documentary sources.[6]

Now sole ruler, Valerian's son Gallienus found himself fighting on several fronts. In the East, the Persian advance was halted by the army of the city of Palmyra, a Roman ally, which then assumed control over Syria and threatened Egypt. In the north-west, the Gallic Empire posed a threat to Italy, whilst on the Danube constant threat of invasion loomed following the arrival of the Goths and Vandals in the area.

To meet these threats Gallienus undertook fundamental, though very sketchily understood, reforms of the army. Firstly, he deprived senators of their military careers. Henceforth, legions and provinces were normally under the control of equestrian officers. This move seems to have been designed to prevent senators with military forces at their command posing a threat to the central government, though we may note that the usurpers Macrinus (217–18) and Maximinus Thrax (235–8) were not senators when they raised their revolts. The real effect was to open a top-rank military career to long-serving professional soldiers. Secondly, he recruited a very large cavalry army which, theoretically, could be switched from

9.2 *The triumphal relief of Shapur I at Bishapur, Iran. The Sassanid king is shown holding the Emperor Valerian captive; before him kneels a supplicant Philip I, whilst the recumbent body of Gordian III lies under the king's horse (After P Brown,* The World of Late Antiquity, *1971)*

front to front as problems arose. This mobile army was the predecessor to that created early in the next century by Constantine the Great.

The source of some at least of the new cavalry will have been the legions. In the early imperial period legions had a mounted component of 120 troopers who served as messengers and scouts. This element was now turned into an independent offensive unit and eventually divorced from the parent legion. Cavalry regiments originating in legionary troops were distinguished by the title *equites promoti* and although not attested before the last years of the third century most probably originate with Gallienus.

The precedent for giving a specialized role to a component of the legion was already established by the first quarter of the third century when a specialized infantry force, the *lanciarii*, was created within individual legions. The creation of these troops in the Severan period has been recognized recently from the tombstones of soldiers of *legio II Parthica*, the imperial escort legion, which on a number of occasions in the first half of the third century wintered at Apamea in Syria.[7] As depicted on their tombstones, the *lanciarii* were equipped not with the two long, heavy *pila* of the traditional legionary but with four or five short, light javelins. In this they seem to be armed in a manner reminiscent of the *velites* of the Republican army. Perhaps at their inception they worked in the same manner, delivering a shower of javelins from close quarters at selected targets with great mobility, probably against the very effective Sassanian cavalry. Alternatively they may have been deployed in rough terrain where youth, fitness and agility will have counted for more than the heavy armoured ponderousness of the ordinary legionary. In any event their tactics had to be learned, since one of the soldiers at Apamea is described as a 'trainee *lanciarius*' (*discens lanchiarium*) (Figure 9.3). By the fourth century, if not earlier, the *lanciarii* were among the élite of the army, their status increasing as they became more and more divorced from legionary attachment.

Before this stage of disintegration was reached the legions were to play a further prominent role in the re-creation of the Roman army. After the confusion of the third century, constitutional stability was re-established by Diocletian (284–305) who, before his retirement to breed rare species of cabbages at his fortified palace at Split, reorganized every aspect of the Roman state. From our point of view the most important element of this reform was that of the army.

9.3 *Tombstone of Aurelius Mucianus, a trainee* lanciarius *of* legio II Parthica, *from Apamea. Mucianus is shown holding five light javelins and a small round shield (photograph: reproduced by permission of J C Balty)*

A contemporary Christian writer, Lactantius, said of Diocletian in his pamphlet *'On the deaths of the persecutors'*:[8]

> 'Diocletian was an author of crimes and a deviser of evils: he ruined everything and could not even keep his hands from God. In his greed and anxiety he turned the world upside down. He appointed three men to share his rule, dividing the world into four parts and multiplying the armies, since each of the four strove to have a far larger number of troops than previous emperors had had when they were governing the state alone.'

The claim that the size of the Roman army was quadrupled by Diocletian has been taken seriously by some modern historians, but other ancient literary sources do not support this view nor indeed, as we shall see, does the archaeological evidence. John Lydus, writing in the reign of Justinian (527–65) records that the Diocletianic army numbered 435,266 (including fleets). This seems to be some 100,000 more than the estimated strength of the Severan army of a century earlier, which is reckoned at 345,500 men. The increase was, therefore, in the order of one third rather than fourfold as implied by Lactantius. Lydus' figures are supported by such sources as Zosimus (late fifth century) and Agathias (sixth century).[9]

One means used to increase the size of the army was to double the numbers of legions from the thirty-three that had existed under Septimius Severus to a calculated sixty-nine or seventy. It is unlikely, however, that these new legions were the 6,000 strong units of the early imperial period. More likely they were 1,000 strong regiments, a fact which, in itself, suggests that many surviving 'classic legions' had been reduced to about that size over the preceding century. It is true that Vegetius states of the pre-Diocletianic period that:[10]

> 'We formerly had two legions in Illyricum consisting of 6,000 men each, which had from their extraordinary dexterity and skill in the use of their weapons (ie lead weighted darts or *martiobarbuli*) ... supported for a long time the weight of all the wars and distinguished themselves so remarkably that the Emperors Diocletian and Maximian on their accession honoured them with the titles Joviani and Herculiani (ie after the emperors who were compared with Jove and Hercules) and preferred them before all the other legions.'

This may just be a roundabout way of saying that these legions were pre-Diocletianic regiments of the same notional strength as the 'classic legion' rather than new creations of the emperors of a diminished nominal strength. Or, since the period at which they stood at full strength before Diocletian favoured them is unspecified, we may interpret the words of Vegetius as implying 'were formerly 6,000 strong' without saying when. The units will certainly have been those which bore the weight of the invasion of the Goths at the end of the third century.

As it is, there is direct, but conflicting, evidence for the size of Diocletianic legions in a number of sources. First in importance is a collection of documents from Egypt called the *Beatty Panopolis Papyri*. Second is the identification and excavation of a newly-built Diocletianic legionary fortress on the frontier in Jordan.[11] To supplement these sources is an inscription relating to the activities of the Diocletianic army in North Africa.[12] The interpretation of this evidence is still under discussion, but its tenor is of diminished unit strength.

The papyri consist of a series of directives from the Procurator of Egypt to regional officials, dated between 298 and 300. These are orders to issue garrison troops, both legionary and auxiliary, with pay, donatives and provisions. Typical of the letters is one authorising pay to *legio III Diocletiana*:[13]

> 'Aurelius Isidorus, Procurator of the Lower Thebaid, to Apolinarius, Strategus, and the receivers of money for the Panopolite Nome. See that you pay the soldiers from *Legio Tertiae Diocletiana* posted in the office of my Lord the most eminent governor of the Thebaid, Julius Athendorus, on account of pay for 1 January in the auspicious pending third consulate of our rulers Constantius and Maximian, the most illustrious Caesars, 34 myriads of *denarii* and 3,300 *atticae*; and pay these over to the leading centurion, Dioscorus, and take from him at the counting out of the money the usual receipts ...'

From the sums of money distributed it is possible to calculate the number of soldiers involved in the payout.[14] In the case of *legio III Diocletiana*, the figure appears to be 1,078 men and for *legio II Traiana*, 1,060 men. Thus both a newly raised unit, *III Diocletiana*, and an old established unit, *II Traiana*, have the same complement of soldiers. Auxiliary units mentioned in the texts have correspondingly low numbers as compared with similar units in the first and second centuries. This appears to be good evidence for unit size from a contemporary source, but other evidence is less clear.

The archaeological evidence comes from the fortress of el-Lejjūn on the *Strata Diocletiana*, the new frontier line established to the east of the *Via Traiana Nova* which had served as the *limes* between the Red Sea and the Jordan Valley from the second century.

The name Lejjūn preserves in Arabic a record of the function of the site as a legionary fortress in antiquity, in the same manner as the name Caerleon preserves the memory of the legion at Isca. Lejjūn was the base of *legio IIII Martia*, built on a virgin site. The dimensions of the fortress are 242 metres by 190 metres, giving an internal area of 4.6 hectares. Caerleon, in contrast, covered 20.5 hectares, and is in the general range of size for early imperial fortresses which were designed to hold about 5,500 men. Lejjūn, at barely a fifth of this size, may have had accommodation for 1,000 soldiers quartered in sixteen barrack blocks occupying the entire *praetentura*.[15] The present estimate is made on the basis of buildings that comprised single rows of rooms arranged either side of a central spine wall, a significant contrast to the double rooms typical of the Early Empire. It must be emphasized that, as yet, there is no information about possible quarters in the *retentura* of the fortress and that estimates for the original size of *IIII Martia* may need upward revision.

Complementary evidence comes from the Danubian frontier where new fortresses were built for *legio II Herculia* and *legio I Jovia* in the Diocletianic period. The base of the former was at Troesmis and encompasses 2.8 hectares; that of *I Jovia* at Noviodunum is of 5.6 hectares. A cohort of *II Herculia* was also deployed at Axiopolis in a fortification which enclosed only 0.6 hectares.[16]

The epigraphic evidence is ambiguous. The inscription from North Africa is a dedication to Mithras by cohorts VII and X of the same *legio II Herculia* which was discussed above. The occasion for the dedication may be related to the campaign of Maximian in Africa in 297 and the cohorts will probably have been detachments assembled for the expeditionary force rather than the whole legion. If, the argument runs, there is evidence for two of the legion's numbered cohorts then the other eight cohorts, which made up a regular legion, must have existed. This may or may not be so, but it does not tell us how large a Diocletianic cohort was, nor whether the numbers of individual cohorts were retained though other cohorts in the regiment had disappeared, perhaps lost whilst on prolonged secondment. Nor can the argument for a full-sized legion, of the old establishment, be reconciled with the size of the fortress at Troesmis designed for its long-term occupation.

The function of this mass of legions, created by Diocletian, was mainly to guard the frontiers in conjunction with other newly raised units. Legislation of the period shows that legions still occupied the highest status in the army ranking above the traditional auxiliary units, the *alae* of cavalry and *cohortes* of infantry. Only the new, and confusingly named, vexillations of cavalry ranked above the legions. But the restored traditional system of frontier defence and the restored status of the legions barely survived this Diocletianic rebirth. Constantine the Great brought about fundamental changes.

The policy of Constantine is neatly summarized by the historian Zosimus, who offers an alternative view of Diocletianic policy from that of Lactantius:[17]

> 'By the foresight of Diocletian the frontiers of the Empire everywhere were covered, as I have stated, with cities, garrisons and fortifications which housed the whole army. Consequently it was impossible for the barbarians to cross the frontier because they were confronted at every point by forces capable of resisting their attack. Constantine destroyed this security by removing most of the troops from the frontiers and stationing them in cities which did not need assistance, thus both stripping of protection those being molested by the barbarians and subjecting the cities left alone by them to the outrages of the soldiers, so that henceforth most of them became deserted. Moreover he enervated the troops by allowing them to devote themselves to shows and luxuries. In plain terms, Constantine was the origin and beginning of the present destruction of the Empire.'

This comment alludes to Constantine's creation of a field army, a mobile strike-force, which enjoyed superior status to the frontier troops and which was stationed in the towns in the interior of the Empire from which, in theory at least, they could hasten to any threatened frontier (Figure 9.4). The reason for this move to a two status army arose from Constantine's political situation. As a usurper, based on the north-west corner of the Empire and controlling Britain, Gaul and Lower Germany, Constantine, from 306, fought his way to the East in a series of civil wars, finally achieving sole rule only in 324 after the defeat of Licinius at the battle of

9.4 *The new Constantinian field army in action during the war against Maxentius. The scene, from a panel of the Arch of Constantine in Rome, depicts the siege of a town in northern Italy. The attacking troops are armed with the typical large round shield of the late army and appear to be protected with helmets but no body armour*

Chrysopolis. This situation made it imperative to maintain a frontier defence which would hold external enemies at bay whilst allowing Constantine to range widely into the territory of his rivals. The inception of the system was, of course, to be found back in the days of Gallienus, who faced very much the same situation.

The field army first saw action in the war against Maxentius in Italy in 312, when units were withdrawn from Britain, Germany and Gaul to form a composite army which moved with what was, to contemporaries, astonishing speed. Among the units in this force were the regiments from the outpost forts on Hadrian's Wall and the detachment of *legio II Italica* from Divitia (Deutz).[18] We do not know if legionaries from Britain fought in this campaign, but it seems very likely. If so, they will not have returned home but formed a permanent part of the new army.

Whilst detachments of legions, especially *promoti* and *lanciarii,* were drafted to the field army, the residue of the frontier legions was excluded, being reduced to limitanean, or border guard, status. In Britain this was the fate of the bulk of *II Augusta* and of *VI Victrix.* We do not know what happened to *XX Valeria Victrix*. It is just possible that the comitatensian unit the *Victores Iuniores Britanniciani*, recorded at the end of the fourth century, derived from this legion, if they were not originally a detached fragment of *VI Victrix.* In most cases it is difficult to specify from which legions the élite corps were drawn; the new units often bore names derived from the base or province in which they had previously served rather than their original regimental titles.[19] For example, in the western field army we find the *Pannoniciani Seniores* and *Moesiaci Seniores* who derived from the legions of Pannonia and Moesia, but since eight legions served in these provinces it is difficult to decide from which these regiments came. As another example of the renaming of late legions we may note that the legionaries of *legio II Italica* from Divitia, who were raised to field army status, were simply called the *Divitenses.*

By the end of this process of military reform, ancient legions, dating back to the earliest days of the Empire, are to be found split apart in such a manner that some parts of legions ranked as superior *comitatenses* whilst others were relegated to limitanean status, this was to be the fate of *II Augusta.*

The rewards of promotion were great. Not only did the *comitatenses* have higher pay and donatives, and better equipment, but also other privileges. In gratitude for their service in his cause, Constantine, as soon as he became sole emperor, conferred important benefits on the *comitatenses,* including the legions. A notable concession was exemption from poll tax, not only for themselves, as was general for soldiers, but also for four of their family or household.[20]

Constantine's fragmentation of the legions was, as we have seen, only the culmination of a long process. There was a long history of vexillations serving away from the parent regiment to the point where they were virtually independent, and even to the extent that they could support claimants to the throne who were regarded as usurpers by the parent legion. Such was the army of Carausius (286–93) which consisted of vexillations of continental legions, whose main bodies were loyal to Diocletian and Maximian. Pre-Constantinian fragmentation can also be traced in the *Beatty Panopolis Papyri*, discussed above, where *legio II Traiana* is divided into contingents serving at Apollinopolis Superior, Ptolemais and Tentyra, towns roughly 140 kilometres apart down the Nile – though it should be noted that for administrative purposes these units were regarded as components of a single legion. For later in the fourth century the *Notitia Dignitatum* furnishes a wealth of evidence for the dispersion of legions. For example, *legio XIII Gemina* had contingents at five locations on the Danubian frontier, one in Egypt and another unit serving in the field army.[21] As we have seen, when the forts of these late units can be identified they are designed to accommodate very small numbers of soldiers.

Constantine's military policy led inevitably to a decline in size and prestige of the frontier legions. Those serving in the field army – the Palatine Legions as they came to be called – still maintained a prestige but even they were less important than the new Germanic regiments (confusingly called *auxilia*), which formed the élite of the late Roman army. Some indication of the size of a limitanean legion after the Constantinian reforms comes from Lejjūn, which was occupied by *legio IIII Martia* to at least the end of the fourth century. Rebuilding after an earthquake in 363 appears to have provided accommodation for only about 600 soldiers, though this number was probably an optimum rather than a reality.[22]

It is from the kind of evidence discussed above that we can hypothesise about the disintegration of *II Augusta*. Presumably, in the third century, vexillations went abroad never to return, the cavalry was detached and raised to the status of *promoti*, the better infantry became *lanciarii* and eventually achieved independent status (though any such unit deriving from *II Augusta* had been lost before the compilation of the *Notitia Dignitatum* in 395). Like the units of *II Traiana* in Egypt, various segments of the legion could have been scattered in Britain, and one element was at Corbridge in the third century.[23] The fate of the bulk of the legion, after the closure of the Caerleon base at the end of the third century, is uncertain but from the evidence of the *Notitia* we can trace two components of *II Augusta* which still existed a the end of the fourth century. Ranked as *limitanei* was the garrison of the 2.5 hectare fort at Richborough,[24] while the *Secundani Iuniores*, as part of the field army of the *comes Britanniae*, ranked as *comitatenses*.[25] We do not know when the latter had separated from the parent legion, but they returned to Britain as part of the field army sent from Gaul following the defeat of the usurper Eugenius who had withdrawn troops from Wales and the west in 392.[26] The *Secundani*

9.5 *Constantine the Great reviewing the army. A silver coin, issued in 317, shows Constantine, attended by Victory, reviewing his cavalry. Scale x 3 (After J P C Kent and M Hirmer,* Roman Coins, *1978)*

Britanniciani who are listed in the *Notitia* under the command of the *magister equitum* in Gaul are presumably identical with the troops in the *comes* command.[27]

We do not know what happened to the Richborough garrison but it seems probable that the mobile army formed the core of the force taken by Constantine III to Gaul in 406 which suffered defeat at the hands of the army of Italy. Since *II Augusta* occupied the crossing point to Gaul perhaps it too joined Constantine and thus, reunited with its long separated component, re-embarked from the very place where it had landed in 43 under Claudius.

We should not confuse structural changes in the legions, or any other regiments, with ineffectiveness in battle. Although Vegetius laments the demise of the *'antiqua legio'* and calls for its restoration there is no lack of evidence for the *esprit de corps* of the late army. This is particularly evident in Ammianus Marcellinus' eyewitness account of the fall of Amida, from which he narrowly escaped. During the siege, the town, normally garrisoned by *legio V Parthica,* held six additional legions of *limitanei* who had retreated before the Persian advance, as well as a unit of mounted archers. In addition to the troops were a mass of refugees, contributing to the 120,000 people crammed inside the defences.

Among these legions, at Amida, were two which had been raised in Gaul by the usurper Magnentius (350–3) which had been transferred for security reasons to the eastern frontier. They were utterly unsuited to service in the East, their whole training having been designed for the open warfare of the West, but their bravery was not in question:[28]

> 'There were with us two Magnentian legions, recently brought from Gaul ... brave, active men, experienced in battle in the open field, but to the sort of warfare to which we were constrained they were not merely unsuited, but actually a great hindrance ... they would sometimes make reckless sallies and after fighting with great confidence return with diminished numbers, accomplishing just as much as would be the pouring of a single handful of water ... upon a general conflagration.
>
> The Gallic soldiers ... demanded that the opportunity be given them of encountering the enemy, threatening death to the tribunes who forbade them, and to the higher officers if they in turn prevented them.
>
> We, at our wits' end and in doubt what opposition ought to be made to the raging Gauls, at last chose this course ... that since they could no longer be restrained they ... attack the enemy's outposts ... with the understanding that if they broke through them, they might keep right on.

9.6 *A late fourth- or fifth-century wooden panel, from a church door, depicting the biblical scene of the relief of the city of Gibeon by Joshua. Expressed in contemporary iconography, the scene shows the late Roman infantry in action. From El Eshmunein, Egypt (After K Weitzmann, ed,* Age of Spirituality: Late Antique and Early Christian Art, *New York, 1979)*

... the Gauls, impatient of delay, armed with axes and swords rushed out through an open postern gate ... they rushed violently upon them (*sc.* the enemy) in close order, and having slain some of the outposts, they butchered the outer guards of the camp in their sleep. ... But the sound of their cautious advance ... was ... heard ... those against whom the surprise was directed were aroused ... now throngs of raging Persians were coming to battle from all sides ... the Gauls faced them ... But when they saw that the whole weight of ... all the troops of the enemy were turned against one spot, although not one of them turned his back, they made haste to get away ... The Gauls entered the gate about daybreak in diminished numbers ... the losses of that night were four hundred.

In honour of their officers, as leaders of the brave deeds, after the destruction of the city the emperor ordered statues in full armour to be made and set up in a frequented spot in Edessa, and they are preserved intact to the present time.'

The Constantinian reforms effectively reduced the function of the legion, whether on the frontier or in the field army to that of any other infantry regiment in the Roman army, neither distinguished in size or in armaments and equipment, which were now supplied as required by state arms factories to a uniform pattern. Nevertheless the aura created by the old legions still had a pervasive force, even to the extent that the word 'legion' became synonymous with 'army' in late Roman classicising historical texts; so making any attempt to disentangle the role of any actual legions in events nearly impossible. A pervasive force in literary circles perhaps, but in the real world legions suffered the crisis of recruitment which characterises the army in the later fourth century.

Diocletian had made military service an hereditary obligation and from time to time those liable to serve were winkled out. A law of 375 ensured that recruits of the best physique would be assigned to the *comitatenses* and the inferior to the *limitanei*.[29] Presumably the latter included those who had cut off fingers to avoid service, and who, under a law of Valentinian,[30] were burned alive but were spared to serve by Theodosius.[31] A quota of mutilated legionaries and physical inadequates presumably made up the late garrison of Richborough.

The demise of the western army in the face of barbarian attack and settlement is not the purpose of this paper. That the memory of the legions of the west lingered on is vouchsafed by a story told by the Byzantine historian Procopius:[32]

'Now other Roman soldiers, also, had been stationed on the frontiers of Gaul to serve as guards. And these soldiers, having no means of returning to Rome, and at the same time being unwilling to yield to their enemy (ie the Visigoths) who were Arians, gave themselves, together with their military standards and the land which they were guarding for the Romans, to the Arborychi (?Armoricans) and the Germans; and they handed down to their offspring all the customs of their fathers, which were thus preserved, and this people has held them in sufficient reverence to guard them even up to my time. For even at the present day they are clearly recognized as belonging to the legions to which they were assigned in ancient times, and they carry their own standards when they enter battle, and always follow the customs of their fathers. And they preserve the dress of the Romans in every particular, even as regards their shoes.'

In the East there is a different story. Here legions were frequently stationed in towns and their longevity is recorded in both papyrological and literary sources. Though the field army of the East had been largely destroyed in 378 at the battle of Adrianople, the frontier forces farther east, facing Persia, had not been affected by this disaster, and survived to the reign of Heraclius (610–41).

At various times we get glimpses of the eastern legions, or rather their attenuated remnants; *legio V Macedonica*, for example, survived from the Republic to the reign of Justinian and possibly later. Virtually the last glimpse that we have of a legion in action is in the war of Maurice Tiberius against the Persians in 586.[33] After a hard fought battle the general Heraclius and his entourage:

'... observed a Roman soldier in the throes of death, his body adorned by four wounds; a Median arrow had penetrated deeply through his helmet and planted itself in his upper lip; another had in turn entered his other lip from below and extended in antithesis, as it were, so that by means of opposing shafts his tongue was marked with a cross by the counterpoised conjunction of the barbs, and hence the hero was unable to shut his two lips. On his left arm he also bore a spear's incursion, and a further wound in the side from a Median javelin ... And so Heraclius' companions ... set him on horseback and carried him to the camp. Next, they drew out and extracted the other missiles implanted in his body, but the one in his side they were unable to withdraw; for those who are instructed in these things ... whispered among themselves that with the departure of the weapon his soul would also pass away. But that ... Roman, when he heard the doctors' words, asked if the Romans had been victorious. When the bystanders assented ... he tested their words on oath. When he learned that the Romans had in reality gained the lighter pan in the balance of war, whereas the Persians had the opposite turn of the scale and were being dragged down to calamity by the weight of defeat, he leapt up with a gasp, saying that the statement was a great consolation and relief for his pain, and that he now awaited death. With a nod he fawned upon the onlookers, as it were, to withdraw from his side without mercy the far-famed Median dart .... They say the hero was on the roll of the Quartoparthoi, which is the appellation borne by the men stationed in the city of Beroe (Aleppo) in Syria. When that fatal weapon was extracted from his side, that great and most noble spirit of the hero sprang forth with it ...'

The Quartoparthoi were *legio IIII Parthica,* a legion raised by Diocletian who, in the late fourth century, are recorded as being based at Circesium in Osrhoene.[34] We do not know when the legion was moved south to Aleppo. By a curious irony it was the Emperor Heraclius, son of the general Heraclius, who was to oversee the destruction of the last legions when at the battle of Yarmuk in 636 the Arabs overwhelmed the Roman Army and conquered Syria, then Palestine and Egypt and eventually the whole of North Africa. After the battle of Yarmuk Heraclius pronounced a tragic epitaph:

'Vale Syria, et ultimum vale' –
Goodbye Syria, goodbye for ever.

He could have said the same about the Roman legionary army, the remnants of which vanished as Palestine, Egypt and North Africa fell to Islamic armies.

ACKNOWLEDGEMENTS

This paper benefited from discussion with a number of scholars; pre-eminent among them was Professor John Mann who offered comment, advice and references. I have on occasion offered, perhaps unwisely, alternative views to those he held. Professor Tom Parker, of the University of North Carolina, has been unstinting with information about his excavations at Lejjūn. Roger Tomlin has, as always, been a beneficial guide to the late Roman world. Finally I must thank the National Museums & Galleries of Wales, and my many friends there, for their kindness in inviting this contribution to their distinguished lecture series.

Notes

1 For recent arguments favouring Theodosius I (379–95) as the dedicatee, see Milner 1993, pp xxv–xxix; for Valentinian III (425–55), see E Birley 1985 and Goffart 1989, but these do not give weight to the account of naval tactics which are described as current practices used in Britain by, it is implied, a Roman fleet. It is hard to credit such operations being maintained after 410.
2 Vegetius, *Epit* 2.3.
3 Jarrett 1964a. Breeze this volume.
4 *RIB* I, 334.
5 Casey and Hoffmann 1995, 74 and 77–9.
6 Kennedy 1987.
7 Balty 1988.
8 Lactantius, *de mortibus persecutorum* 7.
9 Jones 1964.
10 Vegetius, *Epit* 1.17.
11 Parker 1989; 2000, 128–32, including further references.
12 *ILS* 4195.
13 *P Beatty Panop* ii.
14 Duncan-Jones 1978. For the size of late units calculated from the evidence of rations, pay and donatives, see Tomlin 2000, 170–3.
15 Parker 2000, 129.
16 Scorpan 1980.
17 Zosimus, *Hist Nova* 2.34.
18 Casey 1991.
19 For the titles of late legions, see Tomlin 2000, 160–2.
20 *Codex Theodosianus* 7.20.4.
21 *Not Dig Or* 42.34–8, 28.15, 8.6.
22 Parker 2000, 130.
23 Bishop and Dore 1988.
24 *Not Dig Occ* 28.19.
25 *Not Dig Occ* 7.156.
26 Casey 1989.
27 *Not Dig Occ* 7.84.
28 Ammianus Marcellinus 19.5.2 – 6.12.
29 *Codex Theodosianus* 7.22.8.
30 *Codex Theodosianus* 7.13.5.
31 *Codex Theodosianus* 7.13.10.
32 Procopius, *Bellum Gothicum* 5.
33 Theophylact Simocatta 2.6.1–9.
34 *Not Dig Or* 35.24.

CHAPTER 10

THE FUTURE OF ROMAN MILITARY ARCHAEOLOGY . . .

RICHARD REECE

The Tenth Annual Caerleon Lecture, the last of the original series, was a good time to take stock of the archaeology of the Roman army. As in any subject, at a given moment, there are strengths and weaknesses, unexploited opportunities and over-indulged conventions. Every branch of the study of the past needs to re-examine its basic assumptions periodically, however uncomfortable this may be, to make sure that blind alleys have been recognized and new avenues explored. Could the habit of digging up forts and fortresses be a 'branch of ... archaeology (which) seems to have reached a conceptual plateau'?[1] If there is to be criticism, then the rules of the game need to be set out.

Criticism must have a standpoint and must be of its time, and should preferably lead to positive conclusions. It also helps if criticism is informed and, therefore, several people were given the opportunity to comment on this paper in order to arrive at a more enlightened state. To some readers it would be ideal if criticism could be free from current fads and fancies; to others that is either impossible, or obscurantist. In these sentiments lie two different view-points on the whole question of thinking about archaeology which need to be unravelled, for their differing aspects in fact mirror the two approaches to military archaeology. One theme rests in being informed; this includes the listing of facts which to some extent makes up the absolute nature of parts of the pursuit. The other theme, the fads and fancies, emphasizes the large element of interpretation in almost any statement; this is the relative and almost transitory aspect. The factual element comprises sites, structures and finds; the interpretative part, what is made of them.

In many minds a question is bound to follow from these definitions – 'What about the texts, inscriptions and *graffiti*?' In my world these are not part of archaeology, but a complementary part of the study of the past. The past can be studied by one set of methods and rules through material – that is archaeology; or it can be studied by a completely different set of methods and rules through written sources – that is history. Both subjects may have a contribution to make to any study of the past.

While the historical study uses a whole series of models of interpretation, of modern ideas through which to interpret texts from the past, Roman archaeology, and especially Roman military archaeology, has been criticised for not using models. Practitioners of Roman archaeology sometimes glory in the disregard of models, though it would be difficult to find a written example of the boast 'We don't need models, we know what happened'. But both practitioners and critics are, to my mind, wrong. Roman military archaeology does use a model, and it is the failure to recognize this that is the cause of many of the weak points of the subject. It is surprising, therefore, that the critics seem to have been as blind as the practitioners.

The model in general use in military archaeology is the historical model derived from written sources. The misunderstanding, in my view, is to assume that the texts give the main story, while archaeology fills in the decorative details. The true state of affairs is one in which the texts provide the concepts and categories, while the archaeology restricts itself to the elucidation and description of these subjects. It would be quite wrong to accuse the typical military archaeologist of blindly believing what any written text says, for there are so many examples to disprove this that the charge cannot hold. But it does seem fair to accuse the more staid military archaeologists of working within the concepts and categories of the historical model, and with not realizing that it is a model and that it has very severe limitations.

In trying to understand this subject better I want to examine three different aspects of military archaeology, wherever possible using Caerleon and the Second Augustan Legion as examples, in order to make positive suggestions which military archaeologists might like to consider for the future. In brief, these aspects are the definition of things military, the definition of units, and the place of things military within the rest of Roman archaeology.

The Roman army wore certain types of armour, used certain types of equipment, carried out certain duties, and lived in forts, fortlets and fortresses. Some soldiers are known to have been on secondment in the civilian sphere and then returned, in due course, to their military bases. Transferred to material studies this model, derived from written sources, allows us to find the Roman army through tracing particular pieces of metalwork and other finds, and to define their bases. However, by following this route we shall only find that part of the army which was obeying the textual model. I assume that some soldiers are recorded as diverging from this model, but when they do this, the hard-line military archaeologist either cannot find them, or does not want to find them. Thus while pieces of military metalwork are sometimes taken to hint at the presence of forts (yet to be found), even when found on completely civilian sites, they are seldom taken as material examples of the textual evidence for sending soldiers out on jobs in the civilian world.

It might be instructive to look at the example of the troops of the late fourth century in Britain. Caerleon does not figure in the list of offices of the state at the end of the fourth century, as recorded in the *Notitia Dignitatum*. Neither, be it noted, does Cardiff. The interpretative results have been rather different. The late fortification (an interpretative phrase) at Cardiff can hardly be ignored, even after the building and landscaping on the site in the eighteenth and nineteenth centuries. A fortification, recognized as such by comparison with forts of the Saxon Shore named in the *Notitia* such as Richborough, needs both a purpose and a garrison. These cannot be found in military texts, and even the fragments of general historical texts provide only slim guesses as to what might be going on. The context of the fort at Cardiff is taken to be the late third to the middle of the fourth centuries, and that its purpose was therefore to guard the coast against marauders and invaders. The garrison has to be guessed, but Fulford has made use of the low state of Caerleon in the late third and fourth centuries to suggest that the Second Legion, in reduced form, might have moved from Caerleon to the newly built fort at Cardiff.[2] After that there must have been a reorganization, or rationalization, to allow the Second Legion to get to its documentary home, as assigned in the *Notitia*, at Richborough by at least the end of the fourth century.

This model, which makes economical use of the various kinds of evidence, depends partly on the depression of Caerleon after the mid-third century. In turn, the state of occupation at the fortress has to be gauged from material sources, because the written texts are either absent or uninformative. However, it is important to note that the material comes from partial excavation only. Excavation has naturally concentrated on that part of the fortress not subject to medieval and modern settlement, and it is possible that any late activity, so far undetected, could be concentrated in the largely undug area. This interpretation depends on structures, and rather ignores finds.

The basic question which needs to be answered is how can military occupation be found and measured in the absence of written records, especially in the period after the second century. I have suggested that Cardiff is thought to be military on analogy with the forts of the Saxon Shore, whose military purpose is presumably clear from the *Notitia*. This analogy, on grounds of planning and architecture, might only be an indication of its original purpose, especially if we share Cunliffe's doubts as to whether the late fort at Portchester had a continuous military presence after the initial phase of occupation.[3]

The structures at Portchester in the Roman period concentrate within a high wall set round a rectangular area, which is confusingly reminiscent of the playing card shaped fort of the Early Empire. Cunliffe was aware of the difficulties of digging wooden buildings, for he had published the results of earlier work conducted at Richborough in which late structures seemed almost culpably missing.[4] To avoid bias in his sample, he dug a complete eighth of the area inside the fort. Even this strategy failed to produce any convincing buildings and he was reduced to suggesting that the structures that had been there must have occupied the areas between the undisturbed gravel surfaces of the 'roads' and the warren of rubbish and cess-pits. Since he had no internal structures, apart from wells and pits, to consider, Cunliffe looked at the material recovered and the deposits in which it was found. He came to the conclusion that the occupation was of two natures, one clean, and one messy. The initial occupation was clean, that is little rubbish was left lying around and most had been buried or sealed. This clean period was followed by a phase which left a large amount of debris scattered throughout the excavated area. The subsequent phase was different in that it appeared to start with wholesale clearing, when all the old rubbish was sealed under new layers, and another clean phase commenced. Since the first phase was connected with the building of the fort and the time immediately thereafter, the excavator felt it was reasonable to assume that this phase was military. The second, messy, phase was different, and it was suggested that it might have been non-military. The third, clearing-up and clean phase, might again have been military. It must be remembered that this suggestion, like all other interpretations of archaeological material in supposed forts, without garrison inscriptions, is an interpretative hypothesis.

There was one further aspect to these phases which has caused some discussion. The first and third phases were represented by fewer coins than the second phase (324–48). In an appraisal of the evidence, Casey infers that Cunliffe has interpreted his periods of cleanliness and dirt from the coin fluctuations alone.[5] If correct, this would indeed have been a grave error, but in fact the different nature of each of the phases was determined stratigraphically and then compared with the coins. It is curious that the messy phase coincides with the period in which virtually every site in Britain has a peak of coin loss, whereas the clean phases are generally less well represented by coins on most sites.

The Portchester model gives some possible leads and provides a definite warning. The leads grow from the original suggestion that military occupation might be detectable purely through the quantity and nature of the material found. In other words the army may have used particular sorts and combinations of pots, and denominations and quantities of coins. If these peculiarities can be defined, then a material approach to the Roman army might be possible. The warning is that no material may ever be interpreted in an absolute sense; it must be judged on a comparative scale. Thus coins from periods L, M, and N in ratios 1:3:1 do not mean that there was three times the activity in period M. It may be that every site in Britain has the ratio 1L:3M:1N, in which case the figures simply show that the site is close to normality in this particular.

Returning to Cardiff, we might agree that the similarities of the basic structure – a walled rectangle – to the forts of the Saxon Shore suggest that the motives for its construction were military. Before we can populate the structure with soldiers, however, we need to examine the quantity and type of material over several phases, and to compare this with other nearby sites. If we want to populate Cardiff with troops from Caerleon then we need a material fingerprint of the Caerleon garrison while they are still at the fortress, so that we can compare their rubbish at Caerleon with the, at present, anonymous rubbish at Cardiff. While this might seem a good idea, it can only be achieved some time in the future, for the truncations and landscaping to which Cardiff Castle has been subjected have made it very difficult to detect the late levels, and consequently little of them has yet been excavated.

To take the subject forward, we need to know what the material record through time says about the presence or absence of the garrison at Caerleon. Most of the structures, such as barracks, that have been excavated show less activity or occupation in the later third and fourth centuries than before, though the 'Roman Gates' site – lying to the north of the east gate – may be an exception.[6] This immediately takes us into the whole discussion on the size and nature of later Roman army units, and here there are encouraging signs of archaeological reasoning. One side suggests that because late fortifications, such as Richborough, are about one quarter the size of the earlier fortresses, such as Caerleon, then the late legion was a smaller unit of perhaps 1,000 rather than 5,000 men.[7] A change can also be recognized in the pattern of accommodation at some late sites. At Housesteads, for example, the earlier complete barrack blocks were replaced by rows of chalet style blocks. If this were found to be a common change, the early form of barrack block accommodating a century of eighty men each was being replaced by separate houses for seven or eight men, or, as some have suggested, for the families of soldiers. At South Shields there are, however, what appear to be perfectly good early-style barrack blocks built in the fourth century, which suggest continuity of living styles. In these late buildings, remodelled at the same time as the granaries, Bidwell and Hodgson see units of five living rooms, with extra rooms for cooking and storage, which replaced the old ten room barrack.[8] They see similar groupings in the chalets at Housesteads and suggest that this would indicate a reduction in the size of a century from ten to five *contubernia*. This would indicate a drop to about half the earlier troop numbers in the fourth-century units occupying these forts. It is interesting that the Bidwell–Hodgson interpretation holds, without question, to the notion of eight men to a room at all times and in all places (following the textual model?), while the chalet hypothesis moves out to a new model (the army as a holiday camp or Swiss ski compound?).

There is an even deeper layer of interpretation which should be made explicit and is worth exploring. The recent work by Burns on Rome and the Barbarians at the end of the fourth century seems to me to make a clear case for the late Roman privatization of defence.[9] He argues that tribes outside the Empire were invited in and settled as parts of the fighting force. At first they were paid and supplied, but soon this became too much for the state to guarantee so they were given land in exchange for guarding and policing areas of land and sections of frontier. It may be that the structural differences in the accommodation for troops provided at late forts such as South Shields, Housesteads and Birdoswald lie in contrasting approaches to late Roman defence in Britain. South Shields, with its standard barracks and up-to-the-minute fashionable commander's house,[10] might represent the mainstream army in control of an important part of the military network. Housesteads, with its rows of chalets, represents a unit of more or less regular soldiers made into a private limited company and told to run the fort in their own way. Birdoswald on the other hand, with its late timber halls, might represent the hiring of a private firm with no connection to the army, with instructions to hold an area of countryside, whatever the effect on their fellow natives.

The section above was written purely with reference to the archaeology, but Neil Holbrook points out that this evidence displays a remarkable coincidence with the units recorded, or not recorded, at these forts in the *Notitia*. At South Shields, the modernization of the fort was carried out by a new unit transferred there in the early fourth century. At Housesteads, the unit had been in residence since the second century and there is little sign of bright new thinking in the fourth century. At Birdoswald the *Notitia*, as it stands in our present copies, disclaims all knowledge of any unit. If the fort were garrisoned, and the *Notitia* is correct at this point, the people were nothing to do with the mainline Roman administration. Holbrook warns, however, that this fit is clearly too good to be true, and that the whole subject of names of forts and dispositions on Hadrian's Wall in the fourth century is a minefield which should be avoided. I therefore make the point and avoid all further comment.

With the recent publication of the excavations at Birdoswald[11] and with work progressing on the latest phases of South Shields it might soon be possible to establish the material fingerprint that goes with the different types of late military presence. At Birdoswald, the absence of dateable finds makes it very difficult to date the later phases of occupation on the site, and in this regard it may bear strong similarities to the Severn-Cotswold invisible group (see below). When both reports are available, there will be a need to examine the types of pots, the relationships of different forms to one another, supply from near at hand or from a wide area, the denomination and number of coins, and the type of meat in the diet to try to form an idea of the similarities and differences in the material record. Once this is done, then it might be possible to suggest a model for the latest stages at Caerleon. It seems unlikely that the South Shields model applies, because of the general lack of late structures over at least some areas of the former fortress. Neither have any chalets in the style of Housesteads been seen, as yet. The Wild West, or Carousing Barbarian, model from Birdoswald perhaps seems the most likely.

But why do I expect a later presence at Caerleon than already detected. This is hardly as firm as expectation, but a glance at the later material from south Wales does suggest some sort of discontinuity, to put it no higher, east of modern Cardiff. In the western parts of the Cardiff area, at Dinas Powys[12] and Llandough[13] there is clear evidence of the standard early medieval assemblage on the standard sites of hill-top and monastery. Both sites and material, such as imported pottery, are absent to the east, notably at Caerwent and Caerleon. These absences continue further east towards Gloucester and Cirencester, Hereford, Worcester and Bath. The material occurs again to the south in Somerset, across the Severn from Cardiff. It might be, therefore, that the material culture east of Cardiff belongs to a Severn-Cotswold invisible grouping; Celtic early medieval material lies to the west and south. Caerleon is certainly in this frontier zone, even if it is not a frontier outpost. It may, therefore, be the site of a Severn-Cotswold invisible focus of authority.

One way of testing these ideas using material might be through the examination of fortress coin lists. The *Notitia* mentions the Sixth Legion at a place called *Sexta*, which is normally taken to be York. Hence, it is possible that there was a legionary presence at York from the Early Empire up to the bitter end. At Chester there is doubt about the date at which full legionary presence declines or ends. Chester presents a similar problem to that at Caerleon. There is a possible way forward, for a method is beginning to emerge by which coin finds can be turned into fairly simple visual pictures from which comparisons between sites can easily be made.[14] By using this method some military sites clearly stand out from the general provincial background, but this is mainly by virtue of large numbers of early coins (ie first century), which do not seem to be available on civilian sites. There is a need to develop this method further, so that we can identify military peculiarities in the later periods. Another approach has been to study the different denominations found on military sites in the first century,[15] but this type of analysis is not available for the later centuries when different denominations were no longer being supplied.

If we had detailed coin lists from the fortresses, then we might be able to use York, with its continuous occupation to the end of the Roman occupation, as a base-line for legionary coin supply and coin loss. We could then compare this with towns where no military presence is suspected, or needed, or has been found, and so decide whether legionary coin loss is similar to, or different from, civilian coin loss. We could also compare York as the base-line with Chester and Caerleon to see when, and by how much, they deviated from the military norm. This might provide us with indications of changes in the nature of occupation, perhaps from military to civilian, or from full to half complement, or whatever. Unfortunately, this is still some way in the future, though work is in progress. It seems to me a sign of textual imbeddedness that no complete coin lists have been published for the three fortresses, and I have to take it as a sign that their material culture has been thought to have less to contribute than other sites, such as villas, towns or rural settlements. This criticism extends only to the distant past, for at Caerleon George Boon worked on the coins, and no one could possibly have produced more comprehensive information; I am sure that this work will be brought to completion. Work continues at York and Chester which should soon be available in published form.

In pottery studies there are even more gaps in our information, though there have been some interesting suggestions and ideas. Fulford, in his lecture and essay, investigated the place of black-burnished pottery from south-west Britain as an indicator of the activities of the Second Legion.[16] His maps, showing a bulge of BB1 (black-burnished ware category 1) on the north shore of the Bristol Channel round about Caerleon, suggested to him that when the legion moved from Exeter, perhaps via Gloucester, it brought with it reserves of the Dorset pottery and its contracts for supply. Caerleon, for Fulford, formed an island of unexpected Dorset-pottery-importing on the banks of the Severn. This idea had considerable appeal, and I was tempted to label the legion not the Second but the BB1 Legion. The reason for doing this was that the activities of the legion could be traced, even in the absence of inscriptions, by an unusual, out-of-context, amount of BB1 pottery on a site. Since every site produces pottery, while perhaps only one military site in five produces inscriptions, this would clearly be a considerable methodological advance. Subsequently, however, both Webster and Manning took me to task for not digesting properly the published pottery reports from Usk,[17] where it is clear that the Severnside bulge of BB1 is present in the first century. Since the Second Legion is not implicated (at present) at Usk, the bulge of BB1 on the Severn shore must already have existed before the legion arrived at Caerleon. If the army was responsible for movements of BB1, a possible hypothesis but by no means proved, it was not the Second Legion, and this brilliant methodological advance must unfortunately be withdrawn.

Yet, as always, when one door closes, another opens. Charmian Woodfield, intrepid excavator and publisher, in an excellent article on Roman small towns in the East Midlands, makes a more far-reaching and exciting suggestion than mine.[18] Since her ideas are always rooted firmly in material, they often fail to transplant to the more literary minds of students of Roman Britain. Her analysis of pottery demands attention though it needs careful thought because it depends on a method of reasoning similar to that which I suggested for coins. Her ideas can also only be applied to sites for which we have a quantified report on the pottery. We need to know not just what carefully defined forms and fabrics were found, but in what proportions through time. To apply her ideas we therefore need sites which have a well phased sequence with clear separate deposits, published by phase, in which all the pottery found has at least been put in a table by phase, by fabric (eg BB1) and by quantity (eg number of sherds or some more sophisticated measure). This severely limits the sites available for comparison. Indeed, in the present ridiculous state of guidelines for study and publication, few new sites will ever be published in such detail.

Woodfield makes her point in the context of the building of a series of defensive walls round small settlements in the East Midlands, which she argues took place in the years around 160 to 180. Since these walls often pre-date the walls of larger towns, she quite reasonably proposes that their purpose is more likely to be military or defensive than honorific or bureaucratic. She compares pottery deposits of the same date (170–5); that in a latrine pit which cut the back of the rampart at Towcester comprised 22 per cent BB1, whereas 'the normal percentage at that date in the locality, but outside the town, is about 3 per cent or less'. To add to this evidence, she quotes a personal communication from Malcolm Lyne, another intrepid material worker, who states that 'The walling of certain towns in the South, eg Chichester, … Silchester and Winchester, is accompanied by a surge of BB1 to proportions of some 25 per cent'. Do we have here the beginnings of Real Military Archaeology?

Neil Holbrook has two useful, if deflationary, comments on this work. His first remark was 'so there is a burst of BB1 when walls are being built, is there?' This immediately makes the point that while the link between the building of the walls and the burst of BB1 can be accepted, nothing, as yet, ties either the burst of BB1, or the building of the walls to the army. Care must be taken, however enticing the ideas, not to let a circular pattern of reasoning develop in which there are imaginary links. His second comment is more general. He is worried that the burst of BB1 seen in the late second and third centuries comes at a time when there is a general rise in the production, or distribution (or both) of BB1. A site- and event-specific burst of BB1 has to be separated out from a general period of high use of BB1. Also we have to ask whether the rise in the proportion of BB1 is owing to a rise in the amount of BB1 in the 'difficult' times of the early third century, or a fall in the amount of accompanying pottery. Is BB1 more obvious because it is one of the few industries to keep going during this undatable time? Is it perhaps associated with the army because they are some of the only groups of the population to be supplied at this time? It would be helpful to draw information from Fulford and Allen's far ranging study of BB1, but unfortunately it does not take account of chronology in any detail.[19] To redress the balance of the argument, a link might be made between the army, and particularly the legions, and BB1 on the northern frontier. Holbrook points out that Boon first noticed the difference in pottery found on Hadrian's Wall, at the time of its construction, and at the Stanegate forts. BB1 is more common in Wall construction deposits and Boon suggested, in his review of *Current Research in Romano-British Coarse Pottery*, that it might have been the Second Legion which introduced BB1 to the North during its tour of construction duties.[20]

One other piece of research needs a mention here because it takes the subject of pottery analysis a step further. Jeremy Evans[21] – following on from earlier work by, among others, Peter Webster[22] and Charmian Woodfield[23] – has examined both fabrics and forms on different sites in northern Britain and has related his findings to the nature of the site, ie fort, turret, town, or rural settlement. It has to be pointed out that to obtain decent results the researcher needs either access to the full range of pottery found, or a report which describes in detail and quantifies completely. Evans finds that forts 'generally seem to have a fairly high proportion of fine wares', but 'In sharp contrast to the forts are the second-century turret groups which have very low percentages.' The rural groups 'are at a level comparable with the turrets'. When he moved in to a closer examination of the forms (jars, beakers, bowls etc) he found definite differences between the assemblages at different sites and concluded very cautiously that 'there seems to be a likelihood that variations in the functional breakdown of assemblages do reflect, at least in part, the nature of the class of site'. Some of his diagrams go a little further than this. His figure 6 shows a fairly clear distinction between turrets and forts (first – second century) when the proportion of jars is plotted against the proportion of dishes and bowls. Rural and urban sites show a similar difference with only a few dots out of type. Other diagrams show that the difference is not so much civilian *versus* military, but perhaps status within the two categories. Thus rural settlements tend to group with turrets and towns with forts.

Returning to Caerleon, Peter Webster reports an interesting point arising from his current work on samian from the site. In this survey he finds few samian *mortaria* (late second century) in the fortress, but more in the civil settlement. This is not a chronological gap, because other late second-century samian forms are present in both areas, nor is it a dietary variation, because there are plenty of other *mortaria*. Webster suggests that this is an example of the difference between a military and a civilian pottery fingerprint. These areas of research have produced results which to me are exciting; now more people need to follow up the leads.

So far I have tried to look forward to see what an archaeological, rather than a textual, study of the Roman army in Britain might look like. There does seem hope that we can push the subject outwards from written evidence, with all its limitations, to a more general material study. Structures may have to be interpreted by analogy with firm examples defined by text or inscription, and material studies may have to start off from that same base, but there may be a possibility of extrapolating from these beginnings into a wider area. Thus, within military structures there may be different types of occupation at different phases, and not all of these may be military. This is the Portchester model in which one type of occupation within one site is contrasted with another. With coins there may be a military type of coin use at certain times in the occupation of Britain, for example the use of small change and *sestertii* at Exeter and Baginton. With pottery it seems possible that military arrival into a previously civilian area might be detectable by the sources of pottery being used and discarded. A closer look at forms suggests that different categories of site, and even status of each site might be detectable. These elements are to me the building blocks of the future.

All these points concern the army as a whole, even if status within the army might be detectable with detailed study. No mention has been made of individual units, and I think we have to ask whether the study of units has any future in Real Military Archaeology. Perhaps it has a long enough past in the Old Military Archaeology and a future in Roman Military history. The point at issue is whether the unit is a material reality or a textual concept. As we have seen, several attempts have been made to show that the military as a whole, and distinct from civilians, can be studied by material means once these have been calibrated, but I am unaware of any material studies which have successfully been able to identify units, or even categories of unit. I have to leave on one side here the debate on this topic, because it is a substantial subject in its own right, it is well beyond my competence, and it seems to be still in progress.

Some might point to the various Legionary Wares, which seem to rise and fall in pottery publications, as indicators of separate units. Thus the Gloucester wares might, at one point, have defined the Gloucester legion, and there have been further suggestions at Chester (Holt) and York.[24] Apart from the fact that these wares are sometimes short-lived, there is the more serious problem that they are rarely widely traded and do not seem to move with the legion. Furthermore, there is the problem of defining the role of the military in the production of these wares. Ought BB1 to be defined as Exeter Legion ware, just because it is the nearest legion, or the fortress into which a great amount of early production goes, or the legion which seems to have put BB1 on the trading map of Roman Britain? Clearly not, for although those statements are true they avoid the fact that pottery which was black, and burnished, was made in Dorset long before the legions were a nasty cloud on the horizon. At Usk and Caerleon the situation is different, because there were no indigenous pottery makers to exploit the new market. This gives the opportunity to study the pottery used in fortresses which were established in aceramic areas; a subject that provided some early leads, but one which has not been exploited. Certainly an army base with 5,000 men forms a demanding market whose economy needs careful investigation.

In similar vein, Vivien Swan's study of the new Mediterranean cooks arriving at York might be taken to define the Sixth Legion, but that is clearly not the case.[25] She has made a good case for a group of new arrivals in York and the surrounding area, and even at Caerleon, at the end of the second century. These people brought with them, or instigated the production of, a new type of cooking pot. This had a sagging (curved) base, which was perhaps more suited for cooking on a charcoal brazier rather than a flat stove. This type of pot can be found in second-century deposits round the shores of the western Mediterranean, and it is a fair inference that there was a movement of people from that area to Britain at the end of the second century. Since the pots turn up in York and in other military contexts, but seem rare in purely civilian contexts, the new arrivals may well have been soldiers. We might also conclude that they were associated with the Sixth Legion, which was based in York, but they are new arrivals and could not be taken to define the legion in any long-term material sense.

The study of these new cooking pots demonstrates the problems of working with military units by name. The Second Legion came to Britain in 43, after being raised by Augustus and spending some time at Strasbourg. It came to its new fortress at Caerleon after a spell at Exeter and possibly Gloucester. By the time that it settled in Caerleon after 70 there would have been no survivors from the original recruitment. Later recruits, those who were legionaries at the establishment of Caerleon, were raised from different places. Indeed, by the end of the second century and into the early third century there may well have been British recruits in post. If some African recruits had joined the legion in the early third century, the composition of the legion would have changed again, but the information these recruits would leave the archaeologist would be material and not conceptual. That these new arrivals came from the western Mediterranean may be demonstrable in material terms. But would it be possible to show that they joined the Second Legion in a similar way? I very much doubt it, since, in the absence of any serious work or tell-tale inscriptions, the Second Legion remains a concept of doubtful material validity.

What is beyond any doubt whatsoever is that there is in Caerleon, during the second century, a remarkable concentration of 'foreigners' whose impact on the locality must have been tremendous. I use the word 'foreigner' as a native of Cirencester and apply it to anyone different from me, ie not born there. By all means let us continue to call this remarkable concentration of comparatively wealthy consumers the Second Legion, for it is correct. My worry is that, while it sounds helpful and informative, it does not add much to our information. We ought now to look outwards from the military centre to see what effect this imposed settlement had on its surroundings.

The soldiers could be defined in their early years at Caerleon as being different from the local population in many ways. They had far more money, in terms of coinage, and they had a regular supply through their pay. They lived in very crowded conditions, 100 to the acre (0.4 hectare), and this meant that the settlement had to be planned very formally and precisely, something totally different from local farmsteads of whatever status. They dressed differently, probably even off duty. They had a different diet (animal bones and seeds), drank imported wine (wine *amphorae*) rather than local ale, and had lamps which needed oil (oil *amphorae*) rather than tallow candles. They built in monumental forms, which needed major local resources in wood, stone, clay and mortar. They had their own form of burial rite, which diverged sharply from that of the natives in that it is archaeologically visible. When established they consumed enormous quantities of food, drink, and wood for heating, and produced substantial amounts of rubbish and effluent which had to be got rid of.

The huge quantity of resources needed by the army and the impact this might have had on the local native population seem to me to be areas which cry out for investigation. Some work can be done theoretically, but it also needs to be put into practice on and under the ground. Feeding the army was a massive undertaking, for each man in the garrison needed the corn from at least one acre (0.4 hectare) of land to keep him alive for a year. That means that a minimum of 5,000 acres (2,000 hectares) of land somewhere not too far from the fortress were needed for the army. But the army contributed nothing to growing that corn, so you also have to take into consideration the land needed by the native farmers to feed themselves and their dependants. Even if they did nothing but produce food for the army, they would still have had taxes to pay and requisitions to meet. The land to meet those requirements alone would have run to well over 10,000 acres (4,000 hectares). In terms of the whole province that was very little, but in terms of the area in the vicinity of the military establishment it was a substantial chunk of land to set aside. However, grain may have been brought from anywhere and certainly we should avoid the temptation to apply modern ideas of cost and efficiency to such supply, for they are almost certainly anachronistic. There were people and methods of transport whose lives were devoted, willingly for pay, or unwillingly, to the army. The troops themselves could have been sent on food escorting duties with little extra expense. If something was requisitioned by the army, whether food or means of transport, it was only the wealthy and powerful who could argue successfully and avoid the demand – just like the contemporary tax system. So while it is possible to calculate the food needs of a legion, it is impossible to argue for a particular area of land needed to supply that food. Grain can travel for hundreds of miles without unnecessary ill effects; on the other hand, if there were a ration of lettuce leaves for each soldier, they would probably have come from within a circle of a day's journey by ox-cart.

The legionary bathhouse would undoubtedly have been a more reliable drain on the resources of the local environment. The materials for the construction of such a highly visible and wondrous building would have been enormous, but they could have come by sea and river and therefore need not have caused major local disruption, apart from the necessary mess which seems always to follow builders. But once built and in operation it would seem likely that fuel must have come from the immediate locality. From the work of a former heating engineer turned archaeologist, Tony Rook, we are in a position to estimate the quantity of wood used for heating a bath-block.[26] He calculated the fuel needs of a very modest villa bath-building, comprising four small rooms, at Welwyn, Hertfordshire. This block, about 14 metres long by 4 metres wide, needed, if his calculations are correct, somewhere around 114 tonnes of wood to operate at its most efficient throughout the year. He demonstrated that continuous operation was both efficient and convenient and that little was saved by firing at weekends only. For a legionary bathhouse – with 5,000 soldiers wanting to bathe, not counting slaves, local helpers, and paid servants – continuous operation seems almost essential. The 114 tonnes of wood required to operate Welwyn either could have come from chopping down mature trees, in which case the source would be lost for the next hundred years or so while the trees regenerated, or by coppicing. The Welwyn baths would have burnt the wood from about 58 acres (23 hectares) of coppice each year, on the basis of a seven year cycle of coppicing. The 58 acres is roughly the size of a legionary fortress, so the baths of a small villa would need seven fortress areas set aside and managed as coppice for fuel. But, of course, a legionary bathhouse, such as that at Caerleon, is many times the floor area of the Welwyn baths, perhaps around forty times or more. It is not worth attempting accurate calculations at this stage for such a large bathhouse, because the superstructure would have been a far greater drain on fuel than the floor area. The calculations would get very complicated, and progressively erratic (not to mention far beyond me), as they moved from firm comparisons of floor area to cubic volumes of air within the standing baths, which would have to take into account such complex factors as the heat content of the roofs and walls. Even using the simple comparison of floor areas, the Caerleon baths would need forty times the wood of Welwyn and probably considerably more. This would demand either the extinction of local woodland, or the management of well over 14,000 acres (5,600 hectares) of coppice, ie 280 fortress areas, to provide the amenity of baths which soldiers are assumed to have needed – unless of course they used the coal from the Forest of Dean.[27]

Is it sheer accident, we might ask in slightly lighter vein, that the major concentrations of troops in Roman Britain settle near to coal-fields? Was this the only way the soldiers could be kept happy and clean? Whatever the merits of this, the correlation between Caerleon and the Forest of Dean, Chester and the Lancashire pits, York and the Yorkshire pits, and Hadrian's Wall and the mines at its east and west ends are interesting. At Wallsend, where a military bathhouse has recently been reconstructed, coal is known to have fuelled the original stoke-holes. There is of course a much less exciting geological explanation, for the coal measures are associated with rocks older than those which bear the heavily populated and well farmed pastures of the South and East. In the course of events, soldiers settled beyond these densely occupied areas, and were located, whether by chance or design, on or near supplies of coal. Webster also points out the further coincidence of coal and iron, at least in the case of the Forest of Dean.

At Caerleon, it is most unlikely that wood would have been brought from far afield. So we have here a possible direct measurement of the effect of the fortress on the local environment of the type which I suggest needs greater study. I would also have liked to discuss the effect of the fortress on the local population, that is if we knew anything at all about them. Manning has published a map which shows Iron Age settlements and monuments sited around the fortresses of Caerleon and Usk.[28] But, unfortunately, we cannot go on from there to discuss the local population, because we have very little idea how many of those dots on the map were occupied in the first century. Even if we knew that, we have no idea at present of the numbers of people involved in the occupation of any of the sites. In order to understand the full effect of the fortress and its legion on the locality, we require some very basic ideas of the local people living in the vicinity.

The local inhabitants must either have existed in reasonable numbers, or they must have been moved in quickly, for, as a start, about 140 able-bodied adults would have been needed to manage the coppicing alone, as soon as the baths were operating. While the fortress could be seen as almost a quarantine station, provisioned from the sea and sealed off from the surrounding land, this model seems very unlikely indeed. The natives must have been there and they must provide a field of study for looking at the effect of the legion on them, and their reciprocal effect, over the years, on the legion.

This move into the locality brings us back to the question of models and especially the relative merits of the historical model and its archaeological alternatives. There is a case for suggesting that the paucity of information about the surroundings of forts and fortresses pushes any study into the historical model. Texts and inscriptions saw the army base as a far flung tentacle of Rome. The rock on which the tentacle took purchase was unimportant, for it could be made to supply whatever was needed and it was, in any case, a temporary halt before the forces moved on to greater things. The body, the Roman civilian machine, would have drawn up behind the tentacle which could then have relaxed its grip and moved forward to a new foothold. But in Wales in the second century the situation had changed. There was nowhere very obvious, or desirable, for the army to go next unless they all ended up in Ireland. This worrying condition of having to learn to live within boundaries meant that the state's view of the army must also have changed. Webster has suggested to me, however, that when we have local texts, as at Vindolanda, the impersonality and detachment of the tentacle theory breaks down to show the army becoming firmly involved in the local economy, both officially as a body and unofficially as individuals. When such things happen the door is open for private enterprise to flourish. But after the first and second centuries, for which we have written information, the texts and inscriptions little by little fail, and the historical model therefore crumbles. Perhaps it is not so strange that much military archaeology to date has crumbled with the model.

I have expressed dissatisfaction with what I see as a sad state of affairs, but I have tried to put forward for consideration different ways of looking at the army which will be almost independent of the texts. Thus, when the texts fail, or in areas which texts have never illuminated, Real Military Archaeology can go forward to reach parts which have never been reached before.

SPECULATIVE APPENDIX

I have tried to keep the formal text of this paper within the usual bounds of polite academic writing. This means that I have tried to provide references for statements and have taken the advice and editing of friends and colleagues at almost all points. But as a result of writing the formal piece several ideas have bubbled up and I would like to express them in my own way. I know perfectly well that since I am an outsider looking in at military archaeology they cannot be major contributions to the subject. The purpose of putting them down, without the benefit of 'advice', is that one small aspect might at some time in the future fire someone inside the subject with an idea to work on, and I would find that very worth while.

Three points seem to be clear in the present state of studies. The early larger units, like the legions, are much less visible in the later Empire than around 150. The role of the army in building, especially for themselves and for defensive purposes, has always been clear, but it is only very recently that we can recognize just how much of their time and effort this must have taken.[29] In the late fourth century, according to the *Notitia Dignitatum*, there are three main commands, those of the *comes litoris Saxonici*, the *dux Britanniarum*, and the *comes Britanniae*. The Second Legion is associated with the Saxon Shore; the Sixth Legion is associated with the *dux* and the North; but the Twentieth Legion and the *comes Britanniae* are at a loose end. The conjunction of the Second Legion with units, like *limitanei* or 'frontier troops', in fixed forts commanded by a *comes*, makes it clear that the usual army prescriptions can be waived without difficulty. There is, therefore, no objection to suggesting an association of the *comes Britanniae*, the Twentieth Legion and a late field army. These points can be combined in a smooth narrative which no doubt provides many difficulties, but has the benefit of sewing together several disparate ideas.

The arrival of the army in Britain was clearly for the purpose of conquest, whatever that may mean in practice. But as soon as the basic campaigning was over, the army turned to providing itself with accommodation. By the 80s building rather than fighting was top of the agenda, to judge from the tremendous effort of building the new legionary fortress at Inchtuthil.[30] Soldiers were busy building homes for themselves and for their veterans.

Permanent fortresses for the legions were under construction at the end of the first century and the beginning of the second, and the effort which went into these stone structures must have been even greater than that calculated for the timber fortress at Inchtuthil. These projects may not even have been finished when the construction of Hadrian's Wall began. It is now clear that this occupied major elements in the army in Britain for well over a decade.[31] In fact, Kendal suggests that it might not have been finished when the manpower was called away even further north to construct the Antonine Wall. It might be that by the end of the second century Hadrian's Wall was completed, and the troops were once again able to return to their permanent bases and to get them, after a long hiatus, into working order.

By the middle of the third century, there was a call for town defences, which went on for some time. If the army is involved in such building, and it seems an excellent displacement activity, then units were presumably divided up in the usual fashion and sent off to oversee both building and defence in the towns and other settlements. This is the point at which the army becomes much less visible, and the point at which the old fortresses show little more than 'greatly reduced' or 'holding' garrisons. I am obviously suggesting that this is because they are so thinly spread as building and security consultants, and that the chances of seeing them in the tiny sample of discarded material which is archaeology is minimal.

The building of shore defences might have sustained their interest after town walls were completed. But then the addition of towers and other changes to defensive works in the fourth century clearly kept them occupied, and they were probably not brought back into a unified command until the post of *comes Britanniae* was created late in the fourth century, with some additional new units. The army units in the towns are not listed, either because the *Notitia* is notoriously selective in what it lists, or, more likely, because they had been shed from the army pay lists and left to the budgets of the *Civitates*. This process of shedding the financial load from the state to local resources was brought to the inevitable conclusion by the famous letter of Honorius, finally making it explicit that the province must pay for itself or peter out. As always with moribund administrations the paperwork was way behind the practice.

These hypotheses are economical in that they tie up a lot of loose ends. Whether the result is an acceptable pattern or a tangled mess is for others to judge in the future. Military specialists will be glad to know I regard this foray into their territory as *Ave atque Vale*.

ACKNOWLEDGEMENTS

This paper has benefited from the informed criticism of a number of people. I give very grateful acknowledgement to all those who have helped me by reading through drafts of the lecture and the finished text, who have removed some of the mistakes and helped me reach a more informed state. Apart from those directly implicated by mention in the text I am particularly grateful to Richard Brewer and Peter Guest (School of History & Archaeology, Cardiff University).

Notes

1 Mattingly and Hitchner 1995, 209.
2 Fulford this volume, 98–9.
3 Cunliffe 1975, 426–8.
4 Cunliffe 1968, 248.
5 Casey 1986, 98–100.
6 Evans and Metcalf 1992.
7 James 1984.
8 Hodgson, forthcoming.
9 Burns 1994, 264–8.
10 Hodgson 1996.
11 Wilmott 1997.
12 Alcock 1963.
13 Holbrook *et al*, forthcoming.
14 Reece 1995.
15 Reece 1975; 1991.
16 Fulford this volume, 92–5.
17 Manning 1993.
18 Woodfield 1995.
19 Allen and Fulford 1996.
20 Boon 1974b.
21 Evans 1993.
22 P V Webster 1972.
23 Woodfield 1965.
24 Greene 1977; Monaghan 1993, 705–9.
25 Swan 1992.
26 Rook 1978, 281.
27 Zienkiewicz 1986a, 343.
28 Manning 1981, 36, Fig 9.
29 For example, see Shirley 1996; 2001 and Kendal 1996.
30 Shirley 1996, 127–8; 2000.
31 Kendal 1996, 132.

Ancient Sources

Authors and Literary Works

Aelius Aristides, *Roman Oration*
Ammianus Marcellinus
Anonymous, *de re strategica*
Anthologia Latina II.2 (eds F Bücheler and A Riese (1897), Lipsiae)
Appian, *Bella Civilia*
Iberica
Illyrica
Arrian, *Ectaxis contra Alanos*
Caesar, *de Bello Civili*
de Bello Gallico
Cassius Dio, *Historia Romana*
Cicero, *Epistulae ad Familiares*
Claudian, *de quarto consulatu Honorii*
Codex Theodosianus
Digest of Justinian, *Digesta seu Pandectae*
Frontinus, *Strategemata*
Herodian, *ab excessu Divi Marci*
Hyginus, *de Munitionibus Castrorum*
Isidore, *Origines*
Itinerarium Antonini (ed O Cuntz (1929), Leipzig)
Josephus, *Bellum Iudaicum*
Lactantius, *de mortibus persecutorum* (ed and tr J L Creed (1984), Oxford)
Libanius, *Orationes*
Livy
Martial, *Epigrammata*
Maurice, *Strategikon* (ed G T Dennis, *Das Strategikon des Maurikos* (1981), Vienna)
Notitia Dignitatum omnium, tam civilium quam militarium, in partibus Orientis and *in partibus Occidentis* (ed O Seeck (1876), Berlin)
Panegyrici Latini
Pliny (the Elder), *Historia Naturalis*
Pliny (the Younger), *Epistulae*
Plutarch, *Galba*
Polybius, *Historiae*
Procopius, *Bellum Gothicum* (ed and tr H B Dewing (1968), Loeb).
Ptolemy, *Geographia*
Quintillian, *Orationes*
Res Gestae divi Augusti (eds P A Brunt and J M Moore (1967), Oxford)
Sallust, *Bellum Iugurthinum*
Scriptores Historiae Augustae
Silius Italicus, *Punica*
Statius, *Silvae*
Strabo, *Geographia*
Suetonius, *Vitae duodecim Caesarum*
Tacitus, *Agricola*
Annales
Historiae
Theophylact Simocatta (tr by M Whitby and M Whitby (1986), Oxford)
Vegetius, *Epitoma rei militaris*
Zosimus, *Historia Nova*

Bibliography

AE 1888– . *L'Année Épigraphique*, Paris

Alcock, L 1963. *Dinas Powys. An Iron Age, Dark Age and Early Medieval Settlement in Glamorgan*, Cardiff

Alföldy, G 1967. 'Senatoren in der römischen Provinz Dalmatia', *Epigraphische Studien* 5, 99–144

Alföldy, G 1969. *Die Personennamen in der römischen Provinz Dalmatia*, Heidelberg

Alföldy, G 1974. *Noricum*, London

Allen, J R L and Fulford, M G 1986. 'The Wentlooge Level: a Romano-British saltmarsh reclamation in south-east Wales', *Britannia* 17, 91–117

Allen, J R L and Fulford, M G 1996. 'The Distribution of South-East Dorset Black Burnished Category 1 Pottery in South-West Britain', *Britannia* 27, 223–81

Amy, R, Duval, P-M, Formigé, J, Hatt, J J, Piganiol, A, Picard, C and Picard, G-Ch 1962. *L'Arc d'Orange*, Gallia suppl 15, Paris

Anderson, J C 1987. 'The Date of the Arch at Orange', *Bonner Jahrbücher* 187, 159–92

Anderson, A S and Wacher, J S 1980. 'Excavations at Wanborough, Wiltshire: An Interim Report', *Britannia* 11, 115–26

Annable, F 1966. 'A late first-century well at Cvnetio', *Wiltshire Archaeol and Natur Hist Mag* 61, 9–24

Atkinson, D 1914. 'A hoard of samian ware from Pompeii', *J Roman Stud* 4, 27–64

Baatz, D 1962. *Mogontiacum: neue Untersuchungen am römischen Legionslager in Mainz*, Limesforschungen 4, Berlin

Baatz, D 1977. Review of H von Petrikovits 1975 in *Germania* 55, 265–70

Baatz, D 1987. Review of Pitts and St Joseph 1985 in *Antiq J* 67, 170–2

Balland, A 1981. *Fouilles de Xanthos* 7, Paris

Balsdon, J P V D 1934. 'Notes concerning the Principate of Gaius', *J Roman Stud* 24, 13–24

Balty, J Ch 1988. 'Apamea in Syria in the Second and Third Centuries AD', *J Roman Stud* 78, 91–104

Barratt, A A 1989. *Caligula. The Corruption of Power*, London

Bell, H I 1937. 'A Latin Registration of Birth', *J Roman Stud* 27, 30–6

BGU 1895– . *Berliner Griechische Urkunden*, Berlin

Bidwell, P T 1979. *The Legionary Bath-House and Basilica and Forum at Exeter*, Exeter

Bidwell, P T and Boon, G C 1976. 'An antefix type of the Second Augustan Legion from Exeter', *Britannia* 7, 278–80

Bidwell, P, Bridgwater, R and Silvester, R J 1979. 'The Roman Fort at Okehampton, Devon', *Britannia* 10, 255–8

Birley, A R 1971. 'VI Victrix in Britain' in *Soldier and Civilian in Roman Yorkshire* (ed R M Butler), 81–96, Leicester

Birley, A R 1979. *The People of Roman Britain*, London

Birley, A R 1981. *The* Fasti *of Roman Britain*, Oxford

Birley, A R 1988. 'Names at Lepcis Magna', *Libyan Studies* 19, 1–19

Birley, E 1936. 'Marcus Cocceius Firmus: an epigraphic study', *Proc Soc Antiq Scotl* 70, 363–77=Birley 1953a, 87–103

Birley, E 1941. 'The origins of legionary centurions', *Laureae Aquincenses*, 47–62=E Birley 1988, 189–205

Birley, E 1952a. 'The Epigraphy of the Roman Army', *Actes du deuxième congrès international d'épigraphie grecque et latine*, 226–38, Paris=E Birley 1988, 3–11

Birley, E 1952b. 'Some Roman Military Inscriptions', *Trans Cumberland Westmorland Antiq Archaeol Soc* 51, 67–72=Birley 1953a, 125–30

Birley, E 1952c. 'Noricum, Britain and the Roman army', *Beiträge zur älteren europäischen Kulturgeschichte I, Festschrift R Egger*, 175–88, Klagenfurt=E Birley 1988, 284–97

Birley, E 1953a. *Roman Britain and the Roman Army*, Kendal

Birley, E 1953b. 'Britain under Nero: the significance of Q. Veranius' in Birley 1953a, 1–9

Birley, E 1959–60. 'Thomas Pennant, the Hoddam Castle Collection and Roman Antiquities from Birrens', *Trans Dumfriesshire Galloway Natur Hist Antiq Soc* 3 ser, 37, 140–6

Birley, E 1963–64. 'Promotions and transfers in the Roman army II: the centurionate', *Carnuntum Jahrbuch*, 21–33=E Birley 1988, 206–20

Birley, E 1967. 'Troops from the two Germanies in Roman Britain', *Epigraphische Studien* 4, 103–7=E Birley 1988, 251–5

Birley, E 1978. 'The Adherence of Britain to Vespasian', *Britannia* 9, 243–5=E Birley 1988, 256–8

Birley, E 1979. 'Inscriptions Indicative of Impending or Recent Movements', *Chiron* 9, 495–505=E Birley 1988, 130–40

Birley, E 1980. 'Raetian, Britannien und das römische Heer', *Bayerische Vorgeschichtsblätter* 45, 77–89=E Birley 1988, 259–71

Birley, E 1985. 'The dating of Vegetius and the Historia Augusta' in *Bonner Historia-Augusta-Colloquium 1982/83*, *Antiquitas* ser 4, 17, 57–67, Bonn

Birley, E 1988. *The Roman Army. Papers 1929–1986*, Mavors Roman Army Researches 4, Amsterdam

Birley, E and Richmond, I A 1938. 'Excavations at Corbridge, 1936–1938', *Archaeol Aeliana* 4 ser, 15, 243–94

Birley, R E 1962–3. 'Excavations of the Roman Fortress at Carpow, Perthshire, 1961–2', *Proc Soc Antiq Scotl* 96, 184–207
Birley, R E 1993a. *Vindolanda Research Reports, new ser, II, The Early Wooden Forts: Reports on the Auxiliaries, the Writing Tablets, Inscriptions, Brands and Graffiti* (with A R Birley and E Birley), Hexham
Birley, R E 1993b. *Vindolanda Research Reports, new ser, III, The Early Wooden Forts: Reports on the leather, textiles, environmental evidence and dendrochronology* (with C van Driel Murray, J P Wild, M R D Seaward and J Hallam), Hexham
Bishop, M C and Dore, J N 1988. *Corbridge. Excavations at the Roman fort and town, 1947–80*, London
Blagg, T F C 1979. 'The Date of the Temple of Sulis Minerva at Bath', *Britannia* 10, 101–7
Blockley, K, Ashmore, F and Ashmore, P J 1993. 'Excavations on the Roman Fort at Abergavenny, Orchard Site, 1972–73', *Archaeol J* 150, 169–242
Boon, G C 1949. 'A Claudian Origin for Sea Mills', *Trans Bristol Gloucestershire Archaeol Soc* 68, 184–8
Boon, G C 1962. 'Remarks on Roman Usk', *Monmouthshire Antiq* 1.2, 28–33
Boon, G C 1972. *Isca. The Roman Legionary Fortress at Caerleon, Mon*, Cardiff
Boon, G C 1974a. *Silchester: the Roman Town of Calleva*, Newton Abbott
Boon, G C 1974b. Review of A Detsicas (ed), *Current Research in Romano-British Coarse Pottery* in *Archaeol Cambrensis* 123, 184–5
Boon, G C 1978. 'Excavations on the Site of a Roman Quay at Caerleon & its Significance' in *Monographs and Collections I, Roman Sites* (ed G C Boon), Cambrian Archaeol Ass, 1–24, Cardiff
Boon, G C 1984. *Laterarium Iscanum: The Antefixes, Brick & Tile Stamps of the Second Augustan Legion*, Cardiff
Boon, G C 1987. *The Legionary Fortress of Caerleon – Isca. A Brief Account*, Cardiff
Boon, G C and Brewer, R J 1981. 'Two Central Gaulish Bottles from Pennal, Mer and Early Roman Movement in Cardigan Bay', *Bull Board Celtic Stud* 29.2, 363–7
Bowersock, G W 1990. 'The Pontificate of Augustus' in *Between Republic and Empire* (eds K Raaflaub and M Toher), 380–94, Berkeley
Bowman, A K 1994. *Life and Letters on the Roman Frontier. Vindolanda and its People*, London
Branigan, K 1977. 'Britain after Boudicca', *Archaeol Cambrensis* 126, 53–9
Breeze, D J 1969. 'The Organization of the Legion: the First Cohort and the *Equites Legionis*', *J Roman Stud* 59, 50–5
Breeze, D J 1986–7. 'The Logistics of Agricola's Final Campaign', *Talanta* 18/19, 7–28
Breeze, D J and Dobson, B 1969. 'Fort types on Hadrian's Wall', *Archaeol Aeliana* 4 ser, 47, 15–32
Breeze, D J and Dobson, B 2000. *Hadrian's Wall* (4th edn), London
Brereton, J M 1989. *A History of the Royal Regiment of Wales (24th/41st Foot), 1689–1989*, Cardiff
Brewer, R J (ed) 2000. *Roman Fortresses and their Legions*, London
Brewer, R J 2001. 'Caerleon and the Archaeologists: Changing Ideas on the Roman Fortress', *Monmouthshire Antiq* 17, 9–34
Brunt, P A 1971. *Italian Manpower*, Oxford
Brunt, P A 1973. 'The Fall of Perennis: Dio-Xiphilinus 72. 9. 2', *Class Q* 23, 172–7
Bruun, C 1988. '*Caligatus, tubicen, optio carceris*, and the Centurions' Positions; Some Remarks on an Inscription in *ZPE* 71 (1988)', *Arctos* 22, 23–40
Burnham, B C 1993. 'Roman Britain in 1992: Wales', *Britannia* 24, 269–76
Burnham, B C 1995. 'Roman Britain in 1994: Wales', *Britannia* 26, 326–31
Burnham, B C 1997. 'Roman Britain in 1996: Wales', *Britannia* 28, 396–405
Burnham, B C and Davies, J L (eds) 1990. *Conquest, Co-existence and Change. Recent Work in Roman Wales, Trivium* 25, Lampeter
Burns, T S 1994. *Barbarians within the Gates of Rome*, Bloomington
Campbell, B 1978. 'The Marriage of Soldiers under the Empire', *J Roman Stud* 68, 153–66
Casey, P J 1986. *Understanding Ancient Coins*, London
Casey, P J 1989. 'Coin evidence and the end of Roman Wales', *Archaeol J* 146, 320–9
Casey, P J 1991. 'The Coins' in *Bewcastle and Old Penrith. A Roman Outpost Fort and a Frontier Vicus; Excavations, 1977–78* (P Austen), 34–41, 212–18, Kendal
Casey, P J, Davies, J L with Evans, J 1993. *Excavations at Segontium (Caernarfon) Roman Fort, 1975–1979*, CBA Res Rep 90, London
Casey, P J and Hoffmann, B 1995. 'Excavations at Alstone Cottage, Caerleon, 1970', *Britannia* 26, 63–106
CIL 1862– . *Corpus Inscriptionum Latinarum*, Berlin
Coarelli, F 1967. 'Su un monumento funerario romano nell'abbazia di San Gulielmo al Goleto', *Dialoghi di Archeologia* 1, 46–71
Cole, M A and Lonford, N T 1993. 'The Geophysical Survey at Woodbury Farm, Axminster', *Proc Devon Archaeol Soc* 51, 135–48
Collingwood, R G 1932. 'Inscriptions' in Wheeler and Wheeler 1932, 100–4
Collingwood, R G and Myres, J N L 1936. *Roman Britain and the English Settlements*, Oxford
CSIR, I.1, *Hadrian's Wall East.* Phillips, E J 1977. *Corpus*

Signorum Imperii Romani, Great Britain I, 1, *Corbridge, Hadrian's Wall East of the North Tyne*, Oxford

CSIR, I.4, *Scotland*. Keppie, L J F and Arnold, B J 1984. *Corpus Signorum Imperii Romani, Great Britain* I, 4, *Scotland*, Oxford

CSIR, I.5, *Wales*. Brewer, R J 1986. *Corpus Signorum Imperii Romani, Great Britain* I, 5, *Wales*, Oxford

CSIR, I.6, *Hadrian's Wall West*. Coulston, J C and Phillips, E J 1988. *Corpus Signorum Imperii Romani, Great Britain* I, 6, *Hadrian's Wall West of the North Tyne and Carlisle*, Oxford

Cunliffe, B W (ed) 1968. *Fifth Report on the Excavations of the Roman Fort at Richborough, Kent*, Rep Res Comm Soc Antiq London 23, London

Cunliffe, B 1971a. *Excavations at Fishbourne 1961–1969, Volume I: The Site*, Rep Res Comm Soc Antiq London 26, Leeds

Cunliffe, B 1971b. *Excavations at Fishbourne 1961–1969, Volume II: The Finds*, Rep Res Comm Soc Antiq London 27, Leeds

Cunliffe, B 1975. *Excavations at Portchester Castle, Volume I: Roman*, Rep Res Comm Soc Antiq London 32, London

Cunliffe, B 1991. *Iron Age Communities in Britain* (3rd edn), London

Cunliffe, B W, Down, A G and Rudkin, D J 1996. *Chichester Excavations 9. Excavations at Fishbourne 1969–1988*, Chichester

Cüppers, H (ed) 1990. *Die Römer in Rheinland-Pfalz*, Stuttgart

Daremberg, C and Saglio, E 1873–1919. *Dictionnaire des Antiquités Grecques et Romaines* (5 vols), Paris

Davidson, P 1989. *The Barracks of the Roman Army from the 1st to the 3rd centuries AD*, Brit Archaeol Rep Int Ser 472, Oxford

Davies, J L 1991. 'Roman military deployment in Wales and the Marches from Pius to Theodosius I' in Maxfield and Dobson (eds), 52–7

Davies, J L and Kirby, D P 1994. *Cardiganshire County History, Volume 1: From the Earliest Times to the Coming of the Normans*, Cardiff

Davies, R W 1968. 'A note on some Roman soldiers in quarries', *Trans Cumberland Westmorland Antiq Archaeol Soc* 68, 22–6

Davies, R W 1971. 'The Roman Military Diet', *Britannia* 2, 122–42=Davies, R W 1989. *Service in the Roman Army* (eds D Breeze and V Maxfield), 187–208, Edinburgh

Davies, R W 1976. 'A lost inscription from Auchendavy', *Glasgow Archaeol J* 4, 103–7

Decker, K V and Selzer, W 1976. 'Mainz von der Zeit des Augustus bis zum Ende der römischen Herrschaft', *Aufstieg und Niedergang der römischen Welt* II.5.1, 457–559, Berlin

Dennis, G T 1981. *Das Strategikon des Maurikios*, Vienna

Dennis, G T 1984. *Maurice's Strategikon*, Philadelphia

Dennis, G T 1985. *Three Byzantine Military Treatises*, Washington

Devijver, H 1976–93. *Prosopographia Militiarum Equestrium* (5 vols), Louvain

Devijver, H and Wonterghem, F van 1990. 'The Funerary Monuments of Equestrian Officers of the Late Republic and Early Empire in Italy (50 BC – 100 AD)', *Ancient Society* 21, 59–98

Dobson, B 1978. *Die Primipilares*, Beihefte der Bonner Jahrbücher 37, Cologne

Dobson, B 1982. '*Praefectus castrorum Aegypti* – a reconsideration', *Chronique d'Égypte* 57, 322–37= Breeze, D J and Dobson, B 1993. *Roman Officers and Frontiers*, Mavors Roman Army Researches 10, 242–57, Stuttgart

Domaszewski, A von 1885. 'Die Fahnen im römischen Heere', *Abhandlungen des Archäologisch-Epigraphischen Seminars der Universität Wien*, Heft 5, 1–80 (reprint in *Aufsätze zur römischen Heeresgeschichte*, Darmstadt, 1972)

Domaszewski, A von 1899. 'Die Principia des römischen Lagers', *Neue Heidelberger Jahrbücher* 9, 141–63

Domaszewski, A von/Dobson, B 1967. *Die Rangordnung des römischen Heeres* (2nd edn revised by B Dobson), Cologne

Driel-Murray, C van 1988. 'A fragmentary shield cover from Caerleon' in *Military Equipment and the Identity of Roman Soldiers* (ed J C Coulston), Brit Archaeol Rep Int Ser 394, 51–66, Oxford

Duncan-Jones, R P 1978. 'Pay and Numbers in Diocletian's Army', *Chiron* 8, 541–60

Dwyer, E J 1973. 'Augustus and the Capricorn', *Mitteilungen des Deutschen Archäologischen Instituts, Römische Abteilung* 80, 59–67

Eichholz, D E 1972. 'How long did Vespasian serve in Britain?', *Britannia* 3, 149–63

Esmonde Cleary, A S 1998. 'Roman Britain in 1997: England', *Britannia* 29, 381–432

Evans, D R and Metcalf, V M 1992. *Roman Gates Caerleon*, Oxbow Monogr 15, Oxford

Evans, E 2000. *The Caerleon* Canabae. *Excavations in the Civil Settlement 1984–90*, Britannia Monogr Ser 16, London

Evans, E, Dowdell, G and Thomas, H J 1985. 'A Third-century Maritime Establishment at Cold Knap, Barry, South Glamorgan', *Britannia* 16, 57–125

Evans, J 1993. 'Pottery function and finewares in the Roman north', *J Roman Pottery Stud* 6, 95–118

Field, N H 1976. 'The discovery of a Roman fort at Shapwick, near Badbury Rings, Dorset', *Britannia* 7, 280–3

Field, N H 1992. *Dorset and the Second Legion. New Light on a Roman Campaign*, Tiverton

Fink, R O 1966. '*P Mich* VII 442 (inv 4703): betrothal, marriage or divorce?', *American Studies in Papyrology* 1, 9–17

Fink, R O 1971. *Roman Military Records on Papyrus*, Cleveland

Fink, R O, Hoey, A S and Snyder, W F 1940. 'The Feriale Duranum', *Yale Class Stud* 7, 1–222

Forrer, R 1927. *Strasbourg-Argentorate. Préhistorique, Gallo–Romain et Mérovingien* (2 vols), Strasbourg

Fox, A and Ravenhill, W 1966. 'Early Roman Outposts on the North Devon Coast', *Proc Devon Archaeol Soc* 24, 3–39

Fox, A and Ravenhill, W 1972. 'The Roman Fort at Nanstallon, Cornwall', *Britannia* 3, 56–111

Franzoni, C 1987. *Habitus atque Habitudo Militis*, Rome

Frere, S S 1967. *Britannia. A History of Roman Britain* (1st edn), London

Frere, S S 1977. 'Roman Britain in 1976', *Britannia* 8, 356–425

Frere, S S 1978. *Britannia. A History of Roman Britain* (2nd edn), London

Frere, S S 1983. 'Roman Britain in 1982', *Britannia* 14, 280–335

Frere, S S 1987a. *Britannia. A History of Roman Britain* (3rd edn), London

Frere, S S 1987b. 'Brandon Camp, Herefordshire', *Britannia* 18, 49–92

Frere, S S 1987c. 'Roman Britain in 1986', *Britannia* 18, 302–77

Frere, S S 1991. 'Roman Britain in 1990', *Britannia* 22, 222–92

Frere, S S 1992. 'Roman Britain in 1991', *Britannia* 23, 256–308

Frere, S S 1999. *Britannia. A History of Roman Britain* (4th edn), London

Fulford, M G, Allen, J R L and Rippon, S J 1994. 'The Settlement and Drainage of the Wentlooge Level, Gwent: Excavation and Survey at Rumney Great Wharf 1992', *Britannia* 25, 175–211

Fulford, M G and Tyers, I 1995. 'The date of Pevensey and the defence of an "Imperium Britanniarum"', *Antiquity* 69, 1009–14

Garnsey, P 1970. 'Septimius Severus and the Marriage of Soldiers', *California Stud in Class Antiq* 3, 45–53

Gillam, J P 1973. 'Sources of Pottery found on northern military Sites' in *Current Research in Romano-British Coarse Pottery* (ed A Detsicas), CBA Res Rep 10, 53–62, London

Gillam, J P 1976. 'Coarse fumed ware in North Britain and beyond', *Glasgow Archaeol J* 4, 57–80

Gillam, J and Greene, K 1981. 'Roman pottery and the economy' in *Roman Pottery Research in Britain and North-West Europe* (eds A C and A S Anderson), Brit Archaeol Rep Int Ser 123, 1–24, Oxford

Gilliam, J F 1954. 'The Roman Military Feriale', *The Harvard Theological Review* 47, 183–96

Gilliam, J F 1979. Review of *O Flor* in *American Journ Philology* 100, 339–40

Giuliano, A 1984. *Museo Nazionale Romano, Le Sculture*, 1.7 (2 vols), Rome

Goffart, W A (ed) 1989. *Rome's Fall and After*, London

Goldsworthy, A K 1996. *The Roman Army at War 100BC–AD 200*, Oxford

Greene, K 1977. 'Legionary pottery, and the significance of Holt' in *Roman Pottery Studies in Britain and Beyond* (eds J Dore and K Greene), Brit Archaeol Rep Int Ser 30, 113–32, Oxford

Greene, K 1979. *Report on the Excavations at Usk, 1965–1976. The Pre-Flavian Fine Wares*, Cardiff

Greene, K T 1993. 'The Fortress Coarseware' in Manning, 3–124

Griffith, F M 1984. 'Roman Military Sites in Devon: Some Recent Discoveries', *Proc Devon Archaeol Soc* 42, 11–32

Griffith, F M 1997. 'Developments in the study of Roman military sites in South West England' in Groenman-van Waateringe *et al* (eds), 361–7

Griffiths, N 1982. 'Early Roman Military Metalwork from Wiltshire', *Wiltshire Archaeol and Natur Hist Mag* 77, 49–60

Groenman-van Waateringe, W, van Beek, B L, Willems, W J H and Wynia, S L (eds) 1995. *Roman Frontier Studies 1995, Proceedings of the XVIth International Congress of Roman Frontier Studies*, Oxbow Monogr 91, Oxford

Grosse, R 1920. *Römische Militärgeschichte von Gallienus bis zum Beginn der byzantinischen Themenverfassung*, Berlin

Guéraud, O 1942. 'Ostraca grecs et latins de l'Wâdi Fawâkhir', *Bulletin de l'Institut français d'Archéologie Orientale* 41, 141–96

Haalebos, J K 1992. Review of Davidson 1989 in *Bonner Jahrbücher* 192, 653–7

Hanson, W S 1987. *Agricola and the Conquest of the North*, London

Hanson, W S and Maxwell, G S 1986. *Rome's North–West Frontier. The Antonine Wall*, Edinburgh

Hartley, B R 1972. 'The Roman Occupation of Scotland: The Evidence of the Samian Ware', *Britannia* 3, 1–55

Harvey, F D 1981. 'Pegasus: a Coin on a Plate' in *Pegasus: Classical Essays from the University of Exeter* (ed H W Stubbs), 19–24, Exeter

Hassall, M W C 1980. 'Altars, Curses and Other Epigraphic Evidence' in *Temples, Churches and Religion in Roman Britain: Recent Research in Roman*

Britain (ed W J Rodwell), Brit Archaeol Rep Brit Ser 77, 79–89, Oxford

Hassall, M W C 1992. 'Inscribed material: stone and tile' in Evans and Metcalf, 83–4

Hassall, M W C 2000. 'Pre-Hadrianic Legionary Dispositions in Britain' in Brewer (ed), 51–67

Hassall, M W C and Tomlin, R S O 1984. 'Roman Britain in 1983. II. Inscriptions', *Britannia* 15, 333–56

Hassall, M W C and Tomlin, R S O 1986. 'Roman Britain in 1985. II. Inscriptions', *Britannia* 17, 428–54

Hassall, M W C and Tomlin, R S O 1989. 'Roman Britain in 1988. II. Inscriptions', *Britannia* 20, 327–45

Hatt, J J 1964. *Inventaire des collections publiques françaises 9, Strasbourg, Musée archéologique: Sculptures antiques regionales*, Paris

Hatt, J J 1980. 'Strasbourg Romain' in *Histoire de Strasbourg*, Strasbourg

Hatt, J J 1983.'Observations sur quelques critères techniques pour classement et l'étude des sculptures gallo-romaines de Strasbourg', *Cahiers Alsaciens* 26, 39–45

Helgeland, J 1978 'Roman Army Religion', *Aufstieg und Niedergang der römischen Welt* II.16.2, 1470–1505, Berlin

Henderson, C 1988. 'Exeter (*Isca Dumnoniorum*)' in Webster (ed), 91–119

Henig, M 1970. 'The Veneration of Heroes in the Roman Army', *Britannia* 1, 249–65

Henig, M 1971. 'Roman Gems in Dorset', *Proc Dorset Natur Hist and Archaeol Soc* 93, 183–96

Herz, P 1975. 'Honos aquilae', *Zeitschrift für Papyrologie und Epigraphik* 17, 181–97

Hodgson, N 1996. 'A late Roman courtyard house at South Shields and its parallels' in *Architecture in Roman Britain* (eds P Johnson and I Haynes), CBA Res Rep 94, 135–51, York

Hodgson, N forthcoming. *Excavations at South Shields*

Hoey, A S 1937. 'Rosaliae Signorum', *The Harvard Theological Review* 30, 15–35

Hoffmann, D 1969–70. *Das spätrömische Bewegungsheer und die Notitia Dignitatum* (2 vols), Düsseldorf

Holbrook, N *et al* forthcoming. *Excavations at Llandough*

Hübner, E 1881. 'Das römische Heer und Britannien', *Hermes* 16, 513–84

Hurst, H R 1985. *Kingsholm*, Cambridge

Hurst, H R 1988. 'Gloucester (Glevum)' in Webster (ed), 48–73

IDR. Russu, I I 1975–. *Inscriptiones Daciae Romanae*, Bucharest

IGLS. Jalabert, L and Mouterde, R 1929–82. *Inscriptions Grecques et Latines de la Syrie*, Paris

IGRR. Cagnat, R *et al* (eds) 1906–1927. *Inscriptiones Graecae ad Res Romanas Pertinentes*, Paris

ILLRP. Degrassi, A (ed) 1957–63. *Inscriptiones Latinae Liberae Rei Publicae*, Florence

ILS. Dessau, H 1892–1916. *Inscriptiones Latinae Selectae*, Berlin

IMS. Papazoglu, F 1976–. *Inscriptions de la Mésie supérieure*, Belgrade

Inscr Aquil. Brusin, G B (ed) 1991–3. *Inscriptiones Aquileiae*, Udine

ISM. Pippidi, D M and Russu, I I 1980–. *Inscriptiones Scythiae Minoris*, Bucharest

Jackson, R 1990. *Camerton. The Late Iron Age and Early Roman Metalwork*, London

James, H 1990. 'Carmarthen – *Moridunum*' in Burnham and Davies (eds), 86–93

James, S 1984. 'Britain and the late Roman army' in *Military and Civilian in Roman Britain. Cultural Relationships in a Frontier Province* (eds T Blagg and A King), Brit Archaeol Rep Brit Ser 136, 161–86, Oxford

James, T B 1997. *The English Heritage Book of Winchester*, London

Jarrett, M G 1964a. 'Legio II Augusta in Britain', *Archaeol Cambrensis* 113, 47–63

Jarrett, M G 1964b. 'Early Roman Campaigns in Wales', *Archaeol J* 121, 23–39

Jarrett, M G 1968. 'Legio XX Valeria Victrix in Britain', *Archaeol Cambrensis* 117, 77–91

Jarrett, M G and Mann, J C 1968. 'The Tribes of Wales', *Welsh Hist Rev* 4.2, 161–71

Johnson, A 1983. *Roman Forts*, London

Jones, A H M 1964. *The Later Roman Empire 284–602*, Oxford

Jones, B and Mattingly, D 1990. *An Atlas of Roman Britain*, London

Jones, R F J 1976. 'The Roman Military Occupation of North-West Spain', *J Roman Stud* 66, 45–66

Kähler, M H 1931. 'Ein römisches Siegesdenkmal in Mainz', *Germania* 15, 20–8

Kajanto, I 1965. *The Latin Cognomina*, Helsinki

Kendal, R 1996. 'Transport Logistics Associated with the Building of Hadrian's Wall', *Britannia* 27, 129–52

Kennedy, D L 1983. 'Cohors XX Palmyrenorum – An Alternative Explanation of the Numeral', *Zeitschrift für Papyrologie und Epigraphik* 53, 214–16

Kennedy, D 1985. 'C Velius Rufus', *Britannia* 14, 183–96

Kennedy, D 1987. 'The East' in *The Roman World* (ed J Wacher), 266–308, London

Keppie, L J F 1979. *Roman Distance Slabs from the Antonine Wall*, Glasgow

Keppie, L J F 1983. *Colonisation and Veteran Settlement in Italy 47–14 BC*, London

Keppie, L J F 1984. *The Making of the Roman Army. From Republic to Empire*, London

Keppie, L J F 1998. *Roman Inscribed and Sculptured Stones in the Hunterian Museum University of Glasgow*, Britannia Monogr Ser 13, London

Keppie, L J F and Breeze, D J 1981. 'Some excavations on

the line of the Antonine Wall, 1957–80', *Proc Soc Antiq Scotl* 111, 229–470

Keppie, L J F and Walker, J J 1985. 'Auchendavy Roman Fort and Settlement', *Britannia* 16, 29–55

King, A 1990. *Roman Gaul and Germany*, London

Kraft, K 1967. 'Zum Capricorn auf den Münzen des Augustus,' *Jahrbuch für Numismatik und Geldgeschichte* 17, 17–28

Kromayer, J 1896. 'Die Militärcolonien Octavians und Caesars in Gallia Narbonensis', *Hermes* 31, 1–18

Kromayer, J and Veith, G 1928. *Heerwesen und Kriegführung der Griechen und Römer*, Munich

Leach, J D and Wilkes, J J 1977. 'The Roman military base at Carpow, Perthshire, Scotland: Summary of recent investigations (1964–70, 1975)' in *Limes, Akten des XI Internationalen Limeskongresses* (ed J Fitz), 47–62, Budapest

Leach, P 1982. *Ilchester Excavations, Volume I: Excavations 1974–1975*, Bristol

Leask, J C and McCance, H M 1915. *The Regimental Records of the Royal Scots*, Dublin

Le Bohec, Y 1989. *La Troisième Légion Auguste*, Paris

Le Bohec, Y 1994. *The Imperial Roman Army*, London

Le Gros, P 1979. 'Pour une chronologie des arcs de triomphe de Gaule Narbonnaise', *Gallia* 37, 55–83

Lenoir, M 1979. *Pseudo-Hygin, Des fortifications du camp*, Paris

Le Roux, P 1982. *l'Armée romaine et l'organisation des provinces ibériques d'Auguste à l'invasion de 409*, Paris

Lewis, N 1959. 'A Veteran in Quest of a Home', *Trans American Philological Ass* 90, 139–46

MacMullen, R 1984. 'The Legion as a Society', *Historia* 33, 440–56

McWhirr, A 1988. 'Cirencester (*Corinium Dobunnorum*)' in Webster (ed), 74–90

Manley, J and Rudkin, D 1999. *Excavations at Fishbourne Roman Palace 1995–1999*, Chichester

Mann, J C 1963. 'The raising of new legions during the Principate', *Hermes* 91, 483–9

Mann, J C 1983. *Legionary Recruitment and Veteran Settlement during the Principate*, Institute of Archaeology Occas Publ 7, London

Mann, J C 1985. 'Two 'Topoi' in the *Agricola'*, *Britannia* 16, 21–4

Mann, J C and Jarrett, M G 1967. 'The Division of Britain', *J Roman Stud* 57, 61–4

Manning, W H 1976. 'The Conquest of the West Country' in *The Roman West Country* (eds K Branigan and P J Fowler), 15–41, Newton Abbott

Manning, W H 1981. *Report on the Excavations at Usk 1965–1976. The Fortress Excavations 1968–1971*, Cardiff

Manning, W H 1989. *Report on the Excavations at Usk 1965–1976. The Fortress Excavations 1972–1974*, Cardiff

Manning, W H 1993. *Report on the Excavations at Usk 1965–1976. The Roman Pottery*, Cardiff

Manning, W H 1997. 'Ptolemy and the pre-Flavian military sites of Britain' in Groenman-van Waateringe *et al* (eds), 33–40

Marichal, R 1992. *Les ostraca de Bu Njem*, Libya Antiq Suppl 9, Tripoli

Marquardt, J 1884. Römische Staatsverwaltung 2, Leipzig

Marvell, A G and Heywood, B 1992. 'Excavations at Neath', *Bull Board Celtic Stud* 39, 171–298

Mattingly, D J and Hitchner, R B 1995. 'Roman Africa: An Archaeological Review', *J Roman Stud* 85, 165–213

Maurin, L 1978. *Saintes Antique*, Saintes

Maxfield, V A 1981. *The Military Decorations of the Roman Army*, London

Maxfield, V A 1986. 'Devon and the End of the Fosse Frontier', *Proc Devon Archaeol Soc* 44, 1–8

Maxfield, V A 1991. 'Tiverton Roman Fort (Bolham): Excavations 1981–1986', *Proc Devon Archaeol Soc* 49, 25–98

Maxfield, V A and Dobson, B 1995. *Inscriptions of Roman Britain*, Lactor 4, London

Maxfield, V A and Dobson, M J (eds) 1991. *Roman Frontier Studies 1989. Proceedings of the XVth International Congress of Roman Frontier Studies*, Exeter

Milner, N P 1993. *Vegetius: Epitome of Military Science*, Liverpool

Minnen, P van 1994. 'House-to-House Enquiries: an Interdisciplinary Approach to Roman Karanis', *Zeitschrift für Papyrologie und Epigraphik* 100, 227–51

Mitteis, L and Wilcken, U 1912. *Grundzüge und Chrestomathie der Papyruskunde*, Leipzig and Berlin

Mócsy, A 1974. *Pannonia and Upper Moesia*, London

Mommsen, T 1885. *The Provinces of of the Roman Empire from Caesar to Diocletian* (tr W P Dickson, from *Römische Geschichte*, V (Berlin 1885), London. 1886 translation revised and notes on the section on Britain added by F Haverfield (London, 1909)

Mommsen, T 1912. *Gesammelte Schriften* 8, Berlin

Monaghan, J 1993. *Roman Pottery from the Fortress: 9 Blake Street*, The Archaeology of York 16/7, York

Murray, W M and Petsas, P M 1989. *Octavian's Campsite Memorial for the Actian War*, Philadelphia

Nash-Williams, V E 1932. 'The Roman Legionary Fortress at Caerleon in Monmouthshire. Report on the Excavations carried out in the Prysg Field, 1927–9. Part II. The Finds', *Archaeol Cambrensis* 87, 48–104

Nash-Williams, V E 1939. 'An Early Iron Age Coastal Camp at Sudbrook, near the Severn Tunnel, Monmouthshire', *Archaeol Cambrensis* 94, 42–79

Nash-Williams, V E 1940. *The Roman Legionary Fortress at Caerleon, Monmouthshire*, Cardiff

Nash-Williams, V E/Jarrett, M G 1969. *The Roman Frontier in Wales* (2nd edn revised by M G Jarrett), Cardiff

Nesselhauf, H and Lieb, H 1959. 'Dritter Nachtrag zu CIL. XIII. Inschriften aus den germanischen Provinzen und dem Treverergebiet', *Berichte der Römisch-Germanischen Kommission* 40, 120–229

Nischer, E von 1928. 'Die Zeit des stehenden Heeres' in Kromayer and Veith, 470–626

Nock, A D 1952. 'The Roman Army and the Religious Year', *The Harvard Theological Review* 45, 187–252

O Claud. Bingen, J, Bülow-Jacobsen, A, Cockle, W E H, Cuvigny, H, Rubinstein, L and Van Rengen, W (eds) 1992. *Mons Claudianus: Ostraca Graeca et Latina*, I, Cairo

O Flor. Bagnall, R S 1976. *The Florida Ostraca: Documents from the Roman Army in Upper Egypt*, Durham, NC

Ogilvie, R M and Richmond, I (eds) 1967. *De Vita Agricolae*, Oxford

Okamura, L 1991. 'The flying columns of Emperor Gallienus: legionary coins and their hoards' in Maxfield and Dobson (eds), 387–91

Oman, C 1918. 'On the coins of Severus and Gallienus commemorating the Roman Legions', *Numismatic Chronicle* ser 4, 18, 80–96

Oman, C 1924. 'The Legionary Coins of Victorinus, Carausius and Allectus', *Numismatic Chronicle* ser 5, 4, 53–68

Owen-John, H S and Marvell, A G 1997. *Leucarum. Excavations at the Roman Auxiliary Fort at Loughor, West Glamorgan 1982–84 and 1987–88*, Britannia Monogr Ser 12, London

Paget, G C H V (Marquess of Anglesey) 1961. *One-Leg*, London

Parker, H M D 1928. *The Roman Legions*, Oxford

Parker, H M D 1932. 'The *Antiqua Legio* of Vegetius', *Class Q* 26, 137–49

Parker, T 1989. 'The fourth century garrison of Arabia: strategic implications for the south–eastern frontier' in *The Eastern Frontier of the Roman Empire* (eds D French and C H Lightfoot), Brit Archaeol Rep Int Ser 553, 355–72, Oxford

Parker, T 2000. 'Roman Legionary Fortresses in the East' in Brewer (ed), 121–35

Passerini, A 1949. 'Legio', *Dizionario epigrafico di Antichità Romana* 4, 549–627

Paton, G, Glennie, F, Symons, W P *et al* (eds) 1892. *Historical Records of the 24th Regiment*, London

P Beatty Panop. Skeat, T C 1964. *Papyri from Panopolis in the Chester Beatty Library, Dublin*, Dublin

P Col. Bagnall, R S and Lewis, N (eds) 1979. *Columbia Papyri* VII. *Fourth Century Documents from Karanis*, New York

P Dura. Welles, C B, Fink, R O and Gilliam, J F 1959. *The Excavations at Dura-Europos, Final Report V.1: The Parchments and Papyri*, New Haven

Peacock, D P S 1993. 'The site of Myos Hormos: a view from space', *J Roman Archaeol* 6, 226–32

Petrikovits, H von 1975. *Die Innenbauten römischer Legionslager während der Prinzipatszeit*, Opladen

Petrikovits, H von 1976. *Beiträge zur römischen Geschichte und Archäologie 1931 bis 1974*, Bonn

Petrikovits, H von 1980a. *Die Rheinlande in römischer Zeit*, Düsseldorf

Petrikovits, H von 1980b. 'Lixae' in *Roman Frontier Studies 1979. Papers Presented to the 12th International Congress of Roman Frontier Studies* (eds W S Hanson and L J F Keppie), Brit Archaeol Rep Int Ser 71 (iii), 1027–34, Oxford

Petry, F 1985. 'Le grand camp légionnaire' in *Aux Origines de Strasbourg*, 33–45, Strasbourg

P Gen Lat. Nicole, J and Morel, C 1900. *Archives militaires du 1er siècle. Texte inédite du Papyrus Latin de Genève*, Geneva

Picard, G Ch 1957. *Les Trophées romains*, Paris

Piganiol, A 1951. 'Nouvelles inscriptions d'Orange', *Comptes rendus de l'Académie des Inscriptions et Belles-Lettres*, 366–74

Piganiol, A 1962. *Les documents cadastraux de la colonie romaine d'Orange*, Gallia suppl 16, Paris

*PIR*². Groag, E, Stein, A and Petersen, L 1933–. *Prosopographia Imperii Romani, saec I, II, III* (2nd edn), Berlin

Pitts, L F and St Joseph, J K 1985. *Inchtuthil. The Roman Legionary Fortress*, Britannia Monogr Ser 6, London

P Mich. Edgar, C C, Boak, A E R, Winter, J G *et al* 1931– . *Papyri in the University of Michigan Collection*, Ann Arbor

Pontiroli, G 1971. 'Stele di *T. Aponius signifer legionis IX Hispaniensis* nel territorio cremonese', *Rendiconti dell' Istituto Lombardo* 105, 149–56

Porch, D 1991. *The French Foreign Legion*, Basingstoke

P Oxy. Grenfell, B P, Hunt, A S, Bell, H I *et al* 1898–. *The Oxyrhynchus Papyri*, London

Price, J 2002. 'Two vessels from Llandovery, Carmarthenshire and Piercebridge, County Durham: a note on Flavian and later polychrome mosaic glass in Britain' in *Artefacts and Archaeology* (eds M Aldhouse-Green and P V Webster), 121–31, Cardiff

Priest, N 1983. 'A loan of money with some notes on the *Ala Mauretana*', *Zeitschrift für Papyrologie und Epigraphik* 51, 65–70

RCAHMW, *Brecknock* 1986. *An Inventory of the Ancient Monuments in Brecknock. The Prehistoric and Roman Monuments, part ii: Hill-forts and Roman Remains*, Roy Comm Ancient Hist Monuments Wales, London

Reece, R 1975. 'The coins' in 'Excavations at the Lunt' (B

Hobley), *Trans Birmingham Warwickshire Archaeol Soc* 87, 23–5

Reece, R 1991. 'Roman Coins from Exeter' in *Roman Finds from Exeter* (N Holbrook and P T Bidwell), 33–8, Exeter

Reece, R 1995. 'Site-finds in Roman Britain', *Britannia* 26, 179–206

Reinach, S 1920. 'Pégase, l'hippogriffe et les poètes', *Revue Archéologique* 11, 207–55

Rhys, J 1892. 'The Chester Pigs of Lead', *Archaeol Cambrensis* 5 Ser, 9, 165–6

RIB I. Collingwood, R G and Wright, R P 1965. *The Roman Inscriptions of Britain*. I: *Inscriptions on Stone*, Oxford (Index by R Goodburn and H Waugh, 1983)

RIB II.1. Frere, S S, Roxan, M and Tomlin, R S O (eds) 1990. *The Roman Inscriptions of Britain*. II.: *Instrumentum Domesticum:* Fasc 1. *The military diplomata; metal ingots; tesserae; dies; labels; and lead sealings*, Gloucester

RIB II.3. Frere, S S and Tomlin, R S O (eds) 1991. *The Roman Inscriptions of Britain*. II. *Instrumentum Domesticum*: Fasc 3. *Brooches, Rings, Gems, Bracelets, Helmets, Shields, Weapons, Iron Tools, Baldric Fittings, Votives in Gold, Silver and Bronze, Lead Pipes, Roundels, Sheets and Other Lead Objects, Stone Roundels, Pottery and Bone Roundels, Other Objects of Bone*, Stroud

RIB II.4. Frere, S S and Tomlin, R S O (eds) 1992. *The Roman Inscriptions of Britain*. II. *Instrumentum Domesticum*: Fasc 4. *Wooden Barrels, Stilus Tablets, Miscellaneous Objects of Wood, Leather Objects, Oculists' Stamps, Wallplaster, Mosaics, Handmills, Stone Tablets, Stone Balls, Stone Pebbles, Small Stone Votives, Miscellaneous Objects of Stone, Jet Figurine, Clay Figurines, Miscellaneous Clay Objects, Antefixes, Tile Stamps of Legion II Augusta, of Legion VI Victrix, of Legion IX Hispana, of Legion XX Valeria Victrix, Tile Stamps of the Auxiliaries*, Stroud

RIB II.5. Frere, S S and Tomlin, R S O (eds) 1993. *The Roman Inscriptions of Britain*. II. *Instrumentum Domesticum:* Fasc 5. *Tile Stamps of the Classis Britannica; Imperial, Procuratorial and Civic Tile Stamps; Stamps of Private Tilers; Inscriptions on Relief-Patterned Tiles and Graffiti on Tiles*, Stroud

RIB II.6. Frere, S S and Tomlin, R S O (eds), with contributions by M W C Hassall 1994. *The Roman Inscriptions of Britain*. II. *Instrumentum Domesticum:* Fasc 6. *Dipinti and Graffiti on Amphorae, Dipinti and Graffiti on Mortaria, Inscriptions in White Barbotine, Dipinti on Coarse Pottery, Samian Barbotine or Moulded Inscriptions*, Stroud

RIB II.7. Frere, S S and Tomlin, R S O (eds), with contributions by M W C Hassall 1995. *The Roman Inscriptions of Britain*. II. *Instrumentum Domesticum:* Fasc 7. *Graffiti on Samian Ware (terra sigillata)*, Stroud

RIB II.8. Frere, S S and Tomlin, R S O (eds), with contributions by M W C Hassall 1995. *The Roman Inscriptions of Britain*. II. *Instrumentum Domesticum:* Fasc 8. *Graffiti on Coarse Pottery Cut Before and After Firing; Stamp on Coarse Pottery*, Stroud

Richmond, I A 1936. 'Roman leaden sealings from Brough-under-Stainmore', *Trans Cumberland Westmorland Antiq Archaeol Soc* 36, 104–25

Richmond, I A 1943. 'Roman legionaries at Corbridge, their supply-base, temples and religious cults', *Archaeol Aeliana* 4 ser, 21, 127–224

Richmond, I A 1963. *Roman Britain* (2nd edn), Harmondsworth

Richmond, I A 1968. *Hod Hill II: Excavations carried out between 1951 and 1958*, London

Richmond, I A and Birley, E 1940. 'Excavations at Corbridge, 1938–39', *Archaeol Aeliana* 4 ser, 17, 85–115

Richmond, I A and Crawford, O G S 1949. 'The British Section of the Ravenna Cosmography', *Archaeologia* 93, 1–50

Ritterling, E 1906. 'Zur Geschichte des römischen Heeres in Gallien unter Augustus', *Bonner Jahrbücher* 114/115, 158–88

Ritterling, E 1919. 'Ein Amtsabzeichen der beneficiarii consularis im Museum zu Wiesbaden', *Bonner Jahrbücher* 125, 9–37

Ritterling, E 1924/5. 'Legio', *Realencyclopädie der classischen Altertumswissenschaft* 12, 1211–1829

Rivet, A L F 1970. 'The British Section of the Antonine Itinerary', *Britannia* 1, 34–82

Rivet, A L F and Smith, C 1979. *The Place-Names of Roman Britain*, London

RMDII. Roxan, M M 1985. *Roman Military Diplomas 1978–1984*, Institute of Archaeology Occas Publ 9, London

Robinson, D M 1988. 'Prologue notes on Romano-British rural settlement in South-East Wales' in *Biglis, Caldicot & Llandough. Three Late Iron Age and Romano-British Sites in South-East Wales. Excavations 1977–79* (ed D M Robinson), Brit Archaeol Rep Brit Ser 188, vii–xxiv, Oxford

Roldan Hervas, J M 1961. 'El exercitus hispanicus desde Augustus a Vespasiano', *Archivo Español de Arqueología* 34, 114–60

Roldan Hervas, J M 1974. *Hispania y el ejercito Romano*, Salamanca

Rook, A 1978. 'The Development and Operation of Roman Hypocausted Baths', *J Archaeol Science* 5, 269–82

Roth, J 1994. 'The Size and Organization of the Roman Imperial Legion', *Historia* 43, 346–62

Roxan, M M 1981. 'The Distribution of Roman Military Diplomas', *Epigraphische Studien* 12, 265–86
Roxan, M M 1991. 'Women on the frontiers' in Maxfield and Dobson (eds), 462–7
Royle, T 1990. *Anatomy of a Regiment: Ceremony and Soldiering in the Welsh Guards*, London
St Joseph, J K S 1969. 'Air Reconnaissance in Britain, 1965–1968', *J Roman Stud* 59, 104–28
St Joseph, J K 1973. 'Air Reconnaissance in Britain, 1969–72', *J Roman Stud* 63, 214–46
Salomies, O 1992. *Adoptive and Polyonymous Nomenclature in the Roman Empire*, Helsinki
Sander, E 1932. 'Die Hauptquellen der Bücher I–III der epitoma rei militaris des Vegetius', *Philologus* 87, 369–75
Sander, E 1939. 'Die Germanisierung des römischen Heeres', *Historische Zeitschrift* 160, 1–34
Sander, E 1952. 'Triarius Ordo', *Rheinisches Museum* 95, 79–96
Sargent, P 1981. 'Du nouveau sur le combat de Camerone', *Rev Hist des Armées*, numéro spéciale: *La légion étrangere*, 73–89
Sarnowski, T 1985. 'Die legio I Italica und der untere Donauabscnitt der Notitia Dignitatum', *Germania* 63, 107–27
Saxer, R 1967. *Untersuchungen zu den Vexillationen des römischen Kaiserheeres von Augustus bis Diokletian*, Cologne and Graz
SB. Preisigke, F, Bilabel, F and Kiessling, E 1913– . *Sammelbuch griechischer Urkunden aus Ägypten*, Strassburg, Leipzig, Heidelberg, Wiesbaden
Scheithauer, A and Wesch–Klein, G 1990. 'Von Köln-Deutz nach Rom? Zur Truppengeschichte der Legio II Italica Divitiensium', *Zeitschrift für Papyrologie und Epigraphik* 81, 229–36
Schlüter, W 1993. *Kalkriese – Römer im Osnabrücker Land*, Bramsche
Schmitthenner, W 1962. 'Augustus' spanischer Feldzug und der Kampf um den Prinzipat', *Historia* 11, 29–85
Schnitzler, B and Schneider, M 1985. *Le Musée archéologique de Strasbourg*, Strasbourg
Schober, A 1923. *Die römischen Grabsteine von Noricum und Pannonien*, Vienna
Schönberger, H 1969. 'The Roman Frontier in Germany: an Archaeological Survey', *J Roman Stud* 59, 144–97
Schubert, P (ed) 1990. *Les Archives de Marcus Lucretius Diogenes*, Bonn
Scorpan, C 1980. *Limes Scythiae*, Brit Archaeol Rep Int Ser 88, Oxford
Seeck, O (ed) 1876. *Notitia Dignitatum*, Berlin
Sel Pap. Hunt, A S and Edgar, C C 1932. *Select Papyri* I, London and Cambridge, Mass
Selzer, W 1988. *Römische Steindenkmäler: Mainz in römischer Zeit*, Mainz
Sharples, N M 1991. *Maiden Castle: Excavations and field survey 1985–6*, London
Shirley, E A M 1996. 'The Building of the Legionary Fortress at Inchtuthil', *Britannia* 27, 111–28
Shirley, E A M 2000. *The Construction of the Roman Legionary Fortress at Inchtithil*, Brit Archaeol Rep Brit Ser 298, Oxford
Shirley, E A M 2001. *Building a Roman Fortress*, Stroud
Shoesmith, R 1991. *Excavations at Chepstow 1973–1974*, Cambrian Archaeol Monogr 4 [s.l.]
Silvester, R J and Bidwell, P T 1984. 'A Roman Site at Woodbury, Axminster', *Proc Devon Archaeol Soc* 42, 33–57
Simpson, S J and Griffith, F M 1993. 'Trial Excavation at the Roman Fort on St Andrew's Hill, Cullompton', *Proc Devon Archaeol Soc* 51, 149–59
Speidel, M A 1995. 'Ferox: legionary commander or governor? a note on Tab Vindol II 154' in *Römische Inschriften – Neufunde, Neulesungen und Neuinterpretationen: Festschrift für Hans Lieb* (eds R Frei-Stolba and M A Speidel), 43–51, Basel
Speidel, M P 1976. 'Eagle-Bearer and Trumpeter', *Bonner Jahrbücher* 176, 123–63=Speidel 1984, 3–43 with addenda on p 406
Speidel, M P 1977. 'The Roman Army in Arabia', *Aufstieg und Niedergang der römischen Welt* II.8, 687–730, Berlin=Speidel 1984, 229–72
Speidel, M P 1978. 'Felix Legio Vestra. A Building Inscription from Romula – Malva', *Zeitschrift für Papyrologie und Epigraphik* 30, 119–22=Speidel 1984, 77–80
Speidel, M P 1982. 'Legionary Cohorts in Mauretania. The Role of Legionary Cohorts in the Structure of Expeditionary Armies', *Aufstieg und Niedergang der römischen Welt* II.10.2, 850–60, Berlin=Speidel 1984, 65–76 with addenda on p 406
Speidel, M P 1983a. 'The Centurions' Titles', *Epigraphische Studien* 13, 43–61=Speidel 1992a, 21–39
Speidel, M P 1983b. 'Zum Aufbau der Legion und zum Handwerk in Vindonissa', *Jahresbericht der Gesellschaft Pro Vindonissa*, 29–34=Speidel 1992a, 56–61
Speidel, M P 1984. *Roman Army Studies* 1, Amsterdam
Speidel, M P 1985a. 'A Pannonian *Optio Vexillationis* Buried at Stratonikeia', *Epigraphica Anatolica* 6, 75–8=Speidel 1992a, 67–70
Speidel, M P 1985b. 'The Master of the Dragon Standards and the Golden Torc: An Inscription from Prusias and Prudentius' *Peristephanon*', *Trans Proc American Philological Association* 115, 283–7=Speidel 1992a, 390–5
Speidel, M P 1986. 'Rangzeichen für Zenturion und die grosse Weihinschrift aus dem Mainzer Legionslager', *Jahrbuch des Römisch-Germanischen Zentralmuseums* 33, 321–9=Speidel 1992a, 43–55

Speidel, M P 1987a. 'Ein Silberring aus Baden für die Reiter der 21. Legion', *Helvetia Archaeol* 18, 56–8

Speidel, M P 1987b. Spätrömische Legionskohorten in Novae', *Germania* 65, 240–2=Speidel 1992a, 400–2

Speidel, M P 1989a. 'The Soldiers' Servants', *Ancient Society* 20, 239–48=Speidel 1992a, 342–51

Speidel, M P 1989b. 'Hercules with the Hellhound from Viminacium', *Acta Archaeologica Hungarica* 41, 359–63=Speidel 1992a, 298–303

Speidel, M P 1990. 'The Names of Legionary Centuriae', *Arctos* 24, 135–7=Speidel 1992a, 40–2

Speidel, M P 1992a. *Roman Army Studies* 2, Mavors Roman Army Researches 8, Stuttgart

Speidel, M P 1992b. *Die Denkmäler der Kaiserreiter*, Cologne

Speidel, M P 1994a. *Riding for Caesar. The Roman Emperors' Horse Guards*, London

Speidel, M P 1994b. *Die Denkmäler der Kaiserreiter: Equites Singulares Augusti*, Cologne

Steer, K A and Cormack, E A 1968–9. 'A New Roman Distance-Slab from the Antonine Wall', *Proc Soc Antiq Scotl* 101, 122–6

Stevens, C E 1966. *The Building of Hadrian's Wall*, Kendal

Strobel, K 1987. 'Bemerkungen zur Laufbahn des Ti. Claudius Vitalis', *Tyche* 2, 203–9

Strobel, K 1988a. 'Ein weiteres Zeugnis zur Rangordnung im römischen Legionscenturionat der Kaiserzeit', *Epigraphica Anatolica* 12, 43–5

Strobel, K 1988b. 'Zu Fragen der frühen Geschichte der römischen Provinz Arabia, etc', *Zeitschrift für Papyrologie und Epigraphik* 71, 251–80

Swan, V 1992. 'Legio VI and its Men: African Legionaries in Britain', *J Roman Pottery Stud* 5, 1–33

Swinbank, B 1953. 'The Activities of Lollius Urbicus as evidenced by inscriptions', *Trans Architect Archaeol Soc Durham Northumberland Res Rep* 10.4, 382–403

Syme, R 1933. 'Some Notes on the Legions under Augustus', *J Roman Stud* 23, 14–33

Syme, R 1958. *Tacitus*, Oxford

Syme, R 1970. 'The Conquest of North-West Spain' in *Legio VII Gemina*, 83–107, León=*Roman Papers* II, 825–54, Oxford, 1979

Syme, R 1977. 'Helvetian aristocrats', *Museum Helveticum* 34, 129–40=*Roman Papers* III, 986–97, Oxford, 1984

Syme, R 1983. 'Antistius Rusticus: a Consular from Corduba', *Historia* 32, 359–74=*Roman Papers* IV, 278–94, Oxford, 1988

Tab Vindol. Bowman, A K and Thomas, J D 1983. *Vindolanda: the Latin Writing-Tablets*, Britannia Monogr Ser 4, London

Tab Vindol II. Bowman, A K and Thomas, J D 1994. *The Vindolanda Writing-Tablets* (*Tabulae Vindolandenses II*), London

Tassaux, D and Tassaux, F 1983. 'Aulnay-de-Saintonge. Un camp augusto-tibérien en Aquitaine', *Aquitania* 1, 49–95

Tassaux, D and Tassaux, F 1984. 'Aulnay de Saintonge. Un camp militaire augusto-tibérien en Aquitaine', *Aquitania* 2, 105–59

Thompson, F H 1968. 'The Zoomorphic Pelta in Romano-British Art', *Antiq J* 48, 47–58

Todd, M 1984a. 'Excavations at Hembury, Devon 1980–83: a Summary Report', *Antiq J* 64, 251–68

Todd, M 1984b. 'The Early Roman Phase at Maiden Castle', *Britannia* 15, 254–5

Todd, M 1985. 'The Roman Fort at Bury Barton, Devonshire', *Britannia* 16, 49–55

Todd, M 1987. *The South West to AD 1000*, London

Todd, M 1995. 'Charterhouse on Mendip: Interim Report on Excavations in 1994', *Somerset Archaeol Natur Hist* 138, 75–9

Tomlin, R S O 2000. 'The Legions in the Late Empire' in Brewer (ed), 159–81

Ubl, H 1969. *Waffen und Uniform des römischen Heeres der Prinzipatsepoche nach den Grabreliefs Noricums und Pannoniens*, unpublished dissertation, Vienna

Veith, G 1928. 'Die Zeit des Milizheeres' in Kromayer and Veith, 254–469

Veyne, P 1964. 'Epigraphica: Le Pégase de la légion d'Afrique', *Latomus* 23, 37–40

Vita–Evrard, G di 1982. 'Notes sur "trois" sénateurs de Lepcis Magna. Le clarissimat des Plautii', *Epigrafia e ordine senatorio* I, *Tituli* 4, 453–65, Rome

Vorbeck, E 1980. *Militärinschriften aus Carnuntum* (2nd edn), Vienna

Wacher, J 1995. *The Towns of Roman Britain* (2nd edn), London

Wacher, J and McWhirr, A 1982. *Early Roman Occupation at Cirencester*, Cirencester

Waddelove, E, Waddelove, A C and Jones, G D B 1990. 'The Roman Fort at Ruthin, Clwyd', *Britannia* 21, 299–302

Walters, B and Walters, M 1989. 'Ariconium – Military Site Excavation, Interim Report', *Dean Archaeology* 2, 33–45

Waton, M-D 1985. 'Problèmes de l'implantation et de l'occupation du camp romain: l'exemple d'Istra' in *Aux Origines de Strasbourg*, 46–51, Strasbourg

Watson, G R 1969. *The Roman Soldier*, London

Webster, G 1958. 'The Roman Military Advance Under Ostorius Scapula', *Archaeol J* 115, 49–98

Webster, G 1958–9. 'An Excavation at Nunnington Park, Wiveliscombe', *Somerset Archaeol Natur Hist Soc* 103, 81–91

Webster, G 1979. 'Final Report on the Excavations of the Roman Fort at Waddon Hill, Stoke Abbot, 1963–69', *Proc Dorset Natur Hist Archaeol Soc* 101, 51–90

Webster, G 1980. *The Roman Invasion of Britain*, London

Webster, G 1985. *The Roman Imperial Army* (3rd edn), London

Webster, G (ed) 1988. *Fortress into City. The Consolidation of Roman Britain, First Century AD*, London

Webster, J 2001. 'An inlaid iron brooch from Rhyn Park' in *Archaeology of the Roman Empire. A Tribute to the Life and Works of Professor Barri Jones* (ed N J Higham), Brit Archaeol Rep Int Ser 940, 287–8, Oxford

Webster, P V 1972. 'Severn valley ware on Hadrian's Wall', *Archaeol Aeliana* 4 ser, 50, 191–203

Webster, P V 1984. 'The Roman Period' in *Glamorgan County History, Volume II: Early Glamorgan. Pre-History and Early History* (ed H N Savory), 277–313, Cardiff

Webster, P V 1990. 'The first Roman fort at Cardiff' in Burnham and Davies (eds), 35–9

Webster, P V 1993. 'Coarse Pottery' in Casey and Davies, 250–316

Wedlake, W J 1958. *Excavations at Camerton, Somerset*, Bath

Wegeleben, T 1913. *Die Rangordnung der römischen Centurionen*, Berlin

Weinstock, S 1971. *Divus Julius*, Oxford

Welfare, H and Swan, V 1995. *Roman Camps in England*, Roy Comm Hist Monuments Engl, London

Wells, C M 1972. *The German Policy of Augustus*, Oxford

Wells, H G. 1921. *Outline of History* (3rd edn), New York

Wheeler, E L 1979. 'The Legion as Phalanx', *Chiron* 9, 303–18

Wheeler, R E M 1943. *Maiden Castle, Dorset*, Rep Res Comm Soc Antiq London 12, Oxford

Wheeler, R E M and Wheeler T V 1932. *Report on the Excavation of the Prehistoric, Roman, and Post-Roman Site in Lydney Park, Gloucestershire*, Rep Res Comm Soc Antiq London 9, London

White, R B 1978. 'Excavations at Brithdir, Near Dolgellau, 1974' in *Monographs and Collections I, Roman Sites* (ed G C Boon), Cambrian Archaeol Ass, 35–62, Cardiff

Wightman, E M 1985. *Gallia Belgica*, London

Wilcken, U 1894. 'Hypomnematismoi', *Philologus* 53, 80–126

Wilkes, J J 1969. *Dalmatia*, London

Wilmott, T 1997. *Birdoswald. Excavations of a Roman fort on Hadrian's Wall and its successor settlements: 1987–92*, English Heritage Archaeol Rep 14, London

Wilson, D R 1972. 'Roman Britain in 1971', *Britannia* 3, 299–351

Wiseman, T P 1981. 'Titus Flavius and the Indivisible Subject' in *Pegasus: Classical Essays from the University of Exeter* (ed H W Stubbs), 2–18, Exeter

Wood, S 1990. *In the Finest Tradition*, Edinburgh

Woodfield, C C 1965. 'Six turrets on Hadrian's Wall', *Archaeol Aeliana* 4 ser, 43, 87–200

Woodfield, C C 1995. 'New thoughts on town defences in the western territory of the Catuvellauni' in *Roman Small Towns in Eastern England and Beyond* (ed A E Brown), Oxbow Monogr 52, 129–46, Oxford

Worp, K A 1983. 'SPP XXII 80: Revidiert', *Papyrus Erzherzog Rainer: Festschrift zum 100-jährigen Bestehen der Papyrussammlung der Österreichischen National-bibliothek*, 368–70 ,Vienne

Wright, R P 1963–4. 'An Imperial Inscription from the Roman Fortress at Carpow, Perthshire', *Proc Soc Antiq Scotl* 97, 202–5

Wright, R P 1967. 'Roman Britain in 1966. II. Inscriptions', *J Roman Stud* 57, 203–10

Wright, R P 1985. 'A Revised Restoration of the Inscription on the Mosaic Pavement found in the Temple at Lydney Park, Gloucestershire', *Britannia* 16, 248–9

Yalouris, N 1987. *Pegasus: ein Mythos in der Kunst*, Mainz

Zanker, P 1988. *The Power of Images in the Age of Augustus*, Ann Arbor

Zienkiewicz, J D 1986a. *The Legionary Fortress Baths at Caerleon, I. The Buildings*, Cardiff

Zienkiewicz, J D 1986b. *The Legionary Fortress Baths at Caerleon, II. The Finds*, Cardiff

Zienkiewicz, J D 1990. 'The early development of the legionary fortress of Caerleon–*Isca* and consequences for Flavian policy in Britain' in Burnham and Davies (eds), 27–34

Zienkiewicz, J D 1993. 'Excavations in the *Scamnum Tribunorum* at Caerleon: The Legionary Museum Site 1983–5', *Britannia* 24, 1993, 27–140

Index

This index does not contain entries for all the sites or personal names listed in the appendices in chapters 3 and 6.

Abbey Dore, 31, 40, 56–8, 63
Aberfraw, 53
Abergavenny, 31, 40–1, 44, 51–2, 57, 84
Abertanat, 56–7, 59, 65–6
Acci (Guadix), 17, 25
Achaia, 114
Achilles, 20
acies duplex, 133
acies simplex, 133
Adminius, 28
Adrianople, battle of, 175
Aduatuca (Tongres), 146
Aelianus, 108, 135
Aelius Augustinus, 87–8
Aelius Brocchus, 151
Aemilius Arcanus, L., 108
Aemilius Paternus, L., 108
Aeso, 108, 119
Africa, 21, 97, 107, 109–11, 127, 132, 147, 150, 170–1, 176, 186
— *Proconsularis*, 111
Agathias, 170
Agrippina, 149
ala, 34, 91, 105–6, 138, 149–50, 159, 162–3
— *Apriana*, 159
— *Augusta*, 106
— *Hispanorum*, 105
— *I Asturum*, 149
— *Parthorum et Araborum*, 150, 162
— *Sulpicia*, 149, 162
— *Vettonum*, 34, 91
Alabastrine, 155, 157, 163
Alamanni, 168
Alani, 129–30, 133
Alba, 18
Albius, T., 18, 25
Alexander, Severus (emperor), 22, 88
Alexandria, 105, 153, 155–60, 163
Alfenus Senecio, L., 114
Allectus, 98
Amida, 174
Ammianus Marcellinus, 174, 177
Anglesey, 37, 45–6, 50, 53, 83
Anicius Maximus, P., 16, 19, 105
Annius Fabianus, L., 108
Annius Perpetuus, 154
Antioch (Pisidia), 16, 105–6
Antistius Rusticus, L., 106
Antium (Anzio), 107
Antonine Itinerary, 48–50
Antonine Wall, 4, 15, 68, 70–2, 74–7, 81, 83, 92, 95–6, 102, 109–10, 146, 166, 189
Antonius Germanus, 153
Antonius Isauricus, Q., 151, 162
Antonius Primus, M., 22
Antony, M., 11, 22, 141
Apamea, 130–1, 141–2, 169
Aphrodous, 157
Apion (Antonius Maximus), 155–6
Apolinarius, 170
Apollinopolis Superior, 173
Apollo, 76, 114, 157
Apulum (Alba Julia), 161, 163
Aquileia, 23–4, 137, 158
aquilifer, 103–4, 122–3
Aquincum (Budapest), 158, 161
Aquitania, 18, 107, 114
Arabia, 155–6, 159
Arezzo (Arretium), 16
Armenia, 166
Arminius, 146, 149, 165
Armoricans, 175
armorum custos, 135, 142
Arnius Bassus, L., 106
Arrian, 4, 129–30, 132–4, 142–3
Asciburgium (Asberg), 149
Asia, 109, 150
Asseria, 106
Atilia Vera, 108
Atrebates, 29, 30
Auchendavy, 70, 72, 76–7, 81, 112
Augustus (emperor), 11–14, 16–17, 19, 21–2, 24, 28, 97, 106, 159, 163, 186
Aulnay, 18–19
Aurelian (emperor), 97, 142
Aurelius Cervianus, 116
Aurelius Isidorus, 170
Aurelius Polus, Terentianus, Q., 114
Autronius Silo, L., 17–18
Axiopolis, 171
Axminster, 31, 33, 36

Babuleius Garrulus, Ti., 18, 25, 154
Baden-Baden (Aquae), 159, 163
Baetica, 25, 108
Baginton, 185
ballistarii, 137, 140
Balmuildy, 70, 72, 82
Bar Hill, 70, 72, 81
barracks, 37, 97, 116–17, 125–7, 133, 136, 139, 141, 167, 171, 181–2
— first cohort, 126
Batavians, 151
Bath (Aquae Sulis), 30, 33–4, 90–3, 112, 183
Beirut, 16
Belgae, 29–30
Bellerophon, 14
Bellicianus, 88
Bellicius Sollers, Ti., 106
Benwell, 15, 69, 72, 74–5, 82, 108
Beroe (Aleppo), 176
Bewcastle, 69, 73, 80, 95
Birdoswald, 69, 78, 182–3
Birrens, 69
Bishapur, 168
Black-burnished ware 1 (BB1), 92–7, 99–100, 183–6
Blagdon, 34, 43, 89, 102
Blandius Latinus, 106
Bolham Farm, 36, 41
Bologna, 11, 18
Bonn, 23, 108, 148
Bostra, 155–6, 159
Boudicca, 55
Boudiccan revolt, 16, 34, 42, 53, 59, 105
Brampton, 56, 62, 69, 74
Brandon Hill, 52
Brecon, 20, 26, 40, 83
Brescia, 14
Bretzenheim, 17
Bridgeness, 71–2, 110
Briga, 151
Brigantes, 38, 47, 49, 52, 67, 83
Brigetio, 153, 163
Brough-on-Humber, 88
Brough-under-Stainmore, 80, 96
Bulla Regia, 111
Bulmore, 7, 9, 85–6
Bury Barton, 31, 36

Cadder, 70–2
Caecina Severus, 150
Caelius, M., 147–8
Caelius Privatus, M., 148
Caelius Thiaminus, M., 148

Caer Gai, 58, 63, 84
Caer Gybi, 84, 97
Caerhun (Canovium), 49, 84
Caerleon (Isca), 1–8, 35, 39–40, 42, 51, 55, 66–7, 74, 81, 83–4, 86–92, 97–9, 102–3, 107, 110–11, 116, 125–8, 130–1, 136, 139, 141, 145–6, 151–2, 158–60, 167, 171, 173, 180–8
Caerleon Ware, 94
Caernarfon (Segontium), 49–50, 53, 93, 96
Caersws (Mediolanum?), 49–50, 52, 60, 64, 66, 83–5
Caerwent (Venta Silurum), 7, 40, 49, 83, 85, 87–8, 90, 99, 102, 115, 183
Caesar, C. Julius, 11–12, 16–17, 25–6, 28, 43, 46, 54, 64, 125, 129, 132–3, 136, 141–2, 146, 170
Caesius Silvester, C., 113
Caistor-by-Norwich, 88
Caledonian, 16, 67–8, 150
Calpurnius Flaccus, 108
Calvisius Sabinus, 150
Camerton, 31, 34, 43
canabae, 7, 9, 86, 148, 161
Canon Frome, 57
Cappadocia, 4, 106, 113, 154, 162
Caracalla (emperor), 68, 72, 77–9, 83, 87, 90, 95, 142, 152, 166–7
Caratacus, 27–8, 30, 37–8, 46–7, 50, 52, 65
Carausius (emperor), 97–8, 173
Carcassonne, 17–18
Cardewlees, 74, 78
Cardiff, 8, 31, 39–40, 50–2, 54–5, 57, 61, 65, 84, 94, 97–100, 102, 180–1, 183
Carius Scipio, 109
Carmarthen (Moridunum), 48–9, 61
Carnuntum (Deutsch Altenberg), 154, 158, 161
Carpow, 68, 72–4
Carrawburgh, 69, 80
Cartenna (Ténès), 17, 25
Cartimandua, 38, 47, 53
Cassius Dio, 24–9, 43, 46, 64, 68, 72, 82, 142, 146, 149–50, 162
Cassius Saecularis, 103–4, 123
Castell Collen, 14, 83–4, 123
Castellum Arsacalitanum, 111
Castlecary, 70, 76–7, 81, 96
Castledykes, 74
Castlesteads, 69, 74, 129
Catuvellauni, 19, 27–30, 37, 47
centurions, 4, 6, 25, 52, 68, 75–8, 81, 87, 91–2, 103–8, 111–16, 119–24, 126–8, 132–5, 137–41, 143, 150–1, 158–60, 163, 165–6, 170
Chalk, 74
Charterhouse on Mendip, 33–4, 43
Chepstow, 31, 40, 51, 57
Chester (Deva), 7, 49, 57, 61, 83, 88, 91, 93, 95–7, 183, 186, 188
Chichester, 2, 3, 30–1, 33, 90, 184
Chrysopolis, battle of, 171
Cicero, 24, 146
Cilicia, 110–11
Cillium, 111
Circesium, 176
Cirencester, 2, 29, 31, 33–5, 43, 89, 93–4, 112, 153, 183, 186
Cirta, 116
civil war, 15–17, 42, 46–7, 114, 125, 166, 168, 171
Classis Britannica, 94, 96
Claudia Severa, 104, 151
Claudian (poet), 14
Claudian invasion, 1, 11, 15–16, 19–20, 27–32, 45–7
Claudius (emperor), 1, 14, 16–17, 20, 28–30, 33, 39, 45, 47–52, 105–6, 109, 149, 174
Claudius Alpinus, L., 106
Claudius Candidus, Ti., 114
Claudius Charax, A., 109–10
Claudius Fatalis, Ti., 113
Claudius Paulinus, Ti., 7, 87, 114–15
Claudius Terentianus, 158
Clawdd Coch, 59, 65–6
Cleonice, 113
Clifford, 31, 38, 41, 52, 56–7
Clock Mills, 52
Clodius Albinus, 114, 166
Clyro, 31, 38–9, 41, 50, 52–4, 56–8, 61
Cocceius Firmus, M., 76–7, 112–13
Cockersand Moss, 100
Coed-y-caerau, 31, 39, 51, 57
Cogidubnus, 29–30, 47, 64
Cohors
— *I Apamenorum*, 155
— *I Batavorum*, 80, 152
— *I Britannica*, 153
— *I Tungrorum*, 107
— *II Nerviorum*, 80
— *V Bracaraugustanorum*, 105
— *VI Nerviorum*, 76
— *VII Thracum*, 80
— *XX Palmyrenorum*, 22, 159
Colchester (Camulodunum), 27–8, 30, 38, 52, 87–8, 90, 147
Cold Knap, Barry, 95
Cologne, 113, 149, 162
comes Britanniae, 173, 189–90
comes litoris Saxonici, 189
comitatenses, 171–5
Commius, 29
Commodus (emperor), 5, 113–14, 132, 166
Concordia, 116
Congaonius Candidus, 113
Constantine I (emperor), 7, 133, 136, 142, 169, 171–3
Constantine III (emperor), 174
Contrapollonopolis Magna, 155, 157–9, 163
Coptos, 155, 157, 159, 163
Corbridge, 68–70, 78–83, 95–6, 114, 159, 173
Corbulo, 33, 47, 105, 166
Coria, 159
Coritani, 37
Cornasidius Sabinus, 114
Cornelius Saturninus, M., 113
Cornelius Victor, 113
Cornovii, 37, 49
corona civica, 21
Cremona, battle of, 24, 108
Crichton, 74–5
Crowdundle, 74–5, 81, 96
Cudmore Farm, Clayhanger, 36
Cullompton, 31, 36
Cunobelinus, 19, 28
Curiatius Saturninus, C., 92, 112
Curtius Super, 104
Cyrenaica, 111
Cyrene, 156
Cyrus the Great, 168

Dacia, 111, 114, 161
— Superior, 108
Dacian Wars, 108, 113, 153
Dalmatia, 16, 78, 103, 106
Dalmatians, 21, 123
Darius, 168
Decanti, 49–50
Deceangli, 37, 47–9, 53
Decrius Longinus, L., 108, 123
Deganwy (arx Decantorum), 49
Demetae, 48–9, 83
Demetria, 153
Desticius Juba, 116–17
Diana, 76, 116–17
Didius Gallus, 3, 35, 38–9, 52
Dinas Powys, 183

Diocletian (emperor), 7, 136, 139, 169–71, 173, 175
Dioscorus, 170
Divitia (Deutz), 172
Dobunni, 28–9, 35, 38, 49
Dolaucothi, 84, 90
Domitius Potentinus, 116–17
Dorchester (Durnovaria), 2, 31–2, 36, 90
Draethen, 85, 90
druids, 53
Drusus (brother of Tiberius), 106
Dumnobellaunos, 28
Dumnonia, 30, 36
Duntocher, 15, 70
Dura Europos, 22, 159
Durotriges, 3, 28–30, 32–3
dux Britanniarum, 189

Edessa, 175
Egypt, 6, 16, 22, 105, 128, 153–60, 163, 168, 170, 173–4, 176
— Lower, 155
— Upper, 156–7
el-Lejjūn, 8, 170–1, 173
emblema, legionary, 13–16
— boar, 13, 16, 117
— bull, 16
— capricorn, 13–16, 24, 71–2, 74, 97, 117
— dolphin, 13
— pegasus, 13–16, 24, 71–2, 74–5
Epimachus, 155–6
Epona, 76
equites legionis, 4, 127, 132, 138–9, 169
equites promoti, 4, 143, 169
equites singulares Augusti, 76
Exeter, 2–3, 9, 24, 28, 31, 34–7, 39, 41–2, 54, 61, 85, 88–92, 94, 102, 183, 185–6
Exomnius Paternianus, 116

Fabius Agrippinus, C., 108
Falacrinae, 104
Favonius Facilis, M., 147
Fayum, 154–6
Fenius Alexander, 109
feriale Duranum, 22
Ferox, 107
Firma Julia Secundanorum – see Orange
Firmus, 113
Fishbourne, 3, 30–1, 90
Flavius Blandinus, 100
Flavius Candidus, T., 154
Flavius Cerialis, 151
Flavius Lucianus, 76, 81
Flavius Postumius Varus, T., 116–17
Flavius Senilis, T., 100
Flavius Virilis, T., 114
Flavoleius Cordus, 130
Florus, Julius, 13
Forest of Dean, 39–40, 90, 93, 188
Fortuna, 76, 96, 151
Forum Gallorum, 11
Fosse Way, 2, 33–7, 93
Franks, 168
Frisii, 33

Gaius (emperor), 16, 149, 162
Galba (emperor), 14, 24–5, 162
Gallienus (emperor), 97, 104, 116, 139, 142, 167–9, 172
Gaul, 1, 6–7, 11–13, 17, 19, 54, 87, 96, 103, 115, 146, 154, 166–7, 171–5
— Gallia Narbonensis, 87, 108, 115
— Gallia Lugdunensis, 87, 107, 115
Geneva, 106
Germanicus, 149, 162
Germany, 1, 5, 13, 16–17, 19, 64, 106, 132, 145–6, 149, 154, 161, 167, 172
— Lower, 17, 19–20, 113, 171
— Upper, 1, 17, 20, 104–5, 108, 158–9
Geta (emperor), 111, 114, 152
Gibeon, 174
Gittisham, 31, 36
Gloucester (Glevum), 2, 3, 9, 29, 31, 34–5, 38–40, 42, 50–2, 54, 56–7, 61, 87–9, 91–2, 94, 102, 183, 186
Goldcliff, 85–6
Gordian III (emperor), 168
Goths, 168, 170
Great Chesters, 69

Hadria, 114
Hadrian (emperor), 4, 9, 22, 70, 76, 80, 88, 95, 108, 132–3, 135, 143, 153, 166
Hadrian's Wall, 4, 15, 24, 68–77, 79, 81–3, 92, 95, 108–9, 113, 128–9, 135–6, 146, 151, 166, 172, 182, 184, 188–9
Haltern, 17
Halton Chesters, 69, 72, 82
Ham Hill, 31, 34
Hamworthy, 3, 31, 33
hastati, 4, 126–8, 132–4, 140
hastatus posterior, 126–7
hastatus prior, 126, 128, 141–2
hastiliarii, 135, 142
Haterianus, 111
Helvius Rufus, M., 21
Hembury, 31, 36
Heraclius, 175–6
Hercules, 20, 76, 79–80, 170
Hermagoras, 151, 162
Herodian, 68, 82, 142, 152, 162–3
High Rochester, 69, 73, 115, 151
Hirtius, 11
Histria, 76
Hod Hill, 2, 28, 31–4, 43
Honoratus, 109, 151
Housesteads, 69, 77, 80–1, 182–3
Hyginus, 126–7, 138, 141, 143

Ilchester, 31, 33–4, 43, 94
Ilkley, 81
Inchtuthil, 4, 61, 125–7, 139, 141, 189
Interamna, 114
Isis, 157
Isle of Wight, 28
Italy, 6–7, 11, 13–14, 16, 18–19, 24, 87, 103, 113–14, 116, 123, 154–6, 168, 172, 174

Javolenus Saturnalis, C., 92
Jerusalem, 113
Josephus, 141–3, 147, 162
Joshua, 174
Judaea, 107–8, 113, 162
Jugurtha, 147
Julia Domna (empress), 149
Julia Mamaea (empress), 88
Julia Secundina, 86
Julianus, 155
Julius, T., 18, 25
Julius Agricola, Cn., 2, 4, 27, 37, 39, 46–7, 50, 53, 61, 67, 81, 106, 109, 136, 150
Julius Apollinarius, C., 156, 158–9
Julius Athendorus, 170
Julius Candidus, 113
Julius Celer, T., 106
Julius Ferox, Ti., 107
Julius Frontinus, Sex., 2–3, 46, 49, 53, 61, 64, 67, 108, 142
Julius Hiero, M., 113
Julius Honoratus, 78
Julius Julianus, L., 68, 79, 114, 142
Julius Marcellinus, 78
Julius Maritimus, C., 113
Julius Niger, C., 17–18
Julius Quadratus, M., 111
Julius Sacrovir, 13
Julius Severus, 109
Julius Tertullianus, 108–9
Julius Valens, 86
Julius Verecundus, 107
Julius Verus, Cn., 109
Julius Vitalis, 128
Jupiter, 76–80, 96
— Dolichenus, 74, 110
Justinian (emperor), 5, 76, 142, 170, 175

Karanis, 154–7, 163
Kenchester (Magna), 49–50
Kentchurch, 31, 40–1, 56–8
Killerton, 31, 36
Kingsholm, Gloucester, 2, 31, 34, 38, 40, 52, 61, 92
Klis, 104

Lactantius, 169–71, 177
Lake Farm, 2–3, 31–3, 43
Lambaesis, 22, 113–14, 127, 129, 132–3, 141–2
lanciarii, 4, 130, 132, 137, 140, 142, 169, 172–3
Larcius Priscus, A., 107–8
Largennius, C., 18–19, 25, 154
Lavobrinta, 49
legatus legionis, 1, 6–7, 16, 79, 104–11, 113–14, 116, 118, 123, 142, 151
legio
— *I Adiutrix*, 13–14, 24, 112
— *I Italica*, 106, 112
— *I Jovia*, 171
— *I Minervia*, 108, 112
— *I Parthica*, 167
— *II Adiutrix*, 14, 34, 91, 112, 161
— *II Augusta*, (origins, 11–13; title, 16–17; invasion, 1, 11, 19–20, 28–32)
— *II Gallica*, 12–13, 17
— *II Herculia*, 136, 171
— *II Italica*, 167, 172
— *II Parthica*, 130–1, 133, 142, 167, 169
— *II Sabina*, 12
— *II Traiana*, 133, 142–3, 170, 173
— *III Augusta*, 14, 16, 22, 113–14, 129, 132, 160
— *III Cyrenaica*, 159
— *III Diocletiana*, 170
— *III Gallica*, 22
— *III Italica*, 136, 167
— *III Parthica*, 114, 167
— *IIII Flavia*, 113
— *IIII Macedonica*, 14
— *IIII Martia*, 171, 173
— *IIII Scythica*, 14, 16, 24, 108
— *V Macedonica*, 16, 175
— *V Parthica*, 174
— *VI Ferrata*, 22, 112
— *VI Victrix*, 70, 72, 76, 78, 88, 91, 95–7, 102, 106, 113–15, 124, 172
— *VII Galbiana*, 108
— *VII Gemina*, 108
— *VIII Augusta*, 16–18, 25, 108, 129
— *VIII Gallica*, 16
— *VIIII Hispana*, 20, 28, 67, 106
— *X Fretensis*, 107
— *X Gemina*, 112
— *XII Fulminata*, 105
— *XIII Gemina*, 161, 173
— *XIIII Gemina*, 3, 13–14, 16, 18–20, 25, 28, 36, 39, 41–2, 54, 106, 130
— *XV Apollinaris*, 105–6, 154
— *XV Primigenia*, 19
— *XVI Flavia Firma*, 20
— *XX Valeria Victrix*, 1, 3, 9, 13, 16, 19–20, 28, 33–4, 38–9, 42, 52, 54, 70, 72, 77–8, 81–3, 85, 88, 91–2, 95–6, 100, 102, 105–8, 113–14, 117, 136, 167, 172, 189
— *XXI Rapax*, 14, 19
— *XXII Deiotariana*, 108
— *XXII Primigenia*, 14, 19, 111, 114
legio antiqua, 137–9, 159, 174
'Legions', field army, 8, 81, 136, 171–3, 175, 189
— *Divitenses*, 172
— *Moesiaci Seniores*, 172
— *Pannoniciani Seniores*, 172
— *Secundani Britanniciani*, 174
— *Secundani Iuniores*, 8, 173
— *Victores Iuniores Britanniciani*, 172
Leighton, 52, 56–7, 59
Leintwardine (Bravonio), 50, 52, 54, 57, 65
Lepcis Magna, 111
Lepidus, 12
Liber, 114
liberti, 147
Liburnius Fronto, M., 75, 108
Licinius (emperor), 171
Licinius Nerva, 109
limitanei, 173–5, 189
Lincoln (Lindum), 35, 87
Littlechester (Derventio), 49
Llandeilo, 49, 64
Llandough, 183
Llandovery, 49, 57, 61, 66, 84
Llanfor, 50–1, 53–4, 56–7, 59–61
Llanio, 49, 84, 123
Llansantffraid-ym-Mechain, 54, 56–7, 59, 61
Llwyn-y-brain, 50, 57, 59–60, 66
Lollia Bodicca, 114
Lollius Urbicus, Q., 109, 114
Lollius Venator, M., 78, 124
London (Londinium), 29, 85, 87, 90–1, 93, 112, 123, 158–9
Loughor, 49–50, 65
Lucca, 18–19, 154
Luccius Faustus, Q., 13
Lucco, 153
Lucia Macrina, 153
Lucius Verus (emperor), 166
Lucretius Clemens, 153
Luentinum, 48
Lutudarum, 49
Lydney, 99, 100
Lydus, John, 170
Lyon, 13, 154

Macedonia, 11, 112, 165
Machen, 85, 90
Macrinus, 168
Maeatae, 68, 79
magister equitum, 174
Magnentius (emperor), 174
Maiden Castle, 31–2
Mainz (Mogontiacum), 1, 13–14, 17–20, 114, 130–1, 142, 150, 158–9
Manius Dionisias, L., 92
Marcian, 128
Marcius Clemens, T., 110
Marcomannic Wars, 114
Marcus Aurelius (emperor), 22, 26, 76, 166–7
Marinus, 113
Maris, 150, 162
Marius, 126, 133, 136, 141
Marktbreit, 17
Mars, 76, 100
— Cocidius, 77, 135
— Lenus, 88
— Ocelus, 87–8
— Ultor, temple of, 21
Martial, 25, 106, 108
Martialis, 158
Martinoe, 31
Martius Macer, L., 16
Maryport, 82, 95–6
Mauretania, 17
Maurice, 133–5, 142
Maurice Tiberius (emperor), 175
Maxentius (emperor), 172
Maximian (emperor), 170–1, 173
Maximinus Thrax (emperor), 168
Maximus, 157
Medusa, 14
Memmius Fidus Julius Albius, C., 111
Mercury, 76
Metellus, 147
Middlewich (Salinae), 49
Milan, 18, 154
Mildenhall, 31–2
Minerva, 76
Minucius Audens, M., 96–7
Mithras, 91, 171
Moesia, 153, 172
— Inferior, 112
— Superior, 111–12
Monmouth, 31, 39, 41, 51, 56–8, 65
Mons Claudianus, 155, 157–60, 163

Mons Graupius, 64, 67–8, 125
Myos Hormos, 155, 158, 163

Naevius, 90
Nanstallon, 31, 37
Naples, 108, 155
Narbo (Narbonne), 108
Narcissus, 1, 105
natalis aquilae, 22
Neath, 50, 57, 65, 84
Nero (emperor), 17, 26, 34, 39, 42, 47, 52–3, 64–5, 88–90, 105–6, 109, 154, 166
Nerva (emperor), 108
Netherby, 69, 73, 80, 82, 95
Nicopolis, 141, 155, 159
Nijmegen (Noviomagus), 126–7, 141
Nipius Ascanius, C., 88
Nodens, 100
Nonius Romanus, M., 87
Norba (Cáceres), 17
Noricum, 103
North Tawton, 2, 31, 36
Northwich (Condate), 49
Notitia Dignitatum, 8, 97, 135, 173, 180, 189
Novicius, 147
Noviodunum, 171
Numantia, 146
Numerianus, 147, 149
Numidia, 107–8, 111, 114, 116, 160

Ocelus Vellaunus, 88
Octavia Tamusta, 153
Octavian – see Augustus
Octavius Honoratus, C., 111
Octavius Sebanus, 113
Ofillius, 107
Ofillius Felix, L., 107
Okehampton, 31, 36
Old Burrow, 31, 37
Old Penrith, 151
optio, 81, 87–8, 97, 134–6, 142
Orange (Arausio), 12, 17, 23–4, 87
— Arc de Triomphe, 12
Ordovices, 37–8, 48–50, 52
Osrhoene, 176
Ostia, 105, 156
Ostorius Scapula, Q., 29, 33, 35, 37–8, 47, 49, 52, 55
Oxyrhynchus, 155, 159

Palmyra, 168
Pannonia, 20, 22, 102, 112 150, 153, 172
— Inferior, 158
— Superior, 111, 153, 161
Pansa, 11
Parisi, 83
Parthian War, 108, 112, 154
Parthians, 21, 131
Patrae, 109
Pelusium, 155–6
Pennal, 57–9, 84–5, 102
Penrhos, 50, 53, 56, 59, 61
Perennis, 114
Pergamum, 109
Persian Empire, 168
Petillius Cerialis, Q., 4, 67, 162
Petra, 155–6, 158
Petronius Fortunatus, M., 111
Pevensey, 98
phalangarii, 131–2, 140
Philadelphia, 155–6
Philip I (emperor), 115, 168
Philippi, battle of, 12
Piercebridge, 78, 124
pilani, 4, 126, 128, 132–3, 140
pili, 123, 127, 132–4, 143
pilus posterior, 126–7, 141, 143
pilus prior, 126–7
Platorius Nepos, A., 70
Plautius, Aulus, 28–9, 33, 35, 105, 111
Pliny the Elder, 12, 24–6, 64, 107, 123
Plutarch, 150–1, 162
Poenius Postumus, 6, 34, 105
Polla Matidia, 148
Pompeii, 55, 66, 109, 160
Pompeius Ferox, Cn., 107
Pompeius Homullus, Cn., 107
Portchester, 98, 180–1, 185
Poseidon, 14
praefectus Aegypti, 159
praefectus castrorum, 16, 19, 34, 52, 122, 163, 165
primi ordines, 127, 140
primus pilus, 105, 108, 122, 139, 141–2
principes, 4, 127–8, 133–4, 140
Priscus, 114
Procopius, 175, 177
promoti, 137, 172–3
Pselkis (Dakke), 155, 157
Ptolemais, 173
Ptolemy, 30, 32, 35, 43–4, 48–50, 64
Pudens, 81
Pumsaint, 48–9, 90

Quinctilius Varus, P., 17, 21, 25, 146–7
Quintus Veranius, 39

Raetia, 153
Raima, 156
Rammius, 153
Ravenna Cosmography, 49–50, 64
Regensburg (Castra Regina), 153
Regni, 29–30
Rhyn Park, 50, 53–5, 57, 59, 61
Richborough, 8, 15, 28, 97–100, 173–5, 180–2
Risca, 90
Roesius Moderatus, 128, 141
Rome, 14, 21–2, 26–30, 33, 35, 39, 46–8, 53, 64, 76–7, 104, 107–11, 113–14, 116, 122, 125, 132, 150, 156, 166–7, 172, 175, 182, 188
rosaliae signorum, 22
Roscius Coelius, M., 106
Rough Castle, 70, 76
Runcorn, 49

Sabidius Maximus, M., 112, 141
sagittarii, 131–2, 140, 142
St Valéry sur Somme, 34, 89, 102
Sallienius Thalamus, P., 114–15, 151
Salus, 115, 152
Satala, 154
Saturnilus, 157
Saudonio, 49
Savaria (Szombathely), 161
Saxon Shore, 180–1, 189
Scaeva, 18, 25
Scalesceugh, 95
Scipio, P. Cornelius, 146–7
Sea Mills, 31, 40, 51
Sennius Sollemnis, T., 115
Septimius Geta, P., 111
Septimius Severus (emperor), 6, 68, 73, 77, 111, 150, 166–7, 170
Serenus, 153
Severius Emeritus, C., 90, 109, 112
Severus Alexander (emperor), 22
Shapur I, 168
Shapwick, 31–2
Sicily, 12, 109
signum, 13, 133
Silchester (Calleva Atrebatum), 2, 31–2, 90–1, 93–4, 184
Silures, 3, 7, 29, 37–9, 48–52, 61, 64–5, 68, 83, 85, 87, 165
Silvanus, 112
Singidunum (Belgrade), 113
Socrates, 156, 163
Sosia Juncina, 151
South Cadbury, 31, 34
South Shields (Arbeia), 69, 147, 149, 182–3
Spain, 1, 6–7, 17, 19, 24–5, 87, 107–8, 123, 146, 154
Spectatus, 113
speculatores, 135, 142
Split, 169
Stanegate, 69, 185
Stlaccius Coranus, 105
Strabo, 28, 43

Strasbourg (Argentorate), 1–2, 13, 17–20, 105, 129, 154, 159, 186
Strategus, 170
Sudbrook Camp, 31, 40, 51, 65
Suetonius, 1, 24–8, 30, 43, 47, 52, 64–5, 123, 159, 162–3
Suetonius Paulinus, C., 6, 39, 53
Sulis Minerva, 91–2
Sulpicia Lepidina, 104, 151
Summerston, 70–1
Syene (Aswan), 160
Syria, 105–6, 108, 111–12, 129–30, 141, 150, 160–1, 168–9, 176

Tacitus, 1, 9, 17, 24–7, 29, 33, 35–9, 43–4, 46, 50, 52–3, 55, 64–5, 67, 82, 105–6, 123, 125, 143, 146, 150–1, 161–3
Tadia Exuperata, 145, 162
Tadia Vallaunius, 145
Tadius Exuperatus, 145, 152, 154, 161
Tarraconensis, 108
Tentyra, 173
Terentianus, 156–9, 163
territorium, 24, 85
Tertinia Victorina, 116
Tertinius Severianus, 116
Tertius, 113
tesserarius, 81, 135, 142
Thebaid, 153, 156, 160, 170
Thebes, 155, 160
Theodosius I (emperor), 175, 177
Theodosius, Count, 99
Theseus, 20
Thuburnica, 111
Tiberius (emperor), 12, 16, 19, 22, 24, 28, 106
Tifernum, 105
Tincommius, 28
Titus (emperor), 105–6, 108, 162
Tivoli (Tibur), 110
Togodumnus, 28, 30, 47
Topsham, 31, 35
Towcester, 184
Trajan (emperor), 64, 68, 108, 113, 129, 133, 135, 141, 154, 162, 166
Trajan Decius (emperor), 80
Trajan's Column, 26, 129, 133–4, 142
Trebellius Maximus, M., 106
triarii, 132, 137, 140
tribunus
— *angusticlavius*, 6, 104–5, 118, 122
— *laticlavius*, 6, 104, 106, 108, 118, 123
Trier, 88
Trieste, 106
Trinovantes, 27
Troesmis (Igliţa), 141, 171
Tuficum, 113
turma, 138–40, 143

Ulpia Traiana Sarmizegetusa, 154
Ulpius Fronto, M., 152
Ulpius Marcellus, 114
Ulpius Silvanus, 91, 102
Ulucium, 159
Urbino (Urvinum Mataurense), 105
Usk (Burrium), 3, 7, 31, 35, 39–42, 49, 51–4, 56–7, 61, 65–6, 86, 92, 184, 186, 188

Valentinian I (emperor), 175
Valentinian III (emperor), 177
Valerian (emperor), 97, 167–8
Valerius Felix, M., 115–16
Valerius Flavus, 108
Valerius Gemellus, 153
Valerius Longus, 159
Valerius Messalinus, 150
Valerius Palmas, 159
Valerius Paulinus, 156
Valerius Victor, C., 154
Vandals, 168
velites, 169
Ventimiglia, 18
Veranius, Q., 39, 52–3
Verecundus, 147
Verica, 28–9
Vernemetum, 49
Verona, 106, 123
— battle of, 133
Verulamium (St Albans), 27, 90
Vespasian (emperor), 1–2, 6, 14–15, 18, 25, 28–30, 32, 34–5 42–3, 47, 88, 104–7, 123, 127, 142, 162
veterans, 7, 12, 16, 18, 21, 38, 65, 83, 86–8, 91–2, 126, 132, 141, 154, 160–1, 189
Vettius Adiutor, 103–4
Vettius Statura, L., 105
vexillation fortresses, 2–3, 18, 30–1, 33, 36, 38, 41
vexillations, 2, 5, 7, 41, 96, 116, 166–7, 171, 173
vexillum, 15, 133, 166
Vicetia, 106
Victor, 147, 149
Victorinus, 100
Victory, 21, 68, 74, 76–7, 114, 173
Vindolanda (Chesterholm), 6, 15, 65, 69, 78, 103–4, 107, 113, 124, 151, 158–9, 188
Vinius, T., 151
Virgil, 151
Visigoths, 175
Vitellius Atillianus, T., 112
Vitellius Tancinus, L., 34
Vitulasius Laetinianus, 116–17
Vitulasius Nepos, Sex., 116
Vivius Marcianus, 112, 158
Volusius, 108

Waddon Hill, 15, 31, 33, 36
Wâdi Fawâkhir, 157–8
Wall, 59
Wallsend, 69, 78, 188
Walton, 31, 41, 52, 56–7, 59
Wanborough, 31–2
Welwyn, 187–8
Weston under Penyard (Ariconium), 31, 38–9, 41, 51, 56–7, 90
Whitchurch (Mediolanum), 49, 57
Whittington, 56, 59
Wiesbaden (Aquae Mattiacorum), 159, 163
Winchester, 30–2, 184
Wiveliscombe, 31, 36
Woden Law, 166
Wookey Hole, 34, 43
Written Rock of Gelt, 81
Wroxeter (Viriconium Cornoviorum), 3, 28, 35, 39, 41–2, 49–50, 52, 54, 57, 59, 61, 65, 89, 94

Xanten (Vetera), 19–20, 147–8
Xanthus, 105

Y Pigwn, 56, 61
Yarmuk, battle of, 176
Ylas, 151, 162
York (Eboracum), 7, 83, 96–7, 115, 151, 160, 183, 186, 188

Zeus, 14
Zosimus, 170–1, 177